FREGE AND OTHER PHILOSOPHERS

FREGE AND OTHER PHILOSOPHERS

Michael Dummett

CLARENDON PRESS · OXFORD

1991

Oxford University Press, Walton Street, Oxford OX2 6DP
Oxford New York Toronto
Delhi Bombay Calcutta Madras Karachi
Petaling Jaya Singapore Hong Kong Tokyo
Nairobi Dar es Salaam Cape Town
Melbourne Auckland
and associated companies in
Berlin Ibadan

Oxford is a trade mark of Oxford University Press

Published in the United States
by Oxford University Press, New York

British Library Cataloguing in Publication Data
Dummett, Michael, 1925–
Frege and other philosophers.
1. German. Philosophy. Frege, Gottlob, 1848–1925
I. Title
193
ISBN 0–19–824870–9

Library of Congress Cataloging in Publication Data
Dummett, Michael A. E.
Frege and other philosophers / Michael Dummett.
p. cm.
Includes index.
1. Frege, Gottlob, 1848–1925. 2. Frege, Gottlob, 1848–1925—
Influence. 3. Logic, Symbolic and mathematical. 4. Analysis
(Philosophy) I. Title.
B3245.F24D865 1991 193—dc20 90–41695
ISBN 0–19–824870–9

Typeset by Hope Services (Abingdon) Ltd.
Printed and bound in
Great Britain by Bookcraft (Bath) Ltd.
Midsomer Norton, Avon

*For Christopher, Maggie, Louis,
and Michael Orlando*

Preface

This volume contains all the essays I have written that were too late for inclusion in *Truth and Other Enigmas* and are wholly or largely about Frege. All of them concern other philosophers as well, in greater or lesser degree. When Hans Sluga attacked my book, *Frege: Philosophy of Language*, as involving gross misinterpretations of Frege due to its unhistorical approach, my initial reaction was to judge *his* interpretation to be very wide of the mark; this reaction was voiced in Essay 5 of the present collection. Further reflection left me still of the opinion that Sluga was in error in his reading of Frege and in the view that he had been significantly influenced by Lotze, but persuaded that his criticism of my book as unhistorical had some substance.

I had written the book in the belief, which I continue to hold, that the most significant connections were between Frege and later philosophers, not between him and his contemporaries or predecessors, who had contributed little to the formation of his most important ideas. More exactly, I believed this about those of his philosophical views that were not specific to the philosophy of mathematics; I have always thought that his work within the latter branch of the subject needed to be studied in the context of that of his contemporaries. Essay 1, concerning Frege and Hilbert, in fact exemplifies that belief. It was written in 1973, as part of the unfinished version of my still forthcoming *Frege: Philosophy of Mathematics* that I composed in that year. When Professor (then Dr) Matthias Schirn asked me for a contribution to the collection of essays by different hands, *Studien zu Frege*, which he was editing, I simply excerpted it from my typescript, as being the most self-contained section of it.

For all that, whether in the philosophy of mathematics or more generally, the only nineteenth-century writer of whom it would be reasonable to guess, just from the content of his writings and those of Frege, that he had *influenced* Frege, is Bernhard Bolzano, who died in the year Frege was born; but there is no evidence whatever that Frege ever read Bolzano. It was nevertheless borne in on me that, even if I was right to think that Frege had not been greatly influenced by others, it had still been a mistake to attempt to write about his thought concerning less specialized areas of philosophy in disregard of the ideas of his contemporaries: only against that setting was it possible to understand what Frege regarded it as necessary to argue against and why he expressed himself as he did. On one point of history Sluga had convicted me of a definite mistake, namely in thinking that Frege's work had played any part in the downfall of Hegelianism. Sluga's contention that that philosophy had, by Frege's time, long been out of general favour was certainly correct, although he went far astray in understanding me when he maintained that my erroneous historical supposition was my principal ground for interpreting Frege as a realist. He did, however, stimulate my own interest in the history of German nineteenth-century philosophy, and, in particular, in Frege's place in it: and for this I must express my gratitude to him.

The search for influences on Frege's thought, which so absorbed Sluga, may prove to yield some historical facts of interest. I suspect it, all the same, of being largely sterile: it is not there that the fruitful historical questions are to be found. It is frequently forgotten that Gilbert Ryle, who was to become the generalissimo of Oxford ordinary-language philosophy, began his philosophical career as the exponent, for the British philosophical public, of the writings of Franz Brentano and Edmund Husserl, and even published, in *Mind* for 1929, a critical but respectful review of Heidegger's *Sein und Zeit*. This may well seem surprising, not merely because of Ryle's later contempt for Heidegger, but because Brentano's most celebrated idea, that of the intentionality of mental acts, is not well accommodated in *The Concept of Mind*. In the writings of the early Ryle, for instance in his article 'Are There Propositions?' to which I devote a footnote at the beginning of Essay 12, Frege appears as an unexceptional and not especially distinguished member of a school, largely Austrian, initiated by Bolzano and comprising Brentano, Meinong, and Husserl. Ryle's publicity for this school awoke little response among British philosophers, so that it had no greater effect in arousing interest in Frege's work than Wittgenstein's deeply respectful references in the *Tractatus* had had earlier; that interest was born only with John Austin's translation of the *Grundlagen* in 1950, followed by the *Translations from the Philosophical Writings of Gottlob Frege* of Peter Geach and Max Black in 1952.

Personal contact as well as intellectual influence genuinely made

Brentano, Meinong, and Husserl members of a school, and, in his *Logische Untersuchungen*, Husserl acknowledged a profound debt to Bolzano; but, as already mentioned, Frege appears to have been unaware of Bolzano, and, equally, of Brentano and of Meinong. As for Husserl, there was indeed some contact, and Husserl started by holding Frege in great respect, although he appears to have finished by despising him; but there is little enough sign that Frege ever had any high opinion of Husserl. Nevertheless, Ryle was entirely correct in perceiving a certain affinity between some of Frege's ideas and those of the other thinkers he grouped with him. The Husserl who wrote the *Philosophie der Arithmetik* was undoubtedly far away from Frege; it is well known that Frege attacked that book ferociously as a prime example of psychologism, just as Husserl had in it vehemently criticized Frege's *Grundlagen*. The Husserl of the *Ideen* also seems somewhat remote from Frege, if for rather different reasons. But, in the *Logische Untersuchungen*, Husserl expounds views some of which have a strong affinity to those of Frege; indeed, despite the similarity of the arguments used, it was Husserl's *Prolegomena* to that book, rather than any of Frege's assaults upon psychologism, which turned the current of opinion against it.

It is this fact which presents the most perplexing question in the history of modern philosophy. For Frege was unquestionably one of the ancestors of the analytical school of philosophy, and Husserl equally the principal progenitor of the phenomenological school. How, then, did it come about that the work of these two men, who, at one stage, appeared so close to one another in the swirl of conflicting philosophical currents, should have become the head waters of two streams generally regarded as flowing in quite contrary directions?

It is because of my newly awakened interest in historical questions that most of the essays in this collection bear on Frege's intellectual relations to other philosophers, earlier, contemporary, or later. That interest having been awakened by Sluga's criticisms, I was first concerned to arrive at a correct estimate of his theses concerning Frege's relations to earlier and contemporary philosophers; Essays 4, 6, and 7 all resulted from this concern. Essays 4, 5, and 6 all concern the relations between Lotze and Frege. In Essay 6 I argued against the view that Frege's ideas were in any serious way derived from Lotze's. Gottfried Gabriel, who has recently published a detailed study of the relations between them, which he believes to have been significant, remarked in it that it was ironical that, in Essay 4, I had provided the only evidence so far known that Frege actually read Lotze. This evidence strengthens the hand of those who believe, with Gabriel, that there was a genuine influence from the older to the younger man; but I do not think that, of itself, it suggests much in the way of such an influence. Essay 7 compares the views of Frege and Kant on spatial intuition, and tries to glean, from the former's scattered remarks, almost all directed to emphasizing the difference, in his opinion, between geometry and arithmetic, some definite content for his philosophical view of geometry.

Subsequently, however, I became more interested in the writers with whom Ryle had associated Frege; Essays 2 and 13 are fruits of this interest. Essay 2 concerns the status of the definitions of arithmetical concepts given by Frege in his *Grundlagen*; I found it very useful to discuss these in the light of Husserl's criticism of Frege's book in his own *Philosophie der Arithmetik*. In Essay 13 I attempted to set the enquiry in the context of the work of Husserl's mentor Brentano, in order to explore a different aspect of the relation between Frege and Husserl, or rather, the relation between Frege and a different Husserl—the Husserl of the *Logische Untersuchungen* and the *Ideen*. It was in fact from this essay that my *Origins of Analytic Philosophy* later developed, in which I tried to exhibit that philosophical school as arising from the same matrix that also gave birth to phenomenology.

Others among these essays concern yet other historical relationships. As already noted, Essay 1 concerns Frege's clash with Hilbert over the latter's *Grundlagen der Geometrie*. Essay 3 touches on a little-known affinity between some of Frege's work in the second volume of his *Grundgesetze* and an article of Otto Hölder's. Essay 11 embodies some brief remarks on the relation between Frege and Wittgenstein.

Essay 3, though it, too, has a historical interest, has a different character from the rest, being primarily mathematical, and differs also in being the only one written in collaboration. Over very many years, from long before the publication of *Frege: Philosophy of Language*, I have been trying to write something illuminating about Frege's philosophy of mathematics; and I have long believed that the prevailing view of that part of his philosophy has been distorted by the neglect of the uncompleted part III of *Grundgesetze*, in which he expounded his theory of real numbers. Only a short way into the formal development of that theory, the reader comes upon an independence problem that Frege himself declares himself unable to solve. Although Frege did not, in *Grundgesetze*, use the term 'group', the problem in fact concerns groups with right-invariant, but not, in general, left-invariant, partial orderings; the problem is whether certain assumptions are sufficient to guarantee the linearity of the ordering. It long ago appeared to me that it would be wrong to write about that part of Frege's philosophy of mathematics without offering a solution to that problem; but my knowledge of group theory was quite inadequate to enable me to see how to solve it. At the stage at which it was decided that Frege's philosophy of mathematics was to be reserved for a second volume of my book about him, I put the problem aside for many years, as I did the general project of writing about his philosophy of mathematics.

When I took it up again, I found myself as unable to solve the problem as ever. I was very fortunate in consulting an expert in group theory, Dr Peter Neumann, who rapidly perceived the interest of the problem, and produced a solution establishing the independence which Frege suspected but could not prove, having first formulated the question in terms of the notion of an upper semilinear ordering which he and his colleague Dr Samson Adeleke had used in a paper they had been preparing that has yet to appear. Having seen Dr Neumann's solution, I was unsurprised that I had got nowhere in my attempts to tackle it. Given this solution to Frege's original problem, a further independence problem, which he did not expressly formulate, naturally arises, namely whether the linearity of the ordering follows from the stronger assumptions he added to the original ones. This problem was neatly solved by Dr Adeleke, in the opposite sense: in this case, it does follow. It is interesting that Dr Adeleke found it convenient to use in his proof a concept introduced by Frege, namely of a restricted form of left-invariance, to which we gave the name 'limpness', and a theorem proved by Frege about it. The article by Hölder cited in Essay 3 as resembling Frege's enquiry is well known to mathematicians; Frege's superior work, published a little later (though probably carried out earlier), has remained quite unknown. His researches into the theory of right-ordered groups, disguised by the elegant but unperspicuous notation for which he is famous, have been unjustly bereft of acknowledgement in the literature on group theory; I hope that our work may result in his recognition as having been not only a great philosopher but a more than negligible mathematician.

Yet other of the essays in this book concern modern commentators on Frege. As remarked, Essay 5 was my initial response to Sluga, considerably elaborated in *The Interpretation of Frege's Philosophy*, while Essays 6 and 7 were subsequent to that book and constitute, I hope, a more careful exploration of the historical issues raised by Sluga's contentions than I had achieved in it. Essays 8, 9, and 10 comprise critiques of other writers' interpretations of Frege which I consider to be equally deviant, but which appeared too late to be discussed in the *Interpretation*. In writing them, and particularly in writing Essay 8, I consciously tried very hard to make the discussion of interest to those concerned to understand and evaluate Frege's work, even if they were not especially concerned with the writers whom I was criticizing. Essay 13 considers a formulation of John Searle's, as well as touching on views of Ryle and others. The following Essay 14 was a response to an article by David Bell that struck me as being of much interest and raising questions of great general significance; it includes a brief discussion of certain opinions of Stephen Wagner. The final Essay 15 concerns the work of Gareth Evans, and, in particular, a disagreement between him and John Perry. David Bell's recent article in *Mind*, 'How "Russellian" was Frege?', corrects some serious inaccuracies in Evans's account of Frege, while failing, as I see the matter, to acknowledge the power of Evans's own ideas and the good use to which he put those he derived, even if in a slightly distorted form, from Frege. In my view, Evans's contribution to philosophy was of the first importance, one neglected by philosophers in the United States to their considerable loss. His thought derived much from Frege, as well as from Russell and Moore; and the topic at issue in Essay 15 is of central importance in evaluating the significance both of Frege's work and of Evans's.

It is also a topic of central importance to philosophy as a whole. I should not have written so much about Frege, or spent so much time thinking about Frege, were I not convinced that his ideas are of the highest value for the problems that present themselves to us at this stage in the evolution of philosophy. My hope is therefore that at least some of the essays in this book will be judged to be a contribution to philosophy, and not merely to its history.

Oxford, March 1990

Contents

Acknowledgements   xiv

1. Frege on the Consistency of Mathematical Theories   1

2. Frege and the Paradox of Analysis   17

3. On a Question of Frege's about Right-Ordered Groups
   (with S. A. Adeleke and P. M. Neumann)   53

4. Frege's 'Kernsätze zur Logik'   65

5. Frege as a Realist   79

6. Objectivity and Reality in Lotze and Frege   97

7. Frege and Kant on Geometry   126

8. An Unsuccessful Dig   158

9. Second Thoughts   199

10. Which End of the Telescope?   217

11. Frege and Wittgenstein   237

12. Frege's Myth of the Third Realm   249

13. Thought and Perception: The Views of Two
    Philosophical Innovators   263

14. More about Thoughts   289

15. The Relative Priority of Thought and Language   315

Appendix: Writings on Frege by Michael Dummett   325

Index   327

Acknowledgements

The author is grateful to the following for permission to reprint copyright material: Friedrich Frommann Verlag for Essay 1 in this collection; the Council of the London Mathematical Society for Essay 2; Universitets Forlaget, Oslo, for Essays 4, 5, 6 and 7; *The Philosophical Quarterly* and Basil Blackwell Ltd for Essays 8 and 9; Basil Blackwell Ltd for Essays 11 and 13; *Untersuchungen zur Logik und zur Methodologie* for Essay 12; and the *Notre Dame Journal of Formal Logic* for Essay 14.

1

Frege on the Consistency of Mathematical Theories*

Frege's attitude to the problem of the consistency of a theory is very clear, although some features of it may at first be puzzling, because we ourselves have become too sophisticated about such questions. It amounts to a combination of four propositions:

(1) The consistency of a theory requires proof;
(2) the consistency of a theory does not imply the existence of a model for it;
(3) anyway, the only way of proving the consistency of a theory is to provide a model for it; and
(4) even if it were possible to prove the consistency of a theory by some other means, what matters is the existence of a model and not the bare formal consistency.

Proposition (1) would be readily accepted—in fact, too readily—by most people at the present day, although Fitch has claimed the consistency of certain formal systems as 'transparent', and, more importantly, it would be contrary to the outlook of the intuitionists to allow that the consistency of an intuitionistically correct theory stood in need of proof. In any case, we shall see that, for Frege, (1) needs qualification in certain instances. Proposition (2) is a rejection of that variety of formalism according to which the existence of mathematical entities is tantamount to the consistency of the theory relating to them. It is in fact incorrect for a first-order theory, in view of the completeness theorem, but true for a higher-order theory. Frege, however, did not know the completeness theorem for first-order logic, and the proposition is at least true, under the ordinary sense of 'model', even for a first-order theory, if it is taken merely to say that it requires proof, and is not immediate, that, if such a theory is consistent, then it has a model.

Proposition (3) is not only false, but could have been known by

* First published in *Studien zu Frege*, ed. M. Schiru 1 (1976), 229–42.

Frege to be false. He argued, in his lecture series 'Logik in der Mathematik' of 1914, that the use of purely logical inferences must be adequate for the representation of the proofs of any mathematical theory.[1] To this he considered the objection that perhaps there are some forms of inference special to particular mathematical theories; as an example which might be suggested, he gave the principle of induction in number theory. The answer he gave to this objection was that if there is any form of inference peculiar to a particular mathematical theory, then we can formulate the general principle underlying it as a proposition of the theory. We may then be able to prove this proposition; if not, we must incorporate it into the axioms. We can then get the effect of the rule of inference by applying modus ponens to that proposition, whether proved as a theorem or assumed as an axiom. In the case of induction, Frege envisages the statement of the underlying principle as a single proposition involving second-order quantification. He provides no grounds, however, for believing that the principle underlying any putative special rule of inference can always be formulated as a single proposition. If his argument that we can always confine our rules of inference to purely logical ones is to be cogent, it must apply to the general case. In the general case, we should need, for every possible specific application of the putative rule of inference, to add to the axioms of the theory the conditional whose antecedent is the conjunction of the premisses of that application, and whose consequent is its conclusion.[2]

This argument of Frege's thus provided him with a ground for considering infinite axiom-systems (systems containing axiom-schemas) as possibly sometimes being required. But, for a theory with infinitely many axioms, there is always a way of proving the theory consistent without exhibiting any model for it: namely, by showing how to find, for any finite subset of the axioms, a model for that finite subset. For first-order theories, we know, by the

---

[1] *Nachgelassene Schriften*, ed. H. Hermes, F. Kambartel, and F. Kaulbach (Hamburg, 1969), 219–20; *Posthumous Writings*, trans. P. Long and R. White (Oxford, 1979), 203–4.

[2] This is just the way in which induction is usually (though not always) formalized. The schema of induction is: $$\frac{A(0) \forall x[A(x) \to A(x+1)]}{\forall x A(x)};$$ and the usual means of formalizing it is not to adopt it as a rule, but, instead, to take as an axiom the universal closure of every formula of the form: $A(0) \,\&\, \forall x\,[A(x) \to A(x+1)] \to \forall x A(x)$.

compactness theorem, that, if that can be done, then there is actually a model for the whole theory, and it is in applications of the compactness theorem that this kind of argument has become celebrated. The compactness theorem is, indeed, a very substantial result, of which Frege was not aware; but, when we are interested in proving only the *consistency* of the whole theory, rather than the existence of a model for it, then the argument rests on nothing save the soundness of the underlying logic, and the obvious fact that a proof, being finite, can invoke only finitely many axioms; the argument to the consistency of the theory is thus not restricted in its scope to first-order theories, unlike that to the existence of a model. The point was therefore quite open to Frege to realize, and thus allow that the consistency of a theory may be proved without establishing that it has a model. Most consistency proofs that do not proceed by constructing a model (in some often loose sense of 'construct') in fact follow, or can be represented by, just this pattern of a means of finding a model for each finite subset of the axioms.[3]

It could well be retorted that this is not entirely fair to Frege, since his reply to the hypothetical objection about special rules of inference was only *ad hominem*. He did not himself believe that there were any principles of inference peculiar to mathematical theories: in particular, he claimed, from the time of *Begriffsschrift* on, to have reduced argument by induction to purely logical principles (by means of his celebrated device, there introduced, for converting an inductive definition into an explicit one); and he believed, as Russell did, that the principle of induction within number theory was a direct consequence of the *definition* of 'natural number'— a natural number is simply an object for which the principle of induction holds (given that we know what 0 and the successor operation are). Furthermore, because Frege had no qualms about higher-level quantification, axioms which in a first-order formalization would have to be presented as axiom-schemas he could express as single axioms. Hence he would surely not have supposed it ever to be in practice necessary to adopt an infinite axiom-system, and it is therefore not surprising that the possibility of establishing

---

[3] Thus Hilbert's strategy for proving the consistency of arithmetic by substitution of numerical values for ε-terms, as eventually carried through by Ackermann in 1940, involves, in effect, finding, for each formal proof, an interpretation of the ε-operator which satisfies those instances of the axiom-schemas governing it which are actually appealed to in the proof.

consistency in this way did not occur to him. This defence is perfectly valid; but I did not, in any case, intend a serious reproach to Frege. The fact stands that his contention that the only way of proving consistency is by establishing the existence of a model was simply mistaken.

Much the philosophically most important of these four contentions, however, is the last one (4), the thesis, namely, that, even if the consistency of a theory could be proved without establishing that it had a model, what matters is that the theory should have a model, and not merely that it be consistent. Frege's reason for holding this is his general theory of meaning: it is this which is the foundation of his platonism. Once we have rejected radical formalism, we have to acknowledge mathematical propositions as being genuine statements which can be used, like other statements, to make assertions. The questions then arise, what is the correct model for the kind of meanings which mathematical statements have, and how we bestow those meanings on them. For Frege, there can be only one general form of answer for statements of any kind whatever. The sense of a sentence, the thought it expresses, is given by associating with it determinate conditions for its truth, it being understood to be false whenever these conditions fail (at least if it is a sentence of a properly constructed language). These truth-conditions are associated with the sentence via an association made between its constituent words or symbols and their extra-linguistic referents. The sort of thing which constitutes the referent of an expression depends upon its logical type: to a name or singular term is associated an object as its referent; to a (one-place) predicate a concept, under which a given object may or may not fall; to a relational expression, a relation, in which a given object may or may not stand to another; to a functional expression a function; to a sentence a truth-value; to a sentential operator a truth-function; to a predicate of second level, such as a quantifier, a second-level concept; and so on. The manner of association of its referent to an expression is the sense of the expression. What it is to associate an object with a term as its referent, particularly in the case that the object is not a concrete one, is a further question: all that concerns us here is that, for Frege, any legitimate means of conferring a sense upon the expressions and sentences of a language must be such as to bestow suitable references on those expressions, and thus determine each sentence of the language as true or as false. Since this is so, it must apply to (any fragment of) the language of mathematics as to any other part of our language. Any mathematical theory, therefore, if it is to have a specific interpretation which renders the sentences of the theory statements with a determinate meaning, must be related to a definite model: the variables of the theory must be assigned a definite domain over which they are taken to range, and the primitive individual constants, predicate-symbols, function-symbols, etc., of the theory given referents (of suitable types) in or over that domain.[4] To establish a theory as formally consistent is not, in itself, to confer a meaning on it, or to explain the meaning which it has: that can be done only by describing a model for the theory. (The model will of course give the intended meaning of an already existing theory only if it is the intended model.)

Frege did not suppose that a verbal description of a model for a theory played any essential role in our grasp of the meaning of the language of the theory (of the senses of expressions and sentences of that language). If actual *definitions* of the primitive non-logical expressions of the language are possible, then we have a means of displaying the theory as a subtheory of some wider one, as with Frege's own reduction of arithmetic to logic. But, in general, this will not be possible (it will not, on Frege's view, be possible either for geometry or for logic itself). In such cases, our informal explanations of the intended interpretations of the primitives will not amount to *definitions*, but will be what Frege calls 'elucidations' (*Erläuterungen*): they will indicate to the reader what the referents of the primitive expressions are meant to be taken to be, without giving any way of eliminating those expressions in favour of others. (Frege does not say precisely how he conceives of these elucidations as working; in particular, he does not say whether they can actually convey a new sense, or whether they will only work for someone who already grasps the sense which is in fact intended, but is not yet certain which sense is intended.)

This concession is harmless, because Frege does not conceive of a grasp of the sense of an expression as consisting, in general, in a capacity to give a rendering of the expression in other words.

---

[4] Frege did not have the modern conception of a model for a formula of his symbolic language, since he intended its individual variables to range always over all objects whatever, hence obviating the need for specifying the domain. But he was, of course, perfectly well aware that, in ordinary mathematical theories, the variables are intended to have a restricted range.

(To think this would involve an obvious circularity.) To grasp the senses of the expressions of a language is to have a means of associating determinate referents with them, and to grasp the senses of sentences (whose referents are truth-values) is therefore to associate with them their truth-conditions. But the knowledge in which a grasp of sense consists is not, in general, verbalized knowledge: it is not necessarily manifested by an ability to *say* what the referent of each expression is. To describe the intended model of a theory is not, therefore, to set out a series of statements which must have been recognized as true if the senses of the sentences of the theory have been grasped: it is to give an account—perhaps one that is not fully explicit, or one that can be fully understood only when the senses of expressions of the theory have already been understood—of what it is that someone implicitly knows when he understands the language of the theory. A model for a theory, or, rather, a structure for a language, is at the same time, a model of meaning.[5]

The attribution of the propositions (1)–(4) to Frege requires some justification, since he did not use the modern terminology of 'models', 'structures', and 'interpretations'. In several passages, Frege speaks, instead, in terms of concepts, often explicitly in terms of first-level concepts. Expressed in these terms, the four theses become:

(1′) it requires proof that a concept is not self-contradictory;

(2′) one cannot infer, from the fact that a concept is not self-contradictory, that an object falls under it (only that it is possible that one should);

(3′) the only way to establish that a concept is not self-contradictory is to prove that an object falls under it (although, by (2′), the converse inference is a fallacy); and

(4′) even if it could be shown, otherwise than by establishing that an object falls under it, that a concept were not self-contradictory, still, what matters is whether or not any

---

[5] Strictly speaking, this is not completely accurate. The sense of an expression is not uniquely determined by its reference, but by the particular means by which the referent is associated with it. The description of the intended structure for a language is therefore a model of meaning for the language only if the way in which the referents of the expressions of the language are characterized corresponds to the senses of those expressions. However, since sense determines reference, every model of meaning (sense) for a language will determine a structure for that language.

object falls under it, and, if so, whether there is a unique such object, rather than merely whether or not the concept is self-contradictory.

For instance, this is just the way Frege expresses the matter in *Grundlagen*:

Exception must be taken to the statement that the mathematician only counts as impossible what is self-contradictory. A concept is still admissible even though its defining characteristics do contain a contradiction: all that we are forbidden to do is to suppose that something falls under it. But from the fact that a concept contains no contradiction, it cannot thereby be inferred that something falls under it. How, after all, is it to be proved that a concept contains no contradiction? It is by no means always obvious; it does not follow from the fact that one sees no contradiction that none is there, and the determinateness of the definition affords no guarantee against it. . . . The freedom of a concept from contradiction can be rigorously proved only by a demonstration that something falls under it. The converse inference would be a fallacy.[6]

In 'Über formale Theorien der Arithmetik' Frege is concerned more directly with a radical formalist manner of construing auxiliary theories, and so speaks of the consistency, or freedom from contradiction, of rules of calculation; but he tends to convert this into a discussion of the consistency of properties of an object:

Now what means does one have for proving consistency? I see no other principle which could serve this purpose than that properties which are found in the same object do not stand in contradiction with each other. But, if one had such an object, the formalistic theory would be superfluous. For me it is accordingly improbable that a rigorous proof of the consistency of rules of calculation should be attained without abandoning the basis of this formalistic theory. But even if it were attained, it would not suffice, because what is consistent is not thereby true.[7]

However, in neither passage is his true topic the consistency of a first-level concept. In the *Grundlagen* passage, he is discussing an admittedly very woolly statement by Hankel, and applies his remarks to Hankel's account of the introduction of negative integers,

---

[6] *Die Grundlagen der Arithmetik: Eine logische-mathematische Untersuchung über den Begriff der Zahl* (Breslau, 1884), §§94 and 95.

[7] 'Über formale Theorien der Arithmetik', *Sitzungsberichte der Jenaischen Gesellschaft für Medizin und Naturwissenschaft für das Jahr 1885*, Supplement to *Jenaische Zeitschrift für Naturwissenschaft*, 19 (1886), 103.

and to similar accounts of the introduction of fractions and of complex numbers; similarly, in 'Über formale Theorien der Arithmetik', his express topic is formalist explanations of the introduction of fractions, negative numbers, algebraic irrationals, and complex numbers. Here it is not a question of finding an object falling under a well-defined concept: both Frege and his opponents are aware, and explicitly state, that the properties ascribed to the new numbers are contradictory if supposed to hold for the numbers of the base system. It is, rather, a matter of the consistency of a description of a whole mathematical structure; and hence it is more appropriate to talk in terms of a model for a theory than of an object's falling under a concept.

In Frege's articles 'Über die Grundlagen der Geometrie', he comes closer to an exact treatment of the matter, in a style which more resembles a modern approach. He was forced to do so in considering Hilbert's exposition in his *Grundlagen der Geometrie*, which was much more careful than the treatments by the formalist writers whose work Frege had earlier discussed. (There is nothing in Hilbert's book to indicate that he was adopting a radical formalist attitude to geometry, although Korselt, who defended Hilbert against Frege's criticism in the earlier of his two articles, interpreted Hilbert in this manner, and was criticized by Frege in his second article; there Frege expressed doubt whether Korselt's interpretation corresponded with Hilbert's intention.) In his book, Hilbert had said that the axioms he presented constituted a *definition* of the geometrical primitives 'point', 'line', 'plane', 'lies on', 'between', etc. Frege quite rightly points out that this cannot be a correct description of the axiom-system, since we cannot, from the axioms, determine, of a given object, whether it is a point or not. What the axiom-system defines is, rather, a concept of second level, or, more accurately, a second-level relation of a large number of arguments, which may or may not hold between given first-level concepts, relations, and ternary relations.

Now Hilbert is concerned with the consistency and independence of his axioms. How, then, on Frege's view, can such a second-level relation be proved consistent? Frege's answer is: precisely by finding particular first-level concepts, relations, and ternary relations which stand in that second-level relation—the exact analogue, at second level, of finding an object which falls under a first-level concept, or finding two objects which stand in a first-level relation. Independence is to be proved in a similar way. This is an account, in a different terminology, precisely of finding a model for a theory: the theory constitutes a specification of a second-level relation; the various first-level concepts, relations, and ternary relations which are shown to stand in that second-level relation constitute a model for that theory. In fact, it would need only the notion of a sequence of first-level concepts, relations, and ternary relations, considered as a single entity, to provide a direct way of mapping modern terminology on to that used by Frege; though Frege does not himself introduce such a notion of a sequence. A sequence of first-level entities (concepts, relations, and ternary relations) might be thought of as a uniquely specifying second-level relation of appropriate type (i.e. with the appropriate number and types of arguments); where by a 'uniquely specifying' relation is meant one such that, for each argument-place, the existential quantification of all other argument-places would result in a concept (in our case, of second level) with exactly one thing, of the appropriate type, falling under it. Such a sequence would then correspond exactly to a specific mathematical structure of the right similarity type. The axiom-system would then specify a class of structures, i.e. a third-level concept under which some structures of the appropriate type fell, and others did not: the structures falling under this third-level concept would thus be models of the theory. Frege's method of proving the consistency of an axiom-system accordingly consists precisely of proving a theory consistent by finding a specific model of it. Frege's general views about the consistency of concepts then carry over to this case: we cannot infer from the consistency of a theory (of a third-level concept) that there is a model of it (a second-level relation falling under it); we can prove the consistency of a theory only by establishing that it has a model; and, even if the consistency of a theory could be proved in some other way, what is important is that it should have a model, not that it be barely consistent.

However, this account of Frege's views holds only for an axiom-system, or theory, of Hilbert's kind; Frege himself did not want to use the words 'axiom' and 'theory' in this way, and, for what he calls an 'axiom' or a 'theory', his account is significantly different. In his remarks on Hilbert's *Grundlagen der Geometrie*, Frege expends much time discussing Hilbert's use of the word 'axiom'. In the traditional use of this word, to which Frege himself adhered, an axiom is a true proposition—a true thought in Frege's terminology—which does not stand in need of proof and is assumed without proof. (Frege used the term '*Grundsatz*' for the sentence by which the axiom is formulated, i.e. which expresses the thought, and reserved the word '*Axiom*' for the thought expressed.) Frege's only divergence from the traditional conception lay in his not requiring of an axiom that it be incapable of proof. In this respect, axioms resemble definitions. Although he held that there are some notions (such as truth or identity) which are absolutely indefinable, Frege was well aware that it is to some extent a matter of choice what one decides to define in terms of what, and therefore what one starts with as undefined: 'undefined' does not mean 'indefinable', since one might have adopted different primitives, and have defined what one is in fact taking as primitive. It can be demanded of a primitive notion only that it *can* be understood in advance of any definitions, not that it could not be defined. Correspondingly, Frege says in 'Logik in der Mathematik' that the choice of axioms is to some extent arbitrary. Under one choice, a certain proposition A will be an axiom, and B be proved from it and the other axioms; while, under another choice, B might be taken as an axiom, and A be proved from it together with the rest. What is called an 'axiom' is, therefore, relative to a particular system. Nevertheless, only that can be legitimately taken as an axiom which we *can* recognize as true without proof; for, as Frege remarks, if we require a proof in order to recognize a proposition as true, then the premisses of this proof are the real axioms.

Frege insists, again and again, and with perfect justice, that Hilbert's geometrical axioms are not axioms in this traditional sense, despite Hilbert's sometimes so describing them. Since the primitive geometrical expressions occurring in the statements of the axioms are not assumed to have any determinate senses, but to be subject to different interpretations, these statements are not actually complete sentences, and therefore cannot express thoughts which may be judged true or false. Rather, the primitive expressions must be regarded as variables for first-level concepts and relations, or, in Frege's terminology, letters which indefinitely indicate such concepts and relations, without having any determinate reference. The statements of the axioms are then, correspondingly, expressions for second-level concepts and relations; Frege calls them 'pseudo-axioms'. Proving their consistency or independence then becomes a straightforward mathematical problem, the problem, namely, whether there is a structure of such-and-such a kind (whether there are first-level concepts and relations falling under certain second-level concepts and standing in certain second-level relations).

This leads naturally, however, to the question whether the members of a system of *genuine* axioms—axioms in the traditional sense—may be proved independent of one another. In the 1903 article on the foundations of geometry,[8] Frege's answer is apparently a negative one: he says that Hilbert's proof of the independence of his axioms for Euclidean geometry is a proof of the independence only of pseudo-axioms, obtained by varying the interpretations of the primitive expressions. In the actual axioms of Euclidean geometry, however, the primitive expressions have a fixed, determinate sense, and one cannot conclude from the independence of the pseudo-axioms to the independence of the genuine axioms. In his letter to Liebmann of 29 July 1900, he says:

I have reason to believe that the mutual independence of the axioms of *Euclidean* geometry cannot be proved. H[ilbert] contrives to extend the domain, so that Euclidean geometry appears as a special case; and in this extended domain, he can now show consistency by examples; but only in this extended domain; for from consistency in a more inclusive domain one cannot infer to it in a narrower one; for contradictions may enter precisely by the restriction. The converse inference is of course legitimate.[9]

He writes similarly in a letter to Hilbert:

There seems to me to be a logical danger which lies in your speaking of, e.g., 'the axiom of parallels', as if it were the same in each particular geometry. Only the wording is the same; the thought-content is different in every other geometry. . . . Now, even assuming that these axioms were in the particular geometries all special cases of more general axioms, one can indeed infer from their consistency in a particular geometry to their consistency in the general case, but not to their consistency in other special cases.[10]

---

[8] 'Über die Grundlagen der Geometrie', *Jahresberichte der Deutschen Mathematiker-Vereinigung*, 12 (1903), 319–24, 368–75.

[9] *Wissenschaftlicher Briefwechsel*, ed. G. Gabriel, H. Hermes, F. Kambartel, C. Thiel, and A. Veraart (Hamburg, 1976), 148–9; *Philosophical and Mathematicalal Correspondence*, ed. B. McGuinness, trans. H. Kaal (Oxford, 1980), 91.

[10] *Wissenschaftlicher Briefwechsel*, 75–6; *Philosophical and Mathematical Correspondence*, p. 48.

In his notes of 1910 to Jourdain's 'The Development of the Theories
of Mathematical Logic and the Principles of Mathematics: Gottlob
Frege',[11] he was still making observations in the same vein:

> The indemonstrability of the axiom of parallels cannot be proved. If we do
> this apparently, we use the word 'axiom' in a sense quite different from that
> which is handed down to us.[12]

However, in the last part of his 1906 article on the foundations of
geometry,[13] Frege first emphasizes that the investigation of the
independence of genuine axioms is a problem of a sort radically new
in mathematics, but then goes on to discuss it in a vein much more
similar to modern modes of thought on the subject. The reason he
gives, in the first instance, for saying that the problem is of a
radically new character is that genuine axioms are *thoughts*, which
are entities with which mathematics does not normally deal (when
we are discussing the independence of genuine axioms, we cannot
be concerned with the *referents* of the sentences which express
them, for these are truth-values): by contrast, when we discuss the
independence of pseudo-axioms, we are concerned with a relation
between the referents of the (incomplete) sentences which express
them, namely, between second-level concepts and relations, and we
are therefore dealing with a familiar type of mathematical problem.
Having said this, he goes on to describe a possible method for
proving the independence of genuine axioms, which is precisely the
way we should think most natural nowadays. Namely, we set up a
'translation' of the expressions used in the statement of the axioms,
not from one language into another with preservation of sense, but
within one language and involving a change of sense. If we can set
up a translation of such a kind which carries all the axioms but one
into propositions (thoughts) which we can recognize as true, and
that one into a proposition which we can recognize as false, then
the independence of that axiom from the others is proved. It will
immediately occur to us now to describe this process as one of
finding a model in which the given axiom is false but the rest are
true. However, for Frege, it would be very misleading to describe it
in this way, because it would conflate this procedure with what was

---

[11] *Quarterly Journal of Pure and Applied Mathematics*, 43 (1912), 237–69.
[12] Ibid. 240.
[13] 'Über die Grundlagen der Geometrie', *Jahresberichte der Deutschen Mathe-matiker-Vereinigung*, 15 (1906), 293–309, 377–403, 423–30.

for him the totally different one of finding a model of pseudo-axioms, i.e. of finding a structure falling under a third-level concept (or finding first-level concepts and relations standing in a given second-level relation). In the latter case, there is no problem about what expressions it is for which we have to find an interpretation: they are the expressions taken as primitive; or, when the matter is properly expressed, what we are doing is finding values for the variables which mark the argument-places of the expression for the second-level concept or relation. When we are concerned with the independence of genuine axioms, however, the expressions which may undergo 'translation' for the sake of an independence proof are not marked out in any such way: we are confronted with a range of expressions which already have their own proper senses. We may not, however, if we want our translation to establish genuine *logical* independence, adopt a translation without any restriction at all. On the contrary, the senses of expressions which belong to logic—the sign of identity, the sentential connectives, and the quantifiers, for example—must be preserved. Frege expresses this by saying that logic is not purely formal, any more than, on his view, geometry is: there are certain expressions whose *sense* logic requires to be determinate and to be known. Hence, in order to carry out a cogent independence proof, we require a characterization of which expressions are *logical* constants. Frege evidently takes this to be an extremely difficult problem, and uses it as a ground to reiterate his opinion that the investigation of the independence of genuine axioms raises problems of a quite new sort: 'we here find ourselves in a new territory'.

All this represents a partial retraction by Frege of his earlier doubts about the possibility of proving the independence of the axioms of Euclidean geometry; but the doubts still find expression in his remark that it would be necessary first to establish whether the primitive notions of geometry are or are not logical in character, and this may explain why in 1910 he was still asserting that it was impossible to prove the independence of the axiom of parallels. While the problem of characterizing the logical constants is no doubt of some importance, Frege is surely mistaken here. Even if he is correct in saying that the principle of induction in number theory is to be reduced to purely logical inferences, it is surely intelligible, and correct, to say that the principle of induction is independent of the other Peano axioms: in saying this, we are simply prescinding from the possibility of defining 'natural number', in a second-order language, in terms of 0 and successor, and our ground for doing so is just the fact that, in the Peano axioms, all three notions are presented as primitive. Similarly, even on Frege's own view that *all* number-theoretic notions are reducible to, and hence themselves are, logical notions, it would still make sense to say that the unique factorization theorem is independent of the general laws governing multiplication (commutative, associative, and cancellation laws). A question about independence is always relative: a statement A may be independent of some set Γ of statements relative to one fragment of logic, but not relative to a larger fragment (e.g. it obviously might be independent relative to sentential logic, but not relative to predicate logic); and if it is said to be independent relative to one theory, but not relative to another, the *significance* of this statement is not affected by whether or not we take either theory to be part of logic properly so called, although the interest of the statement may be so affected. (The stronger theory might, for example, be set theory, or, again, what is called tense logic.) Similarly, independence is relative to the definitional interconnections taken as assumed: an expression may, in its true sense, be definable in certain terms, logical or otherwise; but it is still legitimate to reinterpret it, for the sake of an independence proof, in such a way as to invalidate this definition, if the independence asserted is not relative to the possibility of such a definition.

Since Frege is able to make sense of the notion of proving the independence of genuine axioms, albeit with the reservations we have noted (and assessed as unnecessary), it might be thought that he would also make sense of that of proving their consistency, since, after all, a consistency proof is only a special kind of independence proof (it shows that a statement of the form 'A and not A' is independent of the axiom-system). This is not, however, the case. To prove the consistency of an axiom-system Γ by his method would be to provide a translation, preserving the logical constants, which converted Γ into a set Γ* of statements which we can recognize as true and such that we can recognize the statement 'A* and not A*' as false. But this is easily accomplished by the identity-mapping: we can already recognize 'A and not A' to be false on purely logical grounds, and the statements in Γ, being axioms, have already been recognized as true. It *needs* no proof, according to Frege, that a set of genuine axioms is consistent: being axioms, they are all true, and hence cannot contradict one another. Thus he says, in a letter to Hilbert of late 1899, 'From the truth of the axioms it follows of itself that they do not contradict one another. This needs no further proof.'[14] It may be thought, in view of what happened to Frege two and a half years later, ironic that he should have said this; but in 1914, in 'Logik in der Mathematik', he was still writing:

The *axioms* serve in the system as premisses for the deductions by means of which the system is constructed, but do not appear as truths to which we have inferred. Since they are to be premisses, they must be true. An axiom which is not true is a contradiction in terms.[15]

One might seek to explain this by saying that, while no axiom can be false, it is often difficult to recognize whether a proposition is an axiom or not; when a contradiction emerges from it, its claim to be an axiom is of course refuted, but it is sometimes hard to see, of a proposition, that it *is* an axiom, even when it is. But it is dubious whether such ideas can be attributed to Frege: for, not only does a proposition lose its status as an axiom as soon as we accept something as a proof that it is true, but an axiom is required to be a proposition which *needs* no proof. It is a pity that Frege did not at least supplement, if not revise, his views on axioms in the light of his experience over the Russell contradiction.

However this may be, it is plain that Frege's view that the consistency of a set of genuine axioms needs no proof is in apparent conflict with the thesis (1), that consistency requires to be proved. The conflict is only apparent, because the thesis (1) is stated by Frege only in the context of a discussion of formalist accounts of mathematical theories: he meant it to apply only to a claim of consistency for assumptions not known to be true, or for pseudo-axioms such as Hilbert's containing expressions functioning as variables for concepts and relations which it makes no sense to speak of as being (absolutely) true, or for a theory construed in a radical formalist manner, when it is not taken as involving meaningful expressions at all. In all these cases, when the axiom-system is not subject to a specific, intended interpretation, or not to one under which it is known to be true, in short, when all that is claimed for it is that it is consistent, not that it is true, it makes sense

[14] *Wissenschaftlicher Briefwechsel*, 63; *Philosophical and Mathematical Correspondence*, 37.
[15] *Nachgelassene Schriften*, p. 263; *Posthumous Writings*, 244.

to speak of finding a model for the axiom-system and so proving it consistent. But, when we are dealing with a genuine theory, that is, one for which we have a definite interpretation, under which we believe its axioms to be true, it makes no sense to talk of finding such a model: for we already have a model. On his own terms, Frege is wholly in the right over this: a consistency-proof achieved by exhibiting a model really is quite pointless in any such case, e.g. for number theory. What non-standard model for number theory could possibly afford better evidence of the consistency of the theory than the standard model we already have? Given Frege's false belief that the consistency of a theory can be proved only by exhibiting a model for it, he was entirely correct in drawing the conclusion that a proof of consistency is neither possible nor needed for a system of what he called genuine axioms. We are, indeed, so accustomed to hearing of consistency-proofs for arithmetic that we tend to overlook the oddity of seeking such a thing at all. Of course, the motivation for such a consistency-proof came originally from Hilbert's finitist philosophy of mathematics, according to which the axioms of arithmetic are not, after all, evidently true, and indeed do not admit of any interpretation as a whole, because of the irreducibly infinitistic use of the quantifiers. Once it is held that we neither have, nor can have, a model for arithmetic, then, naturally, a consistency-proof ceases to be redundant; but, equally, it cannot proceed in the only way envisaged by Frege, namely, by describing a model for the theory.

2
Frege and the Paradox of Analysis*

The Cambridge philosopher G. E. Moore came to the conclusion that philosophers had erred in thinking it the task of philosophy either to refute certain general propositions to which common sense would ordinarily assent, or to defend them against purported refutations. On the contrary, such propositions were not, in his view, to be called in question. What was to be called in question was the correct *analysis* of those propositions, and this was the proper task of philosophy: we could not sensibly doubt the truth of the common-sense propositions, but, without the help of the philosophers, we could not say what precisely it is that they mean. The task of philosophy is thus the analysis of concepts or of meanings.

The idea of analysis led, however, to apparent paradox; and this 'paradox of analysis' greatly preoccupied Moore and others of his general outlook. For the outcome of conceptual analysis must be an analytic truth *par excellence*: and, if so, how could it give us new information? A correct analysis must yield a definition faithful to the meaning of the term defined; how, then, could there be any doubt about its correctness? For, if someone grasps the meanings of two expressions, must he not thereby know whether they have the same meaning or different meanings? If so, then any proposed analysis must be immediately recognizable either as correct or as incorrect. This therefore appeared to leave hardly any work for philosophy to do, if it was to consist in the analysis of concepts; and, even if it were insisted that it is difficult to hit upon the correct analysis, it would make it an utter mystery that there should be disputes in philosophy—any appropriately expressed philosophical theory must be either obviously false or obviously true.

Someone otherwise unfamiliar with Frege's work would conclude, from a reading of his notes for his lecture course 'Logik in der Mathematik', composed, in 1914, towards the end of his career, that he attached little importance to conceptual analysis. In the

* Given as a lecture at Bologna University in 1987.

section devoted to definitions,[1] he distinguishes two types, constructive and analytic. By 'constructive' definitions he means stipulative ones, introducing some new expression or laying down how someone intends to use an old one. Towards such constructive definitions, he adopts a Russellian attitude, regarding them as being, from a logical standpoint, pure abbreviations: the defining expression and that being defined will have the same sense, and so, although they may have great psychological importance, their logical importance is nil. But, in treating of analytic definitions, he runs headlong into the paradox of analysis, and allows this to make him put a very low value on such definitions. An analytic definition is one which attempts to capture the sense attached to a term already in use, but not originally introduced by definition, by means of some complex expression presented as equivalent to it. Frege's comment is that a successful analytic definition must be immediately recognizable as such, for the reason already given: anyone who knows the sense both of the term defined and of the expression by which it is proposed to define it must at once apprehend that they are the same, if in fact they are. At least, this must be so if the sense of the term being analysed was already clearly grasped: if any doubt remains about whether or not the proposed definition really does capture the sense of the existing term, then, provided that the sense of the defining expression is clear, the only explanation must be that we never had a clear grasp of the sense of the term we are trying to analyse. In such a case, Frege's recommendation is that we simply abandon the old term, and employ instead an undisguisedly new one, with the same definition as that we proposed for the old one. When used as the definition of the new term, however, the definition will no longer purport to be an analytic one, but will be a stipulative or constructive one, laid down without any claim that it captures the sense of any existing term; and so the problems of analysis will be circumvented. The labour of analysis will indeed have been fruitful, in that it issued in a clear sense where before there was only a cloudy one; but we should eschew any pretence that the clear sense corresponds to the cloudy sense in any precisely statable manner.

[1] *Nachgelassene Schriften*, ed. H. Hermes, F. Kambartel, and F. Kaulbach (Hamburg, 1969), 224–9; *Posthumous Writings*, trans. P. Long and R. White (Oxford, 1979), 207–11.

Frege is here expressly talking about definitions of mathematical terms; but there is no reason to suppose that he would at that time have adopted any different attitude to definitions of any other terms to be used in rigorous deductive reasoning. By 1914 he had, probably for the preceding eight years, lost his faith in the project towards which he had, until 1903, directed almost all his efforts since the beginning of his career, the demonstration that arithmetic is a branch of pure logic. It is nevertheless astonishing that he could have written in the way I have summarized about conceptual analysis viewed as issuing in definitions; for such analysis had lain at the very heart of the project to which he had devoted his life and which Russell's contradiction had forced him to abandon as unrealizable. This is even clearer in his introductory work *Die Grundlagen der Arithmetik* as in what was intended as the final execution of the project, his *Grundgesetze der Arithmetik*. In *Grundlagen*, the project is formulated as that of making it probable that arithmetical truths are analytic in a sense akin to that of Kant. An analytical truth is defined to be one derivable by means of definitions from the fundamental laws of logic by strictly deductive reasoning. Frege does not ask, in this connection, how a definition may be known to be correct, but treats that as if it were unproblematic; but he makes clear that a great part of the ensuing investigation, devoted to rendering probable the analyticity of arithmetical truths, will be concerned with finding definitions of arithmetical terms.

Starting from these philosophical questions, we come upon the same demand as that which has independently arisen within the domain of mathematics itself: to prove the basic propositions of arithmetic with the utmost rigour, whenever this can be done . . . If we now try to meet this demand, we very soon arrive at propositions a proof of which remains impossible so long as we do not succeed in analysing the concepts that occur in them into simpler ones or in reducing them to what has greater generality. Number itself is what, above all, has either to be defined or to be recognized as indefinable. This is the problem to which this book is addressed. On its solution the decision on the nature of arithmetical laws depends.[2]

By speaking of 'number' here, I believe that Frege has in mind, not a definition of the general term 'number', in the sense either of 'cardinal number' or of 'natural number', but, rather, a general

---

[2] *Die Grundlagen der Arithmetik*: *Eine logische-mathematische Untersuchung über den Begriff der Zahl* (Breslau, 1884), §4.

means of defining individual natural numbers; but that is not of prime importance to us. What matters is that he rates the task of finding appropriate definitions, or of recognizing that no definition is possible, of central importance to the project of determining whether arithmetical laws are analytic or synthetic.

It therefore appears clear that the definitions he has in mind are not stipulative, but analytic, ones. He wants to propose new definitions, which will not be definitions of new terms, but of existing ones. There is no talk of substituting new forms of statement, containing newly introduced terms, for the arithmetical statements we are accustomed to employ, and then deriving statements of these new forms from the fundamental laws of logic: he means to settle the status of the arithmetical laws we already have, involving the arithmetical concepts we already grasp; and, to do that, he must analyse those concepts and supply definitions of expressions long in use but not hitherto defined. Definitions will therefore be among the keenest instruments that he is to employ; and, if such definitions are to serve their purpose, they must surely be analytic ones. This point is succinctly stated by Professor Eva Picardi thus:

Without the premise that definitions afford an analysis or reconstruction of the meaning of the arithmetical sentences which is somehow responsible to the meaning of these sentences as these are understood the logicist idea of providing an analysis of the sense of arithmetical sentences by uncovering the grounds on which a justification for their assertion rests would be incomprehensible.[3]

This is borne out by the course Frege's subsequent discussion takes. From §55 to §83, where his positive theory of the natural numbers is presented, attention is concentrated solely on two types of question: how we are to define arithmetical notions, and how, with the help of the definitions given, we are to prove the fundamental laws of number theory. Definitions are offered of the following expressions:

There are just as many Fs as Gs	the number of Fs
(The concept F is equinumerous	(the number belonging to the
to the concept G)	concept F)

---

[3] Eva Picardi, 'Frege on Definition and Logical Proof', in C. Cellucci and G. Sambin (eds.), *Temi e prospettive della logica e della filosofia della scienza contemporanee*, i (Bologna, 1988), 228.

22 Frege and the Paradox of Analysis

not cause him any uncertainty about whether the proposition that he has proved—that every finite number has an immediate successor—is the same as the proposition that others would express in that way. In this, he has of course followed the ordinary procedure of mathematicians. If you want to prove a theorem stated in terms that are already in use, you may very well need first to give rigorous definitions of those terms, and you do not normally stop to ask yourself whether your definitions really capture the meanings that have long been attached to them, in the absence of any definition. Frege pays hardly more attention to this question in *Grundlagen*, despite the philosophical orientation of the book, than does the ordinary mathematician expounding a proof.

It therefore seems that Frege's definitions in *Grundlagen* must be intended as analytic ones. He is not claiming to demonstrate the analyticity of new propositions that could not have been expressed before his definitions had been given: he is claiming to have demonstrated, or, at least, to have made probable, the analyticity of propositions with which we have been long familiar and to which we have appealed without proof. A possible objection to this interpretation might be that Frege does *not* use everyday expressions, but prefers a jargon of his own—'the number belonging to the concept F' in place of 'the number of Fs', and 'the concept F is equinumerous to the concept G' in place of 'there are just as many Fs as Gs'. This choice of terminology, the objector argues, indicates that Frege's intention was not as I have claimed: rather, by using unfamiliar terminology, he indicated that he was not intending to capture the senses of existing expressions, or in any weaker sense to propose definitions of them. If this were right, we should be faced with a different problem: not that of the nature of analytic definitions, but that of the relation of arithmetical laws expressed in Frege's newly introduced terminology to the laws of arithmetic as they would ordinarily be enunciated. But I do not believe the objection to be sound. Frege's principal motive in employing the jargon is, I believe, to exhibit what he has argued to be the correct logical analysis of the more ordinary expressions. It is to *concepts* that statements of number relate, or to which numbers attach: Frege supposes that the form 'the number belonging to the concept F' brings this out more emphatically than the everyday form 'the number of Fs'. In the same way, cardinal equivalence is a relation, not between objects, but between concepts, and the form 'The concept F is equinumerous to the concept G' makes this explicit as 'There are just as many Fs as Gs' does not. If this was truly the way that Frege thought in writing *Grundlagen*, he was of course mistaken: he was still in a state of innocence, before he became conscious of the troubles with which he tried unsuccessfully to deal in 'Über Begriff und Gegenstand'.

If this is right, it is indeed astonishing that, thirty years later, he could have written as he did about conceptual analysis regarded as issuing in definitions. Admittedly, by 1914, he had long believed that his attempt to derive arithmetic from logic had failed. But what had driven him to this sad conclusion was his recognition that the logic from which he had tried to derive it was unsound; it was not at all a conviction that the whole project had been misguided—the project, namely, of determining the nature and basis of arithmetical truths by discovering, by means of definitions of the terms involved, from what more fundamental principles the most basic laws of arithmetic could be deduced. It is therefore remarkable that he could at that date have written about definitions in a manner that entirely overlooked his own previous attempt to carry out just such a project by means of a suitable chain of analytic definitions.

One explanation might be that, in those thirty years, Frege had come to think that, when he wrote *Grundlagen*, he had misunderstood the character of definition. As Eva Picardi and others have emphasized, a radical change of view is implicit in his ceasing to speak of definitions as fruitful, as he had done in *Grundlagen*, §§70 and 88, and rating them instead as logically (though not psychologically) unimportant. He may equally have come to regard himself as not having apprehended the distinction between constructive (stipulative) and analytical definitions at the time when *Grundlagen* was written. In 'Logik in der Mathematik', an analytic definition is characterized as purporting exactly to reproduce the *sense* that the defined expression bears in its ordinary existing use: if the definitions that he gave in *Grundlagen* lacked this objective, it is misleading to call them analytic. After all, when he wrote *Grundlagen*, he was not yet operating with his later notion of sense, but with the cruder notion of conceptual content; he may therefore simply not have had in mind such a distinction between types of definition.

An alternative possibility is that, at the time of writing *Grundlagen*, he would have rejected the distinction that he later drew. Since, in that book, he is silent on the matter, we cannot tell precisely what he would then have said; but what he wrote concerning definition in 1894, when he did have the notion of sense to hand, contains an explicit rejection of his later conception of analytic definitions. That is to say, he rejected the requirement that the definition of an existing term should exactly capture the sense already attached to that term, and made no assumption that there need be any such unique sense. His remarks on the subject occur in his review of Husserl's *Philosophie der Arithmetik* of 1891. In his book, Husserl had strongly criticized Frege's *Grundlagen*, attacking, in particular, Frege's definitions of arithmetical notions, including the definition of cardinal equivalence (of 'just as many as'). Much of Frege's review is occupied with attacking Husserl's psychologistic treatment, and his consequent failure to distinguish between the objective sense of an expression and the subjective ideas (mental images and the like) which it may call up in the mind of one hearer or another. He therefore naturally rejects the demand that the idea associated with the defining expression should agree with that associated with the term defined. What is important for us, however, is that he goes further than this, and stigmatizes it as an error of psychologistic logicians such as Husserl to demand even coincidence of sense between defined term and defining expression. He characterizes a standard form of objection used by Husserl as follows:

If words and phrases refer to ideas, then, for any two of them, there is no other possibility than that they either designate the same idea or different ones. In the first case, to equate them by means of a definition will be pointless—'an obvious circle' [in Husserl's phrase]; in the other it will be incorrect. These are the two objections, of which the author regularly lodges one or the other. Even the sense is something that a definition is incapable of analysing; for the analysed sense is, as such, not the same as the original one. Either, with the word being defined, I already clearly think everything that I think with the defining expression, and then we have the 'obvious circle'; or the defining expression has a more richly articulated sense, so that with it I do not think the same as with that being defined, and hence the definition is incorrect.[4]

Husserl had clearly faced the paradox of analysis, and had come to the conclusion that it is irresoluble, and hence that analysis is impossible. Frege, in his review, rejects the paradox, and, with it,

---

[4] Review of Edmond Husserl, *Philosophie der Arithmetik* (Leipzig, 1891), *Zeitschrift für Philosophie und philosophische Kritik*, 103 (1894), 319.

the demand that a definition of an existing term should be analytic in the sense of his 1914 lectures. He replies to Husserl as follows:

In this matter there appears a division between psychologistic logicians and mathematicians. The concern of the former is with the sense of the words and with the ideas that they fail to distinguish from the sense. The mathematicians, by contrast, are concerned with the matter itself, that is, with the *reference* of the words. The objection [made by Husserl] that it is not the concept, but its extension, that gets defined is really directed against all mathematical definitions. For a mathematician the definition of a conic as the circumference of the intersection between a plane and the surface of a right cone is neither more correct nor more incorrect than its definition as a plane curve whose equation with respect to rectangular coordinates is of degree 2. His choosing either of these two definitions, or some third one, will be based on convenience, regardless of the fact that these expressions neither have the same sense nor give rise to the same ideas. I do not mean by this that a concept is the same thing as its extension; only that a coincidence of extension is a sufficient and necessary criterion for there to obtain between concepts that relation which corresponds to identity as a relation between objects. (pp. 319–20)

Frege is here plainly unfair to Husserl. Husserl had anticipated Moore's discovery of the paradox of analysis; and the paradox is not to be dismissed as lightly as Frege dismisses it in his review. It is worth noting, first, a rather subtle point concerning which Frege is unfair to Husserl, which, when we look closely at it, does not actually turn on the distinction between stipulative and analytic definitions. Frege meets Husserl's argument that an analysed sense *cannot* be precisely the same as an unanalysed one, not by refuting it, but by simply asserting that a definition need not preserve sense, but only reference; but, by Frege's own standards, he should have accorded the argument sufficient force to block the claim, which he was accustomed to make, that a definition confers on the term defined the very same sense as that possessed by the defining expression. This claim conflicts, even for stipulative definitions, with the doctrine of *Begriffsschrift*, §9. That doctrine was that the distinction, within a complete expression, between a part which refers to an object, and what, in that work, he calls a 'function', 'has nothing to do with the conceptual content, but is solely a matter of our way of regarding it'. When the complete expression to which we apply the distinction is a whole sentence, the 'function' will be an incomplete or unsaturated expression referring to a concept.

Frege's reason for saying that the splitting up of the sentence into two such parts 'has nothing to do with the content' is twofold: that there are distinct equally admissible ways of splitting it up; and that, in general, we do not need to advert to or to be remotely aware of the possibility of splitting it up in a particular way in order to grasp its content. Consider, for instance, the sentence (A):

(A) $19 > 1$, and, for every n, if n divides 19, then $n = 19$ or $n = 1$.

One useful way to split up the sentence (A) is into the numerical term '19' and the incomplete expression (P):

(P) $\ldots > 1$, and, for every n, if n divides $\ldots$, then $n = \ldots$ or $n = 1$.

In order to grasp the content of the sentence (A), however, we do not need to have the possibility of this way of splitting it up in mind; it suffices that we understand each of the simple components of the sentence—the two numerical terms, the relational expressions '>', 'divides', and '=', the two connectives 'and' and 'if', and the universal quantifier. For this reason, the content of the incomplete expression (P) cannot be considered *part* of the content of the sentence (A), a fact that we may express by saying that one does not need to have the concept of primality in order to grasp the content of (A).

If this doctrine of *Begriffsschrift* is to be considered as carrying over to Frege's middle period, from 1891 to 1906, we can express it in the terminology of that period by saying that the sense of the incomplete expression (P) is not part of the thought expressed by the sentence (A). It is not that (P) does not have a sense, or that that sense is not closely related to that of the sentence (A): rather, we can express that relation by saying that the sense of (P) is a function that maps the sense of the term '19' on to the thought expressed by (A), the sense of the term '20' on to the thought expressed by the result of substituting '20' for '19' in (A), and so forth. But, just because the sense of (P) may be regarded as a function having the sense of the sentence (A) as one of its values, it cannot also be *part* of the sense of (A).

To describe the sense of the predicate (P) as a function from the senses of numerical terms to thoughts might appear to conflict with the general requirement that the sense of a predicate must constitute the way some concept is given; for, in general, a function from the senses of terms to thoughts need have no concept corresponding to it. This is because such a function might be referentially opaque: it might, for example, map the sense of the term '19' on to a true thought and that of the term '16+3' on to a false one. But the particular way in which the incomplete expression (P) was obtained, by decomposition of the sentence (A), guarantees that this cannot happen for the associated function. There will be a concept—the concept of a prime number—under which any given natural number will fall just in case the function in question maps the sense of any term referring to that number on to a true thought.

Suppose, now, that we define the predicate '. . . is prime' to be equivalent to the complex predicate (P). What answer is then to be given to the question whether the sentence (B):

(B) 19 is prime

expresses the same thought as the sentence (A)? Plainly, that it does not: for the sense of the newly defined predicate '. . . is prime' evidently *is* a part of the thought expressed by (B): you could not grasp *that* thought without having the concept of primality. It hardly seems to matter whether we say that the predicate '. . . is prime' has the same sense as the expression (P) used to define it, or whether we say that their senses are distinct, though intimately related. If we choose the latter option, we might prefer to say that the sense of the defined predicate is not itself a function, but, rather, a way of determining a concept as that corresponding to the function that constitutes the sense of (P); or, again, we might prefer to regard the sense of (P) in just the same light. What matters is that we cannot, consistently with the doctrine of *Begriffsschrift*, construe the sentences (A) and (B) as expressing precisely the same thought: even if the predicate '. . . is prime' has the very same sense as (P), that sense is a part of the thought expressed by (B), but not of that expressed by (A); and on this fact depends that conviction that definitions can and should be fruitful which Frege voices in the *Grundlagen*.

The point I have just expounded at length is indeed a subtle one; Husserl had, at best, only a hazy perception of it, and, if Frege's unfairness to him were limited to overlooking this point, it would be venial. But it is not: for the criterion that Frege proposes for a successful definition of an existing term, as an alternative to the demand for exact preservation of its existing sense, cannot be seriously maintained. This criterion is the mere preservation of reference. If this were the criterion appealed to in Frege's *Grundlagen* definition of 'analytic', the term, as applied to single propositions, would be quite nugatory; for it is evident that it would always be possible to give reference-preserving definitions of the words occurring in any true proposition whatever that would render it derivable from purely logical principles, so that all true propositions, considered singly, would become analytic in the *Grundlagen* sense.

To this it could with reason be objected that it runs together ideas from different periods of Frege's career, even though, in his review of Husserl, he was seeking to defend his *Grundlagen* from Husserl's criticisms. During his middle period, he never once employed the opposition between analytic and synthetic truths, or that between a priori and a posteriori ones, either as he had drawn it in *Grundlagen* or in any other way. He gave no explanation of his abandonment of these notions; for all we can say, it may have been precisely because he no longer thought that there was any criterion for the correctness of definitions that would give substance to the notion of analyticity or of the a priori as he had defined them. Thus in *Grundgesetze* he still characterized his purpose in the earlier book as having been to make a certain thesis probable: but he no longer stated that thesis as being that the truths of arithmetic, in the plural, are analytic, but, rather, that arithmetic, in the singular, is a branch of logic and does not need to draw upon either experience or intuition for the basis of its proofs.[5] Requiring of definitions only that they preserve reference does not deprive of substance the claim that a whole theory can, by means of definitions, be derived from logical laws alone: for now the question is whether a whole system of definitions can be devised that will have this result. As Eva Picardi remarks,

the 'reconstructed systems' seem to be justifiable only holistically. . . . And hence there is a tension between the descriptive view of axioms, still advocated [by Frege] in 1914, . . . and the conventionalist view according to which sentences have to be interpreted as part of an entire theory obtained from those axioms by means of definitional extension.[6]

Nevertheless, even if we credit Frege with the holistic view that we should enquire into the status of entire theories, rather

---

[5] *Grundgesetze der Arithmetik, begriffsschriftlich abgeleitet*, i (Jena, 1893; repr. Hildesheim, 1966), 1.

[6] 'Frege on Definition and Logical Proof', 230.

than of the individual propositions composing them, the criterion for correct definition that he proposes in his review of Husserl is patently inadequate. The alternative definitions of a conic he provides as an illustration indeed have no pretensions to be equivalent in sense; but they are more closely related than merely by a common reference. They are not merely coextensive: they are *provably* coextensive—provably so, that is, by mathematical means, and hence equivalent a priori even if not analytically so. This is, indeed, for Frege, a weaker relation than being synonymous (having the same sense): but it is a great deal stronger than just being materially equivalent. I doubt if anybody knows how to construct a predicate applying to conic sections and only to conic sections, which nevertheless could not be shown by mathematical means alone, but only, say, by appeal to physical theory, to be true of a curve if and only if its equation is a polynomial of degree 2: but, if such a predicate were constructed, it obviously would not be accepted by mathematicians as an admissible definition of the term 'conic'.

It can plausibly be maintained that the condition upon an admissible definition of an existing term actually stated by Frege in his review of Husserl does supply an applicable criterion for whether or not any given definition should count as admissible. This is to assume that, however uncertain its precise sense, the reference of a term in actual use will be determinate. But the modified criterion will only determine, of two proposed definitions, whether they are equally admissible: if one of them is taken as admissible, then the other will also be admissible if it is provably equivalent to the first, but will be inadmissible if it is not. We cannot by this means establish whether any one definition is admissible or not, since there will be no possibility of proving its equivalence with the existing term we are proposing to define. We could prove the equivalence only if we could state the sense ordinarily attached to the existing term; and, if we could do that, we could make *that* its definition, and, indeed, impose the stricter requirement on an acceptable definition that it preserve sense. Mathematicians may, no doubt, in practice frequently fail to enquire into the theoretical constraints upon admissible definitions, although they sometimes agonize over the correctness of a precise definition of an existing term, for instance 'effectively calculable'; in that instance, the existence of a plurality of provably equivalent definitions was generally hailed as evidence that they picked out the correct extension. However this may be, a philosopher seeking to settle the nature of the laws of arithmetic cannot afford to be casual in this regard.

So far, then, we have failed to find in Frege's writings of any period an adequate account of the status of the definitions that he used in his logical construction of number theory, and hence a resolution of the paradox of analysis. If we cannot find either in his explicit observations, we can scrutinize his practice to elicit from it an attitude to these questions: and, as before, his *Grundlagen* provides the best quarry for this purpose. We may therefore begin by taking a closer look at the definitions of arithmetical notions that he gives in that book.

The structure of the definitions given by Frege in *Grundlagen* can be exhibited in Fig. 2.1. I here use the expressions that are now most natural, rather than Frege's jargon terms. The arrows indicate, not logical implication, but the dependence of certain definitions upon others. The relation between the concepts F and G expressed by 'There are just as many Fs as Gs' will be referred to as cardinal equivalence, and the operator 'the number of . . .' as the cardinality operator. Sentences of the form 'There are just *n* Fs', with which expressions in the bottom left-hand quarter of the diagram are concerned, are called by Frege 'statements of number'; they answer questions of the form 'How many Fs are there?', and will here be called 'A-type sentences'. Sentences of the form 'There are just as many Fs as Gs', stating the cardinal equivalence of two concepts, will be called 'E-type sentences'. Together, A- and E-type sentences stand in contrast to those involving expressions occurring in the right-hand half of the diagram, which will be called 'N-type sentences'. N-type sentences involve singular terms which purport to stand for numbers: both number-words or numerals like '0', '1', '2', etc., used as substantives, and terms of the form 'the number of Fs' formed by means of the cardinality operator. By contrast, number-words occur in A-type sentences only adjectivally.

As the diagram shows, Frege's definition of the cardinality operator rests upon the definition he adopts of the expression for the second-level relation of cardinal equivalence; and all the other definitions depend upon that of the cardinality operator. Although it raises no special issues for us, there are interesting things to be said about Frege's celebrated definition of the predicate

   n is a natural number

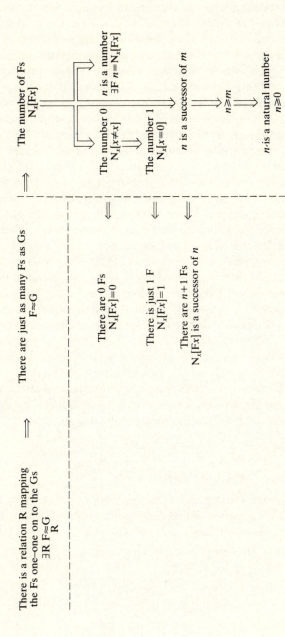

FIG. 2.1. The structure of definitions in *Grundlagen*

There is a relation R mapping the Fs one–one on to the Gs
$\exists R \; F \underset{R}{\approx} G$

$\Rightarrow$

There are just as many Fs as Gs
$F \approx G$

$\Rightarrow$

The number of Fs
$N_x[Fx]$

n is a number
$\exists F \; n = N_x[Fx]$

The number 0
$N_x[x \neq x]$

The number 1
$N_x[x = 0]$

n is a successor of m

$n \geq m$

n is a natural number
$n \geq 0$

There are 0 Fs
$N_x[Fx] = 0$

$\Rightarrow$

There is just 1 F
$N_x[Fx] = 1$

$\Rightarrow$

There are $n+1$ Fs
$N_x[Fx]$ is a successor of n

$\Rightarrow$

in terms of the number 0 and the relation of being a successor. On the other hand, the definitions in terms of the cardinality operator of the other expressions which appear on the right-hand side of the diagram appear relatively uncontroversial, given certain principles governing Frege's whole procedure. The first of these principles is that numerical terms, as they occur in arithmetical equations and other statements, are to be taken at face-value, that is, as genuine singular terms: this is expressed by Frege as the thesis that (natural) numbers are objects, for which he argued in *Grundlagen*, §§55 to 61. The second principle, not distinguished by Frege from the first, is that natural numbers, as the referents of such numerical terms, lie within the domain of the first-order quantifier, as we naturally understand it. The third principle, for which Frege did not argue, but which he simply assumed from the outset of the book, is that the natural numbers are to be regarded as finite cardinals; if so, they can of course be designated by terms formed by means of the cardinality operator. Given these principles, it would be difficult to put up a convincing case that, supposing the cardinality operator to be correctly understood, Frege's definitions of these expressions fail to represent exactly what we do mean by them. I shall therefore concentrate principally on the definitions of cardinal equivalence and of the cardinality operator.

Considered as analytic definitions, or at least as definitions of existing expressions, these two appear strikingly different. Frege gives his definition of the cardinality operator at the end of a lengthy and celebrated section of *Grundlagen*, extending from §62 to §69, in which he asks whether the intuitively evident equivalence

(E)   The number of Fs = the number of Gs
      if and only if
      there are just as many Fs as Gs

could itself serve as a definition of the cardinality operator. The final upshot of the discussion is that (E) cannot count as a definition. Frege therefore substitutes for it the definition

(N)   The number of Fs = the class of concepts G such that there are just as many Fs as Gs

in symbols:

$$N_x\,[Fx] = \{G \mid F \approx G\}.$$

Now the natural, and frequently expressed, reaction to Frege's definition (N) of the cardinality operator is that it could not possibly be claimed as capturing the sense that we ordinarily attach to that expression. Indeed, it could not even be defended in the way he defends his definition of cardinal equivalence against Husserl's objections, namely, that it gives the correct reference to the term defined, and that this is all that can be demanded of a mathematical definition; for, in the present case, it is precisely the reference that Frege's definition ascribes to the cardinality operator which appears contrary to our ordinary intentions. Whatever it is that we ordinarily mean to be referring to when we speak, say, of the number of students presently at the University of Bologna, it is assuredly not the class of concepts G such that there are just as many Gs as there are students at the University of Bologna. And since all the subsequent definitions depend, in the sense stated, upon the definition (N) of the cardinality operator, the same must be said of them. It thus appears that, at best, the definition (N) is an explication in the sense of Carnap. An explication does not seek to render exactly the sense of the existing expression which it explicates. That expression as yet possesses only an imperfect sense: one that is either vague or partial. Since Frege regards sense as directly connected with the determination of truth-value, we may say that the imperfection of the sense of the existing expression consists in the fact that, while we associate with it principles governing the determination of the truth-values of certain sentences in which it occurs, those principles do not suffice to render determinate the truth-values of other such sentences. The explication substitutes a complete and definite sense for the vague or partial one. In so doing, it respects the existing imperfect sense: every sentence which has a determinate truth-value when the expression is understood as bearing that imperfect sense will receive the same truth-value when it is understood in accordance with the explication. But the explication renders determinate the truth-value of *every* sentence in which the expression it explicates occurs; and, in doing so, it is no longer responsible to the original imperfect sense, or to any other principle embodied in our existing use of language.

That, it seems, is the most we can claim for Frege's definition (N) of the cardinality operator; and Frege appears to assess it similarly when he writes, in §69 of *Grundlagen*:

That this definition is correct will perhaps be hardly evident at first. For do we not think of the extension of a concept as something quite different from a number?

By 'the extension of the concept G' Frege of course means 'the class of Gs': since the concept 'equinumerous to the concept F' is one of second level, under which concepts, not objects, fall, a cardinal number is, according to *Grundlagen*, that unusual thing, a class of concepts rather than of objects. Frege goes on to say:

We do not indeed say that a number is more inclusive than another, as the extension of one concept is more inclusive than that of another. . . . The case is conceivable that the extension of the concept *equinumerous to the concept F* is more or less inclusive than the extension of some other concept, which then cannot be a number, according to our definition. It is not usual to call a number more or less inclusive than the extension of a concept; but nothing stands in the way of our adopting such a manner of speaking, should such a case occur.

Frege's attitude appears here to be precisely that his definition (N) renders true certain statements, and false certain others, which we should normally never use at all, and to which our pre-existing understanding of the term 'number' does not require us to assign any particular truth-value. He does not even argue, in this context, that such sentences *ought* to be regarded as having some truth-value or other, and that it therefore constitutes an imperfection in the sense we have hitherto attached to the word 'number' that it makes no provision for the assignment of a truth-value to them. He merely says that there is no obstacle to our so defining the word as to determine some such sentences as true and others as false: the definition therefore appears as an explication in Carnap's sense. This is far from being the only expression in his writings of a conventionalist attitude to definitions. Thus, in §100 of *Grundlagen*, he is discussing the manner in which complex numbers are to be introduced, and makes a somewhat light-hearted suggestion in the following words:

The fact that, simultaneously with the introduction of new numbers, the meanings of the words 'sum' and 'product' are extended, appears to provide a way to proceed. We take some object, say the Moon, and define: let the Moon multiplied by itself be -1. We then have a square root of -1, namely the Moon. This definition seems allowable, since, from the meaning hitherto assigned to multiplication, nothing follows about the sense of such a product, and hence, in extending this meaning, that sense can be stipulated as we choose.

If, then, we take it that Frege's definition (N) of the cardinality operator is to be viewed as an explication, we may ask what comprises the partial sense that we attach to the operator as we ordinarily use it. And to this there appears an easy answer, namely that we understand the cardinality operator as governed precisely by the equvialence (E):

> The number of Fs = the number of Gs
>
> (E) if and only if
>
> there are just as many Fs as Gs

That is to say, our whole understanding of the cardinality operator, as we use it in ordinary discourse, consists in our attaching it to predicates to form expressions that function grammatically as singular terms, and treating any two such terms as having the same referent (standing for the same number) just in case there are just as many things to which the one predicate applies as there are to which the other does.

It follows that, considered as an explication, Frege's definition (N) of the cardinality operator stands on very firm ground. Its two fundamental assumptions, that natural numbers are objects and that they should be construed as finite cardinals, are embedded in our pre-analytic linguistic practice, to which the definition is therefore faithful. Hence, provided these assumptions are sound, there can be no objection to his purported demonstration of the analyticity of arithmetical laws on the score that the definition of the cardinality operator, and hence of the natural numbers, imports something not contained in our ordinary understanding of these laws; for his proofs of the laws make no appeal to it. Having given the definition (N), Frege uses it for one purpose alone, namely, to derive the equivalence (E): having done so, he never adverts to the definition again, but deduces all the rest from the equivalence (E), together with his other definitions. Crispin Wright, in his book *Frege's Conception of Numbers as Objects*,[7] devotes an entire appendix to proving it possible to derive the same theorems as Frege from the equivalence (E), without appeal to definition (N).

---

[7] Aberdeen, 1983.

He could have saved himself the trouble had he observed that that is precisely what Frege himself had already done.

That is not, indeed, to declare his demonstration of the analyticity of arithmetic immune to question: only to say that it is as justified as our pre-analytic use of numerical terms. Frege proves that every natural number *n* has a successor by showing that the number of natural numbers (including 0) less than or equal to *n* is such a successor; but it cannot be claimed that our ordinary use of the cardinality operator forbids our speaking of the number of numbers satisfying a given condition. There is indeed here an assumption embedded in our existing use of terms of the form 'the number of Fs'. That an accepted linguistic usage may yet be unjustified was the lesson so savagely taught by Russell's contradiction.

Why, then, did Frege insist on making the definition (N)? Even if he was right that the equivalence (E) could not constitute a *definition*, could he not have laid it down as an axiom and contented himself with using it, rather than (N), as his starting-point? His 'fundamental laws that neither need nor admit of proof' seem somewhat mysterious: but the epistemological status of such an axiom would surely have been unproblematic, in that it is constitutive of our pre-analytic understanding of the cardinality operator as we use it in ordinary discourse. To have appealed to an axiom of this kind in place of a definition would have required some liberalization of his manner of characterizing analytic truths; but that, though it might have required lengthier discussion, could provoke no objection. Exactly the same perplexity arises over Frege's sketchy discussion of the introduction of complex numbers, and here he expressly evokes it. In §101 he says of the symbol *i* for the square root of −1:

One is tempted to conclude: it is indifferent whether *i* refers to one second, one millimetre or anything else whatever, provided only that our laws of addition and multiplication hold good. Everything depends on that: about the rest we do not need to worry.

And he replies:

One may perhaps be able to lay down the meaning of '*a+bi*', of the operations of sum and product, in different ways, so that in each case those laws will continue to hold good; but it is not indifferent whether we can find at least *one* such sense for these expressions.

Here the laws of addition and multiplication may be taken as constitutive of the partial senses which we attach, in advance of any specific definition, to terms for complex numbers; and the objection is that there is then no need for a specific definition, whose sole purpose will be to serve as a base for the derivation of those laws: we should do better simply to stipulate the validity of the laws. Frege's reply is that we must choose some one specific range of referents for the complex-number terms, even if our choice lies between a number of equally good alternatives: but the objector may still be left wondering why we must.

One part of Frege's reason is more evident from his discussion of complex numbers, embedded as it is in an attack on the procedure of postulating the existence of new mathematical objects, than from the case with which we are concerned, the definition of cardinal numbers. Let it be accepted, at least for the sake of argument, that our pre-analytic conception of the complex numbers is simply as comprising an extension of the field of real numbers to a field containing a square root of -1, that is, a structure containing the real numbers (or surrogates of them) together with such a square root, and closed under operations of addition and multiplication satisfying certain laws. Frege's position is, then, that such a conception is by itself inadequate to guarantee the meaningfulness of terms for and quantification over the complex numbers: we have, in addition, to prove that at least one such structure exists. In doing so, we can take the elements of the structure to be what we please, and define the operations as we wish, provided only that they then satisfy the desired laws: if there is any way of doing this, there will be many. But we cannot omit this step altogether, since, without it, we do not know that we have the right to assume that there is any such structure.

So expressed, the view is now commonplace. It would be generally agreed by mathematicians that, in introducing a new mathematical domain, the preferable procedure is first to give an abstract characterization of it, if possible up to isomorphism, and then to demonstrate the existence of a model. Frege does not clearly separate the two steps, preferring to specify a chosen model, categorically identifying it with the new domain, and to go on to prove that the fundamental laws hold in it: but his acknowledgement of the partly arbitrary character of the choice shows his awareness of the difference in status between the stages of his construction.

In introducing complex numbers, we are starting from within the realm of mathematics; it would be nonsense to speak of the use of terms for complex numbers in everyday discourse. Frege wants to apply the same principles to the natural numbers, which undoubtedly enter the common use of language. The need to display a model of the complex-number field when originally introducing the complex numbers arises in part from our desire to assure ourselves of the consistency of our mathematical theories, and in part from the restrained application of Occam's razor in mathematics: we do not want to have too many independent types of mathematical entity. Most mathematicians would, however, regard the natural numbers as fundamental: we cannot demand an independently describable model of them, because there is nothing in terms of which such a model could be described.

Since Frege is not wishing to treat number theory as absolutely fundamental, he cannot adopt this attitude. His instinct was completely sound: the fact that, together with terms for individual natural numbers, we have for millennia used the cardinality operator under the assumption that terms formed by means of it have a reference, that we are utterly familiar with it, and make that assumption without hesitation, does not by itself ensure that those terms really have a reference. Our ordinary understanding of the cardinality operator is wholly embodied in the equivalence (E); but, as we already noted, the assumption stands in need of a justification which the mere invocation of that understanding cannot provide. It can be provided, Frege believed, only by the specification of a definite reference for each term formed by applying the operator to some predicate: and it is just such a specification that his definition (N) supplies. It was a bitter irony that, having perceived the need for a justification of an assumption embedded even in our pre-mathematical ways of talking about numbers, he should have sought to provide it by means of a theory of classes which proved actually to be self-contradictory.

Frege's definition of course transferred the problem from terms for cardinal numbers to terms for classes: how can we be assured that we are entitled to ascribe reference to *them*? This was the problem with which Frege grappled unsuccessfully in *Grundgesetze*, vol. i, §10; and it is part of a more general problem which, though central to his philosophy, he failed to solve. It cannot be necessary, for every singular term, to secure it a reference by equating its referent with that of some other term: there must be terms whose referentiality is autonomous. Indeed, Frege recognized this fact when he said, in *Grundgesetze*, vol. i, §30, concerning his stipulations of the conditions under which an expression is to be said to have a reference, that:

These propositions are not to be regarded as definitions of the phrase 'to have a reference' or 'to refer to something', because their application always presupposes that we have already recognized some names as referential; they can, however, serve to extend the sphere of referential names. It follows from them that every name constructed out of referential names refers to something.

The question therefore becomes urgent: what conditions must a linguistic term satisfy for us to be entitled to regard it as having a reference without the necessity for expressly stipulating one? The question is urgent, not merely for Frege's philosophy, but for any philosophy: but we can find no clear answer in Frege's writings.

He does, however, propose a partial answer; he is even disposed to think it a complete answer, although reflection shows that it cannot be. The context principle states that it is only in the context of a sentence that a name has a reference. This means that it is only *within* the language that we can ask whether a term has reference, or what its reference is: there is no vantage-point outside the language from which we can answer such questions. And this in turn means that those questions, whenever legitimate, must reduce to ones concerning the truth or falsity of sentences of the language. The doctrine appears at first sight inconsistent with Frege's attempt, in *Grundgesetze*, to use German as a metalanguage in which to state the semantics of his formal language. Whether it is really inconsistent depends upon what, in the formulation I gave, is meant by 'the language'. If, in discussing the reference of terms of Frege's symbolic language, the phrase 'the language' is taken to refer to that symbolic language, there is an inconsistency; but if 'the language' denotes the totality of our linguistic practice, of which the employment of auxiliary languages which we devise and explain in language forms part, there is not.

According to the context principle, the question whether a term of our language refers to a particular object must always reduce to the question whether a certain identity statement of our language is true: namely, an identity statement in which the term in question stands on one side, and a term for the given object on the other. If the question cannot be framed in this way, it is spurious. But, correlatively, we cannot claim to have conferred a definite reference upon a term unless we have determined the truth-value of every identity statement that we can frame in which the term in question stands on one side of the sign of identity. This is why the 'Julius Caesar' problem, which initially strikes every reader as absurd, is so important for Frege, the question, namely, how we can rule out as false such a sentence as 'Julius Caesar is the number of sheep in the field'. His rejection of the proposal to treat the equivalence (E) as itself a definition of the cardinality operator is based on the fact that it affords no way of determining the truth-values of such sentences: he might be prepared to accept appeal to some stipulation that fell short of being a definition, if only it would serve to fix the truth-values of all identity statements involving numbers. But, if we cannot find a way of doing this, we cannot claim to have shown how to assign determinate references to numerical terms.

It is not that Frege intended to make any practical use of the presumed power of his definition (N) to show that Julius Caesar was not a cardinal number. One might think that, if propositions are to be proved concerning all cardinal numbers, it will be necessary first to determine what things are *not* cardinal numbers; but this is not so. If Frege had wished to prove that no cardinal number crossed the Rubicon, he would of course have had to show that no cardinal number was Julius Caesar: but he had no interest in proving that. He defined '*n* is a cardinal number' to mean 'For some concept F, *n* is the number of Fs': hence a statement of the form 'For every cardinal number *n*, A(*n*)' became equivalent to 'For every concept F, A(the number of Fs)'; and this sufficed for the proof of those genuinely mathematical propositions in which he was interested. His objection to treating the equivalence (E) as a basis was that it did not allow us to determine whether or not Julius Caesar was a number: but, as already remarked, he used the definition (N) solely to derive (E). Naturally, therefore, he did not in practice apply the definition to show that Caesar was not a number.

Frege desired, not merely to ensure that it would be *possible* to assign determinate references to such terms, but actually to assign them: not merely to show that there exists a model, but to fasten upon some one model. In view of his recognition of the arbitrary element in the choice of a model, this seems unreasonable. The thought was that, if not every expression in the theory had a determinate reference, then not every sentence would have a truth-value; but that the validity of deductive inferences could be guaranteed only if every sentence occurring in them could be assumed to have a determinate truth-value. An adequate reply would be that it is sufficient for the validity of classical logic that each sentence should be determinately true or false in each model of the theory: but, as we have seen, Frege did not think in terms of alternative models in the manner in which we have become accustomed to do.

It is the definition of cardinal equivalence that raises the paradox of analysis more acutely than that of the cardinality operator. The definition is of course in terms of one–one mapping: specifically, it explains:

> There are just as many Fs as Gs

as meaning

> There is a one–one relation R whose domain consists of the Fs and whose range consists of the Gs.

The use of a relation rather than a function is due to a peculiarity of Frege's logic. For him, every function is defined for every object as argument; to treat of what we should call a function whose domain is less inclusive than the universe, he therefore has to represent it as a many–one relation.

Although Frege probably put up the best philosophical defence of this definition, he did not represent the definition itself as original with him: in the *Grundlagen*, published in 1884, he mentions Kossak, Schröder, and Cantor as having employed it in 1872, 1873, and 1883 respectively; Cantor had in fact used it from 1874 onwards, and Stolz was to do so in 1885. By 1880, it had, in effect, become a mathematical orthodoxy, attacked, however, in his *Philosophie der Arithmetik* by Husserl, who cited Schröder and Stolz as well as Frege. Unlike Frege's definition of the cardinality operator, it does not involve anything arbitrary or extraneous: but there are difficulties, characteristic of the paradox of analysis, in claiming that it gives the ordinary sense of 'just as many'. If you ask a child how one can tell whether or not there are just as many things of one kind as there are of another, it is virtually certain that he will reply that you must count the things of each kind and see whether or not you arrive at the same number in each case; he is very unlikely to think of matching the things of the two kinds directly. Does the child not know the true meaning of 'just as many', then? Or is it, rather, that the definition in terms of one–one mapping does not give the *meaning* of the phrase, but only a logically necessary and sufficient condition for its application?

It is the second alternative that Husserl maintains against Frege and the rest. One might think this a rather weak objection to Frege's project, since, in order to demonstrate the analyticity of arithmetical truths, it is sufficient that the two sides of any definition appealed to be analytically equivalent, even if not synonymous. But this would be to miss Husserl's point, which is that Frege is mistaken concerning the conceptual priority of the notions he defines: he ought not to define the cardinality operator in terms of cardinal equivalence, but cardinal equivalence in terms of the cardinality operator. That is to say, he ought to have used the equivalence (E) the other way round, as a definition, not of the cardinality operator, but of cardinal equivalence, stipulating that

There are just as many Fs as Gs

was to mean

The number of Fs is the same as the number of Gs.

It would then become a theorem, rather than a matter of definition, that there will be just as many Fs as Gs if and only if there is a one–one mapping of the Fs on to the Gs.

Here Husserl was attacking a thesis to which Frege attached great importance. In *Grundlagen*, he is at one with Husserl in regarding it as a requirement on correct definition that it respect the true order of conceptual priority. This requirement goes quite unmentioned in the review of Husserl; but it is the moral of Frege's discussion in *Grundlagen*, §64, of the concepts of parallelism and direction. We must define 'the direction of the line *a*', Frege insists, in terms of the relational expression 'is parallel to', and not conversely, since the latter is conceptually prior to the former. He makes clear that he regards the point as general: in the same way, shape should be defined in terms of geometrical similarity, length in terms of the relation 'just as long as' and cardinal number in terms of cardinal equivalence; in each case, a mistake would be committed by attempting the converse direction of explanation.

The general form is that a certain equivalence relation serves as a condition for the identity of objects of a particular kind—directions, shapes, lengths, or numbers. Frege introduced a particular device, which has subsequently become standard, for effecting the step from the equivalence relation to the new objects, namely, the definition of the latter as equivalence classes; his definition (N) of the cardinality operator is simply one example of the device. Somewhat unfortunately, it has become known as definition by abstraction: we may call it 'definition by logical abstraction' to distinguish it from the quite different operation of psychological abstraction. Husserl makes a general objection, not to the device, but to the order of definition it involves. 'What this method allows one to define', he says, 'is not the content of the concept of direction, shape or number, but its *extension*.'[8] His idea is that in order to recognize, say, the shape of a figure, one does not need to advert to its relation to other figures, but only to attend to *it*: hence a definition in terms of the relation of similarity cannot capture the essence of the concept of shape.

There is here a distinction not drawn by Frege in his review, nor, indeed, at all clearly by Husserl in his book. I earlier picked out three relevant classes of sentence: A-type sentences, called by Frege 'statements of number', which state how many objects there are falling under a certain concept, and in which number-words occur adjectivally; E-type sentences, which state that there are just as many objects falling under one concept as under another; and N-type sentences, in which singular terms are used as standing for numbers, where such terms may be either substantival number-words or terms of the form 'the number of Fs' formed by means of the cardinality operator. Only by the use of N-type sentences do we speak of numbers as objects: by means of A- and E-type sentences, we merely make statements about how many things fall under certain concepts.

Frege's principal interest lay in the transition from making statements about concepts to speaking of numbers as objects, and hence from using A- and E-type sentences on the one hand to using N-type sentences on the other. The thesis on which he so emphatically insisted was the conceptual priority of cardinal equivalence over the cardinality operator, that is, of E-type sentences over N-type ones. It is, however, obscure whether it was that with which Husserl, too, was primarily concerned. He argued that direction, shape, and

[8] *Philosophie der Arithmetik*, 134.

number are not intrinsically relational concepts; that is, that to speak of the direction of a line, the shape of a figure, or the number of elements of a set does not make any tacit reference to a comparison of the line, figure, or set with any other line, figure, or set. In this, Husserl had a valid point: namely, that it is possible to explain what it is to be circular, or rectangular, or of any other particular shape or type of shape, without invoking the relation of similarity; and correspondingly for the other notions. In particular, it is possible to explain what it is for there to be just two things of a given kind, or any other finite number of things, without invoking the relation of cardinal equivalence. That is to say, A-type sentences—'statements of number'—can be explained without appeal to E-type ones.

What Frege insists on is the conceptual priority of cardinal equivalence to the cardinality operator; but what in practice he does, as Fig. 2.1 shows, is first to define the cardinality operator in terms of cardinal equivalence, and then to define everything else in terms of the cardinality operator, thus making the notion of cardinal equivalence the ultimate foundation of all other arithmetical notions. In particular, he explains A-type sentences in terms of N-type ones. But there appears as strong a case for saying that A-type sentences—those of the form 'There are just n Fs'—are conceptually prior to numerical terms of the form 'the number n' as for saying that E-type sentences are conceptually prior to terms of the form 'the number of Fs'. We can understand statements such as 'There are nine planets' without having any conception of the possibility of speaking of numbers as objects by means of the substantival use of number-words; but, if natural numbers are to be taken, as Frege takes them, to be finite cardinals, we cannot understand the term 'the number nine' without knowing what it is for there to be nine objects of one or another kind. In explaining the latter in terms of the former, Frege is open to the charge of violating his own principle of respect for conceptual priority.

If Husserl's concern was the same as Frege's, namely, with the relation of E-type to N-type sentences, then his thesis was that already stated, that E-type ones are to be explained in terms of N-type ones, and not, as Frege thought, conversely: cardinal equivalence is to be explained in terms of the cardinality operator, by means of the equivalence (E). He can, however, be understood to be concerned, rather, with the relation between A-type and

E-type sentences. We have seen that he was right to argue that statements of number (A-type sentences) can be explained without appeal to the notion of cardinal equivalence; he may be interpreted as advancing the further thesis that cardinal equivalence (and thereby E-type sentences) can be explained in terms of statements of number. Suppose that a child says that what it *means* to say that there are just as many nuts as apples in the bowl is that, if you counted each, you would get the same answer. That child is not concerned with the use of number-words as substantives, with referring to numbers as objects: he is attempting to explain E-type sentences in terms of A-type ones. On the interpretation suggested, that is what Husserl was aiming to do.

Frege believed that, to explain the transition from the use of E-type sentences to that of N-type ones, the following steps were necessary: (1) to explain E-type sentences, that is, the binary quantifier 'There are just as many Fs as Gs' signifying the relation of cardinal equivalence between concepts; (2) to explain the cardinality operator in terms of cardinal equivalence; (3) to explain other numerical terms such as number-words (numerals) in terms of the cardinality operator; and (4) to explain adjectival uses of number-words in terms of substantival ones (A-type sentences in terms of N-type ones). He appealed to the requirement to respect conceptual priority only to justify steps (1) and (2); the order of the other steps was determined by lesser considerations. Thus, in taking step (3), Frege is not concerned to deny that it would be possible, without using the cardinality operator, to define the number 2, for example, to be just that class of concepts with which he in fact identifies it; it is merely that it is more convenient to define it in such a way as to make it immediate that 2 is a cardinal number (that is, the number belonging to some concept). Similarly, the point of step (4) is not at all to obscure the fact that A-type sentences—statements of number—are intelligible, and explicable, independently of N-type ones (of the cardinality operator), but to have a simple way of connecting the adjectival use of number-words with their substantival use; for plainly any theory that took no cognizance of the occurrence of the same word in 'The room has two windows' and 'Eight is the cube of two' would be, at least, inadequate.

The question is whether an alternative strategy for explaining fundamental arithmetical notions was really available to Husserl. The child explained what it means to say that there are just as many

Fs as Gs in terms of counting. Aware that counting is unavailable to determine the cardinality of infinite sets, we should find it natural to generalize the child's explanation: this can be done by laying down that there are just as many Fs as Gs just in case the same answer is to be given to the question 'How many Gs are there?' as to 'How many Fs are there?' Husserl, however, states his point by giving the ungeneralized version of the child's explanation, namely, that, to determine that two sets, such as a set of apples and a set of nuts, have the same cardinality, 'by far the superior' method is to count each of them.[9] This enables Frege to answer, in his review, that 'the author forgets that counting itself rests on a one–one correlation, namely between the number-words from 1 to n and the objects of the set' (p. 319).

It may seem then, that Husserl would have done better to employ the generalized form of the child's explanation, suggested above. But reflection shows that this would have done him no good: for we have to ask what constitutes an answer to the question 'How many?' Which properties of a concept F can be cited in answer to the question 'How many Fs are there?'? The only answer to this enquiry is, 'A property such that, if there are just as many Fs as Gs, then the concept G has that property also'. Actually, the generalized form of the child's explanation, as stated, is defective. 'More than a hundred' and 'An even number' are both answers to the question 'How many Fs are there?': but, from the fact that there are more than a hundred Fs and more than a hundred Gs, it cannot be inferred that there are just as many Fs as Gs. The condition for this is that the two questions (how many Fs and how many Gs there were) would have the same *definite* answer; we have therefore to ask what would constitute a definite answer to the question 'How many?' The proper answer to this is that, if something holds good of the concept F, then it is a definite answer to the question 'How many Fs are there?' just in case it holds good of any other concept G if and only if there are just as many Fs as Gs. To put the matter in Fregean terms, we answer the question 'How many Fs are there?' by citing a second-level concept under which F falls; and this second-level concept gives a definite answer to the question just in case all and only those first-level concepts equinumerous to F fall under it. Thus, by remaining at the level of A-type statements, without

		[9] *Philosophie der Arithmetik*, 113.

advancing to speaking of numbers as objects, but considering only the corresponding second-level concepts, we do not escape the necessity to provide a condition for a second-level concept to be one that corresponds in this way to a cardinal number; and this condition can be stated only by appeal to the relation of cardinal equivalence between first-level concepts. The analogy with shape is close: we should have, in a quite parallel way, to explain in terms of geometrical similarity what it is to assign a definite shape to a figure. (The analogy is not precise, in that the explanation of the attribution of a *type* of shape is more complex.)

Could not Frege's whole strategy of definition have been reversed, so that the arrows in Fig. 2.1 would all run in the opposite direction? We have seen that the so-called numerically definite quantifiers— the expressions 'There are 0 . . .', 'There is just 1 . . .', 'There are just 2 . . .', etc.—could all be defined without appeal to any of the other arithmetical notions. These are, in Frege's terminology, expressions for second-level concepts: and, presumably, for Frege every second-level concept has an extension, the class of first-level concepts that fall under it. It may therefore seem that the entire sequence of definitions could be reversed: the last definition in the sequence would then be Husserl's proposed use of the equivalence (E) as a definition of cardinal equivalence. On reflection, however, this alternative strategy would fail to work. We could in this way define the individual natural numbers as classes of concepts: but we could not define the cardinality operator, nor, therefore, the predicate '. . . is a (cardinal) number', unless we could distinguish numbers from all other classes of concepts. For this, we should need first to pick out those second-level concepts under which fall all and only the first-level concepts having some particular cardinality: and, to do that, we should have to appeal to the relation of cardinal equivalence.

Frege's idea, in objecting to Husserl's appeal to counting, is that our sequence of number-words forms a kind of universal tally with respect to which we can compare the cardinalities of different concepts, and which thus provides a means of saying, in the finite case, how many objects falling under a given concept there are. An answer to the question 'How many Fs are there?' can be given only by reference to some arbitrarily picked standard of comparison, just as an answer to the question 'How long is this?' can be given only by the arbitrary selection of a unit: that is why, for Frege, cardinal equivalence is a more fundamental notion than those of specific cardinalities, just as equality of length is a more fundamental notion than those of specific lengths.

This is not to deny the point already conceded to Husserl, namely, that it is possible, for any specific k, to explain the expression, 'There are just k . . .', without appeal to cardinal equivalence. Frege in fact does just this for 'There are 0 . . .' and 'There is just 1 . . .' in §55 of *Grundlagen*. Although he goes on to deny that these definitions can be used as a base for the introduction of the other fundamental arithmetical notions, there is nothing wrong with them in themselves, as Frege contrives to insinuate that there is. He is, indeed, right in objecting to the use of the variable n in the suggested definition of 'There are just $n + 1$ Fs' in terms of 'There are just n Fs'. The difficulty could be overcome by using a variable replaceable by entire expressions such as 'There are just 2 . . .', a variable ranging in effect over all second-level concepts; and then the need for a circumscription of those second-level concepts which determine the cardinality of the first-level ones falling under them would become glaring. But, as Frege allows, the definition of 'There are just $n + 1$ . . .' can in any case be used as a pattern for framing definitions of other expressions of the general form 'There are just k . . .'. This, however, is not the same thing as an explanation of the procedure of counting. We can by this means explain the adjectival use, in statements of number, of any finite number of number-words that we choose: but we cannot so explain the *general* formation of our ordinary number-words, or the *general* procedure of counting by means of them. The latter cannot be done except, as Frege says, by representing counting as the setting up of a one–one map from an initial segment of the sequence of number-words to the objects counted.

From this it is apparent why Frege was right to treat cardinal equivalence as the fundamental notion. His concern was not precisely what he represents it as being, namely, to respect conceptual priority: if it had been, he would not have explained statements of number (A-type sentences) by reference to numerical terms (N-type sentences). He tries to make his readers believe that his definitional strategy is the only possible one. Not only is this not so: the fundamental character of the notion of cardinal equivalence stands out in sharper relief if we consider other possible strategies. In whichever order the definitions are given, the only available means of breaking out of a circle of arithmetical notions into the realm of purely logical ones is by defining cardinal equivalence in terms of one–one mapping: it is not so much that the relation of cardinal equivalence is conceptually prior to the conception of numbers as objects as that it is required for a grasp of the concept of cardinality itself.

For this reason, Husserl's objection, even when it is reconstrued in the way we have been considering, cannot be vindicated. For his argument to succeed, he needed to appeal, not to counting, but to the process of *psychological* abstraction, in which he was a believer. This, too, was an orthodoxy of the time, subscribed to by both Dedekind and Cantor, among others. Dedekind, however, used it in a quite special way, while Cantor was unique in using it in the standard way while yet adopting the definition of cardinal equivalence in terms of one–one mapping. The process was subjected to a devastating criticism by Frege in *Grundlagen*, §§29 to 44; but both Husserl and Cantor failed to perceive the force of the critique. The theory was that, starting with any one particular object, the mental process of closing off attention from any of its features created a mental object like that taken as the starting-point save that it would lack not only the features abstracted from, but any other features in the same range: by abstracting from its position, for example, one obtained an abstract or mental object, not in a different position, but in no position at all. On this theory, a cardinal number is a set of featureless units, a unit being arrived at by a far-reaching act of psychological abstraction, which abstracts from *every* feature the original object possesses. Given any set of objects, we arrive at the number of its elements by subjecting all of them to this process: that number is the unique set of units that can be arrived at from that set and from every other set having just as many elements as it.

A subscriber to this theory could regard the cardinality operator as explicable independently of the relation of cardinal equivalence; that relation is in turn to be explained, not in terms of one–one mapping, but as holding between two sets just in case the number of elements in one is the same as the number of elements in the other. It could then easily be proved that, when there are just as many nuts as apples, there is a one–one map from the nuts to the apples. For, given that there are just as many nuts as apples, the *same* number, or set of abstract units, will be arrived at by abstraction from the nuts as from the apples; hence, by compounding the mapping, by abstraction, of a nut on to a unit with the inverse of the corresponding mapping of an apple on to a unit, we obtain a mapping of the nuts on to the apples.

Psychological abstraction is, of course, a myth: it is astonishing to us that clever men could believe in such internalized magic. Even on its own terms, however, the theory fails to work, as Frege perceived and Husserl was on the brink of realizing. The crucial difficulty is whether the units are the same or different. If, to arrive at the set of units constituting the cardinal number of the set with which we start, we are really to abstract from *every* feature of the elements of the original set, each element will reduce to the *same* featureless unit, and in each case we shall arrive at a set containing a single unit (unless we started with the null set). Accordingly, we must abstract from every feature of each element, save the mere fact of its being distinct from every other object. A unit does not differ from another unit in any *respect*: it *simply* differs from it. In this case, however, if we start from distinct sets, the abstract sets of units at which we arrive will still be distinct; whereas we wanted them to be the *same* provided that the original sets had the same cardinality.

Husserl appears to have perceived this; for, in speaking of cardinal equivalence, he mentions psychological abstraction as the first step in one method of establishing it, but thinks it necessary to add a second step of setting up a one–one map from one set of units to the other, a step that would not be needed if the sets of units were identical. He sees that he therefore cannot represent this as a method independent of one–one mappings, which is why he has recourse to counting; he fails to see that it destroys the entire theory, since sets of units differing otherwise than in cardinality cannot be cardinal numbers. His proposal to treat the equivalence (E) as a definition of cardinal equivalence thus unnecessarily jettisons the project of explaining arithmetical notions in logical terms: having stipulated that there are just as many Fs as Gs if and only if the number of Fs is the same as the number of Gs, Husserl has no legitimate way to explain what the number of Fs is.

Frege was unquestionably right in claiming the notion of cardinal equivalence as more fundamental than the concept of cardinal numbers; the former has therefore to be defined in advance of the latter. What status, then, does a definition of it have? Can it really claim to give the sense that the expression 'just as many' has all along had, even if we were incapable of explaining it in that way? The principle that anyone who grasps the senses of two expressions must be able to recognize that they have the same sense, if they do, is enormously compelling: yet to maintain it appears to rule out the possibility of conceptual analysis, of which the definition of cardinal equivalence is surely a prime example. Certainly we must allow that, when the senses of two expressions are the same, it must be possible for anyone who understands both expressions to come to recognize that their senses are identical: for, if this were not so, how could any conceptual analysis be established as correct, or, for that matter, as incorrect? Frege was anxious to insist that a recognition of synonymy must be immediate; if a proof is needed, we have, not synonymy, but the weaker relation of analytic equivalence. Against this, it is necessary to maintain that reflection may be needed in order to recognize the synonymy of two expressions; if this blurs the boundary between synonymy and analytic equivalence, that is a price that must be paid.

The belief that no reflection is required springs from the picture that Frege has of 'grasping a sense' as a mental act akin to the perception of a material object, whereby the entire sense is apprehended in a single act. On the contrary, the understanding of an expression is manifested in a range of interconnected abilities; and one who has these abilities may well not have apprehended the connections between them. We do not suppose that the child who says that the only way to tell whether there are just as many nuts as apples is to count each of them is even partially ignorant of what 'just as many' means: but we should think that his understanding was seriously imperfect if he failed, when it was pointed out, to see that you could also tell by finding that you could put each nut on top of one of the apples so as to leave no apple without a nut. Suppose that a child has learned to count, and can say, by this means, that there are seventeen chocolate eclairs on the dish set out for his birthday party. His ability does not, by itself, guarantee that he has a clear understanding of such 'statements of number': his understanding would be revealed as clouded if he failed to grasp that there being seventeen eclairs meant that there would be enough to go round, when there were to be sixteen guests. The notion of there being 'enough to go round', in such a context, involves that of a one–one mapping; even to understand number-words, let alone 'just as many', one must in practice grasp the

3

On a Question of Frege's about Right-Ordered Groups*

(*with S. A. Adeleke and P. M. Neumann*)

1. THE PROBLEM AND ITS BACKGROUND

Let G be a group and P a subset of G. We shall be interested in the following assertions:

(1) $p,q \in P \Rightarrow pq \in P$;

(2) $1 \notin P$;

(3) $p,q \in P \Rightarrow pq^{-1} \in P \lor p = q \lor qp^{-1} \in P$;

(4) $p,q \in P \Rightarrow p^{-1}q \in P \lor p = q \lor q^{-1}p \in P$.

---

* It is probably not known to many who have not read part III of his *Grundgesetze der Arithmetik* that Frege raised any questions about groups with orderings. An article with the title of this essay, dedicated with respect and good wishes to Professor Graham Higman to mark his seventieth birthday in January 1987, was published in the *Bulletin of the London Mathematical Society*, 19 (1987), 513–21, under the names of Dr Samson A. Adeleke, Dr Peter M. Neumann, and myself. The article was in three parts; it was thought that a full reprint of it would be out of place in this collection. What follows here, in four parts, is therefore a summary, with a few additional comments. Part 1 is substantially part 1 of the original article, slightly truncated, with the proof of Frege's Theorem 1.5 transferred from part 3 and the list of conditions rearranged. Part 2 of the present version contains a summary, as far as possible in the original wording, of the construction, due to Dr Neumann, that comprised the original part 2, which solves the problem that perplexed Frege. The present part 3 similarly sketches the proof, due to Dr Adeleke, of Theorem 3.1, which resolves, in the opposite sense, a parallel problem not explicitly raised by Frege. It was only after our article had been completed that our attention was drawn by Professor P. M. Cohn to the article 'A Contribution to the Theory of Magnitudes and the Foundations of Analysis' by F. A. Behrend (*Mathematische Zeitschrift*, 63 (1956), 345–62), from whose assertion (A_3) in his §1.6 our Theorem 3.1 may be inferred, although his context and his proof are rather different from ours. Behrend's article is remarkably similar in spirit to the much earlier one by Otto Hölder, 'Die Axiome der Quantität und die Lehre vom Mass' (*Berichte über die Verhandlungen der Königlichen Sächsischen Gesellschaft der Wissenschaften zu Leipzig, Mathematisch-physikalische Klasse*, 53 (1901), 1–64), which we refer to in detail in part 1. Apart from a sentence or two taken from the original part 1, part 4 consists of some additional comments by me. Readers wishing for full details should consult the original article.

Frege's question, which is posed in the second volume of his *Grund-gesetze*,[1] is whether (4) follows from (1), (2), and (3). We shall amplify the question and answer it negatively below.

A binary relation $<$ on G may be defined in terms of P by the rule

$$a < b \quad \text{if and only if} \quad ba^{-1} \in P.$$

It is easy to see that $<$ is right-invariant (that is, $a < b \Rightarrow ag < bg$ for all $g \in G$) and $P = \{p \in G \mid 1 < p\}$. Properties of $<$ may be characterized either directly or in terms of P. For example, as is well known and easy to prove, $<$ is a strict partial order if and only if (1) and (2) hold.

A binary relation ρ on a set A will be said to be *weakly connected* if for any $a, b \in A$ there exists a sequence $a_0, a_1, \ldots, a_n$ connecting a to b, that is, a sequence of members a_i of A such that $a_0 = a$, $a_n = b$ and $a_i \, \rho a_{i+1}$ or $a_{i+1} \, \rho a_i$ for $0 \leq i \leq n-1$.

LEMMA 1.1. The relation $<$ is weakly connected if and only if P generates G.

Proof. Suppose first that P generates G. It is sufficient to show that for each $g \in G$ there is a sequence connecting g to 1. Our supposition means that g may be written as a product $g_0 g_1 \cdots g_m$, where $g_i \in P$ or $g_i^{-1} \in P$ for $0 \leq i \leq m$. We set $a_i := g_i g_{i+1} \cdots g_m$ for $0 \leq i \leq m$, and $a_{m+1} := 1$. Then $a_i \, a_{i+1}^{-1} = g_i$ for each i, so that $a_{i+1} < a_i$ if $g_i \in P$ and $a_i < a_{i+1}$ if $g_i^{-1} \in P$. Thus $a_0, a_1, \ldots, a_{m+1}$ is a sequence connecting g to 1.

Conversely, suppose that $<$ is weakly connected and, for $g \in G$, suppose that $b_0, b_1, \ldots, b_n$ is a sequence connecting 1 to g. We show by indicating that $b_i \in \langle P \rangle$ for each i. Certainly $b_0 = 1 \in \langle P \rangle$. If $b_i < b_{i+1}$ then $b_{i+1} b_i^{-1} \in P$ and if $b_{i+1} < b_i$ then $(b_{i+1} b_i^{-1})^{-1} \in P$. In either case, if $b_i \in \langle P \rangle$ then $b_{i+1} = (b_{i+1} b_i^{-1}) b_i \quad \langle P \rangle$. By induction, $g = b_n \quad \langle P \rangle$. Thus $\langle P \rangle = G$.

Following Adeleke and Neumann's paper 'Semilinearly Ordered Sets, Betweenness Relations and their Automorphism Groups',[2] a binary relation ρ will be said to be a (strict) *upper semilinear ordering* if

[1] *Grundgesetze der Arithmetik, begriffsschriftlich abgeleitet*, ii (Jena, 1903; repr. Hildesheim, 1966).

[2] Forthcoming. See also Manfred Droste, *Structure of Partially Ordered Sets with Transitive Automorphism Groups*, Memoirs of the American Mathematical Society, 334 (Providence, RI, 1985).

(i) ρ is a (strict) partial ordering;
(ii) $a\rho b$ & $a\rho c \Rightarrow b\rho c \lor b = c \lor c\rho b$;
(iii) $a\rho b \lor a = b \lor b\,\rho a \lor (\exists c)\,(a\rho c$ & $b\rho c)$.

LEMMA 1.2. Suppose that P satisfies (1) and (2), and that P generates G. Then (3) holds if and only if $<$ is a (strict) upper semilinear order on G.

Proof. Suppose first that (3) holds. Certainly $<$ is a strict partial ordering of G (because (1) and (2) hold), and (3) says that $<$ is a strict linear ordering of P. Suppose that $a, b, c \in G$, $a < b$ and $a < c$. Then $ba^{-1}, ca^{-1} \in P$, whence $ba^{-1} < ca^{-1}$ or $b = c$ or $ca^{-1} < ba^{-1}$. By right-invariance of $<$ we have $b < c$ or $b = c$ or $c < b$, so that $<$ satisfies (ii). To prove (iii) we use the fact (Lemma 1.1) that $<$ is weakly connected. For $a, b \in G$, let $a_0, a_1, \ldots, a_n$ be a sequence connecting a to b and chosen so that n is as small as possible. Then certainly $a_i \neq a_{i+1}$, if $a_i < a_{i+1}$ then $a_{i+2} < a_{i+1}$, and if $a_{i+1} < a_i$ then $a_{i+1} < a_{i+2}$, otherwise in each case we could have deleted a_{i+1} and obtained a shorter sequence connecting a to b. If $a_{i+1} < a_i$ and $a_{i+1} < a_{i+2}$, however, then (by (ii)) a_i and a_{i+2} would be comparable and so a_{i+1} again could be deleted to give a shorter sequence. Thus the only possibilities are that $n = 0$ (in which case $a = b$), $n = 1$ (in which case $a < b$ or $b < a$), or $n = 2$ and $a = a_0 < a_1$, $b = a_2 < a_1$. Therefore (iii) holds and $<$ is a strict upper semilinear ordering of G.

Now suppose conversely that $<$ is a strict upper semilinear ordering. If $p, q \in P$ then by (ii) we have that $p < q$ or $p = q$ or $q < p$, that is, $qp^{-1} \in P$ or $p = q$ or $pq^{-1} \in P$, which is (3).

LEMMA 1.3. Suppose that P satisfies (1) and (2), and that P generates G. Then (3) and (4) both hold if and only if $<$ is a strict linear ordering of G,

Proof. By an obvious duality, (4) holds if and only if $<$ is a strict lower semilinear ordering of G. Thus if (3) and (4) both hold then $<$ is both an upper semilinear order and a lower semilinear order, hence is a linear order. Conversely, if $<$ is a linear order then it is both an upper and lower semilinear order and so (3) and (4) both hold.

In the light of Lemmas 1.2 and 1.3 we may transform Frege's problem to the question *is there a group with a right-invariant, upper semilinear ordering that is not linear?* It is to this form that we shall give a positive answer in §2 below.

Frege's question comes from his uncompleted logical construction of the real numbers in *Grundgesetze*, ii. Having constructed (in *Grundgesetze*, i[3]) the natural numbers, but not the integers or rational numbers, Frege wished to represent the real numbers as ratios between quantities belonging to the same domain (for example, that of lengths or masses): the problem was then how to characterize a domain of quantities. Unknown to Frege, Hölder had tackled the same problem in his paper 'Die Axiome der Quantität und die Lehre vom Mass' of 1901. He had considered a domain of absolute quantities, not containing a zero quantity, but forming an ordered semigroup, which he described axiomatically in terms of an ordering $<$ and a binary operation $+$ of addition. Frege, on the other hand, considers domains of positive and negative quantities, which he takes to consist of permutations (and which ultimately turn out to be ordered permutation groups—although neither Frege nor Hölder uses explicit group-theoretic ideas). Thus for Frege a domain of quantities is to be, for some set R, a subset, ultimately a subgroup G of the symmetric group Sym (R). He proceeds in two stages, first defining what he calls a 'positival' class, later adding conditions for it to be a 'positive' class.

A *positival* class is a set P of permutations of the set R satisfying conditions (1), (2), (3), (4) above (and Frege's domain of quantities is $P \cup \{1\} \cup P^{-1}$, which is then the group generated by P). However, concerned as he is to ensure the independence of the clauses of his definitions, Frege is perturbed by his inability to establish whether (4) is independent of (1), (2), (3).[4] He therefore proves as much as he can without appeal to clause (4), and he calls attention to the fact that he has not so far invoked it at the point[5] where he first feels compelled to do so.

For the purpose of resolving Frege's independence problem, the fact that P is a subset of Sym (R) may be ignored. For if H is any group with a right-invariant, weakly connected, partial ordering $\prec$, we may take P to be the subset of Sym (H) consisting of the right translations $x \mapsto xp$ by elements p of H with $1 \prec p$. Then P will satisfy (1) and (2), and the subgroup G of Sym (H) generated by P will consist of all right translations of H, hence will be isomorphic to H; moreover, if $a, b \in G$, $a: x \mapsto xg$ and $b: x \mapsto xh$ for all $x \in H$, then $ab^{-1} \in P$

[3] (Jena, 1893.)
[4] See *Grundgesetze*, ii. 172, 243.
[5] Ibid. 207.

if and only if $h \prec g$. This justifies our treatment of Frege's question in the general context of abstract right-ordered groups.

Suppose now that G is a group and that $<$ is a right-invariant, weakly connected, strict partial ordering of it (so that $<$ is determined by a subset P that generates G and satisfies (1) and (2)). We shall be concerned with various further properties that $<$ and G may have:

(a) the relation $<$ is a strict upper semilinear ordering of G;
(b) the relation $<$ is a strict linear ordering of G;
(c) the relation $<$ is limp;
(d) the relation $<$ is left-invariant;
(e) the group G is abelian;
(f) the relation $<$ is archimedean;
(g) the relation $<$ is complete;
(h) the relation $<$ is dense.

Property (c) requires explanation: we say that $<$ is *limp* (*l*eft-*i*nvariant under *m*ultiplication by *p*ositive elements) if for all $p, q, r \in G$ we have that

$$1 < p \ \& \ q < r \Rightarrow pq < pr.$$

We have seen in Lemma 1.2 that (a) is equivalent to the assertion that P satisfies (3), and in Lemma 1.3 that (b) is equivalent to the assertion that P satisfies both (3) and (4). Condition (c) is equivalent to

(5) $$p, q \in P \Rightarrow pqp^{-1} \in P;$$

condition (d) is equivalent to

(6) $$p \in P \ \& \ g \in G \Rightarrow gpg^{-1} \in P;$$

and condition (h) is equivalent to

(7) $$\forall p_{p \in P} \ \exists q_{q \in P} \ pq^{-1} \in P.$$

The proofs are straightforward

Although the language and notation he uses are very different from ours (in particular, he uses the phrase '*p* is grösser als *q*' to describe the relation $pq^{-1} \in P$ rather than using a symbol to denote what we have called $<$), Frege is concerned with these properties (as is Hölder also). He proves the following facts.

THEOREM 1.4. If $<$ is a complete upper semilinear ordering then $<$ is archimedean: that is, (a) & (g) $\Rightarrow$ (f).[6]

THEOREM 1.5. If $<$ is an archimedean upper semilinear ordering then $<$ is limp: that is, (a) & (f) $\Rightarrow$ (c).[7]

THEOREM 1.6. If $<$ is an archimedean linear ordering then $<$ is left-invariant: that is, (b) & (f) $\Rightarrow$ (d).[8]

THEOREM 1.7. If $<$ is a dense archimedean linear ordering then G is abelian: that is, (b) & (f) & (h) $\Rightarrow$ (e).[9]

Since Theorem 1.5 is the least familiar of Frege's results, we give here a version of his proof.

Proof of Theorem 1.5. Suppose that $p, q \in P$, that is, $p, q \in G$ and $1 < p$, $1 < q$. We wish to prove that $pqp^{-1} \in P$. If $p \leqslant q$ then $1 \leqslant qp^{-1}$ and so certainly $pqp^{-1} \in P$. Therefore, we may suppose that $q < p$. Suppose, if possible, that $pq < p$. If $pq^m < p$ then $pq^{m+1} < pq < p$, and so by induction we have that $pq^n < p$ for all natural numbers n. Then $q^{n+1} < pq^n < p$, and this contradicts the assumption that the order $<$ is archimedean on G. Therefore, it cannot be true that $pq < p$, so $p < pq$, whence $pqp^{-1} \in P$. Thus (5) is satisfied and $<$ is limp on G.

The first correct proof of the archimedean law from the completeness of the ordering appears to have been Hölder's,[10] although he used considerably stronger assumptions than Frege's, namely that $<$ is dense, left- as well as right-invariant and linear. Hölder was also the first to prove commutativity from the archimedean law, but he again assumed left-invariance of $<$ as a hypothesis, whereas Frege derived (e) from (b), (f), and (h) alone, because, by Theorem 1.6, left-invariance is automatic. It is well known that the assumption of denseness is not needed: in fact (b) & (f) $\Rightarrow$ (e).[11]

2. FREGE'S INDEPENDENCE PROBLEM SOLVED

Frege's original problem was whether (a) implies (b). To show that it does not, we have to find a group G with a right-invariant semi-

---

[6] *Grundgesetze*, vol. ii, Theorem 635.   [7] Ibid., Theorem 637.

[8] Ibid., Theorem 641.   [9] Ibid., Theorem 689.

[10] 'Die Axiome der Quantität und die Lehre vom Mass', §4.

[11] See E. V. Huntington, 'A Complete Set of Postulates for the Theory of Absolutely Continuous Magnitude', *Transactions of the American Mathematical Society*, 3 (1902), 264–79, proposition 22, case I; or L. Fuchs, *Partially Ordered Algebraic Systems* (Oxford, 1963), 45, 164.

linear order that is not linear. This task reduces to that of finding a partially ordered set $(\Lambda_0, <)$, where $<$ is a semilinear but not linear ordering, that admits G acting regularly as a group of automorphisms. For, if $<$ is a right-invariant semilinear order on G, then the right translations $x \mapsto xg$ form a group of order-automorphisms of $(G, <)$ that acts regularly. Conversely, if $(\Lambda_0, <)$ is semilinearly ordered and G acts regularly as a group of automorphisms, and λ_0 is some fixed member of Λ_0, the prescription

$$a < b \qquad \text{if and only if} \qquad \lambda_0 a < \lambda_0 b$$

describes a right-invariant semilinear order on G. The solution to Frege's problem proceeds by constructing such a set $(\Lambda_0, <)$ on which the free group of rank 2 acts regularly.

The following lemma is needed.

LEMMA 2.1. Let Γ be a free group of rank 2, freely generated by γ_1, γ_2. There is a linear order $\prec$ on Γ such that
   (i) $\prec$ is both right- and left-invariant;
   (ii) $\prec$ is dense;
   (iii) $\{\gamma_1^n \mid n \in \mathbb{N}\}$ is cofinal (that is, unbounded above) in Γ;
   (iv) if $\omega \in \Gamma$ and $1 \prec \omega$ then there exists $n \in \mathbb{N}$ such that $1 \prec \delta_n \prec \omega$, where $\delta_0 := \gamma_2$ and $\delta_{m+1} := \delta_m \gamma_1 \delta_m^{-1} \gamma_1^{-1}$ for $m > 0$.

The fact that a free group is orderable in the usual sense, i.e. carries a linear order that is both right- and left-invariant, has been known for many years (see L. Fuchs, *Partially Ordered Algebraic Systems*, pp. 47–50). Moreover, any such ordering of a group with trivial centre, such as the free group of rank 2, will be dense: for if $1 \quad x$, there exists y such that $xy \neq yx$, and hence either $1 \prec y^{-1}xy \prec x$ or $1 \prec yxy^{-1} \prec x$. The construction described by Fuchs (p. 48) can be adjusted to ensure that (iii) and (iv) hold; there is a special reason, stated below, for including clause (iv).

Where Γ is as in Lemma 2.1, we take Π as the set of all finite subsets of Γ. Given any $\alpha \in \Gamma$, then, where $(\alpha, \infty) := \{\omega \in \Gamma \mid \alpha < \omega\}$, an equivalence relation ρ_α may be defined on Π by setting

$$a \equiv b \pmod{\rho_\alpha} \qquad \text{if and only if} \qquad a \cap (\alpha, \infty) = b \cap (\alpha, \infty).$$

Where $\rho_\alpha(a)$ is the subset of Π which constitutes the ρ_α-class containing a, we may then define

$$\Lambda := \{A \mid \exists \alpha_{\alpha \in I} \cdot \exists a_{a \in \Pi} A = \rho_\alpha(a)\}.$$

Strict inclusion (⊂) may be shown to be a strict semilinear ordering of Λ.

If $\omega \in \Gamma$, right-multiplication by ω induces an automorphism ω^* of $(\Lambda, \subset)$ that maps a set $\rho_\alpha(a)$ on to $\rho_{\alpha\omega}(a\omega)$. We may define a permutation t of Π by

$$t : a \mapsto \begin{cases} a - \{1\} & \text{if } a \cap (1,\infty) = \emptyset \text{ and } 1 \in a \\ a \cup \{1\} & \text{if } a \cap (1,\infty) = \emptyset \text{ and } 1 \notin a \\ a & \text{otherwise} \end{cases}$$

The permutation of t of Π induces a permutation t^* of Λ which is again an automorphism of $(\Lambda, \subset)$. The group G is then to be the group of automorphisms of $(\Lambda, \subset)$ generated by

$$g_1 := \gamma_1^*$$
$$g_2 := t^* \gamma_2^*.$$

G may be shown to be a free group, and to act freely, i.e. to act regularly on every orbit in Λ: that is, if $w \in G$, $\lambda \in \Lambda$ and $\lambda w = \lambda$, then $w = 1$.

When $\lambda_0 := \rho_1(\emptyset)$, we may now take Λ_0 as $\{\lambda_0 w \mid w \in G\}$, that is, as the G-orbit of λ_0. Λ_0 may then be shown to be semilinearly, but not linearly, ordered by ⊂.

This suffices to show that the free group of rank 2 carries a right-invariant strict semilinear order that is not linear, and hence to prove that (4) does not follow from (1), (2), and (3). The theorem may be strengthened by showing that the ordering of G is both limp and dense; it was to prove the latter that clause (iv) of Lemma 2.1 was needed. This shows that (4) does not follow from (1), (2), (3), (5), and (7); equivalently, that (a), (c), and (h) together do not imply (b). The theorem may therefore be stated thus:

THEOREM 2.2. If G is a free group of rank 2 then there is a right-invariant, limp, dense, semilinear order relation on G that is not linear.

3. THE ARCHIMEDEAN CONDITION

The independence problem which so exercised Frege suggests a further question which, somewhat surprisingly, he did not raise. Having defined positival classes and proved a number of theorems about them, he went on to define a *positive* class as a positival class in which < is dense and complete, that is, as one in which (1), (2), (3),

(4), (g), and (h) are satisfied. This raises the question whether there exists a group with a right-invariant upper semilinear ordering that is not linear, but is archimedean or even complete: in other words, whether (4) is independent of (1), (2), (3), and (f), or even (1), (2), (3), and (g). Theorem 3.1 shows that it is not.

THEOREM 3.1. If G is a group with a right-invariant archimedean upper semilinear ordering $<$, G is abelian: that is, (a) & (f) $\Rightarrow$ (e).

This theorem depends on a lemma.

LEMMA 3.2. Let G be a group with a right-invariant limp upper semilinear ordering $<$, and let x, y be elements of G with $1 < x \leqslant y$. If $z := xyx^{-1}y^{-1}$ then z and z^{-1} are comparable. Moreover, if $t := \max (z, z^{-1})$ then $1 \leqslant t < y$.

If $<$ is archimedean, it is also limp, by Frege's Theorem 1.5, and hence Lemma 3.2 may be applied. To prove the theorem, it may be shown by induction on n that, for any x, y, and t

$$1 < x \leqslant y \ \& \ t = \max (xyx^{-1}y^{-1}, yxy^{-1}x^{-1}) \Rightarrow t^n < x$$

for every integer $n \geqslant 0$. It follows by the archimedean condition that, if t satisfies the antecedent, then $t = 1$, and hence that x and y commute. Since this holds for any two positive elements, and the positive elements generate the group G, G must be abelian. Given the commutative law, (4) is a trivial consequence of (3), and hence $<$ is linear: (a) & (e) $\Rightarrow$ (b), whence (a) & (f) $\Rightarrow$ (b). The upshot is that Frege could have defined a positive class P as one that satisfied (1), (2), (3), (g), and (h), and then have proved that a positive class is positival.

4. ALL INDEPENDENCE PROBLEMS RESOLVED

It was remarked in the article that, with these results, all independence problems concerning the properties (a) to (h) are in effect resolved, but not remarked how simple a diagram can be drawn of the logical relations between them. For present purposes, we may assume the weakest condition (a) to be satisfied, and leave it unmentioned in the implications set out below: $<$ is taken to be a right-invariant weakly connected strict upper semilinear ordering of a group G. If $<$ is archimedean, it evidently must be either dense or complete (or both): (f) $\Rightarrow$ (g) $\vee$ (h). With this exception, denseness

(h) is independent of the various possible combinations of the other conditions or their negations: we may therefore set it aside, and consider only conditions (b) to (g). By Theorem 1.4, completeness (g) implies the archimedean law (f): the converse obviously fails. By Theorem 3.1, the archimedean law (f) implies commutativity (e); the failure of the converse is again obvious. Since $<$ is assumed right-invariant, commutativity (e) trivially implies left-invariance (d). Limpness (c) is, of course, a special case of left-invariance (d). Linearity (b) also follows from left-invariance (d), since, if $p, q \in P$, it holds good by left-invariance that $p < q$ if and only if $1 < p^{-1}q$, i.e. if $p^{-1}q \in P$: condition (3) therefore implies condition (4) when $<$ is left-invariant. Conversely, linearity (b) and limpness (c) together imply left-invariance (d): this was proved by Frege in passing from his Theorem 1.5 to his Theorem 1.6. His argument was as follows. Assume that $<$ is linear and limp, and suppose that $q < r$: we wish to show that $pq < pr$ for any p. Since this is given for $p \in P$ and obvious for $p = 1$, we need consider only the case in which $p < 1$. Since $<$ is linear,

$$pq < pr \ \lor \ pq = pr \ \lor \ pr < pq.$$

If $pq = pr$, then $q = r$, contrary to hypothesis. If $pr < pq$, then, since $1 < p^{-1}$ and $<$ is limp, $r < q$, again contrary to hypothesis. It follows that $pq < pr$. Thus left-invariance (d) is equivalent to the conjunction of linearity (b) and limpness (c): (d) $\Leftrightarrow$ (b) & (c).

From all this we obtain a diagram (Fig. 3.1) of the logical relations between the conditions (b) to (g), condition (a) being assumed. Seven possibilities are allowed by the diagram:

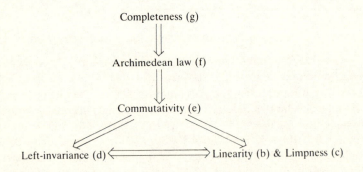

Fig. 3.1. Logical relations between conditions (b)–(g)

(ɪ) $<$ is complete;

(ɪɪ) $<$ is archimedean but not complete;

(ɪɪɪ) G is abelian, but $<$ non-archimedean;

(ɪᴠ) G is non-abelian, but $<$ left-invariant;

(ᴠ) $<$ is linear but not limp;

(ᴠɪ) $<$ is limp but not linear;

(ᴠɪɪ) $<$ is neither linear nor limp.

In case (ɪɪ), $<$ must be dense; in all six other cases, it may or may not be.

Since it is possible to give examples of all seven cases, with dense and discrete subcases save for case (ɪɪ), it follows that no logical relations hold between the various conditions save those shown on the diagram. Cases (ɪ) to (ɪᴠ) are easily illustrated: case (ɪᴠ) is just that of a non-abelian linearly ordered group, in the standard sense. An example may readily be constructed to illustrate case (ᴠ): linearity does not by itself imply left-invariance, nor, therefore, even limpness, and still does not do so when the hypothesis of denseness is added— (b) & (h) $\nRightarrow$ (c). For this, G may be taken as the group of all transformations g of the set **R** of real numbers, where g has the form

$$g : z \mapsto 2^u z + p2^{-n},$$

u and p being any integers and n a non-negative integer. The set P of positive elements will consist of those transformations g for which $\sqrt{2} < \sqrt{2}g$: this has the result that $g < h$ in the group ordering if and only if $\sqrt{2}g < \sqrt{2}h$. Clearly, $<$ is dense and, in virtue of the irrationality of $\sqrt{2}$, linear. Then, where

$$g : z \mapsto 2z - 4$$
$$h : z \mapsto z - 2,$$

$g < h$, but $g^{-1} < h^{-1}$, so that $<$ is not left-invariant.

Frege's problem was whether there was an example of either case (ᴠɪ) or case (ᴠɪɪ). The construction of Theorem 2.2 provides an illustration of case (ᴠɪ), the difficult one, showing that limpness and denseness do not imply linearity: (c) & (h) $\nRightarrow$ (b). To get an example of case (ᴠɪɪ), we may combine cases (ᴠ) and (ᴠɪ). Where G_1 is a group with a right-invariant upper semilinear ordering $<_1$ that is limp but not linear, and G_2 a group with a right-invariant linear ordering $<_2$ that is not limp, we may take G as the direct product $G_1 \times G_2$: the ordering $<$ on G is to be defined lexicographically, so that

$\langle g_1, g_2 \rangle < \langle h_1, h_2 \rangle$ if and only if either $g_1 <_1 h_1$ or $g_1 = h_1$ and $g_2 <_2 h_2$. Then $<$ will be an upper semilinear ordering, but neither limp nor linear.

Frege's theory of real numbers is of interest philosophically, as providing a far clearer insight into the salient role he allotted to the application of mathematics than does his logical construction of the natural numbers: on the basis of a general view about the relation of mathematics to its applications, he treated the applications of the real numbers as far more decisive for the way they should be defined than they are in other theories of the foundations of analysis. Mathematically, his construction of the real numbers, uncompleted because of the disaster wrought by Russell's contradiction, was a pioneering investigation of groups with orderings. His sights were set on ordered groups isomorphic to the additive group of the real numbers; but his interest in what we should call axiomatics, that is, in establishing the most economical base for each theorem he proved, led him into a painstaking investigation, only very partially anticipated by Otto Hölder, of groups not assumed to be abelian with orderings not assumed to be left-invariant. These studies threw out a problem of considerable difficulty and interest; and, in the course of them, he not only employed such subsequently familiar notions as that of a commutator, but hit on the fruitful concept of what we have labelled 'limpness', of which, before the article in which we rounded off his enquiries, it occurred to no other mathematician to make use. It is an injustice that, in the literature on group theory, Frege is left unmentioned and denied credit for his discoveries.

4

Frege's 'Kernsätze zur Logik'*

A puzzling fragment of Frege's *Nachlass*, consisting of seventeen numbered aphorisms on the philosophy of logic, has the rare distinction of having survived the Second World War not only in the form of a typescript but also in that of a photocopy of the original. The editors of the *Nachgelassene Schriften*[1] assign it a date '1906 or earlier', and entitle it '17 Kernsätze zur Logik' (pp. 189–90), translated in the English edition, *Posthumous Writings*,[2] as '17 Key Sentences on Logic' (pp. 174–5). According to a footnote in *Nachgelassene Schriften*, the date 1906 is due to Heinrich Scholz; but the editors point out that the sentence 'Leo Sachse is a man', used by Frege as an example in Kernsatz 10, also occurs in the dialogue with Pünjer on existence,[3] which they date to before 1884 (Pünjer was, according to their note on page 60,[4] Professor of Theology at Jena from 1880 to 1885, when he died at the age of 35); Leo Sachse was a real individual, a Professor at the Gymnasium, who from 1876 was a member of the Jenaische Gesellschaft für Medizin und Naturwissenschaft, to which Frege gave several lectures.[5] For this reason, the editors of *Nachgelassene Schriften* are inclined to assign a considerably earlier date to the 'Kernsätze'. An even better reason for doing so is the fact that the thesis maintained in Kernsatz 10, that a sentence containing an empty proper name does not express a thought, conflicts with that put forward in the 'Einleitung in die Logik', dated by Frege himself to 1906, in which he argues that, if we became convinced that the name 'Odysseus', as used in the *Odyssey*, did stand for an actual man, the thoughts expressed by sentences in that work containing that name would in no way be

---

* First published in *Inquiry*, 24 (1981), 439–48.
[1] Ed. H. Hermes, F. Kambartel, and F. Kaulbach (Hamburg, 1969).
[2] Trans. P. Long and R. White (Oxford, 1979).
[3] *Nachgelassene Schriften*, 67; *Posthumous Writings*, 60.
[4] *Posthumous Writings*, 53.
[5] *Nachgelassene Schriften*, p. 67 n. 1; omitted in *Posthumous Writings*.

altered.[6] For this reason Gottfried Gabriel, in his selection from the *Nachlass*, dates the 'Kernsätze' to 'before 1892'.[7]

The 'Kernsätze' makes a curious impression. Several familiar Fregean theses are expressed, such as the indefinability of truth; but the phraseology is often uncharacteristic, and the sequence of thought seems difficult to follow. If we suppose Frege to have been writing down, in 1906 or even in 1890, what he considered to be the seventeen most important theses he wished to maintain, the principle of selection is perplexing. The opening remark, Kernsatz 1, that 'the combinations which constitute the essence of thinking are characteristically different from associations of ideas', is not in itself surprising: but why should Frege select the word 'combinations' (*Verknüpfungen*)? And why should he go on to observe, in Kernsatz 2, that 'the distinction does not consist merely in an auxiliary thought which adds the ground of justification for the combination'? Why should he suppose that anybody thought it did?

The answers to these questions will be found by comparing the 'Kernsätze' with the Introduction to Hermann Lotze's *Logik*, of which the first edition was published in Leipzig in 1874 and the second in 1880. Provided at least that the comparison is made between the German originals rather than their English translations, it will then become apparent that the 'Kernsätze' form a series of comments by Frege upon Lotze's Introduction, or, more exactly, of remarks prompted by reflection upon it.

Lotze's concern is with the question where the distinction between truth and falsity, or, as he always prefers to say, between truth and untruth, comes from, and with what distinguishes the mental activity of thinking from the mere passage of ideas through the consciousness. He opens by remarking (§I) that in almost every moment of our waking life sensory stimuli arouse in us different ideas (*Vorstellungen*), simultaneously or in immediate succession. Sometimes the simultaneous or immediately successive occurrence of ideas is simply coincidental; sometimes they belong together or are coherent (*zusammengehörig*), because reality always produces their causes together or successively. In either case, the later occurrence of any one idea from such a combination awakens in us the others formerly combined with it: it is upon the recovery of

[6] *Nachgelassene Schriften*, p. 208; *Posthumous Writings*, 191.
[7] *Schriften zur Logik und Sprachphilosophie* (Hamburg, 1971), 23, 174.

coherent connections that our hope of attaining knowledge is based; the merely coincident is the source of error.

In §II, Lotze introduces the term 'stream of ideas' (*Vorstellungs-verlauf*), and remarks that there are presumably general laws, holding for all minds, that govern the succession of ideas, but differ in their application according to the particular nature of each individual mind. If we knew these laws, and the nature of some one given mind, we should be able to predict, from the occurrence in it of certain ideas, which further ideas would succeed them. But these laws would not, in themselves, provide any ground for making a distinction of value (*Werthunterschied*) between these combinations of ideas (*Vorstellungsverbindungen*) in respect of their truth and untruth.

Lotze's problem is, then, where this distinction comes from. He begins §III by observing that 'ordinary linguistic usage ascribes general validity and truth to those combinations of ideas [*Ver-knüpfungen der Vorstellungen*] which it looks to *thinking* to produce'. He thus connects the problem of the distinction between truth and untruth with that of what is distinctive of the activity of thinking. Truth, he says, is usually characterized as 'the correspondence of ideas and of combinations of them with their object [*dem vor-gestellten Gegenstande*] and the relations in which it stands'. He is obviously referring to the correspondence theory of truth, which, later in the book, he rejects. Here he merely says that there may be objections to this formulation, but that this is not the place to go into them: it will be harmless, he says rather disingenuously, if we modify it by saying that 'combinations of ideas are true if they conform to those relations between the contents of the ideas which are the same for every consciousness which has the ideas', rather than to those which hold good for one consciousness but not for another. This characterization of truth is rather obscure; in particu-lar, it faces the objection that Lotze has just talked, in the preceding section, about general laws 'which hold good for all minds alike' but do not provide a basis for the distinction of value between truth and untruth. Presumably, we are meant to distinguish such laws, which govern only the occurrence of ideas, from the relations between the contents of the ideas, which will depend also upon the nature of the individual mind. In any case, the general drift is apparent: an adherent of the correspondence theory might say that Lotze was wishing to replace objectivity by intersubjectivity, although, of course, Lotze uses no such terminology in this connection.

Having given this characterization of truth, Lotze goes on, in §III, to state that thinking is an *activity* of the mind.

The thinking mind is not content to receive and acquiesce in ideas in those combinations into which they were brought by the accident of simultaneous arousal or in which they were reproduced by memory; it sifts them, and dissolves the coexistence of the ideas which have come together only in this coincidental way; but those which belong together in accordance with the relations of their contents it not only leaves together but accomplishes their combination [*Verknüpfung*] afresh, this time, however, in a form which adds to the actual restoration of their connection a consciousness of the ground for their belonging together.

Thus Lotze introduces a rather Kantian idea which he proceeds to develop at some length. In §VI, he focuses on the question by asking after the difference between human thinking and the stream of ideas that occurs in the mind of an animal. 'A common opinion holds that men are capable of thinking, but denies the capacity to animals': without necessarily endorsing this assumption, Lotze will presuppose it in order to illustrate the difference he has in mind. In §VII, he summarizes it by saying that what thinking contributes, over and above the mere stream of ideas, 'consists in auxiliary thoughts which add the ground of justification of their belonging together or not doing so to the restoration or dissolution of a combination of ideas' ('besteht überall in den Nebengedanken, welche zu der Wiederherstellung oder Trennung einer Vorstellungsverknüpfung den Rechtsgrund der Zusammengehörigkeit oder Nichtzusammengehörigkeit hinzufügen'). Later in the same section he says that 'it is in the production of such justificatory auxiliary thoughts that there lies the distinctive characteristic of thinking' ('die Eigenthümlichkeit des Denkens'). In §VI, his two illustrative examples were as follows. An animal may observe a tree covered with foliage in summer and bare in winter, and again in leaf the next summer; at best, it has a combination of ideas which sometimes fails. A man, however, in naming the object a 'tree', and saying of it that it is in leaf or is bare, expresses in this familiar linguistic form 'a conception which contains a mental operation of a quite different kind': for by using the name 'tree', 'he means, not just a constant part of his perceptions, but a *thing* as opposed to its properties'. It is these latter notions of thing and property which here constitute 'the auxiliary thoughts by means of which he justifies both the separation and the conjoining' of the two ideas of the tree and of leaves. The second example is that of a dog who observes a raised stick: past experience associates this in his mind with the idea of pain, and, further, that of running away with that of avoiding pain; he accordingly runs away. But a man who acted similarly in a similar case would, once more, be performing an entirely different mental operation, namely, that of actually reasoning to a conclusion. He connects the blow and the pain, and similarly distance and avoidance of the blow, as cause and effect: he justifies his combination of ideas by appeal to the dependence of the particular upon the general, expressing the general truth in the premiss and the particular instance in the conclusion of an inference. Lotze's 'auxiliary thoughts' thus resemble Kantian categories, although Lotze does not use the term 'category': we distinguish between those ideas which belong together and those which do not, and thus justify a combination of them in the former case, by invoking general forms of thinking (*Formen des Denkens*, a phrase Lotze does use) such as those of thing/property, cause/effect, and general/particular.

Lotze says in §VIII that 'the auxiliary thoughts by means of which we justify combinations of ideas coincide with certain presuppositions' we cannot avoid making. Some hold that 'such forms of thinking, and the auxiliary thoughts which animate them, are immediate copies of the general forms of being'. Others regard them as primarily results of our own mental constitution: but even they do not deny *some* correspondence between them and the nature of existing things. In §IX Lotze excuses himself from resolving this question in his Introduction: he will merely make the assumption that there is some such correspondence, although we may expect to find in our forms of thinking 'some constituents that do not directly reproduce the essence of reality'.

In §X Lotze summarizes the course of his discussion. Even though we may assume that the stream of our ideas is governed by the laws of a psychic mechanism, still

logic itself first begins with the conviction that the matter ought not to rest there, that between the combinations of ideas, however they may have originated, there obtains a distinction of truth and untruth, that there are forms to which these combinations are *supposed* to correspond, laws which they are *supposed* to obey.

We may, indeed, 'seek by a psychological investigation to explain the origin of this lawgiving consciousness in us'; by this Lotze presumably means our consciousness of those laws which our combinations of ideas are supposed to obey, if, that is, we are to be justified in so combining them, so that truth attaches to them. Such an investigation is, however, only of secondary importance, Lotze says, since the correctness of the results of such a psychological investigation could be judged only by the standards set up by that lawgiving consciousness itself: the primary task is to establish the contents of that consciousness; that is, the laws that it imposes.

This ends the substantive part of Lotze's Introduction. He goes on briefly to explain the plan of the book, announcing, in §XI, in a wholly traditional manner, that he will treat, in succession, of concepts, then of judgements, and finally of the syllogism, by which he means the whole of deductive inference.

Two of Frege's 'Kernsätze' echo specific sentences of Lotze's. Kernsatz 12 extracts and endorses part of the sentence quoted above from §X of Lotze's Introduction. The wording almost exactly coincides. Frege writes 'Logic first begins with the conviction that a distinction holds between truth and untruth' ('Die Logik beginnt erst mit der Ueberzeugung, dass ein Unterschied zwischen Wahrheit und Unwahrheit bestehe'). where the relevant part of Lotze's sentence reads 'logic itself first begins with the conviction that . . . there obtains a distinction of truth and untruth' ('beginnt die Logik selbst erst mit der Ueberzeugung, dass . . . ein Unterschied der Wahrheit und Unwahrheit stattfinde'). Kernsatz 2, by contrast, explicitly contradicts Lotze. Frege writes 'The distinction does not consist merely in an auxiliary thought, which adds the ground of justification for the combination' ('Der Unterschied besteht nicht blos in einem Nebengedanken, der den Rechtsgrund für die Verknüpfung hinzufügt'). A comparison with the long sentence from Lotze's §VII, of which the bulk is quoted in German above, will show that Frege took almost all the words of his remark from this sentence, which he is flatly opposing: for Lotze had said that the contribution of thinking 'consists . . . in auxiliary thoughts, which add the ground of justification of their belonging together . . . to the restoration . . . of a combination of ideas' ('besteht . . . in den Nebengedanken, welche zu der Wiederherstellung . . . einer Vorstellungsverknüpfung den Rechtsgrund der Zusammengehörigkeit . . . hinzufügen').

These two instances are enough to show with certainty that, in writing the 'Kernsätze', Frege had Lotze's Introduction in mind.

For the most part, however, one cannot say, of the individual Kernsätze, that Frege is expressing agreement or that he is expressing disagreement with Lotze. Rather, he is striving to attain an accurate formulation of matters which he did not find correctly stated in Lotze's Introduction. Lotze was concerned with what differentiates thinking from a mere stream of ideas. From Frege's standpoint, he was right in fastening, in this connection, upon the distinction between truth and untruth. But what, from the same standpoint, Lotze failed to do was to make any distinction between what occurs in a stream of consciousness and what occurs in thinking, that is, between a combination of ideas and the internal object of thinking. By 'the internal object of thinking' I mean what we refer to in using the cognate accusative of the verb 'to think', that is to say, what we think, as opposed to what we think *about*, which is the external object. I am *not* using 'internal' like 'inner' as in 'inner life' or as opposed to the 'external' of 'external world'. It was to become a fundamental thesis of Frege's that thoughts, which are what we think, are not mental contents, not contents of consciousness. In the 'Kernsätze' he has not yet arrived at that formulation: but he does insist that thoughts are neither ideas nor combinations of them. Because Lotze fails to make this distinction, he treats what occurs in thinking as of the same kind as what occurs in a stream of consciousness, namely a combination of ideas. He therefore describes thinking as differentiated from merely having ideas by its appeal to a means of distinguishing what is true from what is untrue, which is for him a matter of distinguishing between a combination of ideas that genuinely belong together and one in which the ideas have been combined only by chance. The ground of distinction is, for Lotze, nothing intrinsic to the combination of ideas recognized as true, but an extrinsic justification of it. But, for Frege, in arguing thus, Lotze has conflated two separate questions: what allows of our making the distinction between true and untrue; and on what basis we recognize which among the things we think are true and which untrue. Lotze tries to answer the second question, when what he needs to answer is the first.

Frege does not, in the 'Kernsätze', answer the first of these questions. What he does is to observe that, as soon as the distinction between what is true and what is untrue arises, we are concerned with an object of thinking, not with a complex within the stream of ideas. We must distinguish not merely between thinking and having ideas, as Lotze tries to do, but also between that which we think and any combination of ideas. That which we think—the internal object of thinking—he calls a thought (*Gedanke*). Except in the compound *Nebengedanke* (auxiliary thought), reasonably translated by Bosanquet as 'auxiliary notion', Lotze does not, in his Introduction, use the word *Gedanke*, but speaks only of *das Denken*, which, in order to mark the difference from Frege's terminology, I everywhere translated above as 'thinking', sometimes with some awkwardness (e.g. in 'forms of thinking' rather than 'forms of thought'). For Frege, it is the mark of a thought that it is either true or untrue, or at least that it makes sense to ask whether it is true or not. As soon as we have a thought, the question 'True or untrue?' is in place, and wherever that question is in place, what we are concerned with is a thought; a combination of ideas is neither true nor untrue. We may say that, for Frege, Lotze had the right conception of where the answer lay: what he did not have was the right question.

Until we understand their context, the 'Kernsätze' are dead.We can pick out some remarks familiar from Frege's other writings, but, for the rest, it is hard to see what he is getting at, or, therefore, whether what he is saying is right or wrong. As soon as we place them in the context of a reaction to the Introduction to Lotze's *Logik*, they come to life. Kernsatz 1, 'The combinations that constitute the essence of thinking are characteristically different from associations of ideas', announces the principal theme. Frege does not yet use the word 'thought', accepting Lotze's word 'combination' (*Verknüpfung*); but he does not use Lotze's phrase 'combination of ideas'. The internal object of thinking—that which constitutes the essence of thinking—may be regarded as a combination of *something*; but it—the sort of combination that Lotze should be talking about, that, namely, to which truth or untruth can be ascribed—is of an intrinsically different character from an association of ideas. The distinction between them is not to be found where Lotze looked for the distinction between thinking and merely having ideas, namely, an external justification: this is the content of Kernsatz 2, 'The distinction does not consist merely in auxiliary thoughts, which add the ground of justification for the combination'. Indeed, such a combination—the sort which is the object of thinking—is not a combination *of ideas* at all, as is stated in Kernsatz 3: 'in thinking it is not properly ideas that are combined, but things, properties, concepts, relations'. Lotze had in §VI of his Introduction invoked the particular/general distinction as one of the auxiliary thoughts or notions by appeal to which we justify our combinations of ideas; for Frege, the distinction is not a *Nebengedanke*, but intrinsic to thoughts as such: this is the content of Kernsatz 4, 'A thought always contains something that reaches out beyond the particular case, whereby the latter comes into consciousness as falling under something general'.

Kernsatz 5, 'The linguistic expression for what is characteristic of a thought is the copula or the personal inflection of the verb', may strike one as curiously placed: why does Frege start speaking of such matters here? The sentence contains an echo of a phrase of Lotze's, but significantly modified: where Lotze had spoken of 'what is characteristic of thinking' (*die Eigenthümlichkeit des Denkens*), Frege speaks of 'what is characteristic of a thought' (*die Eigenthümlichkeit des Gedankens*). He does not, in this Kernsatz, contradict what Lotze had said, namely, that this characteristic of thinking is the appeal to justificatory *Nebengedanken*, since this had already been denied in Kernsatz 2. He is concerned with a different problem from Lotze: to characterize *thoughts*, the objects of thinking, rather than to characterize the activity of thinking as such. In order to bring out what a thought is, he turns to its linguistic expression: 'The sky is blue' expresses a thought, 'the blueness of the sky' or 'the sky's being blue' does not, for we cannot call it true or false. That, as he says in Kernsatz 6, is the crucial test: 'it may serve as an external criterion for a combination that constitutes a thought that, for it, the question whether it is true or untrue has a sense'; and he adds, to make it clear why combinations of ideas are not thoughts, 'associations of ideas are neither true nor untrue'. The phrase I have clumsily translated 'a combination that constitutes a thought' is, in Frege's German, *die denkende Verknüpfung*, literally 'a thinking combination': Frege means 'the sort of combination that occurs in thinking'. (The phrase would be an extraordinary one for him to use did he not have Lotze in mind.)

In Kernsatz 7, 'What truth is I hold to be indefinable', Frege repudiates Lotze's attempt, or any other, to characterize the notion of truth. This was, of course, to be a position he held throughout his life; but, given that the criterion for whether what we are concerned with is a thought is whether it makes sense to ask if it is true, it is one which makes it that much harder to say what sort of thing a thought is. We can best see what it is by considering its linguistic expression;

as he remarks in Kernsatz 8, 'the linguistic expression of a thought is a sentence'. Nevertheless, as he goes on to say in the same Kernsatz, it is the thought, not the sentence, to which truth primarily attaches: 'one also speaks in a transferred sense of the truth of a sentence'. It is only because the sentence expresses a thought that we call it true or untrue, as he says in Kernsatz 9: 'a sentence can be true or untrue only when it is the expression of a thought'. Indeed, this is shown by the fact that not every sentence *can*, as such, be called true or untrue; when it cannot, it is not the expression of a thought. What is an example of this? Such a sentence as 'This table is round': considered in itself, it makes no sense to call that sentence true or untrue. It can, of course, become an expression of a thought, namely, when used as referring to a particular table. If this is so, then the same must apply to proper names: if the name 'Leo Sachse' did not refer to a definite individual, the sentence 'Leo Sachse is a man' would not express a thought, either. That is how Frege comes to say what he does in Kernsatz 10:

the sentence 'Leo Sachse is a man' is the expression of a thought only when 'Leo Sachse' designates something. In the same way the sentence 'This table is round' is the expression of a thought only when the words 'this table' designate something definite for me, and are not empty words.

Kernsatz 11 asserts the eternity of truth. ' "2 times 2 is 4" remains true even if, as a result of Darwinian evolution, all men came to assert that 2 times 2 was 5.' An arithmetical truth is a good example of those we are accustomed to characterize as eternal truths. But Frege does not admit any distinction between eternal and ephemeral truths: *every* truth is an eternal truth. He continues, in the same Kernsatz, 'Every truth is eternal and independent of whether anyone thinks it and of the psychological constitution of one who thinks it.' The basis of this is given in his later writings: a thought is true or false *simpliciter*. If, then, 'This table is round' is used, on different occasions, to express a thought, it will not, in general, be the same thought that it expresses, since otherwise that thought might at one time be true and at another false, whereas the characterization of a thought as true or untrue admits of no qualification. Frege was to come to assert the same about thoughts as he here asserts about truths: if truth is eternal, then that which is said to be true, namely, a thought, must similarly be eternal, independent of being recognized as true or even of being grasped. In the

'Kernsätze', Frege does not take this step; but he is very close to it.

Frege now turns to what Lotze says about logic, and begins, in Kernsatz 12, by endorsing Lotze's statement about how there comes to be such a thing: 'logic first begins with the conviction that a distinction holds between truth and untruth'. In his §X, from which this observation is extracted, Lotze had written almost as if logic covered all the principles governing the justifications we give for our judgements of truth and falsity, and Frege now proceeds to correct this exaggeration. This is done in Kernsatze 13, 15, and 16. 'One justifies a judgement either by going back to already known truths or without using other judgements. Only the first case, inference, is the subject-matter of logic' (13). Frege now interpolates, as Kernsatz 14, a remark bearing upon Lotze's statement that he will, in his book, treat in succession of concepts, of judgements, and of inferences: 'the theories of the concept and of the judgement serve only as preparation for the theory of inference'. He does not say that Lotze is wrong to proceed as he does, but affirms the subordinate purpose of the first two divisons. One might well object to Frege's claim: no doubt as far as logic is concerned, the notions of concept and judgement are of interest only as bearing upon the validity of inferences, but do they not have a significance in relation to other questions also? In the 'Kernsätze', Frege is considering logic in the traditional manner, as the science of inference. Later, he was to give a broader definition of it. In the fragment 'Logik', probably written about 1882, he says that logic treats of the property 'true' as part of its subject-matter, as physics treats of the properties 'heavy', 'hot', etc., and that 'logical laws are nothing more than a development of the content of the word "true" '.[8] In the 'Logik' of 1897, after some very similar remarks, he declares that 'logic is the science of the most general laws of truth'.[9] We may thus say that Frege came to consider logic as the theory of truth, rather than just as the theory of inference: and, in this spirit, it might appear more reasonable to hold that the notions of concept and judgement were instruments in the development of the theory of truth.

However this may be, Frege returns in the next Kernsatz to the previous point: 'the task of logic is the formulation of laws in accordance with which a judgement is justified by means of others,

[8] *Nachgelassene Schriften*, 3; *Posthumous Writings*, 3.
[9] *Nachgelassene Schriften*, 139; *Posthumous Writings*, 128.

independently of whether they are themselves true' (15). In his §X, Lotze had spoken as though what he called our 'lawgiving consciousness', that is, our consciousness of the laws which our combinations of ideas are supposed to obey, if they are to be true—those laws which it is the task of logic to formulate—could be identified with the procedure of justification in general. Frege is anxious to point out that the kind of justification which is the concern of logic, namely, deductive inference, is only a relative justification (relative, that is, to the truth of the premisses), and hence that there must be another type of justification which logic does not study. The same point is made, in similar words, in the 'Logik' of the 1880s:[10] here he adds, as Kernsatz 16, that 'conformity with logical laws can guarantee the truth of a judgement only in so far as the judgements to which one goes back to justify it are true'. Finally, Frege alludes to Lotze's remark that a psychological investigation of 'this lawgiving consciousness in us' would be possible, but would have only secondary importance, since its results would remain subject to the standards set up by that consciousness itself: the primary task is to discover the content of the laws. Frege's own comment is sharper: a psychological investigation has, not even a mere secondary place, but no place at all, if what we are concerned to do is to justify the logical laws. 'The laws of logic cannot be justified by means of a psychological investigation' (17).

Seen in the light of their true context, of which I trust that the foregoing comparison will have convinced the reader, Frege's 'Kernsätze' present a coherent sequence of theses, developing a definite argument, instead of being, what at first sight they appear, a somewhat desultory set of random observations. To when should we date the 'Kernsätze'? As pointed out by Gabriel, they must be from before 1891, since they plainly precede the drawing of the distinction between *Sinn* and *Bedeutung*. The use in them of the word '*Gedanke*' might suggest that they were written when Frege was on the verge of making that distinction. From the *Begriffsschrift* (1879) and throughout the 1880s, including in *Grundlagen* (1884), his usual word was 'content' (*Inhalt*), qualified, when necessary, by 'judgeable' (*beurtheilbarer*) to distinguish the content of a sentence from that of a subsentential phrase: he later described himself as having split up the judgeable content into the thought and the truth-

---

[10] *Nachgelassene Schriften*, p. 3; *Posthumous Writings*, 3.

value.[11] I believe, however, that the 'Kernsätze' were written *before* Frege had come to adopt the 'content' terminology used in *Begriffsschrift*; what more natural than that, when he abandoned it, he should employ, for one of the two constituents into which he had now split judgeable contents, the word he had employed before he used the word 'content' in that connection? Indeed, as Mr Justin Broackes has pointed out to me, although in the 'Logik' of the 1880s 'judgeable content' is the official term, Frege does also use the term 'thought' (*Gedanke*) in less formal contexts,[12] which, in view of the relatively close connection between it and the 'Kernsätze', should probably be stated by saying that he was still sometimes using the word '*Gedanke*'. I believe that the 'Kernsätze' form the first piece of writing from Frege's pen on the philosophy of logic that survives to us. Since Lotze's *Logik* was first published in 1874, that gives us the earliest possible date for them; and probably Frege did not meet Leo Sachse until 1876. On the other hand, the complete absence of the 'content' terminology suggests that the work was composed well before the *Begriffsschrift*, and hence before the second edition of Lotze's *Logik* appeared: 1876 or 1877 thus seem reasonable dates. If Frege wrote the 'Kernsätze' in 1876, it was not a precocious work: he was then 27. We see in it the first effort on Frege's part, of which we have any knowledge, to attain clarity about a problem which, however expressed, concerned him all his life, the nature of a thought. How far he was stimulated to think about it by reading Lotze's Introduction, and how far he had already thought about it, and found Lotze's remarks a useful peg on which to hang his reflections, it is impossible to say: but in the 'Kernsätze', although he does not resolve his problem, he has gained much greater clarity about it than Lotze ever did, and has arrived at some formulations which he was to maintain throughout his life.

Hans Sluga has maintained that Lotze was one of the great formative influences on Frege's philosophy. Since Frege never mentions Lotze by name, at least in any of the writings that have come down to us, it is difficult to find direct evidence for how Frege regarded him. The 'Kernsätze' form the only such piece of direct evidence known to me. What should we judge, from it, Frege's evaluation of Lotze's philosophical work to have been? This is, of course, a matter of inference. I should judge that Frege regarded

---

[11] *Grundgesetze der Arithmetik*, i (Jena, 1893), p. x.
[12] *Nachgelassene Schriften*, p. 6; *Posthumous Writings*, p. 6.

5
Frege as a Realist*

In two articles,[1] Hans Sluga has maintained that, in my book *Frege: Philosophy of Language*,[2] I completely misunderstood Frege's place in the history of philosophy, and, as a result, misinterpreted Frege's doctrines.

Sluga speaks of my 'repeated claim that Frege's logic was directed against a dominant Hegelian idealism which was, somehow, associated with psychologism',[3] and gives three page references to my book (pp. 197, 470, 683) to substantiate this attribution. On the contrary, Sluga says, 'Hegelian idealism had . . . completely collapsed in Germany twenty-five years before Frege ever set pen to paper',[4] while psychologism is not to be linked to the idealistic tradition.[5] In point of fact, however, of the three references to my book given by Sluga, only one, almost at the end of the book, mentions *Hegelian* idealism specifically (the only allusion to Hegel in the entire book). What it says is that 'in the early years of the present century, it would have been impossible to see Frege's significance in the way' I there explained it, and that 'rather, it would have been natural to lay emphasis upon Frege's realism, seeing his chief importance as lying in the part he played in bringing about the downfall of Hegelian idealism'; this, which Sluga represents as the core of my whole historical misunderstanding of Frege's significance, was thus an assessment which I expressly rejected: I allowed merely that 'in so far as Frege's realistic philosophy played a part in' the overthrow of Hegelianism—something I did not attempt to assess—'that is also an ingredient in its historical importance'. What Sluga dislikes is my describing Frege as a realist, which he calls an

* First published in *Inquiry*, 19 (1976), 455–68.
[1] 'Frege and the Rise of Analytical Philosophy', *Inquiry*, 18 (1975), 471–87, and 'Frege as a Rationalist', in M. Schirn (ed.), *Studies on Frege*, Problemata (Stuttgart, 1976), i. 27–47.
[2] (London, 1973).
[3] 'Frege and the Rise of Analytical Philosophy, 477.
[4] 'Frege as a Rationalist', p. 28.
[5] 'Frege and the Rise of Analytical Philosophy', 477.

'unsubstantiated (though widely accepted) claim':[6] but it is tendentious of him to represent this alleged error in my interpretation of
Frege as springing from my supposedly faulty historical assessment,
since, in the same passage, I specifically said that Frege's realism
was not a logical, but at most a historical, precondition for what I
took to be his principal achievement. That is, while I regarded
Frege as a realist, and continue so to regard him, I did not see his
realism as essential to the main significance of his work; hence, even
if I were wrong in thinking him a realist, and had been misled into
that error by a historical mistake, that error could not have underlain
any misconception on my part of his significance.

As for the other two passages to which Sluga refers, I there
indeed spoke of a prevalent idealism associated with psychologism;
but no mention was made of the Hegelian variety, nor was any
intended. In associating psychologism with a species of idealism,
and in describing it as dominant, I may have been in error; but, if so,
it was an error shared by Frege. In *Grundgesetze*, he speaks of the
school of logicians of whom he takes Erdmann as a representative
example as 'the dominant logic', and immediately says that it is
'infected through and through with psychology' (vol. i, p. xiv).
Later he says that, on Erdmann's view, 'everything drifts into
idealism' (p. xix), and, of Erdmann himself, that 'he is therefore an
idealist' (p. xxi), and goes on to argue against idealists. Perhaps it
can be argued that the historical picture I gave was wrong: but, if so,
no one would be likely to be led into misinterpreting Frege by
adopting it, since it was a picture held by Frege himself.

Since Sluga is so inaccurate in his exegesis of me, it is not very
surprising that he also goes astray in his exegesis of Frege. As
already remarked, the nub of my misunderstanding of Frege is said
to lie in my supposing him to have been a realist. 'In calling
Frege a realist', Sluga says, 'Dummett has laid much stress on the
supposed ontological implications of Frege's doctrines'.[7] Sluga
feels 'acutely uncomfortable about the fact that Dummett puts
ontological considerations at the heart of Frege's thought'.[8] I should
not be sure what these accusations amounted to, were it not
that Sluga makes explicit what he means. 'Frege's theory of the
objectivity of numbers, value-ranges, functions, etc.', he tells us,

---

[6] 'Frege and the Rise of Analytical Philosophy', 478.
[7] 'Frege as a Rationalist', 29.
[8] 'Frege and the Rise of Analytical Philosophy', 477.

'was never intended as an ontological theory.'[9] He goes on to say that it may have been derived from Lotze's theory of validity, and, in any case, 'must . . . be compared with' that theory. For Lotze, he explains, 'ideal objects are not real, but merely possess validity'. The issue between realism and nominalism was, for Lotze, a metaphysical, not a logical, one, whereas the notion of validity belongs to logic. The comparison of such views with Frege's is based on the claim that Lotze's distinction 'is paralleled by Frege's distinction between reality and objectivity as he makes it in the Preface to the *Grundgesetze*'; hence, Sluga concludes, 'it is obviously a mistake to regard' 'Frege's and Lotze's doctrines' 'as ontological theories, at least according to the intentions of their authors'.[10] This remarkable piece of misapplied history rests on a tendentious translation. The word used by Frege, and here translated 'real' by Sluga, is '*wirklich*', translated 'actual' by Austin and Furth; Frege expressly associates *Wirklichkeit* with *Wirkung* (being actual with acting on things). Abstract objects are not, for Frege, *wirklich* (they have no causal effects): for all that, they are just as objective as concrete ones, and exist in just as great independence of our thinking about them. Whatever Lotze may have thought, Frege would strenuously have denied that there is any place for a further philosophical inquiry, say a metaphysical one, which could have shown that, while from a merely logical point of view 'the number one' is a proper name standing for an object, there is no real object for which it stands. To suppose that he would have allowed for such a possibility is to miss the entire point of his use, in *Grundlagen*, of the principle that a word has meaning only in the context of a sentence, to justify regarding abstract terms as standing for genuine, objective objects. If there is any obvious mistake being made, it is Sluga's, not mine.

Sluga's blindness, in this crucial connection, to the significance of the context principle is all the more remarkable in view of the fact that one of his principal charges against me is that I failed to give due weight to that principle. Now the context principle was explicitly stated only in *Grundlagen*, before Frege had arrived at the distinction between sense and reference: hence, as I remarked in my book (p. 496), we have to decide whether to take the principle as one about reference or only about sense. Construed as a

---

[9] 'Frege as a Rationalist', 29.   [10] Ibid.

thesis about sense, it enshrines the principle of the central role of sentences in any theory of meaning. So understood, Frege's views on sense and reference cannot be made coherent without it; that is why I repeatedly called Frege's failure (as I then believed) to reiterate the principle a disaster. On this aspect of the context principle, Sluga is not in fact in disagreement with what I said, save over the historical question whether, in his later period, Frege explicitly maintained the principle. I did not say in my book, as Sluga alleges,[11] that it was Frege's realism that led him to abandon the context principle; still less did I say, as he also alleges,[12] that it was the distinction of sense and reference which had this effect: on the contrary, I said that this distinction 'is entirely consonant with the doctrines of *Grundlagen*, and supplies a necessary complementation of them' (pp. 643–4). On many different pages (7, 196, 644–5) I emphasized that what conflicted with the context principle was the assimilation of sentences to proper names, or, otherwise expressed, the doctrine that truth-values are objects. I also stressed that this doctrine was a dispensable part of Frege's later philosophy (pp. 411–12). Sluga expresses himself[13] as at a loss to understand why the doctrine that sentences are a special kind of complex proper names should war with the context principle. The reason is that Frege was unwilling to admit any logically significant distinction between expressions save those that showed a difference of type; so sentences, when no longer thought of as comprising a separate logical type, could no longer be allotted any distinguished role. Hence, in §10 of *Grundgesetze*, to which I referred (pp. 196, 645), Frege says that, in order to fix the reference of all value-range terms, we must fix the reference of all expressions resulting from putting them in an argument-place of a primitive functional expression, with no restriction to primitive *predicates*. This is, as I remarked, a kind of ghost of the context principle, namely, a principle to the effect that the reference of a proper name is fixed by fixing the reference of any more complex proper name containing it; but it precisely lacks any recognition of the special role of *sentences*.[14]

---

[11] 'Frege and the Rise of Analytical Philosophy', 478.

[12] Ibid. 485.   [13] Ibid. 478.

[14] Since this article was originally published, I have somewhat altered my view on the historical question. It still appears to me, for the reason given in the text, that Frege abandoned the context principle, construed as a thesis about reference; but I now think it equally plain that he maintained it as a thesis concerning sense.

As I argued in my book, the use to which the context principle is put in *Grundlagen* depends on taking it as a thesis about reference, not just about sense, since it is used in effect to justify ascribing a reference to abstract terms. Here, as I observed (p. 500), there really is some tension with Frege's realism. The reason is obvious: if, as appears, we are justified in taking abstract names at their face-value and ascribing reference to them simply on the ground that we have provided determinate truth-conditions for sentences containing them, then the means by which such truth-conditions were laid down cannot itself have involved any appeal to the notion of reference for such names. Whether this was what Frege intended, however, is far from clear, since he does not achieve, in *Grundgesetze*, a means of stipulating the truth-conditions of sentences containing names of value-ranges in terms that do not presuppose that we know what, in general, value-ranges are: the reason is that, for the stipulations to be successful, we must already take the individual variables as ranging over a domain including value-ranges (or at least over an equally large domain). (In fact, this assumption makes the domain impossibly large, and hence the contradiction.) It seems probable that Frege's views were not, at this point, in complete harmony. In order to restore harmony, we must make some modification. If we choose to stress the use of the context principle as a thesis about reference, namely, as serving to justify taking abstract terms at their face-value, then we must, contrary to Frege's own practice, admit only such abstract terms as are genuinely eliminable. (At least, if we do not do this, it is not clear just what the justification is.) This has the effect of *increasing* the disanalogy between terms for concrete objects and those for abstract ones. As I remarked in my book (p. 500), if the context principle 'is taken in the very strong sense in which Frege appears to take it in *Grundlagen* . . . then it seems to provide a way of dispensing with reference altogether': that is, the notion of reference will not be appealed to in laying down the truth-conditions of sentences. But, in fact, we have no conception of how the truth-conditions of sentences containing names of concrete objects would, in general, be determined without invoking the notion of reference for such names; and so the disanalogy between abstract and concrete terms would be much greater than I should wish to allow.

I stated in my book that one of the ingredients in Frege's notion of reference is the principle that the reference of a proper name is its bearer. I should have thought this evident enough from even a cursory reading of Frege; but it especially incenses Sluga. If it is right, then a more promising way of restoring the harmony is to try to show, as I did, that the conception of identifying an object as the bearer of a name covers a family of cases, for names of different sorts, and that some content can be given to it even in the case of names of abstract objects, or at least of some such. If it is wrong, then we await some account, at which Sluga does not even hint, of how we can grasp the condition for the truth of sentences containing names of concrete objects independently of any conception of identifying an object as the bearer of such a name.

If it is true, as I think, that Frege's notion of reference for proper names implicitly appeals to the name/bearer relation, we are entitled to ask in what this relation consists and with what right Frege appealed to it. I attempted to explain the relation as embedded in very basic linguistic practices, including the use of ostension to identify an object as the referent of a name. Sluga objects[15] that he knows no place in Frege where ostension plays such a role. I did not purport, however, to be reproducing anything in Frege in this discussion, only to be bringing to light something I believed must underlie his use of the notion of reference.

I gave as the other main ingredient in the notion of reference the conception of what I called 'semantic role', and should now prefer to call 'semantic value'. The semantic value of an expression is its contribution to determining any sentence in which it occurs as true or false; the theory of reference is an attempt to give an account of the way in which a sentence is determined as true or otherwise in accordance with its composition. It is this which explains why it seems so clear to Frege that every genuine constituent of a sentence must have a reference of some kind. But this notion, as thus formulated, is as yet no more than programmatic: Frege had specific views about what the reference of expressions of various types was to be taken to be. The two most important are that the reference of a sentence is its truth-value, and that of a name its bearer (if any). Sluga wholly fails to notice my repeated observation that Frege's notion of reference has these distinct ingredients, which, for the most part, complement one another,[16] although there is sometimes

---

[15] 'Frege and the Rise of Analytical Philosophy', 479–80.
[16] *Frege: Philosophy of Language*, e.g. pp. 199–200, 223, 401.

some tension between them; on the contrary, he assimilates the conception of reference as semantic value to its identification with the name/bearer relation,[17] and inveighs against it as yet another instance of my mistakenly realistic interpretation of Frege. It is difficult to be clear what Sluga does think, however, since he also commends Tugendhat for offering an interpretation of Frege's views on sense and reference in the light of the context principle,[18] and rebukes me for rejecting it and persevering with the 'standard interpretation' which ignores that principle. (It was not so standard in the days when Grossmann could claim that it was certain that Frege drew no distinction between sense and reference for incomplete expressions.) I devoted many pages[19] to explaining why Tugendhat's account appeared to me inadequate, particularly because it omits the appeal to the name/bearer relation: Sluga does not answer my arguments; it is sufficient criticism, it appears, that I did not at once rally to the support of a fresh, new, non-standard interpretation. In fact, however, Tugendhat offers no account whatever of the notion of sense, and his account of reference amounts simply to construing it as semantic value, programmatically conceived, that is, without any specification of what the reference of any type of expression actually is (save for his erroneous claim that he can prove that the reference of a sentence is its truth-value). If Tugendhat's interpretation is an adequate one, therefore, Frege provided no explanation of how a sentence is determined as true or false in accordance with its composition, but merely contented himself with introducing the abstract notion of the contribution which an expression makes to this. If, on the other hand, Tugendhat's reading is to be supplemented by a specific account of the reference of each type of expression, it still remains to be seen whether that account differs substantially from that which I attributed to Frege.

Frege takes it for granted that the *Bedeutung* of 'Jupiter' is a planet, that of 'Socrates' a man, etc.: but, from a purely programmatic conception of semantic value, there would be no presumption that the semantic value of 'Socrates' would be a man, or anything resembling one; if any case, how could we have any idea of what a man was, independently of having *some* means of referring to particular men? Frege appeals to what a speaker intends to talk about as showing what the *Bedeutung* of a name he uses is, or at

---

[17] 'Frege and the Rise of Analytical Philosophy', p. 479.
[18] Ibid. 478.   [19] *Frege: Philosophy of Language*, 199–203, 401–7.

least what it is not: but where do we get the notion of talking about something from, and why should we connect it, let alone identify it, with semantic value? As Geach has stressed, Frege assumes that any expression '. . .' may be replaced by '*die Bedeutung von* ". . ."', or by '*was* ". . ." *bedeutet*' without change of *Bedeutung*: what reason is there to assume that the semantic value of the phrase 'the semantic value of ". . ."' will be the same as that of the expression '. . .' itself? Frege uses the word '*Bedeutung*' in such a way as not to allow for any distinction between the reference of a word and its referent; he uses this noun, and the verb '*bedeuten*', in such a way as to make it possible, without being false to his thought, to translate them as 'reference' and 'stand for'. Frege holds that, even though a proper name has sense, it is without *Bedeutung* if it is empty, e.g. if it is 'King Arthur' and there is no *man* whom we may use that name to speak about; and he draws the consequence that *any* sentence in which that name occurs will not merely fail to be either true or false, but will have no truth-value at all, not even an intermediate one. Starting from a merely programmatic notion of semantic value, however, we should have no ground to deny a semantic value to such a name, and to do so involves us in many awkwardnesses; not only must we deny a truth-value to the thought expressed by such a sentence as 'If King Arthur defeated the Saxons, then the Saxons were not always victorious', but we shall be embarrassed to say whether someone who expresses a thought, and attaches assertoric force to his utterance, always makes an assertion. Above all, Frege takes it as inescapable that occurrence within *oratio obliqua* causes a name to have a non-standard *Bedeutung*. If we start with a programmatic notion of semantic value, then, by definition, two expressions can have the same semantic value only if they are intersubstitutable in all (standard) contexts without change of truth-value; hence the existence of intensional contexts would provide strong prima-facie evidence that, for two names to have the same semantic value, it is not enough that they have the same bearer. Of course, we can escape this consequence by reserving intensional contexts for special treatment, and it is possible that we should encounter some strong motive for doing so. But this is not the way in which Frege argues: he simply *starts* from the assumption that the *Bedeutung* of a name is its bearer; and he does so because that is where he got the notion from, a notion he proceeded to extend, by analogy, to other types of expression.

The notion of reference is of relatively little interest unless it plays a role in the account of sense; otherwise it is idle, and does not belong to the theory of meaning. Sluga says that 'Frege never formulated a general theory of meaning'[20]: this is correct in so far as it is meant that he did not give a complete theory of meaning, but conveys a false impression that he was not interested in contributing to such a thing (in fact, his contribution is of overwhelming importance). Indeed, it seems to me that the notion of reference is of little or no interest if it is not viewed as belonging to the theory of meaning. The point is of immense importance, and I had hoped I had succeeded in conveying this: it concerns the relation of sense to reference. Sense, Frege says, determines reference: but this could be understood in either of two ways. On the strong interpretation, to know the sense is to know the condition for the expression to have a given reference; on the weak interpretation, it is just that two expressions with the same sense could not have different references. It is clear to almost everyone that we need the strong interpretation so far as the sense of a sentence—a thought—is concerned: to grasp a thought is to know the condition for it to be true. But what about a proper name? I think that Frege intended us to adopt the same interpretation here: to know the sense of the name is to know the condition that must hold of any given object to be the referent of that name. What is in favour of this? First, it accords with those well-known passages in which Frege says that the sense of a word is the mode of presentation of the referent—the way in which it is given to us (e.g. 'I compare . . . the . . . image projected by . . . the telescope . . . to the sense').[21] And, secondly, it gives us some conception of what the sense of a proper name consists in; if we reject this suggestion, we simply have no idea what the sense of a name is. Now let us consider a predicate, say 'ξ stammers'. In what does its sense consist? There is a temptation, which I combated in my book, to say that the sense of such a predicate is a function which carries us from the sense of a name, say 'Mrs Thatcher', to the sense of the sentence formed by putting that name in the argument-place of the predicate. Certainly there must be such a function: but is that how the sense of the predicate is given to us? Suppose that it is. Then the sense of the predicate carries us from the sense of the

[20] 'Frege and the Rise of Analytical Philosophy', 474.
[21] 'Über Sinn und Bedeutung', *Zeitschrift für Philosophie und philosophische Kritik*, 100 (1892), 30.

name 'Mrs Thatcher' to the thought expressed by the sentence 'Mrs Thatcher stammers', that is, to the condition for that sentence to be true. But what is that condition? What does determine that sentence as true or as false? On this picture of the sense of the predicate, we are left unable to say: or, if we can say, then it must be the satisfaction of some condition, given by the predicate, by the *sense* of the name 'Mrs Thatcher'. The reference of that name does not come into the determination of the truth or falsity of the sentence: at best, it is relevant only to how we grasp the sense of the name. Obviously, this is wrong: the determination of the truth-value of the sentence goes via the referent of the name. The sense of the name determines an object as its referent; and the sense of the predicate determines a mapping from objects to truth-values, that is to say, a concept; the sentence is true or false according as the object does or does not fail under the concept, i.e. according as it is mapped by it on to the value *true* or the value *false*. The mapping of objects on to truth-values is not the *sense* of the predicate, but its referent: the sense is, rather, some particular way, which we can grasp, of determining such a mapping. But the sense of the predicate is to be thought of, not as being given directly in terms of a mapping from the *senses* of names on to anything (e.g. thoughts), but, rather, in terms of a mapping of *objects* on to truth-values. Thus in all cases we need the strong interpretation of the thesis that sense determines reference. If there were any type of expression for which this were not so, then the notion of reference, though it might be defensible, would play no part in the theory of meaning as it related to expressions of that type. The vehemence of Sluga's objections to taking the referent of a name to be its bearer suggests to me that he has not understood this, or even asked himself the question 'What do we need the notion of reference *for*?'; and I should despair of the chances of producing any account of sense which did not do justice to the connection between sense and reference, as just explained, and yet had a plausible claim to being a development of Frege's views.

To say, as was said above, that to know the sense of a name is to know the condition for a given object to be the referent of the name is intelligible only in the presence of some means of picking out an object (of a suitable kind) otherwise than by means of the name. In general, to say, of any condition whatever, that one knows what it is for an object to satisfy that condition, presupposes that one has the conception of referring, by some means, to a particular such object. Hence, to explain the notion of the sense of a name in this way is tacitly to appeal to some other means of picking out an object than by the use of that, or a similar, name—the means by which the object is 'given'. I thought that, in some cases, a suitable variety of ostension would serve this purpose. That suggestion is not so important, however, as the fact that, for an account of sense of this kind, *something* must serve that purpose. If nothing does, then the notion of the sense of a name is left completely unexplained.

Sluga connects my description of Frege as a realist with what he calls 'epistemological atomism'; Frege on the contrary belonged to 'the anti-atomistic tradition characteristic of classical German philosophy',[22] and it is his anti-atomism which is expressed by the context principle. I should say, rather, that it comes out in his making the distinction between sense and reference, and in his views on criteria of identity. Sluga characterizes epistemological atomism as the doctrine that 'knowledge is . . . in the first instance knowledge of objects and their properties',[23] as opposed to the view that 'knowing is in the first instance always knowing that'. I wholly agree that Frege was not an atomist in this sense: I remarked in my book (p. 179), in connection with Frege's view that the sense of a proper name determines a criterion of identity, that Mill's view involved that 'the world already came to us sliced up into objects', whereas, on the basis of Frege's view, we see that 'the proper names which we use . . . determine principles whereby the slicing up of the world is to be effected, principles which are acquired with the acquisition of the uses of these words'.[24] Moreover, in a subsequent article on Frege,[25] I attributed to Frege, as part of a reconstruction of one of the arguments for the sense/reference distinction, the view that all theoretical knowledge is propositional knowledge (p. 163)—although, contrary to Sluga's claim, I should not regard knowledge-how as always reducible to knowledge-that. It is unclear to me whether, when Sluga says[26] that Frege had no model theory, he intends to deny that Frege offered an account of the way in which a sentence is determined

[22] 'Frege and the Rise of Analytical Philosophy', 485.
[23] Ibid. 479.
[24] See also pp. 504–5, 577.
[25] 'Frege', *Teorema*, 5 (1975), 149–88; repr. in English as 'Frege's Distinction between Sense and Reference', in M. Dummett, *Truth and Other Enigmas* (London, 1978).
[26] 'Frege and the Rise of Analytical Philosophy', 479.

as true in accordance with its composition, or only that this account resembled that of classical semantics. He goes on to claim that (classical?) model theory 'essentially presupposes an atomistic theory of knowledge'. Since a semantic interpretation corresponds to the assignment of *references*, not of *senses*, and since it is sense, not reference, that is the cognitive notion, this accusation seems preposterously wide of the mark. In any case, even a notion of sense which connects the sense of a proper name with the identification of an object as its bearer does not entail epistemological atomism as defined by Sluga. I can only suppose that Sluga's impression to the contrary derives from his very odd denial[27] that Frege believed that proper names have associated with them a criterion of identity, although Frege's enunciation of the principle is perfectly general: 'If we are to use the sign a to designate an object, we must have a criterion for deciding in all cases whether b is the same as a'.[28] He might otherwise have noticed that, on the very same page of my book (p. 406) as that on which I spoke of ostension and its connection with the notion of a bearer, I said that:

the objects which serve as referents cannot be recognized quite independently of language: it is only because we employ a language for the understanding of which we need to grasp various criteria of identity . . . that we learn to slice the world up, conceptually, into discrete objects.

What, then, does Sluga take the content of the context principle to be? He spells this out in detail:

From a logical point of view, Frege argued, a proposition was, to begin with, a unity. For many logical purposes it was, of course, necessary to distinguish parts in the sentence and the judgment expressed by it. From a grammatical point of view one could regard the sentence as built up from words according to the rules of syntax. But the logical point of view was a slightly different one. In logic we must first speak of a judgment in which a whole thought is grasped. When we account for the logical relations that hold between judgments or the thoughts expressed by them, we may be forced to conceive of the judgment as falling apart into constituents. In a particular case, the logical constituents we have to distinguish in a judgment may closely correspond to the words out of which the grammarian sees the sentence composed. But there is no need to assume a general correspondence

---

[27] 'Frege and the Rise of Analytical Philosophy', 486.
[28] *Die Grundlagen der Arithmetik: Eine logisch-mathematische Untersuchung über den Begriff der Zahl* (Breslau, 1884), §62.

between the 'synthetic', aggregative point of view of the grammarian and the analytic point of view of the logician.[29]

. . . what constituents we distinguish in a thought in logic does not depend on the words out of which a sentence expressing it is composed, but entirely on the logical consequences that are derivable from the thought.[30]

It is difficult to sort out the terminology employed in the first of these passages, let alone to reconcile it with Frege's. Apparently a sentence expresses a judgement and a judgement expresses a thought: with which of these three entities the proposition referred to at the outset is to be identified is obscure. But the general intention is plain enough. A thought is grasped as a whole: if there is complexity in it, an awareness of this complexity is inessential for grasping the thought. In fact, the attribution of complexity is warranted only as a means of representing the logical relations of the thought to other thoughts. Presumably, in grasping any two thoughts, we are to be supposed to be capable of recognizing any logical relation, e.g. of entailment, that may hold between them: it is only when we do logic, i.e. when we are concerned to make a systematic map of these logical relations, that we have any motive for regarding the different thoughts as complex; and we so represent them as a means of exhibiting, not their *internal* structure, but, rather, their *external* relations to other thoughts. Whether the representation so arrived at bears any analogy to the structure of the sentence expressing the thought is a matter of chance.

It is plain that, if we adopt such a view, the study of *language* can have no relevance to the study of *thought*. Hence to devote a volume to the discussion of Frege's philosophy of language must reveal a complete misunderstanding of him; so, even more, must advocacy of a view which makes of him a great innovator who made the theory of meaning the starting-point of all philosophy. Someone who makes these mistakes must, on such a view as Sluga's, have been misled by the merely superficial appearance in much of Frege's writing that he devotes a great deal of attention to various types of linguistic expression. On Sluga's account, Frege's symbolic notation could not be seen as a purified form of language. Rather, the formula corresponding to any given thought would be a means of representing the logical relations of that thought to others, an expression of that complexity which we attribute to the thought in

---

[29] 'Frege and the Rise of Analytical Philosophy', 483.　　　　[30] Ibid. 484.

virtue of its having those relations, but which we do not need to discern within it in order to grasp the thought itself. When Frege appears to be talking about linguistic expressions, he is usually talking about this or that ingredient of such formulas, and not about any part of a genuine language, natural or artificial; when he slips into discussing expressions of actual language, this presumably constitutes a digression from the serious business of analysing thoughts independently of language.

There would still remain a problem about language, indeed: but its resolution would not contribute to the analysis of thought. Even if thoughts are unitary, few would deny that *sentences* are complex. (Sluga does, however; he attributes to Frege the view that even sentences are 'primarily simple'.)[31] Since it is by means of sentences that we convey our thoughts, they must serve to identify the thoughts they convey by means of some systematic code, which must relate, not to any complexity internal to the thought (it has none, on this view), nor to its logical relations to other thoughts (otherwise there would be a correspondence between the structure of the sentence and the logical representation of the thought), but to some other feature of the thought which Sluga does not specify. It is interesting to speculate what this could be.

On this account, we should have to take Frege's ascription of reference to the 'constituents' of sentences as relating, not to the parts of sentences in any actual language, natural or artificial, but, rather, to the parts of those *formulas* by means of which he represents the logical relations of thoughts, and which, by a misleading analogy, he also calls 'sentences'. What shows this approach to be mistaken is the fact that Frege also ascribed *senses* to the constituents of sentences. The notion of sense is not required for explaining how the truth-value of a sentence is determined in accordance with its composition: that of reference is sufficient for this purpose. It has to do, rather, with our understanding of how the truth-value of our sentences is determined: it is a consequence of the context principle, taken as a thesis about sense, that to ascribe sense to a constituent of a complex is intelligible only as part of an account of how we grasp the thought expressed by the whole. It can have that role if, as I think, Frege is concerned with how we come to recognize the thought expressed by a genuine sentence in accordance

---

[31] 'Frege and the Rise of Analytical Philosophy', 480.

with its composition: it cannot have that role if the constituents are constituents only of a symbolic representation of the results of an analysis of the logical relations of the thought to other thoughts, arrived at only after the thought has already been grasped as a unity.

Sluga bases his interpretation of the context principle on the *Begriffsschrift* and the writings immediately following its publication; if defensible at all, it could be justified only as relating to Frege's ideas in this early period. Even so restricted, it is false to Frege's views. Thus Sluga says[32] that in the essay 'Booles rechnende Logik und die Begriffsschrift' of 1880–1 'Frege relates his own conception . . . to the linguistic doctrine that the "sentence word" is the primary form of speech' and that he 'refers, in this connection, to a book by . . . A. H. Sayce'. He does indeed mention this doctrine; but in the very next sentence he repudiates it—'The expression of the judgeable content must, indeed, in order to be able to be so analysed, already be composite'.[33]

The passages which Sluga cites from these writings in support of his interpretation all relate to Frege's idea that the general conception of a predicate is that of an expression formed, not by being put together out of its constituents, but by omitting one or more occurrences of some proper name from a complete sentence which *is* to be viewed as built up from its parts. This is a doctrine which I expounded in my book.[34] It certainly does *not* imply that no thought has any intrinsic complexity: the fact that a thought expressed by a sentence which can be viewed as containing a proper name standing in the argument-place of a predicate is not, in general, to be regarded as having been constructed out of the senses of that name and that predicate does not, as Sluga supposes,[35] show that it is not compound in any way. (In fact, it was precisely to distinguish the way in which a sentence is constructed out of its parts from the way in which it may subsequently be decomposed that I introduced my distinction between simple and complex predicates. The subsequent decomposition has, indeed, as I said, to do with the role of the sentence in inference; its construction out of its parts has to do with how its sense is determined and is grasped.)

[32] Ibid. 481.
[33] *Nachgelassene Schriften*, ed. H. Hermes, F. Kambartel, and F. Kaulbach (Hamburg, 1969), p. 19; *Posthumous Writings*, ed. P. Long and R. White (Oxford, 1979), 17.
[34] *Frege: Philosophy of Language*, pp. 15–16, 23, 31.
[35] 'Frege and the Rise of Analytical Philosophy', p. 480.

There are two distinct aspects to the composition of sentences: the formation of complex sentences from atomic ones, and the formation of atomic sentences from their subsentential constituents. In view of Frege's persistent assertion of the complexity of the thoughts expressed by complex sentences, it is hard to see how Sluga can deny (as he does)[36] that there is any complexity of sense of the former kind: in his 'Logik' of 1897,[37] Frege headed a section 'Verbindung von Gedanken'; the last essay he ever published was entitled 'Gedankengefüge'. So the only substantial question is whether Frege believed the thoughts expressed by atomic sentences to be complex also, whether they contain component senses corresponding to the component words. It is difficult to dispute that Frege did hold just this in his later period: a characteristic statement of it comes from the 'Aufzeichnungen für L. Darmstaedter' (1919), in which he says:

When an astronomer says something about the Moon, the Moon itself is not part of the thought expressed. The Moon itself is the reference of the expression 'the Moon'. This expression must therefore have, besides its reference, a sense, which can be a constituent of a thought. The sentence can be treated as the representation of a thought in such a way that to the relation of part to whole between the thoughts and the parts of the thoughts correspond by and large the same relation between the sentence and the sentence-parts.[38]

This doctrine that the sense of the whole is compounded of the senses in its parts, the truth of which Geach has also called in question, means that in grasping the thought expressed by a given sentence, we grasp it as something expressible only by a sentence having just the same (logical) complexity. In explaining my slogan that while, in the order of explanation, the sense of the sentence is primary, in the order of recognition the sense of the word is primary, I referred in my book (p. 4) to just this doctrine of Frege's explained in just this way. The remark that in the order of explanation the sense of the sentence is primary was intended, on the other hand, to embody the context principle, taken as a thesis about sense. It is therefore either disingenuous or unobservant of Sluga to say that 'there is little indication in Frege's words that he ever made

---

[36] 'Frege and the Rise of Analytical Philosophy', 480.
[37] *Nachgelassene Schriften*, 137–63.
[38] Ibid. 275.

such a distinction':[39] what is needed, if I am to be shown wrong, is a different interpretation of Frege's notion of sense that will fit what he does say at least as well as mine does.

Even in Frege's pre-*Grundlagen* period, there is clear indication that he did not take the content of an atomic sentence as unitary. To quote once more from 'Booles rechnende Logik und die Begriffsschrift',

The expression of the judgeable content must, indeed, in order to be able to be so analysed, already be composite. One can infer from this that at least the properties and relations which are not further analysable must have their own simple designations.[40]

Here we have an explicit acknowledgement of the existence of simple predicates and relational expressions. 'Contrary to what Dummett says', Sluga writes 'this distinction' between simple and complex predicates 'has no basis in Frege's text.'[41] Actually, I said (p. 27) that 'Frege himself was at no great pains' to draw this distinction and (p. 30) that 'Frege himself did not draw attention to' the difference in the role of the notion of a simple and that of a complex predicate. Nevertheless, even though, in general, a (complex) predicate is to be thought of as extracted from a sentence by omission of one or more occurrences of a name, it remains that, if we are to follow Frege in the highly natural view that we grasp the thought expressed even by an atomic sentence by understanding its component words (in a logical sense of 'word') and the way they are put together, then we are forced to recognize that there are some, primitive, predicates and relational expressions which we understand otherwise than by extracting them from some previously understood sentence. (Exactly the same applies to functional expressions: we should not have any complex functional expressions unless we had some primitive functors; Sluga thus needs further argument for saying[42] that Frege's replacement of the subject/predicate distinction by the argument/function one obviated the need for taking 'the content of a sentence' to be 'composed out of previously given constituents'.)

As already remarked, on Sluga's understanding of the context principle, Frege's doctrines did not constitute a philosophy of

---

[39] 'Frege and the Rise of Analytical Philosophy', 479.
[40] *Nachgelassene Schriften*, 19.
[41] 'Frege and the Rise of Analytical Philosophy', 480.   [42] Ibid. 484.

language at all. This makes it less surprising that he dismisses
Frege's account of sense and reference as being, not 'the centre of a
philosophy of language', but merely 'an appendix to a philosophy of
mathematics';[43] and hence disputes that my order of exposition,
from the more to the less general, 'can really do full jusice to Frege's
thought'.[44] In terms of doing justice to Frege, Sluga's assessment is
surely the more at fault. It was indeed a concern with the foundations
of mathematics that motivated Frege's researches into logic and the
theory of meaning in the first place: but it is also clear, from his
published and unpublished writings, that these researches took on
for him an interest of their own, and that he believed himself to have
constructed a system of doctrines of quite general application.[45]
Indeed, that he had failed to do so would itself be a criticism of his
philosophy of mathematics, which involved the claim that arithmetic
(including analysis) is reducible to a logic that is not specific to
mathematics. Frege himself repeatedly presented his views on that
part of philosophy which he called 'logic' without any special
reference to mathematics and with hardly any mathematical examples, as in the 'Logik' of the 1880s,[46] that of 1897,[47] the 'Einleitung
in die Logik'[48] of 1906 and the 'Logische Untersuchungen' of the
late years. Sluga evidently believes that Frege overvalued the
significance of this part of his work: I do not.

Sluga's account of Frege's views appears to serve the purpose of
playing down his originality and placing him as one among many
members of the school of 'classical German philosophy'. Such a
purpose, if it be Sluga's, has the unfortunate effect, at least as Sluga
pursues it, of rendering Frege's doctrines a confused tangle of
incoherent errors. The interpretation of Frege I gave in my book
had at least the merit of presenting him as a great philosopher, who
deserves the esteem in which he was held by Russell, Wittgenstein,
and others, and the great posthumous reputation which he enjoys;
but I do not think that, under Sluga's interpretation, either the
esteem or the reputation would be merited. For this reason, even if
others were inclined to interpret Frege in Sluga's way, in the words
of Kai Lung 'this person would unhesitatingly prefer his thoughts
to theirs'.

---

[43] 'Frege and the Rise of Analytical Philosophy', 475.   [44] Ibid. 474.
[45] If the conclusions reached in the preceding essay are correct, this interest goes
back to an early point in Frege's career.
[46] *Nachgelassene Schriften*, 1–8.   [47] Ibid. 137–63.   [48] Ibid. 201–12.

6

Objectivity and Reality in Lotze and Frege*

In a series of articles[1] and in his recent book,[2] Hans Sluga has argued that Hermann Lotze had a deep influence on Frege's philosophy. For the most part, these claims, if correct, would, while detracting from Frege's originality, leave the interpretation of his philosophy unaffected. One of them, however, if accepted, would have profound consequences for our understanding of Frege. This is Sluga's comparison of Frege's notions of objectivity and of *Wirklichkeit* with related notions employed by Lotze and expressed by him in the same or different words; for Sluga uses it as a ground for denying that Frege was a realist concerning either logical objects or thoughts and their constituent senses. In a recent book,[3] I have contested Sluga's claims. Here I wish, without enquiring into the general question of Lotze's influence on Frege,[4] to go into rather closer detail concerning this particular comparison of Sluga's, which, for the reason just stated, is by far the most important of those he makes.

Frege employs two terms, '*objectiv*' and '*wirklich*', between which he makes a sharp distinction, and which are also used by Lotze. '*Objectiv*' can safely be translated 'objective' without begging any questions; I shall, in this article, use that English word and its

* First published in *Inquiry*, 25 (1982), 95–114.
[1] 'Frege and the Rise of Analytical Philosophy', *Inquiry*, 18 (1975), 471–87; 'Frege as a Rationalist', in M. Schirn (ed.), *Studies on Frege*, Problemata (Stuttgart, 1976), i. 27–47; 'Frege's Alleged Realism', *Inquiry*, 20 (1977), 227–42.
[2] *Gottlob Frege*, The Arguments of the Philosophers (London, 1980).
[3] Michael Dummett, *The Interpretation of Frege's Philosophy* (London and Cambridge, Mass., 1981).
[4] Save to mention a verbal coincidence I have noticed. In his *Metaphysik* (Leipzig, 1879), §1, Lotze speaks of 'truths that neither need nor admit of proof' ('Wahrheiten, die eines Beweises weder bedürftig noch fähig sind'); in *Grundlagen*, §3, Frege refers to 'general laws, which themselves neither admit of nor need proof' ('allgemeinen Gesetzen . . ., die selber eines Beweises weder fähig noch bedürftig sind'). Even if this is not accidental, it does not follow that Frege read the *Metaphysik*: he may have heard Lotze use the phrase in a lecture at Göttingen, and have retained it while forgetting its source.

cognates always and only as a rendering of '*objectiv*' and its cognates as they occur in the writings of both Frege and Lotze. '*Wirklich*' is a perfectly ordinary German word for 'actual' or 'real', and I think that, as used by Lotze, it is quite correctly translated 'real' by Bosanquet. As it is used by Frege, on the other hand, its translation is a sensitive matter, depending on what one takes him to mean by it: the example of the word '*Bedeutung*' is sufficient warning that Frege's systematic uses of common terms are not always to be taken at face-value. I shall therefore here always leave the word '*wirklich*' and its cognates, whether in reference to Frege or to Lotze, in their German forms, except of course in actual quotations from Sluga.

Frege describes physical objects as *wirklich*,[5] and comes close to saying that perceptions and subjective ideas are, too.[6] As examples of what is not *wirklich* he instances the axis of the earth, the centre of mass of the solar system, and the equator.[7] He denies that numbers of any kind, or logical objects in general, are *wirklich*.[8] Of thoughts, he says that they can be called *wirklich* only in a special sense,[9] and that, although they are not altogether *unwirklich*, their *Wirklichkeit* is of a quite different kind from that of things.[10] Sluga believes that, for Frege to have been a realist about objects of a given kind, it is necessary, but not sufficient, that he should have regarded them as *wirklich*. Thus he regards Frege's denial of *Wirklichkeit* to logical objects (value-ranges and, among them, classes and numbers) and to thoughts as showing him not to have been a realist concerning either category; but he also thinks, on quite different grounds, that Frege was not a realist about material objects either, despite his having considered them *wirklich*. Gregory Currie appears to take the opposite point of view. Disregarding Frege's caveats, he advances his ascription of *Wirklichkeit* to thoughts as a ground for regarding him as a realist concerning them;[11] but his

[5] *Grundgesetze der Arithmetik, begriffsschriftlich abgeleitet*, i (Jena, 1903), §74.
[6] 'Le Nombre entier', *Revue de Métaphysique et de Morale*, 3 (1855), 74. I assume that Frege used *réel* as the French equivalent of *wirklich*.
[7] *Die Grundlagen der Arithmetik: Eine logisch-mathematische Untersuchung über den Begriff der Zahl* (Breslau, 1884), §26.
[8] Ibid., §§85, 109; *Grundgesetze*, ii, §74.
[9] 'Logik', 1897, in *Nachgelassene Schriften*, ed. H. Hermes, F. Kambartel, and F. Kaulbach (Hamburg, 1969), 138, 149–50, English trans. *Posthumous Writings* (Oxford, 1979), 127, 137–8.
[10] 'Der Gedanke: Eine logische Untersuchung', *Beiträge zur Philosophie des deutschen Idealismus*, 1 (1918), 77.
[11] G. Currie, 'Frege's Realism', *Inquiry*, 21 (1978), 218–21.

account of why, having ascribed *Wirklichkeit* to thoughts, Frege had no need to ascribe it also to logical objects suggests that he regards Frege as a realist equally about such logical objects.[12] If this interpretation of Currie is correct, he must take Frege's holding objects of a given kind to be *wirklich* as a sufficient, but not a necessary, condition for him to have been a realist concerning them.

1. SLUGA'S CLAIMS

In his 1976 article 'Frege as a Rationalist', Sluga says that 'Frege's theory of the objectivity of numbers, value-ranges, functions, etc., . . . must . . . be compared with Lotze's theory of validity, from which it may be historically derived' (p. 29). His later book, *Gottlob Frege* (1980), contains a stronger historical claim, remarking that 'some insight into how the notion of objectivity' as it occurs in Frege 'is to be understood can be derived from the fact that Frege took it from Lotze's *Logik*' (p. 118). On the face of it, the claims differ, not only in strength, but in content, since the second compares Frege's notion of objectivity with Lotze's, while the first compares it with Lotze's notion of validity, this term being used as a translation of the words '*Gelten*' and '*Geltung*' employed by Lotze. Sluga's 1977 article 'Frege's Alleged Realism', however, reconciles the two claims by equating Lotze's notions of objectivity and of validity, saying that the distinction drawn by Lotze in §3 of his *Logik* between objectivity and *Wirklichkeit* is the same as that drawn by him in §316 between validity (*Gelten*) and being (*Sein*), although the terminology has changed (p. 232). In more detail, he says that Lotze uses three pairs of terms to express the same distinction: in §3, objectivity (*Objectivität*) and the reality of things (*Wirklichkeit der Dinge*); in §316, validity (*das Gelten*) and being (*das Sein*); and in §§319–20, validity (*Geltung*) and reality (*Realität*). He subsequently modifies this, however, by remarking (p. 233) that the later distinction between validity and being or reality (*Realität*) is a wider one that replaces the earlier distinction between objectivity and *Wirklichkeit*, though he does not clearly explain in what way it is wider. To make the matter more confusing, he adds a footnote that he is deliberately ignorning Lotze's (later) use of '*Wirklichkeit*' to cover both validity (*Geltung*) and reality (*Realität*); he evidently regards this use of the

[12] G. Currie, 'Frege on Thoughts', *Mind*, 89 (1980), 234–48.

term '*Wirklichkeit*' by Lotze as essentially different from, and broader than, that employed by him in §3 of the *Logik*. It is at least clear that Sluga does not see the claims made in his article of 1976 and in his book of 1980 as differing substantially.

What light, then, in Sluga's view, does this comparison throw upon Frege's intentions? In 'Frege as a Rationalist', he says that 'Frege's theory of the objectivity of numbers, value-ranges, functions, etc., was never intended as an ontological theory' (p. 29); in the same vein, he says in 'Frege's Alleged Realism' that 'the doctrine of the objectivity of numbers, concepts, and thoughts is not an onto-logical one for Frege' (p. 236). He thus denies that Frege was a realist concerning logical objects (numbers and value-ranges); con-cerning the referents of incomplete expressions (functions and concepts); or concerning thoughts. Frege indeed says of things of all three kinds that they are objective; but those three kinds are of such a different nature in his philosophy that the ascription of objectivity to them can hardly rate as a single thesis, but, rather, as three distinct theses. For Frege, logical objects and functions, things of the first and second of these kinds, belong to the realm of reference, being referred to but never expressed; things of the third kind, thoughts, belong to the realm of sense, since, although they can be referred to (and thus also being of the realm of reference), they are more often, and typically, expressed. On the other hand, both value-ranges and thoughts are objects, since they are complete; functions and concepts are incomplete or unsaturated. Frege's three theses might, indeed, be *opposed* by a single thesis, advanced by a philosopher who did not admit any radical distinction between these kinds of thing; but they could hardly *coincide* with any single thesis advocated by another philosopher.

What, in detail, is Sluga's account of the interpretation of Frege's views to which a comparison of them with Lotze's should lead us? In 'Frege as a Rationalist', he explains this as follows:

According to Lotze, ideal objects are not real, but merely possess validity. Lotze thought that drawing this distinction (which is paralleled by Frege's distinction between reality and objectivity as he makes it in the Preface to the *Grundgesetze*) preserves what is true in Plato's theory of ideas while being beyond both realism and nominalism. The latter are, according to Lotze, predominantly concerned with metaphysical issues, that is, with something that has 'other than purely logical importance', whereas presum-ably the notion of validity is not a metaphysical but a logical one.

Sluga here gives, in a footnote, a reference to Lotze's *Logik*, §340, from which the phrase 'other than a purely logical importance' is taken. He continues, 'That is not to say that Frege's and Lotze's doctrines are at all clear, at least according to the intentions of their authors'.[13]

In *Gottlob Frege*, the matter is set out as follows. In his *Logik*, Sluga states, 'Lotze says explicitly that objectivity "does not in general coincide with the *Wirklichkeit* that belongs to things". And he maintains that the objective is that "which is the same for all thinking beings and which is independent of them"'.[14] He here supplies a reference to §3 of the *Logik* for the two quotations. 'In other words', Sluga continues, Lotze 'endorses all three of Frege's assertions about the objective'. These three assertions have been stated by Sluga as follows:

1. The objective is that which can be grasped by more than one human (rational) being. The objective, in other words, is the intersubjective.
2. The objective is that which does not require a bearer.
3. The objective must be distinguished from that which is *wirklich*, i.e., actual or real.[15]

After remarking that 'at the same time Lotze makes clear that the doctrine of objectivity is not to be taken as ontological, but rather as epistemological', Sluga proceeds to an exposition of Lotze's discussion of Plato's theory of ideas and a consequent explanation of how, in view of the presumed affinity between Lotze and Frege, we ought, in his opinion, to understand Frege. I shall consider this aspect of his comments in a later section.

2. LOTZE ON OBJECTIVITY

'Objective' is a key term for Frege, even though he does not use it very often, because it is a key thesis in his philosophy that what is not *wirklich* may be objective.[16] Contrary to what one might suppose from Sluga's account, 'objective' was not a key term for

[13] 'Frege as a Rationalist', p. 29.
[14] *Gottlob Frege*, p. 118.
[15] Ibid. 117–18.
[16] *Grundlagen*, §26; *Grundgesetze der Arithmetik, begriffsschriftlich abgeleitet*, i (Jena, 1893), xviii; 'Logik', 1897, *Nachgelassene Schriften*, p. 149, *Posthumous Writings*, p. 137.

Lotze: it is virtually only in §3 of his *Logik* that it occurs at all.[17] In §1 he says that

what thinking accomplishes usually reveals itself to us in the relations of a manifold; from this one may believe that we must look for the very earliest of its operations in the simplest kind of combination of two ideas [*Vorstellungen*]. A straightforward consideration prompts us to go back one step further. A heap can easily be put together from mere spheres, if it is indifferent how they lie; a building of regular shape, on the other hand, can be constructed only out of building-blocks which have already been formed individually in such a way that their surfaces will fit together in a secure attachment to one another. One must expect something similar in our case. As mere internal excitations the states which result from external stimuli may, without further preparation, exist in us alongside one another, and act upon one another in whatever way the general laws of our mental life allow or demand. If, on the other hand, they are to become combinable into the definite form of a *thought*, they require a prior individual formation, by which they are for the first time converted into logical building-blocks [*Bausteinen*],[18] converted from *impressions* into *ideas*. Nothing is more familiar to us, fundamentally, than this first operation of thinking; we are wont to overlook it only because it has already been permanently effected in the formation of our customary language, and therefore seems to belong among self-evident presuppositions rather than to the activity of thinking, properly so called.

Lotze is thus singling out, as the most primitive operation that can be said to be part of the activity of thinking, the formation of ideas as opposed to mere sensory impressions. He elaborates this in §2.

What immediately arises in us under the influence of external stimuli, a sensation or sensory feeling, is in itself nothing but a state of our awareness, a way we feel. We do not always succeed in finding a name for what we thus experience. . . . But in the more favourable cases in which we do succeed in constructing a name, what operation is thereby effected and reveals itself precisely in the construction of the name? Nothing else but precisely what we are here looking for, the transformation of an *impression* into an *idea*.

[17] There is an occurrence of the verb 'to objectify' in *Logik* (Leipzig, 1874), §105, with a plain allusion to §3; 'objective' occurs in §11 of the Introduction to *Metaphysik*. As far as I have been able to discover, these are the only occurrences, outside *Logik*, §3, of 'objective' or its cognates. The fact that objectivity is not a key notion in Lotze makes it far less plausible that Frege borrowed it from him.

[18] Anyone eager to catch echoes of Lotze's words in Frege's writings will think of Frege's use of the phrase 'building-blocks of thought' (*Gedankenbausteine*) in the 'Logik in der Mathematik' of 1914 (*Nachgelassene Schriften*, p. 243; *Posthumous Writings*, p. 225).

As soon as we give the name 'green' or 'red' to the different excitations to which the light-waves give rise in us through our eyes, we have separated something that was previously unseparated: our sensation from the sensible to which it relates. We now represent [*stellen . . . vor*] the sensible to ourselves, no longer as a state of our feeling, but as a content [*Inhalt*], which is in itself what it is[19] and means what it means, and continues so to be and to mean independently of whether our consciousness is directed towards it or not. In this may easily be discovered the necessary beginning of that activity which in general we attribute to thinking; it cannot as yet be directed towards transforming the manifold of what occurs together into one that belongs together: it solves the prior problem of giving to each individual impression the meaning of something independent [*Gleichgültigen*], without which the fact of genuinely belonging together, as opposed to merely occurring together, could not subsequently have any explicit sense for us.[20]

It is in §3 that the terms 'objectivity' and '*Wirklichkeit*' are brought into play; one could hardly understand the distinction here drawn by Lotze without his previous explanation of the mental operation of which he is speaking. 'One may denominate this first operation of thinking a beginning of an *objectification* of the subjective; I use this expression in order to ward off a misunderstanding and thereby to make clear the plain sense of what I have said,' he begins. We shall see that Sluga comes close to falling victim to the very misunderstanding Lotze is seeking to avert. 'By the logical act which reveals itself in the construction of a name', he continues,

there is not conferred on the content of the idea arising precisely from that construction any objectivity in the sense of a real existence [*wirklichen Daseins*] of any kind whatever that would obtain even if no one had any thought of it. What this first act of thinking truly means is most readily made clear in languages which have retained the use of the article. For by means of the article, which in general originally had the value of a demonstrative pronoun, the word to which it is attached is picked out as the name of something to which it refers; but we refer to that which may be perceptible to another as it was to us. Admittedly this happens most easily in respect of things,[21] which in fact stand in external reality [*Wirklichkeit*] between the speakers; but developed language objectifies in the same manner every

---

[19] Similarly, in the 'Logik' of the 1880s, Frege, speaking of the objectivity of the sun, says, 'To one it may *appear* in one way, to another in another: it *is* what it is' (*Nachgelassene Schriften*, p. 7; *Posthumous Writings*, p. 7).

[20] It is difficult to understand these remarks about belonging together (*Zusammengehörigkeit*) and occurring together (*Zusammensein*), translated by Bosanquet as 'coherence' and 'coexistence', without having read Lotze's Introduction.

[21] By 'things' (*Dinge*) Lotze always means physical objects.

other content of thinking also. The objectivity which is indicated in such cases, too, by the use of the article does not therefore coincide with the *Wirklichkeit* that belongs to things; it coincides, rather, with the mere fact of a claim to such a status, given to them by the distinctive character of their true [*realen*] nature, and expressed in the nominalization. We do not speak in such a way of pain, of brightness, of freedom,[22] as if pain could exist if no one felt it, brightness if no eye saw it, freedom if there were no creature who either himself enjoyed a lack of restraint upon his actions or caused others to experience it. Still less, when we speak of 'the indeed', 'the but', and 'the however',[23] do we mean by the article to indicate an existence [*Dasein*] independent of any idea, somehow ascribed to the thought-contents denoted by these words; by means of these forms of expression, we are saying only that certain characteristic resistances and tensions, felt by us in the stream of our ideas, are not mere peculiarities of our condition and inseparable from it, but, rather, depend on the relations to one another of the contents of the different ideas, relations which everyone who thinks those ideas will discover between them just as we do. The logical objectification which reveals itself in the construction of a name thus does not move the content named into an external *Wirklichkeit*; the common world in which others are to recognize what we refer to is in general only the world of the thinkable; here there is ascribed to it only the first trace of an existence [*Bestehen*] of its own and an inner regularity which is the same for all thinking beings and independent of them, and it is here quite irrelevant whether particular parts of this world of thought designate something which in addition possesses an independent *Wirklichkeit* outside the thinking minds, or whether its entire content exists [*Dasein hat*] at all only in the thoughts of the thinkers, but with the same validity [*Gültigkeit*] for all.

Because what is at issue is the interpretation of Lotze, as well as of Frege, the translation has been made as literal as possible. Lotze is concerned to characterize what he takes to be the first operation in that mental activity which, in his Introduction, he has stated to constitute thinking. This, for him, is the initial formation of ideas: merely to have sense-impressions is not yet to have ideas. There is no trace in Lotze of a distinction corresponding to that drawn by Frege between the *Sinn* and the *Bedeutung* of an expression. He indeed admits a distinction between an idea and its content. It will have been seen from the foregoing, however, that he expressly allows that the content may exist only in the thoughts of those who

---

[22] 'von dem Schmerze, der Helligkeit, der Freiheit': all three expressions carry the definite article in German, but not in English, giving some difficulty to Lotze's English translator.
[23] Of course we do not so speak in English.

have the idea; we cannot usefully ask whether the content is, in general, to be taken to correspond to Frege's *Sinn* or to his *Bedeutung*, any more, indeed, than we can ask this about the notion of content as employed by Frege before he distinguished *Sinn* from *Bedeutung*. Moreover, Lotze does not succeed in maintaining a sharp distinction between an idea and its content, at least in any case in which the content does not possess an independent *Wirklichkeit*: he does not draw the sharp distinction made by Frege between a sense (*Sinn*) and idea (*Vorstellung*), earlier expressed as that between conceptual contents and ideas or, in the second footnote to *Grundlagen*, §27, as that between ideas in the objective and in the subjective sense. Thus, while Lotze does not regard every idea as constituting a concept, he takes a concept to be a particular kind of composite idea;[24] and while, in his Introduction, he is preoccupied with distinguishing the activity of thinking from the mere occurrence of a stream of ideas, he takes that which is true or untrue to be a combination of ideas. Lotze's first operation of thinking, the conversion of impressions into ideas, is for him a necessary condition for our employment of a linguistic term. It might seem, from his speaking repeatedly of names and from his emphasis on the significance of the definite article, that he is concerned specifically with our use of singular terms, including abstract ones; but it is apparent, from the example in §2 of 'green' and 'red', which appear in his text as adjectives, not as nouns, that he means his remarks to apply quite generally to our employment of all words whatsoever, or at least to those which may be held to correspond to ideas arising from impressions, taken as the material not only of sensation but of all experience. Thus the remarks about 'but', etc., should be taken, not as comments solely on the peculiar German expression '*das Aber*', and the like, but on our use of such conjunctions in general, for which he has a psychologistic explanation reminiscent of Russell's *Enquiry into Meaning and Truth*. Lotze is very far from Frege's principle that the *Bedeutung* of a singular term must be fundamentally different from that of a cognate expression of a distinct logical type.

Lotze is at pains, in §3, to impress upon his readers how restricted are the claims he is making for what his first operation of thinking accomplishes. It does not confer upon the content of the idea which it forms a place in external reality (*Wirklichkeit*). Lotze is *not*

---

[24] *Logik*, §25.

maintaining that 'the objective is that "which is the same for all thinking beings and independent of them" ', as Sluga says he is.[25] True enough, the words quoted by Sluga occur in Lotze's text; but they occur in the context 'what we do here is to ascribe . . . the *first trace* of an existence . . . which is the same for all thinking beings and is independent of them' (my italics). The term to which Lotze attaches a special significance is not 'objectivity' but, rather, 'objectification'. He has no particular opinion about whether or not 'objectivity' should be used to signify that *Wirklichkeit* which is possessed by what exists independently of being thought of at all; but he is anxious to ward off the misunderstanding that the objectification which he regards as being effected by his first operation of thinking involves an ascription of objectivity in that sense. The first operation of thought converts an impression into an idea, and shows itself in the formation of a name; Lotze is concerned with a feature that attaches to all our ideas, to everything we express by means of a word, or, as he says, a name. If that feature is spoken of as objectivity, then it is objectivity only in a restricted sense; to ascribe objectivity in this sense to something is not yet to ascribe to it a fully independent existence. Lotze conceives of impressions as subjective and incommunicable until they have been converted into ideas; ideas are thus to be distinguished from impressions as having an objectivity of this restricted kind. He in no way insists that it is rightly to be called 'objectivity'. It would be natural to comment that it would be better called 'intersubjectivity', since Lotze says explicitly that it is a matter only of what is in common to all thinkers who have the idea. The idea is to be regarded as independent of any one particular thinker, in the sense that it is the same for all, but not as having a content independent of *all* thinkers, since it may exist 'only in the thoughts of those who think it'.

What here preoccupies Lotze is the communicability of ideas, as opposed to mere impressions. Frege of course laid great stress on the communicability of senses and of thoughts, but for just this reason held them to be essentially distinct from ideas, which he regarded as ineradicably subjective and which he did not distinguish in any essential manner from impressions. 'By objectivity', Frege explained, 'I understand independence from our sensation, intuition and ideation [*Vorstellen*] and from the delineation of interior images

[25] *Gottlob Frege*, 118.

from the memories of earlier sensations';[26] similarly, in the 1897 'Logik', he characterizes it as 'what is independent of our mental life', 'what does not belong to our minds', what 'does not belong to the individual mind . . . but [is] independent of thinking'.[27] The objectivity which Frege ascribed to thoughts does involve independence from all thinkers. Having said, in the 'Logik' of the 1880s, that a judgeable content is 'something objective, that is, something that is exactly the same for all rational beings that are able to grasp it', he adds, to make his meaning clear, 'as, say, the Sun is something objective'.[28] The first part of the sentence Lotze could agree to; but he could not accept the comparison with the Sun without blurring precisely that distinction he is so concerned to emphasize between *Wirklichkeit* and the restricted type of objectivity conferred upon an idea by the first operation of thinking. In the 1897 'Logik' Frege makes a similar comparison.

Not only do thoughts—e.g. natural laws—not need to be recognized by us in order to be true: they do not need to be thought by us at all. A natural law is not created by us, but discovered. And just as a desolate island in the Arctic Ocean was there long before it was seen by men, so the laws of nature and in the same way those of mathematics hold from eternity and not just from the time of their discovery. We may deduce from this that thoughts are not only true, when they are true, independently of our recognition, but that they are altogether independent of our thinking.[29]

In order to equate Frege's notion of objectivity with the restricted type of objectivity spoken of by Lotze in §3 of his *Logik*, Sluga had to give a misleading impression of Lotze's use of the word, representing it as if it were for him a technical term to be employed only in the restricted sense in which, in fact, Lotze uses it only with hesitation and hedged about with caveats. What is more important is that Sluga had to distort Frege's views even more. Of the three theses on objectivity cited above and attributed by him to Frege, the first was the 'the objective . . . is the intersubjective'. For Lotze, as we have seen, 'objective', in the restricted sense, does indeed mean

---

[26] *Grundlagen*, §26. I have used the unprepossessing word 'ideation' to make clear the connection with ideas (*Vorstellungen*): ideation is having ideas just as thinking is grasping thoughts.

[27] 'Logik', 1897, *Nachgelassene Schriften*, 149, 155, 160; *Posthumous Writings*, 137, 144, 148.

[28] 'Logik', 1880s, *Nachgelassene Schriften*, 7; *Posthumous Writings*, 7.

[29] 'Logik', 1897, *Nachgelassene Schriften*, 144–5; *Posthumous Writings*, 133.

'intersubjective', whereas '*wirklich*' means for him 'existing independently of being thought at all'. It is plain, however, that it is the latter which Frege means by 'objective', a term which, on his use of it, means more than merely 'intersubjective': Frege's 'objective' thus corresponds, not to 'objective' in Lotze's restricted sense, but to his '*wirklich*'.

3. LOTZE'S NOTION OF VALIDITY

Do the passages in which Lotze speaks, not of something's being objective, but of its holding or being valid, lend any colour to Sluga's claims? Lotze raises his question in this way

How are we properly to conceive of colours when no one sees them, or of notes and their intervals when the former are heard by no one and the latter are not perceived by anyone's comparing them? Are we to say that both are then nothing, or that they are not,[30] or does some predicate, difficult to make precise, some sort of being or *Wirklichkeit*, attach to them even in that case?[31]

His answer is that

we call a thing *wirklich* if it *is*, in contrast to another which is *not*;[32] we call an event *wirklich* if it *occurs* or has occurred, in contrast to one which does not occur; we call a relation *wirklich* if it *obtains*, in contrast to one which does not obtain; and finally we call a proposition really true [*wirklich wahr*] if it *holds* [*gilt*], in contrast to one whose validity [*Geltung*][33] is still open to question. This linguistic usage is intelligible: it shows that by *Wirklichkeit* we always intend an affirmation, the sense of which, however, varies greatly according to which one of these different forms it assumes; it must assume some one of these, and none of them is reducible to the others or contained in it. For we can never make an occurrence out of being, and the *Wirklichkeit* which belongs to things, namely *being*, never attaches to events; events never *are*, but *occur*; a proposition neither *is*, like things, nor

---

[30] This is a literal translation, of which 'that they do not exist' would of course be a more idiomatic version, which, however, would destroy the verbal connection with 'being'. I have translated similarly in other passages.

[31] *Logik*, §316.

[32] For Lotze's restricted use of 'thing', see n. 21 above; for his use of 'is', see n. 30 above.

[33] For 'validity' Lotze uses, interchangeably, two words, '*das Gelten*' and '*die Geltung*'. The former is simply the verbal noun for 'holding', corresponding to 'holds' just as 'being' (*das Sein*) corresponds to 'is' (*ist*). '*Die Geltung*' is the cognate abstract noun, which we do not have in English; it therefore becomes necessary to use 'validity' for it, destroying the verbal connection with 'holds'.

occurs, like events; . . . in itself . . . its *Wirklichkeit* consists in its *holding* and its opposite's not holding.[34]

This is a doctrine about modes of reality: entities of different logical types have different sorts of reality according to their type. In his *Metaphysik*, Lotze puts this doctrine to work in order to call in question the reality of space, on the ground that it fits into none of these categories. He asks 'in what the alleged being of space might consist, if it is not to be the active being of a thing nor the mere validity of a truth nor yet its being presented [*Vorgestelltwerden*] to us': he considers, but rejects, the objection that the example of 'space demonstrates to us . . . that there are other and special kinds of *Wirklichkeit* besides these'.[35] In the *Principles of Mathematics* Russell considers this and other arguments of Lotze's against an objectivist view of space, and dismisses each of them in turn.[36] To this particular argument Russell replies that 'there is only one kind of being, namely, being *simpliciter*, and only one kind of existence, namely, existence *simpliciter*'.[37] At this time Russell admitted a distinction between being and existence, which Frege would never have done. For Frege, existence is a concept of second level: more exactly, the existence of objects is for him a second-level concept, not coinciding with, but only analogous to, the third-level concept of the existence of unary functions (including concepts) or that of the existence of binary functions (including relations). Thus Frege, like Lotze, recognized a distinction between kinds of existence corresponding to the distinction of logical type between what is said to exist. There is, however, no place in his philosophy for a distinction of logical type between events or thoughts and physical objects: 'the storming of the Bastille' and 'Pythagoras's theorem' stand for objects of particular kinds and, in saying that their referents exist, we are using 'exist' in the same sense as if we say that the referents of 'Venus' and 'Mars' exist, that, namely, expressed by the existential quantifier of lowest level. For Frege, an appeal made, as by Lotze, to the linguistic usage according to which we say of physical objects that they exist, but of events that they occur, would be irrelevant. Existence is not a property of an object: for Frege, the only sense to saying that objects of some given kind exist is to say that there are

[34] *Logik*, §316.
[35] *Metaphysik*, §109.
[36] Bertrand Russell, *Principles of Mathematics*, 2nd edn. (London, 1950), ch. 51.
[37] Ibid. 449.

objects of that kind; if, then, we allow as well formed singular terms for events, the sense of asking whether an event of a certain kind occurred will similarly be to ask whether there was any such event. Lotze uses the verb 'to hold' of propositions to mean that they are true: he considers their holding in this sense to be the analogue to material things' being or existing. It is quite certain that Frege did not equate the existence of a thought with its truth. 'It would be wrong to think that only true thoughts had an existence [*Bestand*] independent of our mental life.'[38]

The categorization quoted above from Lotze does not include ideas: what kind of reality do they possess? Frege regarded ideas as being within the mind of some one individual, their bearer. Lotze neither distinguished between ideas and concepts in the way Frege did, nor had Frege's distinction between ideas and senses, but operated, as we have seen, with a rather hazy differentiation between an idea and its content, in terms of which his answer is given.

To ideas [*Vorstellungen*], inasmuch as we have and grasp them, there belongs *Wirklichkeit* in the sense of an event: they occur in us. . . . But their content, in so far as we consider it as detached from the activity of ideation[39] that we direct to it, no longer occurs; nor, however, *is* it as things are: it merely *holds* [*gilt*].[40]

The concept of validity, that is, of holding good, is thus to be employed to explain the kind of *Wirklichkeit* possessed, not only by propositions, but by the contents of ideas, considered in contrast to the ideas themselves regarded as ingredients in the stream of consciousness. We may certainly doubt, with Sluga, whether this doctrine of Lotze 'is at all clear'. Lotze does not face the question how the validity of a proposition relates to that of the content of an idea until §321 of his *Logik*. There he admits that 'it is only with imperfect clarity that this expression', namely, 'to hold' (*gelten*), 'can be transferred' from propositions 'to individual concepts'. He attempts an explanation by adding that

---

[38] 'Logik', 1897, *Nachgelassene Schriften*, p. 150; *Posthumous Writings*, p. 138. Russell, commenting on Lotze, says similarly that 'as regards being, false propositions are on exactly the same level, since to be false a proposition must already be. Thus validity is not a kind of being' (*Principles of Mathematics*, 450).

[39] 'von der vorstellenden Thätigkeit'.

[40] *Logik*, §316.

of them we can only say that they *mean* something; but they mean something only in virtue of propositions' holding *of* them, e.g. the proposition that every content of a concept is identical with itself and is contained in invariable relationships to or contrasts with others.[41]

Sluga, after quoting this last passage, remarks that 'the similarity of this thesis to Frege's contextual principle needs no stressing'.[42] The context principle, as enunciated by Frege in *Grundlagen*, says that it is only in the context of a sentence that a word has meaning. He applies this to argue that we may ascribe a meaning to a word provided that we have found a means to fix a sense for all sentences in which it occurs. Although he had not yet drawn his distinction between sense and reference, we may reasonably describe him as stating a sufficient condition for a term to have a reference, and hence, in Quinean terminology, for us to admit the referent of that term into our ontology; but he is not concerned, as is Lotze, with explaining in what sense that referent may be said to exist or to be real. That is not a problem for him: indeed, the whole point of the application which he makes in *Grundlagen* of the context principle is that any such problem is spurious; if we really have fixed the senses of sentences in which the term occurs, including identity statements, no further question about the existence of the object designated by the term remains to be settled. It is for this reason that Sluga's comparison, as explained in 'Frege as a Rationalist', between Frege's notion of objectivity and Lotze's notion of validity was so wide of the mark: for, according to it, all that logic guarantees to such 'ideal objects' as numbers is validity, and they await a further, metaphysical, investigation, whose result will in their case be negative, to determine whether they are real. There could be no more resolute neglect of the use to which, in *Grundlagen*, Frege puts his context principle.

Lotze, on the other hand, is concerned to *explain* in what sense the contents of concepts can be said to be real (*wirklich*); and his explanation is that they are *wirklich* in the sense of 'holding' or of 'meaning something', and that, in turn, they 'hold' or 'mean something' in the sense that certain propositions (which exactly, I am not sure) are true of them. By contrast, Frege says nothing about the

[41] I am uncertain of the meaning of this last clause: Bosanquet, Lotze's English translator, has 'stands' for 'is contained', but possibly Lotze intends something stronger.

[42] 'Frege's Alleged Realism', 234.

truth of the sentences whose senses we have fixed, and does not believe that any explanation of the sense in which numbers exist is required. There is a faint similarity in the words used by the two writers, but none in the theses for which they are contending.

4. LOTZE ON PLATO

In his *Logik*, Lotze proceeds to apply the distinction he has drawn between holding and being to Plato's theory of Ideas (*Ideen*).[43] He argues that Plato has been misunderstood as ascribing to the Ideas 'an existence [*Dasein*] separate from things and yet . . . similar to the being [*Sein*] of things'.[44] In fact, Plato intended to ascribe to them, in so far as they exist eternally and unchangingly, only validity and not being, but lacked the terminology to draw the distinction.

Sluga comments on this that Lotze takes Plato's theory of Ideas

as an epistemological, rather than an ontological, theory, and therefore he is an epistemological rather than an ontological Platonist. That is to say he believes that empirical knowledge of temporal, changing things presupposes some knowledge of non-temporal, non-changing things. On this view, the timeless and non-historical is conceived as the foundation of the temporal and historical.[45]

The last sentence certainly accords with what Lotze says; for instance, that the

world of Ideas . . . forms at the same time the permanent and inexhaustible store from which are distributed to each thing in the external world all the different predicates with which it at varying times is clothed, and also to every mind the different states which it is to be able to experience.[46]

Here, however, the dependence holds good not only in the psychic but in the physical realm. It would be intelligible to say that Lotze was *not only* an ontological but also an epistemological Platonist, but hard to understand the allegation that he was an epistemological *rather than* an ontological one, since it is difficult to see how knowledge of temporal things could be taken by anyone to pre-suppose knowledge of non-temporal entities unless he thought that

---

[43] Following Bosanquet, I write 'Idea' with an initial capital when it represents '*Idee*' in Lotze's text, in which case it means a Platonic Idea; 'idea' without a capital will continue to represent '*Vorstellung*'.

[44] *Logik*, §317.

[45] *Gottlob Frege*, 119.

[46] *Logik*, §318.

there were some non-temporal entities. This is the view adopted by Michael Resnik, who regards the Frege of *Grundlagen* as an onto-logical but not an epistemological Platonist.[47] Sluga, however, does not share Resnik's opinion that epistemological Platonism is a stronger doctrine than the ontological variety: he continues:

In accordance with medieval usage the doctrine of ideas interpreted ontologically is often called a realist doctrine. It is in this sense that Frege is usually considered a realist. But, given the close connections between Frege and Lotze, we may wonder whether this is the correct interpretation. . . . Is it possible that Frege, like Lotze, was an epistemological, and not an ontological, Platonist?[48]

After reiteration of his claim for Frege's intellectual debt to Lotze, Sluga concludes, 'On the basis of these affinities it seems plausible to hold that Frege's doctrine of objectivity, like Lotze's, was intended as an epistemological thesis and that he was a critical rather than a dogmatic thinker.'[49]

Lotze does indeed reject the choice between realism and nomin-alism in the scholastic sense, as involving a confusion between validity and being:[50] he thinks of realism as ascribing being to Platonic Ideas, and nominalism as denying them *Wirklichkeit* altogether. Frege, though he never discusses the dispute between realism and nominalism, as conducted by the scholastics, would have concurred with Lotze in rejecting both options, but on quite different grounds; for him the very notion of a universal must involve a confusion between the *Bedeutung* of an incomplete ex-pression and that of a cognate singular term. That does not imply that, in a broader sense of 'realist', not tied to realism concerning universals in the scholastic style, Frege was not a realist concerning logical objects or concerning thoughts.

5. OBJECTIVITY AND INTERSUBJECTIVITY

Something is indisputably amiss with Sluga's account. Even when it is used in its restricted sense, the term 'objective' does not, for

---

[47] M. Resnik, 'Frege as Idealist and then Realist', *Inquiry*, 22 (1979), 350–7.

[48] *Gottlob Frege*, 119–20. Here, of course, Sluga means by 'ideas' Platonic Ideas. For myself, I have never considered Frege to have been a realist in the scholastic sense, and have never intended this when characterizing him as a realist: I should imagine the same to be true of many other commentators.

[49] Ibid. 120.   [50] *Logik*, §340.

Lotze, imply, but merely allows, that what is so characterized exists only in our thoughts: to call something 'objective' in this sense is not, therefore, to deny that it is *wirklich*. Similarly, although Frege insists that not only what is *wirklich* is objective (in *his* senses of these words), he nowhere suggests that, just because something is *wirklich*, it cannot, for that reason, be objective. On the contrary, as we have seen, he frequently cites, as a paradigm of what is objective, an astronomical body like the sun or a terrestrial one like an island, in either case for him unquestionably *wirklich*. Now Lotze expressly says that what is cannot hold, and what holds cannot be: Sluga therefore cannot be right to equate his distinction between holding and being either with his own earlier distinction between being objective in the restricted sense and being *wirklich*, or with Frege's distinction between objectivity and *Wirklichkeit*. Sluga himself, indeed, in commenting on Frege, has a tendency to oppose the objective to the *wirklich*. For instance, he attributes to him the view that 'the objective is not something alien or external to the mind, but constitutive of it: it is its most characteristic possession'.[51] It is hardly likely that Sluga was intending to credit Frege with the view that the sun and an undiscovered island in the Arctic are constitutive of the mind and among its most characteristic possessions. The context has to do with thoughts, and Sluga may have been thinking of logical objects also; but, perhaps misled by his own equation of Lotze's validity and being with Frege's objectivity and *Wirklichkeit*, he was surely forgetting that, for Frege, physical objects are objective as well as *wirklich*. However that may be, it is beyond doubt that being objective did not, for Frege, exclude being *wirklich*, and that therefore those two notions cannot be the same as those of validity and being as employed by Lotze.

Sluga could meet this difficulty by modifying his position. He could say, instead, that what should be equated with Lotze's notion of validity is not simply his earlier notion of objectivity in the restricted sense, but, rather, that of being objective in this sense but yet not *wirklich*. On the face of it, however, even this modified position would involve a blunder. Lotze presents his distinction between being, occurring, obtaining, and holding as a subdivision of *Wirklichkeit*: he is not using the term '*wirklich*' in some new and far more general sense, but making distinctions within *Wirklichkeit*

---

[51] *Gottlob Frege*, 121.

as previously understood. This point is not to be pressed too hard against Sluga, however. Lotze's official position, both in the *Logik* and in the *Metaphysik*, is indeed as stated; but there are places where he appears to forget that validity is a species of *Wirklichkeit* and presents them as opposed to one another. One such passage is §1 of the *Metaphysik*, whre he says that a 'tranquil self-subsistence [*Bestehen in sich selbst*], impervious to any alteration, is quite properly the character of that world of Ideas [*Ideen*] which we contrast with *Wirklichkeit* in that it is eternally valid [*gültig*] but is not'.[52]

Sluga indeed gives a confused account of Lotze's not altogether consistent terminology, and renders it far more inconsistent than in fact it is; but it is not by disentangling that terminology that we shall come upon Sluga's principal error. It will be recalled that he identifies objectivity, as spoken of both by Frege and by Lotze, with intersubjectivity. This identification is certainly correct for the restricted notion of objectivity of which Lotze treated in §3 of his *Logik*; but further reflection shows that it is just here that the crucial difference lies between the two philosophers. The difference does not concern merely the way they use the word 'objective': it is a fundamental difference of doctrine. For Lotze, it is not merely that to recognize something as intersubjective, as the same for all thinking subjects, is not yet to attribute to it an existence altogether independent of our thinking: it is that there is no argument from the first to the second. Consider, for instance, the following passage, which occurs in Lotze's argument for the celebrated idealist view that, as it is often expressed, relations are purely ideal.

If *a* and *b* are . . . not things possessing an external permanent *Wirklichkeit* independent of our thinking, but are only contents of ideas [*vorstellbare Inhalte*], like red and yellow, straight and curved, then a relation *between* them obtains only inasmuch as we think it and in virtue of our thinking it. But our own mind is so constituted, and we assume every other to be so constituted, that whenever anyone has an idea of the same *a* and *b*, they will always give rise to the same relation in his thinking, a relation capable of obtaining only through thinking and only in thinking. This relation is thus independent of the individual thinking subject and of the individual phases of his thinking. It is in this alone that there lies what we suppose when we consider it as in itself obtaining between *a* and *b* and conceive of it as an

[52] 'als ewig gültig aber als nicht seiend', i.e. 'in that it is eternally valid but has no being'.

enduring object discoverable by our thinking; it really does persist, but only as an event, which will always repeat itself in thinking in the same way under the same conditions.[53]

Lotze does not here use the word 'objective', or even 'objectification': but the conception to which he is appealing is the same as that presented in §3 of the *Logik*. It is, namely, that we can be assured of the intersubjectivity, and of the constancy over time, of that to which we deny any existence save in our thought of it: something of this kind will therefore be independent of any particular thinker, but not independent of thinking altogether.

For Frege, the matter stands quite differently. He indeed repeatedly emphasizes that a thought, unlike an idea, is the same for all; a number, similarly, is the same for all. That thoughts are the same for all is what primarily interests Frege about them: if they were not, we could not communicate with one another, or could do so at best imperfectly and uncertainly. Similarly, if numbers were not the same for all, a mathematical theorem which held for one person might fail for another.

One will not easily regard . . . the number one as *wirklich*. . . . On the other hand, it is impossible to ascribe to each person his own number one; for then it would have first to be investigated how far the properties of these ones coincided. And if one person said, 'Once one is one', and another 'Once one is two', one could only note the difference and say: your one has that property, mine this. . . . One, as the same for all, stands over against [*gegenübersteht*] all in the same way.[54]

A thought does not belong to one who thinks it in the special way in which an idea belongs to one who has it, but stands over against [*steht . . . gegenüber*] all who grasp it in the same way and as the same. [Otherwise] two people would never connect the same thought with the same sentence, but each would have his own: and if, e.g., this man advanced $2.2 = 4$ as true, whereas the one denied it, there would be no contradiction, because what the former asserted would be distinct from what the latter rejected. . . . A contradiction occurs only when it is of the very same thought that one asserts the truth and the other the falsity.[55]

If the thought which I express by the theorem of Pythagoras can be recognized as true by others exactly as it can by me, it does not belong to the content of my consciousness; I am not its bearer and can nevertheless recognize it as true. If, however, it is not the very same thought which is

[53] *Metaphysik*, §80.   [54] *Grundgesetze*, vol. i, p. xviii.
[55] 'Logik', 1897, *Nachgelassene Schriften*, p. 145; *Posthumous Writings*, 133.

taken by me and by another as the content of the theorem of Pythagoras, then one ought not properly to say 'the theorem of Pythagoras', but 'my Pythagorean theorem' and 'his Pythagorean theorem', and these would be different.[56]

The crucial difference between Frege and Lotze lies in the fact that Frege admits no category of the intersubjective intermediate between what is private to some individual subject and what is independent of all subjects. Lotze's '*wirklich*' corresponds to Frege's 'objective': but Frege has no notion corresponding to 'objective' understood in Lotze's restricted sense. For him, what is subjective has a bearer, and so is not literally the same for different individuals. 'If two were an idea, it would then, in the first place, be mine alone. Another man's idea is, as such another idea. . . . We should then have to say: my two, your two, a two, all twos.'[57] We have no way of assuring ourselves that other people's subjective ideas resemble our own in essential respects. 'Could the sense of my Pythagorean theorem be true, that of his false?', Frege asks in 'Der Gedanke', immediately after the passage quoted above. His reply is that, if the words 'true' and 'false' were fitted to characterize the contents of my consciousness at all, they would be applicable only within the domain of my consciousness: 'truth would then be confined to the content of my consciousness, and it would remain doubtful whether anything in the least similar occurred in the consciousness of another'.[58] The reason is that I have no way of directly comparing that of which I am the bearer with that of which you are the bearer. 'It is . . . sometimes possible to establish differences in the ideas . . . of different people; but an exact comparison is not possible, because we cannot have these ideas together in the same consciousness.'[59] 'Even if it were possible to make an idea vanish from one consciousness and to make an idea simultaneously appear in another, the question whether it were the same idea would still remain unanswerable.'[60] The only way, therefore, to guarantee that something is the same for all is to take it to be objective in a sense that goes beyond mere intersubjectivity, and involves its independence from all thinking minds. Otherwise expressed, there is for Frege an inference from

[56] 'Der Gedanke', 68.   [57] *Grundlagen*, §27.
[58] 'Der Gedanke', 69.
[59] 'Über Sinn und Bedeutung', *Zeitschrift für Philosophie und philosophische Kritik*, 100 (1892), 30.
[60] 'Der Gedanke', 67.

something's being the same for all to its being objective in this stronger sense. It is to just this inference that he repeatedly appeals: from the fact that a thought, or the object to which it relates, is independent of any particular thinker, he deduces its independence from all thinkers; it 'stands over against' them all. 'Thoughts do not belong, like ideas, to the individual mind (are not subjective), but are independent of thinking, and stand, objectively, over against everyone in the same way; they are not made by thinking, but only grasped by it.'[61] 'The thought of the Pythagorean theorem is the same for all men, and stands, as objective, over against them all in the same way. . . . We grasp thoughts, but we do not create them.'[62]

The question whether intersubjectivity is possible without objectivity in the full sense remains a live one. Those who agree with Frege in thinking that it is not will, for example, criticize intuitionist mathematicians for describing numbers as mental constructions: for they will fail to see how, if that were what they were, there would be any guarantee that an arithmetical proposition which held for one mathematician would hold for another.[63] A philosopher of mathematics who agreed with Lotze, on the other hand, would perceive no difficulty in this. It is precisely because Frege did not admit any realm of entities which are intersubjective without being wholly objective that he *was* a realist both about thoughts and about numbers, and was so utterly opposed to psychologism in mathematics or logic. It is because he did admit such a realm that the path lay open for Lotze to be an idealist. Sluga, in assimilating their notions of objectivity, has contrived to obliterate *the* essential difference between them.

Of the three theses concerning objectivity cited by Sluga as held in common between Lotze and Frege, the first, that objectivity is intersubjectivity, thus involves a crucial misunderstanding of Frege and of his divergence from Lotze. The second, that the objective requires no bearer, is quite correct for Frege, but wrong for Lotze, when 'objective' is understood in its restricted sense, to the extent that it may require some bearer or other, although it requires no *particular* one: for Frege, on the other hand, whatever requires a

    [61] 'Logik', 1897, *Nachgelassene Schriften*, p. 160; *Posthumous Writings*, 148.
    [62] 'Kurze Übersicht meiner logischen Lehren', 1906. *Nachgelassene Schriften*, 214; *Posthumous Writings*, 198.
    [63] See Michael Resnik, 'Mathematical Knowledge and Pattern Cognition', *Canadian Journal of Philosophy*, 5 (1975–6), 25–39, esp. pp. 27–8.

bearer at all can have no other bearer than it has. As for the third thesis, that the objective need not be *wirklich*, it means something different as stated by Lotze and by Frege.

6. FREGE'S NOTION OF *WIRKLICHKEIT*

There is no room for serious doubt about what Frege meant by '*wirklich*': he tells us quite explicitly. In the Preface to *Grundgesetze* he glosses it as 'capable of acting directly or indirectly upon the senses';[64] in 'Le Nombre entier', he explains its equivalent '*réel*' as meaning 'that which can exert influence and be subject to it' (p. 74); in 'Der Gedanke' he says that 'the world of the *wirklich* is a world in which one thing acts upon another, changes it and itself experiences reactions and is changed by them' (p. 76). All this agrees with the characterization in *Grundlagen*, §85, of the *wirklich* as 'that which acts upon the senses, or at least gives rise to activity of which sense-perceptions may be near or remote consequences'; in this and all the foregoing renderings, the verb 'to act', and all other cognate words, represent German words etymologically related to '*wirklich*' as the English words are to 'actual'. (It is a mistake to cite §85 of *Grundlagen*, as Currie has done,[65] to show that Frege sometimes admitted numbers to be *wirklich*. He is here agreeing with Cantor, as against Kronecker and currently received opinion generally, that natural numbers are not *wirklich* in any sense in which negative numbers, etc., are not: but he immediately explains that, on his own preferred understanding of '*wirklich*', none of them are.) When Frege refuses *Wirklichkeit* to objects of some given kind, he is thus not claiming that they should be extruded from our ontology; he is merely denying that they are involved in causal interactions. The comparison of what Lotze calls 'being' to Frege's *Wirklichkeit* is not altogether unreasonable, since there is a suggestion in Lotze of a connection between being and activity.[66] The important difference is that Frege does not see this characteristic of physical objects as explaining what it is for them to exist: he does not think that there is any room for asking in what the existence of an object of any kind consists. '*Wirklich*' is for him a predicate applying to the object, or not

---

[64] *Grundgesetze*, vol. i, p. xviii.

[65] 'Frege on Thoughts', pp. 234–48; see 236–7.

[66] Thus in *Metaphysik*, §109, he speaks of 'the being of a thing, as capable of action' ('das wirkungsfähige Sein eines Dinges').

applying to it, whereas 'exists' does not stand for a concept under which the object falls. Not even objectivity is to be equated with existence: there are ideas, even though they are subjective. *A fortiori*, since not everything objective is *wirklich*, *Wirklichkeit* is not to be equated with existence: to say of something that it is not *wirklich* is not to say that it is not real in the sense that there is not really any such thing. Contrary to Sluga's opinion, however, objectivity is in Frege's philosophy a type of ontological status, that of independence from any conscious subject. We may therefore look to Frege's assignment of objectivity to ascertain his ontological views: since thoughts, logical objects, and concepts are all of them objective, they can none of them be identified with ideas, and so must form distinct ontological categories.[67]

7. LOGICAL OBJECTS AND FUNCTIONS

It was earlier questioned whether one could usefully discuss Frege's views of numbers, concepts, and thoughts in a single breath. Numbers, for him, are objective but not *wirklich*; but, while he calls concepts 'objective',[68] he nowhere says outright of them that they are not *wirklich*. On the contrary, he says of '*wirklich*' that 'it is only one predicate out of many':[69] this appears to imply that it is a genuine first-level predicate, true of some objects and not of others, but for that reason making no sense when applied to concepts or functions.

If, like Lotze and the great majority of philosophers, one does not sharply distinguish the content of a predicate from that of the corresponding abstract noun, one will be disposed to classify it as abstract, in contrast to concrete individual objects or things. Frege, who insisted upon such a distinction, had no reason to conflate any differentiation among objects with the more fundamental distinction between objects and functions, including concepts and relations. The distinction, which is not exhaustive, between physical objects and logical ones, can presumably be extended to one between physical properties and relations and logical properties and relations

---

[67] It is because philosophers are prone to identify things of all these types with ideas or contents of consciousness that Frege's claim that they are objective, while ideas are not, is a guide to his opinions about ontology. If it were a common opinion that numbers are a kind of material objects, then his thesis that physical objects are *wirklich*, but numbers not, would also serve as such a guide.

[68] *Grundlagen*, §47.   [69] *Grundgesetze*, vol. i, p. xix.

(and doubtless properties and relations of many other kinds): once one has firmly grasped the radical difference between an object and a concept or property, one will have no motive to lump all properties together with abstract objects. There is therefore no ground to saddle Frege with the view that the physical world contains physical objects, but is devoid of physical properties and relations.

When we say, 'Jupiter is larger than Mars', what are we there speaking of? Of the heavenly bodies themselves, of the *Bedeutungen* of the proper names 'Jupiter' and 'Mars'. We are saying that they stand in a certain relation to one another, and we do this by means of the words 'is larger than'. This relation holds between the *Bedeutungen* of the proper names, and must therefore itself belong to the realm of *Bedeutungen*.[70]

The relation holds between physical objects, in virtue of their physical constitution: it is therefore a physical relation, and bears no similarity to any abstract or logical object. It is *not* to be classified together with numbers as an example of that which is objective but not *wirklich*.

Against this two passages may be quoted from *Grundlagen*. In the first, to which my attention was drawn by Miss Ulrike Kleemeier, Frege is arguing the numbers are not 'properties of external things'. 'It would indeed be remarkable', he observes, 'if a property abstracted from external things could without change of sense be transferred to events, to ideas and to concepts. . . . It is absurd that what is by nature sensible should occur in what is non-sensible. . . . If we supposed that, when we look at a triangle, something sensible corresponds . . . to the word "three", we should have to find this again in three concepts; something non-sensible would then have something sensible in it.'[71] Concepts are here said to be non-sensible. It follows that, *if* it can be intelligibly asked whether they are *wirklich*, the answer must be negative.

In a later passage, Frege declares that 'in the external world, the totality of what is spatial, there are no concepts, no properties of concepts, no numbers'.[72] He is here concerned to point out that if, as he has been maintaining, arithmetical laws are analytic, they do not need to be confirmed by observation and are not laws of nature; but, as a ground for this, the contention that concepts are

---

[70] 'Einleitung in die Logik', 1906, *Nachgelassene Schriften*, 209–10; *Posthumous Writings*, 193.
[71] *Grundlagen*, §24.
[72] *Grundlagen*, §87.

non-spatial and do not form part of the external world is less than cogent. After all, in the earlier passage he had denied events to be external things, which certainly does not exclude the possibility of natural laws governing them. Nor can the absence of concepts from the external world render all statements about them analytic; elsewhere Frege had invoked the objectivity of concepts to explain how, by predicating something of a concept, e.g. that there are nine objects falling under it, we may state a fact about the external world.[73] Even to ask whether or not concepts are 'in' the external world has a curious ring. It would seem more reasonable to hold that it made no sense to say that they are or that they are not. Frege's outright assertion that they are not is surely attributable to his not yet having attained clarity about what he understood by the word 'concept', since he had not yet won through to the distinction between *Sinn* and *Bedeutung*. If one were pressed to answer the question whether or not there are relations in the external world, one would be much more likely to give an affirmative answer than to the corresponding question about concepts, unless one bore firmly in mind that concepts belong, like relations, to the realm of *Bedeutungen* and not to the realm of sense. It is, indeed, improbable that Frege would have used 'concept', rather than 'property', for the one-argument analogue of a relation if he had had the *Sinn/Bedeutung* distinction from the outset. In most of the important occurrences of 'concept' in *Grundlagen*, it would remain intact under a revision of the book to accord with his later terminology; but there are many other occurrences in which it plainly means what he would later have called the sense of a concept-word; it represented a notion within which he had not yet separated the sense from the referent. In the course of such a revision, the statement about the content of the external world would surely have had to be eliminated.

More difficult to explain is a remark from the Preface to *Grundgesetze*, to which again Miss Kleemeier drew my attention. It is a central thesis of that Preface that a failure to recognize that what is objective need not be *wirklich* leads to one of two errors concerning numbers, the empiricist (which makes them *wirklich*) and the psychologistic (which makes them subjective). Most of the Preface is an attack on psychologism; and Frege applies his diagnosis to explain the confusion between concepts and ideas. 'Because the

---

[73] *Grundlagen*, §47.

psychologistic logicians fail to recognize the objective but non-*wirklich*, they regard concepts as ideas and thereby assign them to psychology', he says.[74] The apparent implication is that concepts, though objective, are not *wirklich*. If so, the statement on the next page that ' "*Wirklich*" is only one predicate among many and no more belongs to logic than does, say, the predicate "algebraic" applied to a curve' is not to be taken at face-value, since no ordinary predicate can be univocally applied to objects and to concepts, as 'non-*wirklich*' would have to be. It therefore seems better to interpret the earlier remark, not as committing Frege to saying that concepts are non-*wirklich*, but simply as criticizing the psychologistic logicians for believing that only what is *wirklich* is objective.

8. FREGE'S NOTION OF OBJECTIVITY

The remark about the absence of concepts from the external world raises the possibility that the views Frege expressed in *Grundlagen* diverged from those which he later maintained. The passage in which he there explains what he means by 'objective' runs in full:

By objectivity I understand an independence from our sensation, intuition and ideation, and from the delineation of interior images from the memories of earlier sensations, but not an independence from the reason; for to answer the question what things are independently of the reason would be as much as to judge without judging, to wash the fur without wetting it.[75]

Sluga's reading of this remark is 'that it is incoherent for us to try to say what things are in themselves, independent of our judgements, and that the claim that something is objective is not a dogmatic metaphysical claim'.[76] He therefore, in a passage already quoted, attributes to Frege the view that 'the objective is not something alien or external to the mind, but constitutive of it. It is its most characteristic possession.'[77] The question at issue, however, is

---

[74] *Grundgesetze*, vol. i, p. xviii.

[75] Ibid., §26. There is an unfortunate ambiguity in the second half of the sentence, as here translated: does the adverbial phrase 'independently of the reason' qualify 'what things are' or 'to answer the question'? The German is less ambiguous than the English. Although, on the face of it, the characterization 'to judge without judging' would fit much better if the latter interpretation were intended, the syntax, so far as I am able to judge, allows only the former interpretation.

[76] *Gottlob Frege*, p. 120.

[77] Ibid. 121. In Sluga's text, the quotation relates directly to a passage from 'Der Gedanke' (p. 74 n.), in which Frege contrasts the use of 'what my hand contains' to

whether the mind constitutes logical objects and thoughts, not whether they constitute it. Not only in his writings after 1890, which have already been quoted, but already in the 1880s, Frege made plain that he rejected the view that the mind constitutes that which, though not *wirklich*, is objective, such as numbers and the contents of sentences. 'A judgeable content . . . is . . . not the result of an inner process or the product of a mental act which men perform, but something objective,' he wrote in the 1880s;[78] and *Grundlagen* itself contains the famous declaration that 'the mathematician cannot create things at will, any more than the geographer can; he too can only discover what is there and give it a name'.[79]

Nevertheless, Frege does say that the objective is not independent of the reason, which is the faculty by means of which we are aware of logical objects.[80] Michael Resnik is disposed to believe that, at the time of writing *Grundlagen*, Frege was what he calls an 'objective idealist' in the sense of holding 'that Mind or Reason constructs the whole world of mathematical objects prior to our "experiencing" it'; 'the effect of this', he explains, 'would be to make such a world *objective* in the sense of being "independent of our sensation, intuition and imagination" . . . but still not a world of things in themselves'.[81] It appears to me impossible to construe Frege in this way as having been, at any stage, a transcendental idealist about numbers without also making him a transcendental idealist about the external world. The context principle involves that it is by our grasp of the contents of sentences containing numerical expressions that numbers are given to us; among such sentences are statements of number by means of which we express judgements about the external world. The laws of arithmetic hold for everything think-able,[82] including physical reality. Hence, if it is our reason that

mean 'what I hold in my hand' with its use to mean 'what my hand is composed of', viz. bones, muscles, etc. Sluga remarks that 'Frege does not hold that thoughts are in the mind as the bird is in the hand, but rather as the muscles and bones are in the hand' (*Gottlob Frege*, p. 121). He has it the wrong way round: for Frege, thoughts are not mental contents, like ideas, that go to constitute our consciousness, but objects existing independently of us which we grasp in a sense analogous to that in which the hand may grasp a cricket ball.

[78] 'Logik', 1880s, *Nachgelassene Schriften*, 7; *Posthumous Writings*, 7.
[79] *Grundlagen*, §96.   [80] Ibid., §105; *Grundgesetze*, vol. ii, §74.
[81] Resnik, 'Frege as Idealist and then Realist', 351.
[82] *Grundlagen*, §14; 'Über formale Theorien der Arithmetik', *Sitzungsberichte der Jenaischen Gesellschaft für Medizin und Naturwissenschaft für das Jahr 1885*, Supplement to *Jenaische Zeitschrift für Naturwissenschaft*, 19 (1886), 94.

constructs the numbers in the only relevant sense, namely, that their properties and their very existence depend upon our making the judgements that we do, then, at least in part, it constructs the external world also, indeed everything of which we can think.

To read all this into Frege's remarks that objectivity does not entail independence from the reason is to be deaf to what he says earlier, in the very same section, in introducing his term 'objective'.

I distinguish what is objective from what is palpable, spatial or *wirklich*. The axis of the earth and the centre of mass of the solar system are objective, but I should not like to call them *wirklich*, in the way the earth itself is. One often calls the equator an *imagined* [*gedachte*] line; but it would be wrong to call it an *imaginary* [*erdachte*] line:[83] it was not brought into existence by thinking as the result of a mental process, but was only recognized, apprehended, by thinking. If its being recognized had been its coming into existence, we should be unable to say anything positive about it with respect to any time earlier than this alleged beginning of existence.[84]

Frege here states quite clearly that he does not consider the existence of that which is not *wirklich* to depend upon our thinking of it. His final characterization of objectivity, in this section, comes at the end of a paragraph in which he has been discussing the senses of colour-words, and maintaining that, in communication with one another, we use them in an objective sense not to be explained in terms of our private sensations, and hence accessible to a colour-blind person. The colours denoted by colour-words used in this objective sense are therefore themselves objective in two respects, not clearly distinguished by Frege. First, their existence is independent of our sensations; and, secondly, they can be apprehended without reference to our sensations. In saying that what is objective is not independent of the reason, Frege does not mean that its existence depends upon our thinking about it, for he has already clearly repudiated that view: he means that it cannot be apprehended save by, or by reference to, rational thought.

---

[83] 'Imagined' and 'imaginary' are not quite accurate translations of '*gedachte*' and '*erdachte*', but a precise rendering is hindered by our careless habit of speaking of the equator in English, as an 'imaginary line'. The contrast is between being conceived in thought (*gedachte*) and invented by thought (*erdachte*).

[84] *Grundlagen*, §26.

7

Frege and Kant on Geometry*

1. FREGE'S TERMINOLOGY

Hans Sluga has maintained that, on the realist/idealist axis, 'Frege's position must be akin to' that of Kant,[1] i.e. that he was a kind of transcendental idealist. His principal ground is that 'throughout his life Frege held to the Kantian thesis that space and time are *a priori* intuitions and that geometrical and temporal propositions are, therefore, synthetic *a priori*'; and he comments that anyone who commits himself to the Kantian thesis in question 'commits himself to something like the belief that objects, in the normal, empirical sense, are mere appearances and do not exist apart from cognition'.[2] Similarly he declares, in his book on Frege, that 'he held a Kantian view of space and hence a transcendentally subjective view of the objects that occupy it'.[3]

In one respect, it is very easy to evaluate such claims. References to philosophers, rather than to mathematicians and logicians, are extremely sparse in Frege's other writings; but they are plentiful in *Grundlagen*. He is there at particular pains to clarify his philosophical position *vis-à-vis* that of Kant. It is surely for this reason that, in that work, he makes extensive use of the Kantian terms 'analytic', 'synthetic', 'a priori' and 'a posteriori', which virtually never occur in his other writings.[4] While he was concerned to determine the

---

* First published in *Inquiry*, 25 (1982), 233–54.
[1] 'Frege's Alleged Realism', *Inquiry*, 20 (1977), 227–42; see 237.
[2] Ibid. 236.
[3] *Gottlob Frege*, The Arguments of the Philosophers (London, 1980), 45.
[4] An exception is his letter to Marty of 1882, in which he uses the terms 'analytic' and 'synthetic' (*Wissenschaftlicher Briefwechsel*, ed. G. Gabriel, H. Hermes, F. Kambartel, C. Thiel, and A. Veraart (Hamburg, 1976), 163; *Philosophical and Mathematical Correspondence*, ed. B. McGuinness and H. Kaal (Oxford, 1980), 99–100); he was here expounding *Grundlagen*, which he was in the course of writing. Another exception is the reference to a priori knowledge in the 'Zahlen und Arithmetik' of 1924–5 (*Nachgelassene Schriften*, ed. H. Hermes, F. Kambartel, and F. Kaulbach (Hamburg, 1969), 297; *Posthumous Writings*, ed. P. Long and R. White (Oxford, 1979) 277. In *Begriffsschrift*, §23, Frege speaks of 'synthetic judgements', 'making use', as he says, 'of Kant's term'.

grounds of our knowledge, and particularly of our knowledge of arithmetic (number theory and analysis), he was not deeply interested in the notion of necessity. His comparison, in *Grundlagen*, of his own views with those of Kant is not merely tacit, however: he endeavoured, in many passages, to make it explicit.

In another respect, we face a certain difficulty in evaluating Sluga's remarks. His reference to 'temporal propositions' is gratuitous, since Frege nowhere says anything about them;[5] but, although there are scattered observations about geometry in several of his writings, usually by way of contrast with arithmetic, it is difficult to elicit from them any very definite doctrine. The two series of articles, of 1903 and 1906, on the foundations of geometry, are of little help, preoccupied as they are with general questions about the nature of axioms and the sense, if any, in which an axiom-system implicitly defines the primitive terms. Since, after *Grundlagen*, Frege never used the terms 'analytic' and 'synthetic a priori', it is somewhat tendentious to describe him as holding throughout his life to the thesis that geometrical propositions are synthetic a priori. In *Grundlagen* itself, the principal thesis of the book is stated to be that 'arithmetical laws are analytic judgements';[6] in *Grundgesetze*, on the other hand, it is cited as having been that 'arithmetic is a branch of logic',[7] a stronger thesis, of course also maintained in *Grundlagen*. In respect of geometry, it is the other way about. In *Grundlagen*, Frege expressed his agreement with Kant that the truths of geometry are synthetic a priori, and praised Kant for having propounded that thesis.[8] But, except in the very late writings composed in the last year of his life, Frege never later made so definite a claim. He did, indeed, declare, in one of his notes to Jourdain's article about him, that 'the truths of geometry, in particular the axioms, are not facts of experience, at least if by that is meant that they are founded on sense-perceptions';[9] so we can confidently say that he did not regard them as a posteriori in Kant's sense. It is,

---

[5] Save for a brief allusion at the very end of his 'Erkenntnisquellen' of 1924–5 (*Nachgelassene Schriften*, 294; *Posthumous Writings*, 274).

[6] *Die Grundlagen der Arithmetik: Eine logische-mathematische Untersuchung über den Begriff der Zahl* (Breslau, 1884), §87.

[7] *Die Grundgesetze der Arithmetik begriffsschriftlich abgeleitet*, i (Jena, 1893), 1.

[8] *Grundlagen*, §89.

[9] In P. E. B. Jourdain, 'The Development of the Theories of Mathematical Logic and the Principles of Mathematics: Gottlob Frege', *The Quarterly Journal of Pure and Applied Mathematics*, 43 (1912), 241. The original German version of Frege's notes is contained in a letter to Jourdain in *Wissenschaftlicher Briefwechsel*, 114–24.

undoubtedly, very unlikely that he at any time considered them to be analytic in the sense of *Grundlagen*: but it is going very far beyond the demonstrable facts to assert that, throughout his life, he held them to be synthetic a priori; we have no positive reason to affirm, though no specific reason to doubt, that he continued to view the Kantian trichotomy analytic/synthetic a priori/a posteriori with favour.

It is, nevertheless, quite likely to be true that Frege always regarded the truths of geometry as synthetic a priori. That he always connected our knowledge of them with intuition in anything like a Kantian sense is very much more dubious. It is doubtful whether he at any time subscribed, as Sluga alleges, to 'the Kantian thesis that space and time are a priori intuitions'; but from 1873, the year of his first publication, to 1885, when he delivered the lecture on formal theories of arithmetic, he certainly held that our knowledge of geometrical truths rests on intuition. During that period, he operated with a notion of intuition very similar to Kant's and embodying a certain epistemological conception. After that year, however, occurrences of the word 'intuition' (*Anschauung*) in his writings become very rare indeed. It occurs, in a negative context, in the opening sentence of *Grundgesetze*, where he says that he had sought, in *Grundlagen*, 'to make it probable that arithmetic is a branch of logic and does not need to borrow any ground of proof either from experience or from intuition'.[10] In the unpublished 'Logik' of 1897, he draws a distinction between an 'idea' (*Vorstellung*) and an 'intuition' (*Anschauung*): 'by an idea I understand an imaginative picture, which does not consist of present sensations, like an intuition, but of reawakened traces of past sensations or activities'.[11] Here '*Anschauung*' is used in a far more restricted sense than in *Grundlagen*, and indeed the English translators render it 'perception';[12] the passage therefore supplies positive evidence that Frege no longer adhered to the notion of intuition that he had employed in that book. There are two occurrences of the word in a letter from Frege to Hilbert, dated December 1899. The first[13] is simply an allusion to Hilbert's statement, quoted in 'Über die Grundlagen der Geometrie' (1903), that each of his five groups of axioms 'expresses certain corresponding basic facts of our intuition'.[14]

[10] *Grundgesetze*, i. 1.   [11] *Nachgelassene Schriften*, 142.
[12] *Posthumous Writings*, p. 131.
[13] *Briefwechsel*, 61; *Philosophical and Mathematical Correspondence*, 35.
[14] D. Hilbert, *Grundlagen der Geometrie*, 7th edn. (Leipzig, 1930), §1, 2.

Frege asks how the word 'point' should be understood, as Hilbert uses it, and comments, 'One first thinks of points in the sense of Euclidean geometry, and this is confirmed by the statement that the axioms express basic facts of our intuition.'[15] In the second instance, however, Frege is speaking on his own account. He says, 'I call axioms propositions that are true, but which are not proved, because the knowledge of them flows from a source of knowledge [*Erkenntnisquelle*] which is quite different from the logical one, and which one may call spatial intuition'.[16] The word occurs again in a letter to Hilbert of 1900, in which Frege remarks that 'it seems to me that you want to detach geometry entirely from spatial intuition and to turn it into a purely logical science like arithmetic';[17] here, for all the context reveals, it could mean the same as in the 1897 'Logik'. In the published articles about Hilbert, Frege is careful to avoid any positive assertions about intuition. Save in reference to a use of it by Hilbert, it appears in the 1903 'Über die Grundlagen der Geometrie' only in the evasive remark, 'The question on what the justification rests for taking axioms to be true will not here be gone into: as the source for geometrical axioms, intuition is most often cited.'[18] Even in the very late writings, there is only one explicit reference to intuition, where it is equated with the geometrical source of knowledge,[19] about which Frege speaks a great deal, but of whose nature he tells us little. These late writings should not, of course, be taken as a guide to Frege's opinions at any earlier period, representing as they do a wholly new approach on his part to the philosophy of mathematics; we should note, however, that, in the fragment 'Zahl' of 1924, he observes that 'even the objects of geometry, points, lines and planes, etc., are not strictly speaking perceptible by the senses'.[20] From all this it appears probable that Frege came, after 1885, to regard as dubious that notion of intuition which he had inherited from Kant and had made use of in *Grundlagen* and earlier writings, perhaps returning to something resembling it in 1924. That is, indeed, no more

[15] 'Über die Grundlagen der Geometrie', *Jahresberichte der deutschen Mathematiker-Vereinigung*, 12 (1903), 321.

[16] *Briefwechsel*, 63; *Philosophical and Mathematical Correspondence*, 37.

[17] *Briefwechsel*, 70; *Philosophical and Mathematical Correspondence*, 43.

[18] Über die Grundlagen der Geometrie', *Jahresbericht der deutschen Mathematiker-Vereinigung*, 12 (1903), 319.

[19] 'Neuer Versuch der Grundlegung der Arithmetik', *Nachgelassene Schriften*, p. 298; *Posthumous Writings*, 278.

[20] *Nachgelassene Schriften*, 285; *Posthumous Writings*, 265–6.

than surmise: what is quite certain is that we have little warrant to ascribe to him, in the years 1886–1923, any positive views connecting our knowledge of geometry with intuition.

It nevertheless remains of interest to enquire whether Sluga's interpretation can be sustained for that period, from 1873 to 1885, when Frege did employ a notion of intuition and did make positive, though passing, observations concerning geometry. The question may seem unimportant; after all, Frege said even less about physical objects than he did about space. It would be a mistake to dismiss it in this fashion. *Grundlagen* already enunciates Frege's crucial thesis that not only what is actual (*wirklich*) is objective, and that numbers, in particular, though not actual, are objective.[21] For him, physical objects are not only the paradigm example of actual things, but equally the paradigm of what is objective. Naturally, since he maintained that 'objective' was a broader term than 'actual', he cites other examples, such as the axis of the earth, to illustrate the difference between the two features; but, whenever he is wishing to assert the objectivity of numbers or of thoughts, without stressing their lack of actuality, it is to the material world that he turns for comparison. The mathematician can only discover what is there, just as can the geographer;[22] a judgeable content is objective, just as the sun is objective;[23] a law of nature held good before it was discovered, just as an island in the ocean was there before it was seen by any human being.[24] If, then, Frege's view of physical objects were, or ever had been, as Sluga maintains, a 'transcendentally subjective' one, that would necessarily colour our understanding of what he meant by affirming thoughts and logical objects such as numbers to be as objective as they.

2. RELATIVE AND ABSOLUTE JUSTIFICATION

Whether Sluga is right to characterize the thesis expressed by Frege in *Grundlagen* by saying that geometrical truths are synthetic a priori as 'Kantian' depends upon whether he used 'synthetic a priori' in the same sense as Kant. In the first footnote to §3 of

---

[21] *Grundlagen*, §§26, 61, 85, 109; *Grundgesetze*, vol. i, xviii.
[22] *Grundlagen*, §96. Compare the title of J. H. Conway, R. T. Curtis, S. P. Norton, R. A. Parker, and R. A. Wilson, *Atlas of Finite Groups* (Oxford, 1985).
[23] 'Logik', 1880s, *Nachgelassene Schriften*, 7; *Posthumous Writings*, 7.
[24] 'Logik', 1897, *Nachgelassene Schriften*, 144; *Posthumous Writings*, 133.

Grundlagen, Frege professes not to be assigning new senses to the terms 'analytic', 'synthetic', 'a priori', and 'a posteriori', but only to be hitting off 'what earlier writers, Kant in particular, have intended' by them. In §88, on the other hand, he is quite willing to say that Kant defined 'analytic' too narrowly, and to speak of 'the wider concept' that he himself has employed, and this seems to accord much better with the facts of the case. He further says that 'on the basis of [Kant's] definition, the division of judgements into analytic and synthetic is not exhaustive'. If so, it would be necessary, in order to make it exhaustive, to redefine at least one of the two terms, though possibly not both; at any rate, it cannot be assumed without argument that Frege meant the same by 'synthetic a priori' as did Kant.

Frege falsely believed that every proof must have initial premisses. He believed this because he recognized no rule of inference which discharges a hypothesis, that is, whose conclusion depends on fewer hypotheses than those on which the premisses of the inference depend; although we frequently employ such forms of inference in informal argument, it was not until Gentzen that they came to be recognized and systematically treated by logicians. Given Frege's mistaken belief, it becomes impossible to comply with St Paul's admonition to 'prove all things'. The question then is whether it is possible to comply with the weaker admonition 'Prove everything that can be proved'. One possibility would be that every proposition that we can know to be true is capable of proof. If that were so, even compliance with the weaker admonition would be impossible: in order to give any proofs at all, we should have to accept as true some propositions which, though capable of proof, we had not proved. Frege rejected this possibility, and so conceived of the weaker admonition as capable of being followed. He held that there are some propositions which are intrinsically incapable of proof, but need no proof for us to recognize them as true. These are of two kinds: 'general laws, which . . . neither need nor admit of proof'; and 'facts, i.e. unprovable truths that lack generality, whose contents are predications concerning particular objects'.[25] On these two kinds of knowable but unprovable truths all our knowledge rests.

---

[25] *Grundlagen*, §3. Strictly speaking, I have in the text stated the alternatives too crudely. Restricting our attention to proofs involving no inference that discharges a hypothesis, let us call such a proof 'irredundant' if, when set out in tree form, no proposition appears more than once on any branch; and let us call a sequence of

Frege defines an a priori proposition as one which is capable of being proved, by appeal only to definitions of the terms involved, from fundamental general laws, i.e. ones neither needing nor admitting of proof: he obviously intends that such a proof shall be of a purely deductive or logical character. An a posteriori truth is one whose proof necessarily involves some appeal to 'facts' (in the special sense of this word explained above). Among a priori truths, the analytic ones are distinguished by its being possible to prove them from 'general logical laws' alone, together with the definitions to which one may always appeal; the synthetic ones are those which cannot be proved without appealing to 'truths which are not of a general logical nature, but relate to a particular domain of knowledge'. Thus the general laws which neither need nor admit of proof can be divided into those which are logical in character and those which are not, the logical ones being those whose range of application is unrestricted. The definitions display an uncharacteristic careless-ness, in that no provision is made for the status of those truths which are incapable of proof: obviously the fundamental laws of logic should be included among the analytic truths, fundamental general laws which are not logical among synthetic a priori ones, and particular 'facts' among a posteriori truths. All this is set out in §3 of *Grundlagen*. In the second footnote to that section, Frege argues that we must admit the existence of fundamental laws if we are to acknowledge any general truths,[26] since nothing follows from an individual fact save on the ground of a general law. He instances, as an example of such a fundamental (non-logical) general law, 'the general proposition that this procedure [induction] can establish the truth or at least the probability of a law'. This is the only quite

irredundant proofs an 'extension chain' if each term is a (proper) extension upwards of its predecessor. Then the relevant possibilities are: (1) that there are infinite extension chains; and (2) that every extension chain is finite. On hypothesis (2), it might be true that every individual proposition we can know to be true was capable of proof; but we could still comply with the yet weaker admonition 'Prove *as much* as can be proved', which we could not do on hypothesis (1). From remarks in Frege's later writings, it is apparent that it is hypothesis (2) that he is really concerned to maintain, rather than the stronger thesis that there are specific propositions which cannot be proved but can be known; see in particular the discussion of axioms in 'Logik in der Mathematik', *Nachgelassene Schriften*, 221–2; *Posthumous Writings*, 205–6.

[26] Austin's translation, 'if we recognize the existence of general truths at all', involves a mistake. The point is not that we acknowledge that there are some true general propositions, but that we acknowledge certain general propositions as true.

specific example of such a non-logical fundamental law ever cited by Frege.

As everybody knows, the fundamental problem of the *Kritik der reinen Vernunft* is how synthetic a priori judgements are possible. This problem is, in the first instance, an epistemological one: the problem is not, at the outset, what makes synthetic a priori propositions true, but how we are able to judge them to be true. Now Frege was a logician rather than an epistemologist. Some commentators, such as Gregory Currie, have called this characterization in question on the ground of his concern with the basis of our knowledge of arithmetical truths. That was indeed one of his principal concerns; but it was properly his concern as a logician, since he proposed to justify those truths by deriving them from the fundamental laws of logic.

The grounds which justify the recognition of a truth often lie in other truths already recognized. But if truths are known by us at all, this cannot be the only kind of justification. There must be judgements whose justification rests on something else, if indeed they require a justification at all. It is in this that the task of epistemology lies. Logic has to do only with those grounds of judgement which are truths. To judge when one is aware of other truths as grounds of justification is called *inferring*. There are laws governing this kind of justification, and it is the aim of logic to set out these laws of correct inference.[27]

The justification of a judgement, whether analytic, synthetic a priori or a posteriori, that is capable of proof is the proper concern of a logician, since proof is his subject-matter. But, since any proof has initial premises, this will never be more than a relative justification, relative, namely, to the justification of the initial premises. At least, that will be so if those initial premises, which are either fundamental general laws or particular 'facts', require any justification. If they are general logical laws, then, again, the question whether they need a justification, and, if so, what it can be, is obviously one for the logician. The question is one for the epistemologist if they are non-logical laws or particular 'facts'.

Of such 'facts', and of the fundamental general laws, Frege says in §3 of *Grundlagen* that they do not admit of proof. But he also says that they do not need proof. This leaves it in question whether it is possible to recognize that they need no proof without adverting to

---

[27] 'Logik', 1880s, *Nachgelassene Schriften*, 3; *Posthumous Writings*, 3.

the principle that you cannot be in need of that which it is impossible in principle for you to have: could we recognize that these truths needed no proof in advance of realizing that none was possible? It is difficult to see how one could do so save by recognizing that they needed no justification whatever; but Frege's text leaves it open whether that is so, or whether they can be justified by one of those other means referred to in the passage quoted above from the 'Logik' of the 1880s, means which involve neither proof nor appeal to other truths. On the face of it, one would be disposed to say that the individual 'facts' could be justified by perception or observation: and this leaves it open that the general laws, whether logical or non-logical, can be justified by reference to other faculties of ours for the direct apprehension of truth.

As regards the fundamental laws of logic, Frege gives no answer to this question in *Grundlagen*; but he does do so in the Preface to *Grundgesetze*. 'The question why and with what right we acknowledge a law of logic to be true, logic can answer only by reducing it to another law of logic. Where that is not possible, logic can give no answer.'[28] This is quite explicit: no justification can be given for accepting those laws of logic which cannot be derived from other laws. If someone denies one of them, one can only say, 'We have here a hitherto unknown type of madness.'[29] Frege goes on to reject a particular putative justification.

Stepping aside from logic, one may say: we are compelled to make judgements by our own nature and by external circumstances, and, when we judge, we cannot reject this law—e.g. that of identity—but must acknowledge it, unless we wish to bring our thought into confusion and finally renounce all judgement. I do not wish either to dispute or to endorse this view; I wish only to observe that we do not here have a logical deduction. What is given is not a ground for the law's being true, but for our taking it to be true. Moreover, this impossibility of rejecting the law, which constrains us, does not in the least prevent us from supposing beings who do reject it; but it prevents us from supposing that such beings are right to do so; and it also prevents us from doubting whether it is we or they who are right.[30]

[28] *Grundgesetze*, vol. i, xvii. In the original version of this essay, I here falsely accused Furth of making 'one of his rare slips in translation'; I take this opportunity to apologize.

[29] Ibid., xvi.　　　　　　　　　　　　　　　　　　　　　　　[30] Ibid., xvii.

Frege has already insisted on the sharpest distinction between being true and being taken to be true: 'being true is something different from being taken to be true, whether by one person, by many or by all, and can in no way be reduced to it'.[31] The fact, if it be a fact, that we cannot but take the fundamental laws of logic to be true, is no ground for their truth, for their being what we take them to be: in the nature of the case, no ground for that can be given, and hence no justification for our taking them to be true, if by a justification be meant something that goes to show that we are right to do so. This should not, however, push us into logical relativism. It must not be concluded that these laws are only true for us: the predicate 'true' does not admit of such a qualification. It is incoherent to say that we cannot but take the laws to be true, and in the same breath to disparage them as only true for us on the ground that other beings might reject them; if we are compelled to take them as true, then we take them to be *true*, and must thereby regard anyone who denies them as wrong.

The question is, therefore, how the matter stands with those fundamental general laws which are not logical in character, and particularly those which relate to space and underlie the science of geometry. Kant believed that he could explain how we come by a knowledge of such synthetic a priori truths. If Frege believed the same, and accepted the same explanation, then he was, in the respect that interests Sluga, a Kantian; if he believed that it could not be explained, or that there was a quite different explanation, he was not. Neither in Kant's nor in Frege's definitions of the terms 'synthetic' and 'a priori' is there any appeal to a positive thesis about how we come by synthetic a priori knowledge, save by deduction from more fundamental synthetic a priori truths. Hence, simply to believe that geometrical truths are synthetic a priori does not make one a transcendental idealist: all depends upon the explanation of our knowledge of those truths. Specifically, it depends on whether it is our knowledge of them, or at any rate some feature of our constitution, that makes them true, or whether, as on the realist view, they are true quite independently of us.

[31] Ibid., xv.

3. THE JUSTIFICATION OF NON-LOGICAL LAWS

In the 'Logik' of the 1880s, Frege suggests, as we have seen, that there are non-deductive justifications for certain truths. It would have been consistent for him to hold that judgements based on sense-perception are justified simply by being so based. Admittedly, although it is by means of our logical faculties or our reason that we acknowledge the truth of the fundamental laws of logic,[32] Frege does not say that they are justified by being directly apprehended by the reason, but that they are incapable of justification at all. Reason is not, however, a true parallel to sense-perception: to ascribe reason to an individual just is to ascribe to him a capacity to grasp thoughts and to make judgements on the basis of other judgements from which they follow. Reason does not *prompt* us to do such things, but *consists in* our doing them, whereas sense-perception prompts us to make observational judgements rather than itself consisting in our making them. Frege insisted on the distinction between what brings about and what justifies a judgement:[33] with what right, then, might what prompted a judgement be cited in justification of it? There can be only two possibilities. Either we assume, or have reason to believe, that what prompts the judgement is a reliable sign that it is true; or we take the judgement as relating solely to the occurrence of that which prompts it. The former is the realist option, the latter the idealist one. For the realist, sense-perception supplies a justification for observational judgements because it is intrinsic to the concept of perception that to perceive things is a ground for taking them to be as we perceive them, and because this presupposition is confirmed by our ability to explain how physical things affect our senses as they do. For a Berkeleyan idealist, on the other hand, the justification lies in the fact that, in speaking of material objects, we are doing no more than speaking about our sensations.

It is not certain that Frege would have allowed sense-perception as a justification for observational judgements, though, if not, it is obscure how there can be any non-deductive justifications for epistemology to investigate. On the hypothesis that he would have done so, our question must be whether the faculty by means of

[32] *Grundgesetze*, ii (Jena, 1903), §§74, 147.
[33] 'No . . . description of the inner processes which precede the delivery of a judgement . . . can ever be adduced in proof', *Grundlagen*, §26.

which we acknowledge synthetic a priori truths resembles reason or the perceptual faculties. In the last year of his life, Frege returned to the philosophy of mathematics which he had abandoned for eighteen years, ever since, in 1906, he had become convinced of the inadequacy of his attempted solution of Russell's paradox and thereby of the failure of his reduction of arithmetic to logic. He bravely undertook a new unification of mathematics on a geometrical basis, and wrote for publication an article on the sources of mathematical knowledge. In this he distinguishes three sources of knowledge: sense-perception; the logical source; and the geometrical and temporal source. Sense-perception is not needed for mathematical knowledge. The geometrical source is, of course, that from which the axioms of geometry derive, and only it or the temporal source, and neither the logical one nor sense-perception, can furnish us with the infinite.[34] The fragment 'Zahlen und Arithmetik', of the same date, identifies knowledge derived from the geometrical source as a priori;[35] and, as already observed, a final fragment identifies the geometrical source of knowledge with intuition, and, in doing so, retracts the declaration in *Grundgesetze* that 'arithmetic does not need to draw any ground of proof . . . from intuition'.[36]

In these very late writings, then, it is intuition on which our knowledge of synthetic a priori truth is based, and, specifically, spatial and temporal intuition. That does not, in itself, settle the question whether, in this last period, Frege regarded intuition as *justifying* such knowledge or simply as *consisting in* the ability to attain it: he asserts the existence of a geometrical source of knowledge, but says little to explain its nature, and it is therefore difficult to be sure in just what sense he is using the word 'intuition'. Friedrich Kaulbach has argued that his identification of intuition with the geometrical source of knowledge indicates that the latter is closely connected with the 'sensible a priori intuition of which Kant spoke and which he designated one of the "sources" from which flows the knowledge not only of geometry but also of arithmetic'.[37] Kant indeed says that 'time and space are two sources of knowledge [*Erkenntnisquellen*] from which different synthetic a priori cognitions

---

[34] 'Erkenntnisquellen der Mathematik', *Nachgelassene Schriften*, 286–94; *Posthumous Writings*, 267–74.

[35] *Nachgelassene Schriften*, 296–7; *Posthumous Writings*, 276–7.

[36] See nn. 10 and 19, above.

[37] *Nachgelassene Schriften*, xxxi.

can be drawn'.[38] Kaulbach is very likely right that, in speaking of his three 'sources of knowledge', Frege was intending an allusion to Kant. He had made an express reference to Kant when, forty-two years before, he had used the same expression in a letter to Anton Marty.[39] This is not at all to say that, in these late writings, Frege was in complete agreement with Kant. Kant did not think, as Frege plainly implies, that all our synthetic a priori knowledge is derived from intuition. He did think intuition necessary for *self-evident* synthetic a priori truths: that is why mathematics has axioms, but philosophy does not, and why the categories require a transcendental *deduction*, while the axioms of geometry and the fundamental truths of arithmetic stand in no such need.[40] In Frege's late writings, on the other hand, not only does all synthetic a priori knowledge rest on the geometrical and temporal source, that is, on intuition, but there is no hint of the possibility of anything resembling a transcendental deduction.

4. GEOMETRY FOUNDED ON INTUITION

In *Grundlagen*, equally, a transcendental deduction could find no place in Frege's account, since he says explicitly that all a priori propositions either can be deductively derived from, or themselves are, truths incapable of proof. It might be argued that, from Frege's standpoint, Kant's deductions of the categories do rest upon an unproved premiss, namely that experience is possible at all; but it would be special pleading indeed to try in such a manner to find room in Frege's theory for transcendental deductions of the Kantian type. The difference between the *Grundlagen* account and that given in Frege's writings of 1924 lies in the absence, from *Grundlagen*,

---

[38] *Kritik der reinen Vernunft*, B 55.

[39] Mentioning that he has nearly completed a book, evidently *Grundlagen*, he asserts what he also says there (§§88–9), that Kant placed too low a value on analytic judgements, that arithmetical truths are analytic, not synthetic as Kant thought, but that Kant deserves great credit for having recognized geometrical propositions as synthetic. 'The two cases are quite different. The domain of geometry is that of the spatially intuitable; arithmetic knows no such restriction. . . . The domain of what is countable is . . . as broad as that of conceptual thought, and a source of knowledge [*Erkenntnisquelle*] of more restricted extension, such as spatial intuition or sensory perception, would not suffice to guarantee the general validity of arithmetical propositions' (*Wissenschaftlicher Briefwechsel*, 163–4; *Philosophical and Mathematical Correspondence*, 100).

[40] *Kritik der reinen Vernunft*, B 760–1.

of any suggestion that all synthetic a priori knowledge rests on intuition; it would be implausible to claim the one specific example cited by Frege of a fundamental non-logical law—the principle underlying induction—as so founded. What matters for present purposes, however, is not how far Frege disagreed with Kant about other synthetic a priori knowledge, but how much he agreed with him about geometry; and he does, in *Grundlagen*, repeatedly connect geometrical truths with intuition.

Frege made this connection in his earliest writings. His doctoral dissertation of 1873 begins with a Kantian enough statement that 'the whole of geometry rests ultimately on axioms which derive their validity from the nature of our intuitive abilities';[41] this raises the problem how we are able to speak of imaginary points of intersection of a circle with a straight line, or of points at infinity, which do not occur in the space of our intuition. In his Habilitationsschrift Frege wrote that

there is a remarkable distinction between geometry and arithmetic as regards the basis of their fundamental principles. The elements of all geometrical constructions are intuitions, and geometry appeals to intuition as the source of its axioms. Since the subject-matter of arithmetic is not intuitable, its fundamental principles cannot spring from intuition.[42]

In the lecture 'Über formale Theorien der Arithmetik', Frege argued for the logical character of arithmetic, contrasting it with geometry; the negation of certain geometrical axioms would be logically possible, that is to say, would involve no contradiction. Arithmetic has no special domain of applicability, but extends to everything thinkable, whereas geometry applies only to what is spatial. If arithmetic were not reducible to logic, the ground of our knowledge of its correctness would be in question: it could not be spatial intuition, for then arithmetic would be restricted to the geometrical; nor could it be physical observation, for it would then apply only to the physical.[43]

This contrast is drawn in much the same way in *Grundlagen*, §14. Arithmetical laws are neither empirical nor synthetic, being

[41] *Über eine geometrische Darstellung* (Jena, 1873), 3.

[42] *Rechnungsmethoden* (Jena, 1874), 1.

[43] 'Über formale Theorien der Arithmetik', *Sitzungsberichte der Jenaischen Gesellschaft für Medizin und Naturwissenschaft für das Jahr 1885*, Supplement to *Jenaische Zeitschrift für Naturwissenschaft*, 19 (1886), 94.

distinguished both from empirical propositions and from geometrical truths by their range of applicability. Empirical propositions hold good only of physical and psychological reality.[44] Geometrical truths govern the domain of what is spatially intuitable, both reality and the products of pictorial imagination. So long as they remain intuitable, the wildest flights of fancy are still subject to the axioms of geometry. Conceptual thought, however, can break loose from these axioms, as when it assumes a space of four dimensions or of positive curvature.[45] Such reflections, though far from useless, 'leave the ground of intuition behind': if we do make use of intuition in this connection, 'it is still the intuition of Euclidean space, the only one of which we have a picture'. For purposes of conceptual thought we can always postulate the opposite of one or another axiom of geometry without inconsistency: this proves both that those axioms are independent of one another and that they are synthetic. By contrast, we cannot deny any of the basic laws of arithmetic without falling into a confusion in which thought is no longer possible. The basis of arithmetic lies deeper, not only than that of the empirical sciences, but also than that of geometry: the domain of arithmetical truths is the widest of all, for it embraces not only what is real, like that of empirical science, nor even only what is intuitable, like that of geometry, but everything that is thinkable.

In *Grundlagen*, §90, Frege concedes that he has not so far conclusively demonstrated the analytic character of arithmetical propositions: that can be done only when proofs are completely formalized so as to preclude the occurrence of any gaps in them. In common mathematical practice, the mathematician is content so long as each transition in the proof is self-evident, without enquiring whether this self-evidence is logical or intuitive. Since the steps within the proof are longer than the simplest possible steps into which they could be broken down, two opposite mistakes are liable to be made. One is to take such a complex single step to be purely logical, when in fact some element of intuition has crept into it, the step representing a combination of simple inferences and of axioms

---

[44] *Wirklichkeit*: for once this word is better translated 'reality' than 'actuality', since Frege is concerned, not with the difference between that which is causally efficacious and that which is not, but with that between what exists and what is only imagined.

[45] By the axioms of geometry Frege always understands those of three-dimensional Euclidean geometry: see the fragment 'Über Euklidische Geometrie', *Nachgelassene Schriften*, 182–4; *Posthumous Writings*, 167–9.

of intuition. The other occurs when a complex inference involves no intuitive element, being applicable beyond the realm of what can be intuited, but we wrongly regard its self-evidence as intuitive, and accordingly rate the truth derived by means of it as synthetic. This can happen because, while its correctness is self-evident to us, we recognize that it does not conform to any of the standard forms of logical inference, and have failed to analyse it into its simple component steps. Relying only on informal proofs, we shall not succeed in distinguishing what is synthetic and rests on intuition from what is analytic, nor in compiling a complete list of axioms of intuition from which, together with the laws of logic, every mathematical theorem can be derived. Frege goes on, in §91, to report his formalization of logical inference in *Begriffsschrift*, by means of which it is possible to ensure that no unnoticed premiss creeps into any proof. He gives as an example of a theorem which might at first sight be taken to be synthetic, but which he had proved 'without borrowing any axiom from intuition', the proposition that the ancestral of a many–one relation is a simple ordering when restricted to the objects to which a given individual is ancestrally related. His conclusion is that 'the contents of sentences which extend our knowledge can be analytic judgements', something already asserted in §88.

5. WHAT IS INTUITION?

If we are to elicit from these allusions to geometry a definite doctrine concerning it, we must understand Frege's use, up to 1885, of the word 'intuition'. His insistence that geometrical laws apply, not only to what we actually observe, but to all that we can imagine shows plainly that he was not then using the word in the restricted sense of the 1897 'Logik', in which it is, rather, '*Vorstellung*' that applies to the products of visual imagination. He certainly did not intend, however, to use the term in any vague, indeterminate sense. In *Grundlagen*, §12, he objects to Hankel's use of the expression 'pure intuition of magnitude', and comments that 'we are all too ready to invoke inner intuition whenever we cannot produce any other ground of knowledge. But we have no business, in doing so, to lose sight altogether of the sense of the word "intuition".' He then proceeds to cite the explanation of the term given by Kant in his *Logik*, namely, that 'an intuition is an individual idea [*Vorstellung*]

. . . a concept is a general . . . or reflective idea'. Although Frege thus appeals to Kant as against Hankel, he was very dissatisfied with Kant's terminology. In the second footnote to §27, he objects to Kant's use, for both intuitions and concepts, of the word '*Vorstellung*', observing that he associated both an objective and a subjective meaning with the word, and that, in consequence, 'he gave his theory a very subjective, idealist colouring and made it difficult to hit on what his true opinion was'. Frege was not, of course, objecting merely to a defective terminology on Kant's part, but to an unclarity of thought. Unfortunately, Frege's own terminology in *Grundlagen*, though an improvement on Kant's, was still defective, because he had not yet won through to his distinction between *Sinn* and *Bedeutung*; and the footnote in which he comments on Kant's use of '*Vorstellung*' is the plainest example of this. Throughout *Grundlagen*, there is an oscillation in his use of the word 'concept' (*Begriff*) to be observed in his earlier writings also: in some passages it means what he would later have called the *Bedeutung* of a concept-word, in others its *Sinn*. In the footnote the same ambiguity affects the word 'object' (*Gegenstand*) also: we find him surprisingly saying that 'objective ideas can be divided into objects and concepts'. Frege explains that he himself will reserve the word 'idea' (*Vorstellung*) for its subjective sense: but it is evident that, by 'objective idea', he here means what he would later have called the sense (*Sinn*) of an expression, so that an objective idea of an object is what figures in his later writings as the sense of a proper name; here, however, it is not distinguished from the object itself, the *Bedeutung* of the name.

By 'intuition' Kant meant 'cognition of an object'; as stated in the passage of the *Logik* quoted by Frege, the distinction between intuitions and concepts is that the latter are general, the former individual. The same principle of distinction is maintained in the *Kritik*: 'an objective perception is a *cognition*. This is either an *intuition* or a *concept*. . . . The former relates directly to an object and is individual; the latter relates to it indirectly by means of a characteristic [*Merkmal*] which can be common to several things.'[46] Kant's distinction between intuitions and concepts thus corresponds to Frege's distinction, among ideas in the objective sense, between

---

[46] *Kritik der reinen Vernunft*, B 376–7. Here a perception (*Perception*) is an idea of that particular kind which involves awareness (*Vorstellung mit Bewusstsein*). Such a perception may be either a sensation (*Empfindung*) or a cognition (*Erkenntnis*), the latter being subdivided into intuitions and concepts.

objects and concepts. It is for this reason that Frege observes, in *Grundlagen*, §12, that, in the sense of 'intuition' explained by Kant in the *Logik*, 'we might perhaps be able to call 100,000 an intuition; for it is certainly not a general concept'.

'An intuition in this sense, however,' Frege goes on to say, 'cannot serve as the ground of our knowledge of arithmetical laws.' What is missing from the definition given in the *Logik* is any mention of a 'relation to sensibility, which, on the other hand, is included in the notion of intuition in the "Transcendental Aesthetic"'. He quotes Kant as there saying, 'It is by means of sensibility that objects are *given* to us, and it alone furnishes us with intuitions',[47] and concludes that 'the sense of the word "intuition" is wider in the *Logik* than in the "Transcendental Aesthetic"'. It is only in the narrower of the two senses, that involving sensibility, that intuition 'can serve as the principle of our knowledge of synthetic a priori judgements'.

Since Frege himself believed intuition to be the basis of our knowledge of certain a priori truths, namely geometrical (though not, of course, arithmetical) ones, he evidently attached to the word 'intuition' the narrower of the two senses. This, however, creates a problem for Kant's classificatory scheme: how do numbers fit into it? As Frege remarks in *Grundlagen*, §104, natural numbers, at least very large ones like $1000^{1000^{1000}}$, are not intuitable: hence, as he says in §12, our awareness (or objective idea) of a number is neither a concept nor an intuition in the narrower sense;[48] and, as he says in §89, the number itself is not a concept, but an object, which, however, is not given to us either in sensation or in intuition. This shows that Kant was wrong in asserting that 'without sensibility no object would be given to us', and also in requiring of concepts that we should attach their objects to them in intuition,[49] unless, indeed, he used the word 'object' in a different sense from Frege. This last supposition would not resolve the difficulty: this would now take the form that there is no place for numbers in Kant's scheme.

Thus, for Frege, as for Kant, an intuition is of something particular or individual, and, as for Kant, it involves some relation to our sensory awareness; but, just because of this second feature, it

---

[47] Ibid., B 33. [48] 'I cannot allow an intuition of 100,000.'
[49] Both remarks are cited from ibid., B 75, where Kant also says that 'our nature is so constituted that intuition can never be anything but sensible, i.e. it contains the only way in which we are affected by objects'.

cannot be equated with our awareness of objects of every kind. It is on the ground of the great generality of the notion of magnitude that Frege objects, in *Grundlagen*, §12, to Hankel's speaking of an 'intuition of magnitude':

if we consider all the different things that are called magnitudes—numbers, lengths, areas, volumes, angles, curvatures, masses, velocities, forces, intensities of illumination, electric currents, etc.—we can well understand how they can all be brought under the single *concept* of magnitude; but the term 'intuition of magnitude' . . . cannot be recognized as appropriate.

Furthermore, intuition involves not only particularity but also immediacy. As already noted, Kant held that a synthetic a priori truth can be self-evident to us only when it is founded upon an intuition; and Frege similarly requires a truth based on intuition to be immediately evident, though not conversely. In *Grundlagen*, §5, he remarks that Kant regarded numerical equations as unprovable and synthetic, though hesitating to call them axioms, since they are not general and there are infinitely many of them.[50] He goes on to observe that 'Kant wishes to call the intuition of fingers or of points in aid,[51] thus running the risk of making these propositions appear empirical, contrary to his own opinion; for the intuition of 37,863 fingers is certainly not a pure one.' The clinching refutation is that, if we had such an intuition, and others of 135,664 and of 173,527 fingers, the correctness of the equation '135,664 + 37,863 = 173,527' would have to be 'immediately evident, at least for fingers', which it is not.

The immediacy of intuition is reflected, not only in our immediate recognition of truths derived from it, but also in the unmediated application of the notions in terms of which we characterize it. That is why, in the section just quoted, Frege denies that we have any intuition of 135,664 fingers. The same point underlies his discussion of the notion of direction in §64 of *Grundlagen*. Frege remarks that 'many scholars give the definition: parallel straight lines are those which have the same direction'. It is possible that he was here thinking, among others, of Hermann Lotze, who, in §131 of his *Metaphysik*, wrote that 'we call parallel two straight lines *a* and *b* which have the same direction in space'; if so, Frege is being slightly unfair, since Lotze goes on to give a criterion for having the same

---

[50] *Kritik der reinen Vernunft*, B 205.
[51] An allusion to ibid., B 15.

direction. In any case, Frege's comment on a definition of this kind is that 'the true state of affairs is thereby turned on its head'. In arguing this, he first states that 'everything geometrical must originally be intuitable', and then goes on to ask whether 'anyone has an intuition of the direction of a straight line'. His answer is that we have an intuition of a straight line, but do not distinguish in intuition the direction of the line from the line itself; he concludes that 'direction' is not a primitive geometrical notion, but that 'this concept is discovered only by means of a process of mental activity which takes its start from intuition'. The upshot is that the term 'direction' requires definition: in defining it, we may use the relational expression 'is parallel to' because 'we do have an idea [*Vorstellung*] of parallel lines'. Frege's statement in the late fragment 'Zahl' that points, lines, and planes are not, properly speaking, perceptible by the senses[52] represents a more cautious attitude than his blithe statement in *Grundlagen* that we can have an intuition of a straight line, but is based on the same guiding principle.

This feature of intuitions, as Frege conceived them, comes out most sharply in the philosophical discussion of the concept of magnitude which introduces *Rechnungsmethoden*, a work which foreshadows his uncompleted treatment of real numbers in *Grundgesetze*, part III. Frege there uses the argument from generality he was to use again against Hankel in *Grundlagen*: 'so comprehensive and abstract a concept as that of magnitude cannot be an intuition'.[53] More interestingly, he also argues that even specific types of magnitude, such as length, area, and size of angle, are not derived from intuition: these concepts have been gradually disentangled from intuition, the intuitability formerly ascribed to them having been only apparent. 'Bounded straight lines and plane surfaces enclosed within curves are indeed intuitable; but the notion of magnitude as applied to them, something common to lengths and areas, eludes intuition.' The key notion, in grasping the concept of magnitudes of a given kind, such as length, is that of adding two such magnitudes. Angles provide a clear example: one cannot convey to a beginner a correct idea of an angle just by showing him a figure; one has to show him how to add angles, and then he knows what they are.

We may thus characterize that notion of intuitions with which Frege operated up to 1885 as follows. An intuition is a direct

---

[52] *Nachgelassene Schriften*, 285; *Posthumous Writings*, 265–6.
[53] *Rechnungsmethoden*, 1.

presentation, after some sensory mode, of a particular object or collocation of objects. Sense-perception is undoubtedly one species of it: but since it also occurs when we form mental pictures, it need not be the apprehension of any actual object or collocation of them. It can, however, be only of what can be immediately recognized: what is intuited cannot be characterized by appeal to any concept which it requires a further mental operation either to attain or to acknowledge as applying to the particular case. Such a notion of intuition does not appear to have assumed a major role in Frege's thought during this early period, since he was principally concerned with logic and arithmetic, in which, for him, intuition plays no part; his observations about geometry are motivated by the desire to contrast it with arithmetic. It appears, nevertheless, to have been the notion of intuition which he employed: one that embodies a particular conception of how we arrive at certain concepts and how we recognize certain truths. If that is right, the conjecture that he later became dissatisfied with it should occasion no surprise.

6. OUR KNOWLEDGE OF GEOMETRY

In order to determine whether Sluga correctly interprets the views held by Frege during the period that includes *Grundlagen*, we have to extract from that and his earlier writings a coherent theory of our knowledge of geometry. It was reasonable for him to argue from the universal applicability of arithmetical truths to the reducibility of arithmetical notions to purely logical ones; indeed, his criterion in *Grundlagen*, §3, for a truth's being logical in character is precisely that it be of unrestricted application, so that, in default of any alternative characterization of logical notions, no step is involved in such an argument. The converse argument, not expressly advanced by Frege, from the fact that geometry applies only to what is spatial to the impossibility of defining geometrical notions in purely logical terms would, in itself, be fallacious. This is because the expressibility of arithmetical truths in purely logical terms and their being analytic are two independent theses: an axiom of infinity, for example, might be formulable in logical terms, and yet not analytic in the epistemic sense given to that word by Frege. He appealed to the fact that arithmetical truths apply to everything thinkable in support of their analyticity, as well as in support of their logical expressibility: for if they rested on sense-perception, they would apply only to the actual world, and if on intuition, then only to what is intuitable. This is an epistemological argument, concerned with the grounds of our knowledge. Suppose that there were some synthetic truth, say A, which was nevertheless expressible in purely logical terms. Then, if we knew A at all, we could not know it in virtue of our logical faculties alone, but on the basis of observation or by appeal to intuition. Because we knew it in this way, we should not take it as holding good of everything thinkable; but, by hypothesis, we should be mistaken if we inferred from that that it could not be expressed in logical terms. It would therefore involve a fallacy to infer from the fact that geometrical truths relate only to what is spatial that they cannot be expressed in purely logical terms. It is nevertheless evident that they cannot. That does not imply, under Frege's definitions of 'analytic' and 'synthetic', that they are synthetic: a deep logical analysis might uncover interrelations between the different geometrical notions that could be embodied in a system of definitions by appeal to which the axioms of geometry could be shown to be analytic. For this reason, the converse of Frege's argument from the universal applicability of arithmetic to the analyticity of its truths could not be used to show geometry to be synthetic. There are two distinct reasons why a truth may not be universally applicable. It may involve notions whose range of application is restricted; or our knowledge of it may rest on other than purely logical grounds. These reasons are independent: there can be no valid inference from either to the other.

What does show the synthetic nature of geometrical propositions is the logical consistency of a denial of the axioms of geometry. Frege later became dubious about the proofs of independence of the Euclidean axioms;[54] but whether or not the possibility of *proving* the consistency of non-Euclidean geometries be admitted, to assert that the Euclidean axioms are synthetic is equivalent to asserting, as Frege did in *Grundlagen*, §14, that their negations are logically consistent. That they are synthetic is shown by the fact that we can consistently describe a world in which they fail; that we cannot *imagine* such a world shows that they are nevertheless

[54] Thus in a letter to Liebmann of 1900 he wrote, 'I have reason to believe that the mutual independence of the axioms of *Euclidean* geometry cannot be proved' (*Wissenschaftlicher Briefwechsel*, 148; *Philosophical and Mathematical Correspondence*, 91); and in his notes to Jourdain's article he says, 'The indemonstrability of the axiom of parallels cannot be proved'. See Jourdain, 'The Development of the Theories of Mathematical Logic', 240.

a priori, since, if they rested upon empirical observation, they would apply only to the actual world, not to everything imaginable. That, at any rate, appears to be the argument that Frege is implicitly advancing. As he wrote in his doctoral dissertation, their validity derives from the nature of our intuitive abilities.

The particularity of intuitions seems to present an obstacle to their being the foundation of *general* laws such as underlie all synthetic a priori truths and are embodied in the axioms of geometry. Frege resolves this difficulty in *Grundlagen*, §13. One of the differences between arithmetic and geometry is that each number has an individual character of its own, whereas a geometrical point, line, or plane cannot, in itself, be distinguished from any other point, line, or plane:

> it is only when several points, lines, or planes are simultaneously grasped in a single intuition that one distinguishes them. When in geometry general propositions are derived from intuition, it is evident from this that the points, lines, or planes that are intuited are not really particular ones and hence can serve as representatives for the whole of their kind.

What makes it appropriate to speak of intuition here is that the spatial configuration is presented to us as a particular one; but we apprehend in it only such features as are invariant under Euclidean transformations, and hence can base general laws upon it.

If our a priori knowledge of geometry rests upon intuitions, those intuitions must themselves be a priori, pure intuitions in the sense in which Kant explains that he calls all ideas *pure* in which 'nothing is met with that belongs to sensation'.[55] In *Grundlagen*, Frege uses the term 'pure intuition' only to deny that it applies in certain cases.[56] In §12, however, he remarks that Kant, having opted for the synthetic a priori character of arithmetical laws, had no alternative 'but to invoke a pure intuition as the ultimate ground of our knowledge'; it would seem to follow that Frege was under the same compulsion in respect of geometry. Kant, in the passage just cited, says that 'the pure form of sensible intuitions' is found in the mind a priori, and that 'this pure form of sensibility is itself called a *pure intuition*'. His justification for calling it an intuition is, in so far as it assumes a spatial form, that he does not regard space either as a property of

---

[55] *Kritik der reinen Vernunft*, B 34.

[56] *Grundlagen*, §§5 and 12 (in the latter against Hankel's 'pure intuition of magnitude').

material things or as a system of relations between them, but thinks that we conceive of it as a kind of receptacle, an all-embracing object containing them.[57] There is, however, no suggestion anywhere in Frege's writings that he shared Kant's conception of a single pure intuition of space as a whole. The intuitions upon which, for Frege, geometrical laws depend appear to be of particular spatial configurations; they are pure only in the sense that they may be constructed by the imagination and that it is irrelevant whether they are ever encountered in observation.

Frege claims to be able to show that the informal reasoning we employ in proofs of arithmetical theorems can be validated by rigorous analysis. In informal reasoning about geometrical propositions, on the other hand, we take steps that are not always deductively valid: they may appear so only because we advert to figures drawn on paper or visualized in the imagination. Certain logical possibilities cannot be represented in such an actual or mental picture, and we therefore leave them unconsidered. An exact logical analysis, appealing to a formalization of deductive inference, would expose the points at which we were making a surreptitious appeal to synthetic laws, and would enable us to systematize, as a set of axioms, the laws so appealed to. Our acceptance of such fundamental laws rests on the impossibility of our imagining them to be violated, and hence on a priori intuitions, where 'intuition' is used as comprehending both spatial perception and spatial imagination. Such intuitions are a priori in that the constraints that govern them do not depend upon our observation of any particular facts; that is why they continue to apply to all that we can imagine, not just to the world as we find it to be.

7. IDEALISM

To hold our knowledge of geometrical truths to be founded upon intuition no more entails adopting a transcendentally idealist view

---

[57] *Kritik der reinen Vernunft*, B 38–9, 42. How far this committed him to a full acceptance of absolute Newtonian space is open to argument. Frege maintained that Newton's absolute space was not wholly transcendent, but was connected with experience via the law of inertia; on the other hand, 'in Newton's assumption of a single absolute space more is contained than is necessary for the explanation of the phenomena' ('Über das Trägheitsgesetz', *Zeitschrift für Philosophie und philosophische Kritik*, 1018 (1891), 149). In the context, this reads as an admission that Newton's hypothesis is partly, though not wholly, superfluous: but anyone determined to interpret Frege as a Kantian could read it to mean that it was a priori.

of space than does regarding them as synthetic a priori. Once more, all depends upon what explanation, if any, is given for intuition's yielding such knowledge. This is, indeed, the weak point in the account of geometry which we have seen to be implicit in the passing remarks Frege made about it up to 1885. The transcendental idealist explains the matter by treating the ground of our knowledge as also being the ground for the truth of the propositions known, that is, by identifying that whereby we know them with that in virtue of which they are true. On Kant's view, to have admitted a gap between these would deprive us of any reason to take synthetic a priori propositions, in particular the laws of geometry, to be true.

Assume, then, that space and time are objective in themselves, and are conditions of the possibility of things in themselves, . . . Since the propositions of geometry are known synthetically a priori, . . . I ask: from where do you obtain such propositions, and on what does our understanding rest, in order to attain such absolutely necessary and universally valid truths? . . . It is therefore indubitably certain . . . that space and time . . . are merely subjective conditions of all our intuition.[58]

This is why, for Kant, geometrical laws hold only of the phenomenal world, of the world as it appears to us. Space is not objective, not a feature of things as they are in themselves; rather, we construct it from our a priori intuitions and impose it on the external world, which, in consequence, is only the world of appearances and not reality as it is in itself and independent of us.

Such an account would accord very badly with Frege's general outlook as expressed in the Preface to *Grundgesetze*, in which, as we have seen, he insists upon the gap between being true and being taken to be true. This was not a new attitude on his part: in the 'Logik' of the 1880s, he says, in just the same spirit, that the sense of the word 'true' precludes any reference to the knowing subject.[59] Is it not possible, nevertheless, that his attitude was less inflexible at the time of writing *Grundlagen*? As Kant says, if we assume that space is a feature of an objective reality independent of us, it is hard to see why 'the nature of our intuitive abilities' should afford us any sure guide to its constitution. It may have been the difficulty of answering this question that led Sluga to assume that Frege must have shared Kant's transcendental idealism. A realist must either

---

[58] *Kritik der reinen Vernunft*, B 64, 66.
[59] *Nachgelassene Schriften*, 5; *Posthumous Writings*, 5.

refuse to offer any explanation, or assume an intrinsic harmony between independent reality and the form of our intuitions. It is conceivable that Frege would have denied that any justification could be given for fundamental non-logical laws any more than for the fundamental laws of logic; but such a position would undeniably be even less satisfactory in the former than in the latter case. The laws of logic are the laws of the laws of nature,[60] laws of truth which which we must comply if our judgements are to be true.[61] Even if, then, we can in certain cases give no answer to the question why we take a given law to be a law of logic, there is no general problem with what right we assume the laws of logic to be objectively true. Physical objects, as being actual (*wirklich*), act upon the senses;[62] it is therefore reasonable to take the sense-perceptions to which they give rise as indications of their existence and their properties. Moreover, as Frege observes in his 'Erkenntnisquellen' of 1924, sense-perception yields knowledge only when corrected by our knowledge of natural laws, which, he says, depends in part upon the logical and geometrical sources of knoweldge and enables us to detect illusions.[63] To maintain, in the context of a realist philosophy, that a priori intuitions yield genuine knowledge of objective reality is far more problematic. Synthetic a priori laws are not laws of truth itself; if the intuitions on which rests our acceptance of geometrical laws as true are a priori, it is not physical reality which has directly given rise to them: why, then, should we take them as revealing the truth about that reality?

According to Frege, we cannot imagine space as other than three-dimensional and Euclidean; *a fortiori*, we cannot perceive it otherwise. The truth, and even the meaning, of this contention are open to question. In one sense, our visual perception of space is not three-, but two-dimensional; it is reasonable to say that, in that sense in which we perceive it as three-dimensional, we have learned to do so, and hence, if our experience had been different, we could have learned to perceive it as four-dimensional.[64] Frege also held it

[60] *Grundlagen*, §87.

[61] 'Logik', 1897, *Nachgelassene Schriften*, 157; *Posthumous Writings*, 145.

[62] *Grundgesetze*, i, xviii; *Grundlagen*, §85; cf. 'Der Gedanke: Eine logische Untersuchung', *Beiträge zur Philosophie des deutschen Idealismus*, 1 (1918), 76.

[63] *Nachgelassene Schriften*, 287; *Posthumous Writings*, 268.

[64] For a sketch of how this might be possible, see the excellent, and neglected, article by Honor Brotman, 'Could Space be Four-Dimensional?', *Mind*, 61 (1952), 317–27.

to be logically possible for space not to conform to the laws of three-dimensional Euclidean geometry. We may therefore intelligibly ask how things would be for us if it did not. Frege never asked this question; any answer to it weakens his position, if that position is interpreted as realistic. One answer would be that we should fall into complete confusion, continually misinterpreting our sensations or unable to interpret them at all. Another would be that, in such a case, we should both imagine and perceive space as conforming to whatever was the true geometry. Yet a third answer would be that we should continue to perceive space as three-dimensional and Euclidean, but that we should be able to discover its true character and to arrive indirectly at correct judgements about the spatial disposition of objects. Given Frege's assumption that three-dimensional Euclidean geometry correctly describes actual physical space, any one of these three answers would furnish us with a posteriori grounds for accepting that assumption. A fourth possible answer is that, if the geometry of physical space were, say, elliptic, or if it had four dimensions, we could never become aware of the fact. This answer would deprive us of any ground whatever for taking physical space in fact to be as our intuitions represent it. It is to this dilemma that the doctrine that geometry is synthetic a priori and rests on intuition leads, when understood against the background of a realist view of the physical universe. Frege's logicist theory of arithmetic is not caught in this fork. One cannot argue against it that, if the laws of arithmetic did not hold, then either we should be aware of their failure, in which case arithmetic is an empirical science, or it would make no difference to us, in which case we have no reason for believing those laws to hold: for, on Frege's account, the failure of arithmetical laws is a logical impossibility. The thesis that geometry is synthetic a priori *is* impaled upon the fork: it is unclear that Frege was ever conscious of the fact.

This, then, is a good prima-facie reason for regarding the view of geometry suggested by Frege's scattered remarks about it in *Grundlagen* and elsewhere as untenable save in the context of transcendental idealism. It is not, however, a good reason for interpreting Frege as having subscribed to that or any other form of idealism. This is apparent from *Grundlagen*, §26, of which we have so far taken no account, and which includes Frege's most sustained discussion of space. He begins by remarking that 'according to

Kant, space belongs to appearance'.[65] 'For other rational beings', he continues, 'it might take some form quite different from that in which we know it.' This is not a Kantian thesis. Kant says that it is possible that all thinking beings must necessarily have a mode of spatial and temporal intuition like the human mode, but that we cannot decide the question;[66] but Frege is asserting the thesis on his own account. He goes on to say that 'we cannot even know whether [space] appears the same to one man as to another; for we cannot lay one man's intuition of space beside another's in order to compare them'. 'Nevertheless', he declares, 'there is something objective in space all the same.' 'What is objective in it', he says, 'is what is subject to laws, what can be conceived, what can be judged [*Das Gesetzmässige, Begriffliche, Beurtheilbare*], what can be expressed in words. What is purely intuitable [*Das rein Anschauliche*] is not communicable.' He justifies this by saying that 'everyone recognizes the same geometrical axioms, even if only by his behaviour, and must do so if he is to find his way about the world'; and he proceeds to illustrate it by an example. He supposes two rational beings for whom only projective properties and relations are intuitable; and he supposes further that what one intuits as a point appears to the other as a plane and conversely, so that what for one is the line joining two points is for the other the intersection of two planes, and so on. He comments that 'they could understand one another very well'; because of the principle of duality in projective geometry, 'they would never become aware of the difference in their intuitions'. In particular,

they would be in complete agreement concerning all geometrical theorems; they would merely translate the words differently into their intuitions. With the word 'point', for example, one would connect this intuition, the other would connect that one. We can therefore still say that this word means something objective for them; it is just that we must not understand by this meaning anything peculiar to their intuitions.

Frege goes on to compare this case with that of colour.

The word 'white' ordinarily makes us think of a certain sensation, which is of course wholly subjective; but even in ordinary linguistic usage, it seems to me, an objective sense frequently predominates. When we call snow white, we wish to express an objective state which we recognize, in ordinary

---

[65] See, e.g., *Kritik der reinen Vernunft*, B 59–60.   [66] Ibid., B 72.

daylight, by a certain sensation. When the light is coloured, we allow for that in the judgement that we make: we say, for instance, 'It *appears* red at present, but it *is* white'. Even a colour-blind man can speak of red and green, although he does not distinguish these colours in sensation; he recognizes the distinction by the fact that others draw it, or perhaps by means of a physical experiment. Often, therefore, the colour-word does not signify our subjective sensation, of which we cannot know that it agrees with that of someone else, . . . but an objective state.

The whole discussion is summed up by a formulation of what Frege means by 'objective':

by objectivity I thus understand independence from our sensation, intuition and imagination [*Vorstellen*], and from the delineation of inner pictures from memories of earlier sensations, but not independence from reason; for to answer the question what things are independently from reason would be to judge without judging, to wash the fur without wetting it.

According to Frege, then, we associate certain sensations or intuitions with certain words, such as 'white' or 'point'; but we cannot rely upon such associations to convey our sensations to someone else, since he may connect a different sensation or intuition with the same word, and we can never know that this is not so, sensations and intuitions being subjective and incommunicable. Hence, in order to communicate successfully, we must accord to our words an objective sense, one that is independent of our own sensations and intuitions. Successful communication occurs when there is agreement on how to judge the truth of what is expressed by the words; a word such as 'point' or 'white' thus bears an objective sense when it is used in sentences in such a way as to convey by means of them an objective state of affairs, about which all agree how to determine whether or not it obtains. Space is objective in so far as we can state its properties in words bearing an objective meaning; and the axioms of geometry state just such properties. Everyone must acknowledge their truth, even if only implicitly, in his actions; in doing so, he acknowledges what holds objectively and can be wholly grasped by conceptual thought independently of intuition or imagination.

Many objections can be brought against this argument of Frege's: that it rests on an untenable view of the privacy of inner sensations; or that, to move about the world successfully, we need assume at most that space approximates to being Euclidean in small regions, just as the surface of the earth approximates to a plane over small areas. But §26 is no aberration on Frege's part. Given his unwavering conviction of the ineradicable subjectivity of ideas, where 'idea' is understood in the generic sense, as covering sensations, intuitions, and mental images, he could say no other; the alternative would be to allow that a geometrical axiom might be true for one person and false for another. It might seem surprising, in view of Frege's various statements that it is on intuition that our knowledge of geometrical axioms rests, that he should say in §26 that their contents relate only to those features of space which are independent of sensation and intuition. The surprise is merely superficial. We cannot imagine what it would be like for the axioms of geometry to be false, but we can conceive of their falsity, that is, we can think their negations: it follows that their senses are capable of being wholly grasped by conceptual thought in a manner that involves no allusion to our intuitions. It is on the basis of a priori intuitions of space that we accept those axioms as true; but the features of those intuitions which the axioms capture are ones which, as being expressible in words, are common to all and could, therefore, be grasped even by a subject whose intuitions differed from ours.

None of this, admittedly, extricates Frege's account from the fork, 'either empirically based or groundless', discussed above; in itself, it is even compatible with a transcendentally idealist account of what makes geometrical propositions true. The passage was not, however, written without Kant in mind: it opens with a reference to him, and Frege was as concerned here as throughout *Grundlagen* to relate his views to Kant's. Kant quite rightly said that his explanation of why our a priori intuitions of space and time are sources of knowledge entails that 'space and time . . . are merely subjective conditions of all our intuition' and that 'as phenomena [*Erscheinungen*], they cannot exist in themselves, but only in us'.[67] Hence, when Frege repudiates Kant's view that space belongs to appearance (*Erscheinung*), and opposes to it the thesis that it is in certain respects, including those expressed in the axioms of geometry, objective, where objectivity involves independence from intuition, he can only be meaning to reject Kant's account of what makes the laws of geometry true. From the 'Logik' of the 1880s onwards, Frege always understood 'objective' in the same way as Kant, namely, as meaning what is

---

[67] *Kritik der reinen Vernunft*, B 66, 59.

altogether independent of us: thus in the 1897 'Logik' he characterizes it as 'that which is independent of our mental life', and says later that 'thoughts do not belong like ideas to the individual mind (are not subjective), but are independent of thinking, and stand (object-ively) over against everyone in the same way'.[68] In speaking of space as objective, therefore, Frege must be taken as asserting that it possesses those of its properties which are expressed in words and stated by geometrical laws independently of our mode of appre-hending it. It is not, for him, our recognizing those laws as true that makes them true; we do not construct physical space, let alone the physical universe, any more than we construct the numbers, but, in both cases, give a name to what is there independently of us. In speaking about space, as described by geometry, we are not, for Frege, speaking of our intuitions or sensations. If this leaves it obscure why we should treat our intuitions as a ground of know-ledge of geometry, that is a lacuna that Frege might have filled had he ever written positively about geometry. It is also perhaps a reason why, from 1885 to 1924, he ceased to assert that our knowledge of geometry is founded upon intuition: but it is not a ground for construing him to have meant the opposite of what he said.

In the unfinished 'Logik' of the 1880s, probably written close to the time when *Grundlagen* was composed, Frege explained why he called the sun 'objective' as follows:

Is not the sun for some people a beneficent or malignant deity, for others a shining disk hurled into the heavens from the east and rolling down again towards the west, for yet others an immense spherical white-hot body enveloped by a cloud of incandescent gases? No. To one person it may *appear* one thing, to another, another: it *is* what it is.[69]

One who subscribed to a transcendentally subjective view of physical objects could find a way of assenting to that; for he could explain that what the sun *is*, as here contrasted with how it *appears*, is still only a matter of appearance, of how things are in the phenomenal world. The contrast drawn between its objective and its apparent character, he could say, is really only that between intersubjective judgements on which all can come to agree and personal ones which

---

[68] *Nachgelassene Schriften*, 149, 160; *Posthumous Writings*, 137, 148.
[69] *Nachgelassene Schriften*, 7; *Posthumous Writings*, 7.

are to be abandoned.[70] In this way, such a one could assent to the passage while still maintaining that physical objects are mere appearances: it would be psychologically impossible for him to have written it.

[70] Thus Kant: 'We indeed ordinarily distinguish, among phenomena, that which belongs essentially to the intuition of them, and holds good for every human mind, from that which attaches only accidentally, in that . . . it holds only for a particular state . . . of this or that mind' (*Kritik der reinen Vernunft*, B 62). In fact, however, 'we have to do with nothing but phenomena; . . . the transcendental object remains unknown to us' (B 63).

8

An Unsuccessful Dig

A review of G. P. Baker and P. M. S. Hacker, *Frege: Logical Excavations**

1. GENERAL AIMS

Frege's work has had a notoriously bizarre fate. Neglected in his lifetime and for long afterwards by all but a very few, in recent years not only acclaimed but studied, it seemed that it had at last received its due as a classic contribution to philosophy. The appearance was premature; for, in the past few years, it has been made into a battleground for exegetes. No philosophical writer can less have deserved this fate, so great are the clarity of his style and the pains he took to be explicit; yet book succeeds article and article succeeds book, each declaring that every previous exponent has misunderstood Frege from start to finish. Dr Baker and Dr Hacker's book *Frege: Logical Excavations* is squarely in this tradition. The authors announce, in their first chapter, that Frege has been converted into a mythological figure, and that their task will be to demythologize him. Previous writers have fashioned him in their own image, that of twentieth-century analytical philosophy: Baker and Hacker will tell us, for the first time, what Frege really meant.

This adversarial approach is to be deplored. It obstructs progress and provokes pointless controversy. Frege is so interesting a writer because we have got so comparatively short a way beyond the point he reached. To be more exact, we have sent out forays far ahead of that point, but have secured very little further territory. Wittgenstein, in particular, made very bold expeditions into unknown country; but we are still struggling with his work, which we have not yet mastered and cannot properly evaluate. Frege's problems are therefore still our problems; his thoughts still answer to our concerns. His work was deep, and rewards sustained reflection, which can discern

---

* (Oxford and New York, 1984.) I have made minor revisions to the review as originally published in *Philosophical Quarterly*, 34 (1984), 379–401.

new aspects and uncover new connections. Such reflection is hampered by the din of battle as exegete smites exegete; and the clash of arms is unnecessary. When Frege's work was as yet generally unfamiliar, bad mistakes were indeed made: and, just because his work was so profound, anyone writing about Frege is liable to miss important points and to misrepresent his ideas to some degree. It really is not likely, however, that, at this date, any serious commentator will have gone utterly astray. The line between exposition and comment is thin, but there is nevertheless an important difference between a contribution to philosophy and an account of the views of an individual philosopher, in that the former, if wrong, is likely to be completely—though, perhaps, fruitfully—wrong, whereas the latter, even if not wholly right, may well be nearly so. It ought to be easy for those interested in Frege's work to arrive at a consensus about his meaning, a consensus that need not be static, but may be modified by new insights as they occur, but which excludes the production of radically new interpretations backed by claims that every previous writer has totally misunderstood Frege. The rule of the game, as it is now played, demands such a new interpretation from every new player, a demand which prompts not only misplaced ingenuity but unbridled exaggeration. It is controversial whether there can be progress in philosophy, but it ought to be uncontroversial that there can be progress in the understanding of a particular philosopher; the game of Frege exegesis, under the present rules, makes such progress extremely difficult.

Frege: Logical Excavations aims to expound and criticize certain aspects of Frege's philosophy, including, in particular, the context principle: the book scrutinizes the notions of conceptual content, assertoric force, sense, reference, concept, function, and truth-value. Other aspects, such as the definitions of 'analytic' and 'a priori', the notion of a criterion of identity, and virtually the whole of Frege's philosophy of mathematics, are passed by in silence. It differs from previous entries in the competition for new interpretations in rating Frege as of low importance, philosophically or historically. The book advances two principal second-order theses:

(A) that Frege's philosophy has no genuine affinity, and no important links, with the work of subsequent philosophers and logicians; and

(B) that his philosophy is irretrievably confused, incoherent, and self-contradictory.

'The foundations' of Frege's thought 'are rotten', we are told, 'the principles unsound, the supporting members flawed and cracked' (p. 365); hence 'any attempt to build on his writings any weighty philosophical principles is doomed to sink into a quagmire of sophisticated nonsense' (p. 260). These charges, typical of those that frequently recur throughout the book, are absolute. Baker and Hacker hold that many of the doctrines of modern philosophy of language are irremediably confused and incoherent, and that the very questions to which they are addressed are nonsensical. One might therefore be charitably disposed to read their condemnations of Frege as issued, not *in propriis personis*, but only as from the point of view, which is not theirs, of modern logic and philosophy of language; in other words, to interpret thesis (B) as no more than a gloss on thesis (A). This more benign interpretation unfortunately fails to square with the text. Modern ideas do not resemble those of Frege as closely as is generally supposed, Baker and Hacker argue; but it is particularly when the resemblance is closest that the latter are flimsiest. 'To the extent that modern ideas rest on the same foundations as Frege's, they are supported neither by cogent argument nor by compelling insight' (p. 260).

It is impossible, even in a lengthy review, to deal with all the topics discussed by Baker and Hacker; I shall omit their treatment of assertoric force and of the context principle (the least interesting sections of the book). I have selected two clusters of topics, each crucial to one of the second-order theses. If, as I shall try to show, they are wrong about the topics in the first cluster, then thesis (A) fails; similarly, if they are wrong about those in the second, so does thesis (B). Before treating of these, however, I will consider one of the main issues concerning interpretation.

Save for an introductory and a concluding chapter, the book is divided into two parts: part 1 deals with Frege's early period, up to 1886, and part 2 with his later period, from 1891 to his death. Now the principal problems in the exegesis of Frege turn on the relation between his earlier and later views. These problems fall under two heads. First, there are certain theses propounded in *Die Grundlagen der Arithmetik* which make no overt appearance in the later writings: the context principle; the doctrine of criteria of identity; the definitions of analyticity and aprioricity; and the dependence of geometry on a priori intuition. The exegete needs to decide how far their disappearance reflects a genuine change in Frege's philosophical beliefs.

The only one of these discussed by Baker and Hacker is the context principle, in respect of which they see great continuity from the earlier to the later period.

Secondly, we must ask how far the salient addition to Frege's doctrines, the distinction between sense and reference, represented a mere clarification and how far a repudiation of earlier ideas. Frege's later comments suggest that he himself took the former view of the innovation. We are not bound by this judgement, even if it be truly Frege's: it is quite possible for someone to misinterpret his own earlier work. There is nevertheless a presumption in favour of it, and, in my opinion, it was correct. In certain respects, the ideas expressed in *Begriffsschrift*, *Grundlagen*, and the other early writings had not been fully worked out; when Frege attempted to work them out, he found himself forced to draw a distinction between sense and reference, not only for 'proper names', but for expressions of all types. If this is right, it is a methodological mistake to try to extract from Frege's early writings a complete systematic theory of philosophical logic comparable to, and in competition with, that propounded by him from 1891 onwards. The assumption on which Baker and Hacker proceed is the opposite. They treat Frege's early writings as embodying a fully worked-out system of philosophical logic, of which many features survived the transition to the mature theory, but some were rejected and replaced by new doctrines.

If, by adopting the sense/reference distinction, Frege was replacing one fully worked-out theory by another, it is quite out of order, in expounding, say, *Grundlagen*, to appeal to that distinction in order to elucidate the theses Frege advanced in that book; that, naturally, is how Baker and Hacker see it. If, on the other hand, the distinction constituted a clarification of a theory not yet fully elaborated, it will be legitimate to make such an appeal, in full awareness that Frege had not made the distinction when he wrote *Grundlagen*. Moreover, on this hypothesis, any attempt to depict the early writings as embodying a complete systematic theory will be bound to smuggle in some of the later ideas, representing them as already present in the early period. This is in fact just what the authors do: they import into Frege's early doctrine a use of the notion of a function which is only to be found in the mature writings.

They regard the notion of judgeable content used by Frege in his early period as equivalent to that of a thought as used from 1891 onwards. They expressly say (p. 279) that truth and falsity were, for

Frege, externally related to the judgeable content. They note that he later said that he distinguished the thought and the truth-value *within* the judgeable content, which would suggest that the truth-value of a judgeable content was integral to its identity; but, although they offer no grounds, they are confident that, if Frege meant this, he was misunderstanding his earlier thinking. They declare that Frege included judgeable contents 'within the category of *objects*' (pp. 148–9) and treated sentences as 'names of objects' (pp. 124–5): his assimilation of sentences to proper names was thus not a feature of his mature doctrine, but 'was present in his work in *Begriffsschrift*' (p. 289). An occasional note of warning is sounded, to the effect that Frege did not actually *say* these things, although it is clear that he meant them: but these notes are drowned by the repeated emphasis placed on these claims.

All this represents a massive importation into Frege's early period of ideas stemming from his subsequent writings. The mature period opened with *Funktion und Begriff*, which enunciates all the salient theses of the logical doctrine maintained by Frege throughout the period, which he had been working out during the silent years from 1886 to 1890. The early period, on the other hand, was one of steady development. In *Grundlagen*, Frege set his whole discussion against the background of Kant's philosophy, and used a Kantian terminology. It is probably for that reason that he employed the word 'object' (*Gegenstand*), which he had not previously used in any systematic way; in earlier writings he had preferred 'thing' (*Ding*) or 'individual thing' (*Einzelding*).[1] So far as I am aware, he nowhere describes a judgeable content as an object or individual thing, or raises the question whether it should be so classified: there is no presumption that he took everything to be either a concept or else a thing or object. Similarly, he did not, in his early writings, call sentences 'names'. His terminology, before *Grundlagen*, was very loose. In *Begriffsschrift* he speaks of a formula, and also of a sentence, as 'expressing' (*ausdrücken*) or 'meaning' (*bedeuten*) a judgement, of its 'meaning' a circumstance, of its 'stating' (*angeben*) 'indicating' (*andeuten*), 'having' or 'meaning' a content (the last is by far the most frequent); sometimes he speaks of the content when he means the expression, as when he speaks of it as being preceded

---

[1] As I remarked in *The Interpretation of Frege's Philosophy* (London, 1981), 321, Frege was probably right, in *Grundlagen*, §89, to surmise that Kant used the word '*Gegenstand*' in a sense different from his own.

by the content-stroke. Plainly, we have here no systematic termin-ology, and no evidence of an intention to represent sentences as names. It is strong evidence against such an intention that whereas, in *Grundgesetze der Arithmetik*, there is no distinction recognized by the formation rules between sentences (there called by Frege 'names of truth-values') and singular terms (names of other objects), in *Begriffsschrift* there is such a distinction, residing in the principle that the judgement-stroke may precede only an expression for judgeable content.

What makes Baker and Hacker so anxious to date Frege's assimilation of sentences to names as early as *Begriffsschrift* is their contention that, from that work onwards, he regarded concepts as functions. According to them, the only change, from the early to the mature period, lay in what the values of these functions were taken to be. In the mature doctrine, concepts are functions from objects to truth-values, that is, from the references of names to the references of sentences. In the early period, according to Baker and Hacker, they were similarly functions from the contents of names to the contents of sentences; since the content of a name was an object, they were functions from objects to judgeable contents. In this manner, they furnish Frege's early period with a logical doctrine almost as fully articulated as that expounded after 1890.

The notion of a function is used in *Begriffsschrift* to explain the process of decomposing a sentence or judgeable content to obtain a predicate or concept, a process to which Frege attached fundamental importance. The process itself is explained again in 'Booles rechnende Logik und die Begriffsschrift', and referred to in *Grundlagen*, §70. Did Frege conceive of the process as being applied to judgeable contents or to sentences? Baker and Hacker insist that it is applied to judgeable contents, rather than to their linguistic or symbolic expressions; but Frege surely viewed it as applying to both. Thus in his letter to Russell of July 1902, having discussed the decomposition of two sentences, he added that 'to the decomposition of the sentence there corresponds a decomposition of the thought'. In his early writings, he expressed himself in both ways. In 'Booles rechnende Logik', he spoke of decomposing the judgeable content, as he also did in a single sentence in the Preface to *Begriffsschrift* (p. xiii). Even in §§9 and 10, where the process is explained in detail, he occasionally deviates into talking in terms of conceptual contents or ideas. Nevertheless, he there speaks so persistently in terms of *expressions*, and does so, in particular, in the four italicized formulations, that it is impossible to doubt this way of expressing himself to be deliberate. The first of the italicized formulations, for instance, runs:

> If in an expression, whose content need not be judgeable, a simple or complex sign occurs in one or more places, and we think of it as replaceable by another expression in all or some of these places, but always by the same one, we call the invariant part of the expression the function, and the replaceable part its argument.

It is stretching credulity to ask us to believe that he meant us to understand by this that we should think of an object as replaceable by another object in one or more of its occurrences within a conceptual content, judgeable or otherwise.

Baker and Hacker deliver a rebuke to Geach (p. 172 n.) for crediting Frege with 'the notion . . . of a function whose arguments and values are expressions': they insist that, on the contrary, Frege intended both function and argument to be taken as unjudgeable contents of different kinds, and the value as a judgeable content; he simply exhibited the typical mathematician's carelessness about use and mention. Although, indeed, he had not yet acquired that care in this regard on which he was later to be the first to insist, the fore-going quotation makes that quite implausible. Now, unfortunately for Baker and Hacker, *Begriffsschrift* is the only one of Frege's early writings (save for a passing reference to that work under example 19 of 'Booles rechnende Logik') in which he uses the term 'function' in this connection:[2] the place in which he talks of functions is therefore that in which the arguments and values, and indeed the function itself, are treated as being linguistic or symbolic expressions. Baker and Hacker thus have only the flimsiest case for attributing to him an interpretation of concepts as functions whose values are judgeable contents. This of course hangs together with the assimilation of sentences to names, for whose dating to the time of *Begriffsschrift* they have no better case: for a predicate literally represents a function from objects to objects only if a sentence resulting from it by inserting a name of an object in its argument-place is itself a name of an object.

---

[2] In their reply, 'Dummett's Dig', to the present review, Baker and Hacker noted one another (*Philosophical Quarterly*, 37 (1987), 88), in the lecture 'Anwendungen der Begriffsschrift' Frege gave in 1879 (*Sitzungsberichte der Jenaischen Gesellschaft für Medizin und Naturwissenschaft*, NS 6 (1879), 30).

In his early period, Frege undoubtedly recognized an analogy between functions and expressions for concepts (which, in *Begriffs-schrift*, he could hardly call 'predicates' after he had declared the subject/predicate distinction irrelevant to logic). It was not part of any systematic doctrine, however; it is scarcely mentioned save in *Begriffsschrift*. From the text of that work, there is no saying whether we are meant to take it as more than an analogy. It is pointless to subject the use of the word 'function' in *Begriffsschrift* to close scrutiny; it is far from certain that Frege himself had at that date yet attained his later clarity about the nature of functions in general. It would have been natural if Frege had also drawn an analogy between functions and concepts themselves; but there is no actual evidence that he did so. The principle of extracting concepts from judgements is indeed a definite doctrine, and appears in 'Booles rechnende Logik' as well as in *Grundlagen*: but in both these works it is stated without appeal to the notion of a function. Baker and Hacker have simply transposed to Frege's early period certain of his mature doctrines, modulated to suit the lack of the sense/reference distinction. The result is not a representation of Frege's thought, as it was at any stage, but a construct of the authors' own minds.

2. UNDERSTANDING

One of Baker and Hacker's main grounds for maintaining thesis (A) is their denial that Frege was concerned with the notion of understanding, at least until late in his life. They divide his career into two periods, before and after 1891: it would have been more natural to recognize three, allowing his recognition in 1906 of the failure of his logicist programme to count as a turning-point. In fact, they see his work from 1914 onwards as, in the present respect, different in character. He acquired at this time, they say, a new interest in the concept of understanding, and proposed 'to appeal to [his notion of the] senses of expressions in order to explain the understanding of sentences' (p. 382). To see his work before that date as intended to bear upon that concept is, however, a misinterpretation, according to them: on the contrary, 'he was not concerned with understanding or knowing meanings' (p. 288), but 'severed the internal connection between meaning and understanding' (p. 60).

It is difficult to make clear sense of this contention, let alone to reconcile it with the view, which they ascribe to Frege in his mature period (p. 247), 'that the business of logic is closely entwined with the analysis of [natural] language'. What is it to analyse a sentence of natural language, if not to explain how its composition serves to determine what thought it expresses? And is not the identification of that thought a major part of understanding the sentence? Is not the notion of sense, or at least of meaning, simply correlative to that of understanding? That is, is not understanding a sentence simply knowing, or grasping, its meaning, and is not its sense, in Frege's special use of the term, a major ingredient of its meaning?

The answers to these questions are not, indeed, quite straightforward. There are two correct points to be made apropos of them, and Baker and Hacker indeed make both. First, Frege 'regarded the task of clarifying the nature of understanding as belonging to the province of psychology, not of logic' (p. 376): for, as he confesses in a celebrated passage in his unpublished 'Logik' of 1897,[3] quoted by Baker and Hacker on p. 60, he is content to leave the act of grasping a thought mysterious, on the ground that 'just because it is mental in character, we do not need to trouble ourselves about it in logic'. This remark does not stand unqualified in the passage quoted, however; for he also says of this act that it 'cannot be completely understood from a purely psychological standpoint'. This might suggest that the remark of Baker and Hacker quoted above is not wholly correct. It is correct, however, when construed in a suitably restricted sense. The point is that, even if meaning is correlative to understanding, that need imply no more than that we have to explain meaning in order to explain understanding. We thereby explain what must be known or grasped if an expression is to be understood, but may leave aside the problem of accounting for the nature of that knowledge or the mental act of grasping. In the same way, what someone has to know in order to be able to play chess, namely, the rules of the game, may be stated without any enquiry into the character of his knowledge. Similarly, Frege did not propose to explain sense by explaining what constitutes an individual speaker's mastery of a language, or any aspect of it: he was concerned only with what it is that he grasps in virtue of that mastery.

---

[3] *Nachgelassene Schriften*, ed. H. Hermes, F. Kambartel, and F. Kaulbach (Hamburg, 1969), 157; *Posthumous Writings*, trans. P. Long and R. White (Oxford, 1979), 145.

Baker and Hacker's observation is thus true if construed to mean that Frege concerned himself with what is *understood*, as a matter for logic, but not with *understanding*, as a matter for psychology. But it is now unclear that he changed his mind on the matter in the last twelve years of his life. When he said that we understand sentences by understanding the words of which they are composed, did he mean this as a contribution to psychology? The observation is surely not so intended; it belongs to an account of *what* it is someone must know in order to grasp what thought a sentence expresses, namely, the senses of the constituent words and the manner of their combination, rather than to an explanation of the nature of that knowledge. If so, however, the present point tells not at all against Frege's having been interested in understanding before 1914 in just that way in which he was interested in it after that date: both before and after, what interested him was its content.

The second point, equally correct in itself, is that a 'judgeable-content is neither identical with, nor part of . . . the meaning of a sentence' and we must similarly 'sharply differentiate the later notion of the sense of a sentence from that of sentence-meaning' (p. 132): a judgeable content or a thought is a matter, not of the meaning of a (type-) sentence in the language (as someone learning the language might encounter it in an exercise), but 'of what someone meant by the utterance of a token of it' (p. 131). This phrase is itself ambiguous; but sense, for Frege, embodies only what bears on the truth or falsity of what is said, and not, for instance, on what relevance it was intended to have to what had gone before. Since a thought must always have an absolute truth-value, an indexical or demonstrative must have different senses in relevantly different contexts: none of these senses can therefore coincide with its (constant) meaning in the language. This does not show, however, that sense is not correlative to understanding, since the bifurcation of the notion of meaning, acknowledged by Baker and Hacker in the passage just quoted, affects that of understanding equally: understanding a (type-) sentence—knowing what the words mean—differs in just the same way from understanding what someone said on a particular occasion. In *The Varieties of Reference*, for instance, Gareth Evans concentrates on that notion of understanding what is said according to which one does not understand unless one knows enough to identify the references of the indexicals and demonstratives; and he quotes Moore as using the word 'understand' in the same manner. It is undoubtedly to understanding as so construed that Frege's notion of sense is correlative, rather than to a bare grasp of linguistic meanings.

Understanding, so construed, does not consist in merely knowing the meanings of the words in the language; as Baker and Hacker say (p. 279), 'to grasp a thought . . . is not to grasp the meaning of a type-sentence (though it may presuppose that)'. It does not in the least follow that it does not comprise it, as the authors themselves acknowledge in their parenthesis; it is in fact quite evident that it does. What is needed, to grasp the thought expressed by an utterance—to understand it in Moore's and Evans's sense—is to know the meanings of the words, to know the relevant constructions, and to apprehend in the appropriate way the reference of the indexicals and demonstratives; and Frege's whole use of the term 'sense' accords with this. It is certainly wrong to overlook the respects in which his notion of sense diverges from that of linguistic significance: but to exaggerate the divergence distorts Frege's thinking just as badly. When he has in mind neither indexicals nor indirect speech, he repeatedly speaks of the senses of words or of expressions quite independently of context, as a glance at, say, 'Über Sinn und Bedeutung' will confirm; indeed, the requirement on a language apt for deductive reasoning that every word should bear the same sense in all contexts suggests that the use of indexicals is an imperfection of natural language.

In any case, Baker and Hacker once more face a difficulty created by their having conceded that Frege became interested in understanding in his very late period. If by 'understanding' they mean what Moore and Evans do, there is no difference between this late period and that which began in 1891. If, on the other hand, they mean that Frege acquired a new interest in the knowledge of linguistic meaning, as manifested by the understanding of a type-sentence, there is nothing to be said in favour of such a contention. He indeed always had an interest in it, as the principal and often the only ingredient in a grasp of sense: but there is no change in this regard from the mature to the late period. In only one of the passages cited by Baker and Hacker on pp. 381–2 from Frege's late writings does he use the word 'understand': in the rest, he speaks, as he had always spoken, of grasping a thought. 'Der Gedanke' bears witness that he had not abandoned the principle that a thought is true or false absolutely; and this entails that the thought expressed by a sentence containing an indexical or demonstrative depends on the context of utterance. It follows that he retained exactly the same conception of grasping a thought as he had had in the 1890s, a conception that corresponds to one, but not, in general, to the other, sense of 'understanding'.

The two points here discussed thus wholly fail to establish Baker and Hacker's contention that Frege was uninterested in understanding before 1914: they point only to necessary glosses on the claim that he had a consistent interest in it. Those two points are not, indeed, the only ones on which they rely; but the others are exceedingly flimsy. They observe, for instance (p. 129), that sentences such as imperatives and optatives, which do not, for Frege, express thoughts, nevertheless have meanings. More to the point, it might be added, most of the words in them obviously bear the same senses as they do in assertoric sentences; but, though this is a severe difficulty for Frege's position, it is no ground for denying him an interest in meaning or understanding.

3. SEMANTIC THEORIES

A major pillar of thesis (A) is Baker and Hacker's claim that there are 'no grounds for asserting that [Frege] advanced . . . to any conception that the true business of logicians is a science of language (semantics) . . . The hypothesis that he intended to lay the foundations of logical semantics is implausible' (pp. 248–9). The word 'semantics' is used in several different ways, but the references to logic and logicians suggest that what they have in mind is a semantic theory for a formal language as conceived in contemporary model theory. If so, their assertion is very surprising, since part I of *Grundgesetze* appears to contain a semantic theory for the formal language, clearly separated from the account of its formation rules, axioms, and rules of inference: this theory is stated by stipulating what references the primitive symbols are to have, and laying down how the reference of a complex expression is determined from the references of its constituents. In addition, Frege gives a general framework for such a theory, namely, an account of the various possible logical types of expression, of their nature and how they are formed, and of what it is to assign a reference to an expression of any one such type; this is similarly clearly separated from the specific stipulations governing the primitive symbols of the system.

One reason why Baker and Hacker do not see the matter in this light is that they conflate a semantic theory with a semantic definition of logical consequence. They are quite right in saying that Frege lacked the latter notion. He lacked it because he did not operate with the conception of a range of possible interpretations of a formal language; a symptom of this is that, contrary to what Baker and Hacker say (pp. 112 and 205), he did not use free variables or schematic letters in his formalism: what look like them he officially interpreted as bound by tacit initial universal quantifiers. If, however, he had formed this conception, he would have had very little more work to do to arrive at the semantic notion of validity: for the background theory stated in part I of *Grundgesetze* would immediately have yielded a formulation of what, in general, any one such interpretation should consist in. It is precisely because of the presence of this background theory, and its close, though not complete, resemblance to the notion used by modern logicians of an interpretation of a formal language within classical two-valued semantics, that Frege's work can be fruitfully compared with that of later logicians.

4. REFERENCE

The foregoing claim that part I of *Grundgesetze* contains a semantic theory rests on the equation of Frege's notion of reference with that of semantic value, so that a stipulation of the references of expressions of a formal language constitutes an interpretation of it in the model-theoretic sense. A more profound reason for Baker and Hacker's denial of the claim lies in their summary rejection of this conception. In their sole allusion to it, they speak (p. 106) of the need that it should 'be supported by an argument showing that conceptual content can be equated with the "semantic value" assigned to symbols in the predicate calculus, not treated as a self-evident axiom in the interpretation of Frege's logic', and give a footnote reference to my book *Frege: Philosophy of Language*. The equation proposed was between semantic value and the later notion of reference, not the earlier notion of conceptual content; it was not assumed as an axiom, but argued for at some length, both in that book and in my later book *The Interpretation of Frege's Philosophy*. I am not alone in having argued for it: Ernst Tugendhat, who is not mentioned in *Frege: Logical Excavations*, has done so, too, in a well-known article. I have, indeed, contended that he erred by going too far in the opposite direction, ignoring the contribution, to Frege's complex notion of reference, of the name/bearer prototype. However this may be, the equation of reference with semantic value is the principal premiss for the claim that Frege propounded a semantic theory; and Baker and Hacker have no business to dismiss the claim without examining that premiss. Unless it lacks all prima-facie plausibility, no idea ought to be rejected out of hand, even if it has *not* been argued for; the grounds for it, even if not stated, may be evident and compelling.

The grounds for seeing Frege's notion of reference as corresponding to that of semantic value, as it figures in standard classical two-valued semantics for formal languages, are twofold. Anyone reading Frege for the first time will naturally take the notion of reference as modelled on the relation of name to bearer, since it is always as applied to proper names that it is first introduced. He will then be struck by the fact that Frege goes on to ask what constitutes the reference of a sentence and what that of a predicate or of a relational or functional expression, almost always without stopping to justify the assumption that such a thing is to be ascribed to an expression of any of these types at all. The assumption that there is anything to which a sentence or a predicate stands in a relation remotely analogous to that of a name to its bearer will seem at first sight absurd to him, and yet more puzzling Frege's apparent assurance that there is a unique correct way to draw the analogy. When Frege's work was as yet not widely known, it was, perhaps, excusable to stop at this point, condemning Frege for making a large, unjustified, and implausible assumption. At the present stage in the history of Frege exegesis, it is surely inexcusable: yet this is just what Baker and Hacker do. They treat the prima-facie absurdity as a conclusive refutation, saying that Frege 'offers no argument whatever for supposing that' a predicate 'stands for or designates any entity at all' and asking, 'Is not this (traditional) idea absurd?' (p. 257). (The parenthetical adjective imports a further error, since Frege's theory differs crucially from the doctrine of universals, which can serve both as subject and as predicate.) They go on to comment that 'to describe predicates as referring to concepts' obscures the 'fundamental distinction' between 'the role of referring', allocated to names, and 'that of predicating', allocated to predicates, and ask rhetorically how 'the sophistication of what predicates are supposed to stand for' can compensate for 'the gross crudity' of 'thinking that their logical significance should be explained solely in terms of what they stand for'. The single paragraph from which these remarks are taken forms their entire treatment of the ascription of reference to incomplete expressions. They indeed discuss the notion of a concept, and its identification as a function whose values are truth-values, at considerable length: but they say no more than has here been indicated about the thesis that a concept is the reference of a predicate. If there is crudity here, it lies in their imperceptive comments, not in Frege's theories.

Anyone not ready to dismiss Frege without further ado as in the grip of a crude Augustinian model of how language works will ask what understanding he had of the notion of reference that made it appear so obvious to him that expressions of quite different logical types all have a reference; and he will seek the answer by looking to the work Frege made the notion do. As soon as we make this enquiry, we find that it did for him the same work as that of semantic value. This results from the combination of three fundamental theses:

(1) the reference of a complex depends uniquely on the references of its constituents;
(2) if a part lacks reference, the whole lacks reference;
(3) the reference of a sentence is its truth-value.

Now the semantic role assigned to an expression by a semantic theory is that feature of it that goes to determine any sentence in which it occurs as true or otherwise; when this is taken to consist in the association of a suitable entity to the expression, that entity constitutes its semantic value. In the light of the foregoing theses concerning reference, it is apparent that Frege's notion of reference serves exactly the same purpose: an assignment of references to the constituent parts of a sentence displays how that sentence is determined as true or false in accordance with its composition. The reference of an expression is thus its semantic value according to the semantic theory propounded by Frege; for its having that reference constitutes that feature of it which goes to determine any sentence in which it occurs as true or as false. It is also plain why the denial of reference to any part of a sentence whose removal or replacement by another expression could affect whether the sentence was true or false is not a serious possibility, unless its presence has the effect of depriving the sentence of truth-value: otherwise, it must contribute in *some* way to determining the truth or falsity of the whole.

Frege remarked that it is just as bad to draw distinctions where none are needed as to fail to draw them when they are. In the same way, it is as bad to introduce technical notions that do no work as to omit to frame ones that are required. To understand a philosophical notion, we must therefore ask what work it does; the answer to this question, when it is asked about Frege's notion of reference, is that it does precisely the work of the notion of semantic value. Baker and Hacker's failure to ask this question leads them to miss the point of this whole ingredient of Frege's mature logical doctrine, and quite mistakenly to reiterate that he had no semantic theory and that the notions he used admit no fruitful comparison with those employed by modern logicians.

In what respects is the relation of name to bearer the prototype for Frege of the relation of reference? It is so, principally, in that, in introducing the notion of reference, he always begins with proper names; in doing so, he explains the reference of a name as what it designates, or as what we are thinking or talking about. If Frege had, at the outset, explained the notion of reference quite generally as semantic value, he would have had to *argue* that the reference of a proper name is its bearer; as it was, he took it for granted, because this was for him part of the very notion of reference. In fact, he did not explain reference as semantic value even at a later stage: this is what makes it natural to take him, at first reading, as generalizing the name/bearer relation from proper names to expressions of other kinds. It is only by reflection on the role which the notion plays in his theory, and, in particular, on the three theses concerning it enunciated above, that we can recognize that the role is precisely that of semantic value. Having recognized this, we can then see that the assignment of references to expressions other than proper names is governed by the need for them to fulfil this role, and not at all by appeal to an analogy with the name/bearer relation. Without an appreciation of this, it is impossible to understand Frege's theory of reference.

5. CONCEPTS

How, then, has it come about that Baker and Hacker have missed the point of Frege's theory of reference so widely and taken it as a mere generalization of the relation of name to bearer? It was said in the preceding section that the remarks embodying this misconception form their entire treatment of the ascription of reference to incomplete expressions; but this might be objected to as an illusion due to their unusual viewpoint: their treatment of it lies, it may be said, precisely in their extensive discussion of the notion of a concept. To understand this objection, a certain digression will be necessary.

What did Frege do when he introduced the sense/reference distinction into his logical theory? If we concentrate on proper names, in terms of which he first explains it, we shall give the wrong answer. In their case, he already considered the object named as the content of the expression naming it: so, concentrating on this case, we shall say that the innovation was the notion of sense, foreshadowed by the talk in *Begriffsschrift* of 'modes of determination' (*Bestimmungsweisen*). Frege indeed needed such a distinction for names: his explanation in *Begriffsschrift* of identity-statements is lame, and it is amazing that he could speak in *Grundlagen* of 'objective ideas' as divided into objects and concepts (§27, second footnote). We should not therefore exclude these as motivations for introducing the distinction; but to regard them as primary is to miss the point. It lay to hand to make some distinction between the meaning of a proper name and the object to which it referred, as Husserl did, at least when 'proper name' is understood in Frege's extended sense. What is important about Frege's notion of reference, however, is precisely that he applied it to expressions of all logical types.

At this point we must ask: Does the important innovation lie in the kinds of thing Frege took to be the references of the various types of expression? Or does it lie in his regarding them all as terms of a single relation of reference (more exactly, of a number of analogous relations)? We speak of *the* distinction between sense and reference, but in fact there are many distinctions: that between the sense of a name and an object, that between a thought and a truth-value, that between the sense of a predicate and a concept, and so on. Our question is then this. Suppose that Frege had made all these particular distinctions, but had not tied them together by describing objects, truth-values, concepts, etc., as all being the references of expressions of different types: would he have had essentially the same theory, or would the very core of it be lost?

Plainly, the very core would be lost. It would, indeed, be an overstatement to say that all the particular distinctions already existed: that the notion of an object was no new invention; that it did not need Frege to point out the difference between the thought expressed by a sentence and its truth or falsity; and that, equally, everyone was familiar with the distinction between the extension of a concept and the concept considered intensionally. Such an overstatement would ignore important innovations by Frege: his admission of abstract (*unwirkliche*) objects, including logical ones; the difference between truth-values considered as objects and the conventional notion of the properties of being true and of being false; and the unsaturated character of concepts. Important as these innovations are, however, their importance is subordinate: for there would be no point in these refinements or eccentricities (whichever they may be) save in the presence of a general doctrine concerning reference. A name cannot bear the very *same* relation to its bearer as does a predicate to the concept for which it stands: but the point lies in the analogy between those relations, an analogy encapsulated in general principles such as those enumerated in the preceding section. What counts as an object matters only if it is crucial to an account of what determines certain sentences as true or as false, and, in consequence, to an account of their senses; the unsaturated character of concepts matters only because it plays a role in explaining the unity of sentences and of thoughts; it would lack all significance to take truth-values to be objects if that did not carry with it taking concepts to be functions whose values they were.

As for the notion of sense, the innovation does not lie in the use of such a notion, since the intuitive conception of meaning is already present. It does not even lie in the differentiation between sense and tone, since that was present in the distinction between conceptual and non-conceptual content, or in that between sense and force, since that was present also. It lies, rather, in the fact that the notion of reference yields a general account of what the sense of an expression consists in, namely, in the way in which its reference is given.

Not to see reference as semantic value is merely to miss an important affinity between Frege's theories and the work of later logicians: to fail to see the notion as a theoretical one whose whole substance derives from the general theoretical principles that govern it is to misunderstand Frege altogether. If one sees it thus, one will acquiesce in Frege's admittedly eccentric terminology: his quasi-technical terms mean just what his theory entails that they mean, and nothing more. A concept, for instance, is merely a function from objects to truth-values, considered extensionally: its being called a 'concept' is no more than a historical accident. Frege had used the term, in his early period, as part of the accepted terminology which divided the subject-matter of logic into concepts, judgements, and inferences, itself an inheritance from Kant. In *Grundlagen* he had advanced part of the way towards his later notions, without being aware where he was heading, and so had used the word 'concept' sometimes for what he was afterwards to call the sense of a predicate, sometimes for its reference. Presumably because he had used it in the latter way in formulating several important theses, he reserved it exclusively for that use in his mature theory, greatly as that diverged from its traditional use in philosophy, let alone its non-philosophical uses.

These last observations may seem to labour the obvious. It is not obvious to Baker and Hacker, however; and this is not a minor oversight, but integral to their entire approach to Frege's theory of reference. They complain bitterly about the eccentricity of Frege's use, in his mature period, of the term 'concept', asking (p. 255) how 'Frege's definition of concepts as functions [can] be accepted as an analysis of our concept of a concept', denying that it clarifies 'the real nature of concepts', and objecting (p. 254) that 'concepts are objects of understanding, not what we speak *about* in typical assertions; they more closely resemble the senses of concept-words rather than the references'. At first sight, these are mere cavils at Frege's terminology; but Baker and Hacker do not so intend them. They are convinced that Frege suffered from 'philosophical schizo-phrenia' (p. 270). The task undertaken by one half of this split personality was precisely that of 'analyzing the notion of a concept which we already possess'. Since his theory is in fact 'at odds . . . with our conception of a concept', the other half views it as that of 'replacing our defective conception of a concept with something more adequate'. This, however, destroys the point of his use of the notion: 'both the interest and the intelligibility of his thesis that count-statements ascribe properties to concepts presupposes that we have a prior grasp of what concepts are'.

The reader may well regard these contentions as bizarre. It is true enough that we cannot understand the thesis that the content of a statement of number consists in predicating something of a concept unless we grasp what Frege means by 'concept': it does not follow that we must take him to be using the word for an object of the understanding. If he were, he would be saying that a statement of number, such as that Mars has two moons, is a conceptual observation; so preposterous an interpretation is excluded by his explanation, in §47 of *Grundlagen*, of the factual character of many statements predicating something of a concept. Admittedly, the notion of a concept here being employed was not made wholly clear, and probably was not wholly clear to Frege, until the mature writings: that is why Frege found it necessary to introduce the notion of reference in order to clarify it, and why we need to invoke that notion in order to elucidate it.

Baker and Hacker cannot take this route, however. It is agreed on all hands that, in Frege's mature theory, a concept is a function from objects to truth-values. The question at issue is the status, and thereby the substance, of this thesis. If it were a mere *definition* of the word 'concept', it would as yet have no substance; this would be a shallow interpretation, which Baker and Hacker rightly reject. On the view of Frege's theory of reference as a semantic theory—one explaining the determination of the truth-values of sentences in accordance with their composition—the thesis is to the effect that, in such a theory, the semantic value of a predicate should be taken to be such a function. Baker and Hacker, however, have denied that this conception provides a general rationale for the notion of reference: and they have no other general account of the notion to put in its place. They have, therefore, to explain the substance of the thesis in a different way: their unconvincing explanation is that Frege thought he could best elucidate our pre-existing notion of a concept in this manner.

The key sentence for an understanding of Baker and Hacker's view is: '[Frege] saw the sense/reference distinction as an adjunct of his redefinition of concepts and relations . . . not as the ultimate philosophical foundation of his logical system' (p. 237). They do not see the general notion of reference as having any importance: for them, the important change lay in what Frege now took concepts and relations to be. Objects were already in place; Frege's essential new idea was that concepts ought to be identified as functions from objects, not to judgeable contents, but to truth-values. This went along with construing sentences as names of truth-values rather than of judgeable contents, a step made possible only by classifying truth-values as objects. These steps taken, the theory had now to be supplemented with a notion of sense, on to which could be loaded all the tasks previously assigned to conceptual content but which truth-values and concepts as now conceived could obviously not perform (p. 279).

According to this view, Frege was not conferring a new use on the word 'concept': he already knew what he meant by it, but had, rather, formed a new belief about what concepts really are. Baker and Hacker have difficulty, however, in conveying in what they take his understanding of the word, constant from his early to his mature period, to consist. The suggestion that it consisted in simple fidelity to the standard use of the word is highly implausible; instead of withdrawing it, as they ought, they ascribe to Frege a schizophrenic vacillation between such fidelity and a desire to replace the standard notion by a 'more adequate' one. (As so often with their criticisms of Frege, the vacillation is all on their part.) This prompts the question 'More adequate for what purpose?' Frege must, when this half of his personality was dominant, have had some purpose in mind: the role that he intended the notion of a concept to play must have constituted his constant understanding of the word. To this question Baker and Hacker give no answer. The answer is not provided by the connection, which they emphasize (e.g. on pp. 271–2 and 283), between taking sentences as naming truth-values and taking concepts as functions whose values are truth-values. The latter follows from the former *if* concepts are functions at all: but since the former has no intrinsic plausibility, the whole doctrine is pointless unless concepts, so construed, serve the explanatory or theoretical purpose for which they are needed; and we still have not been told what that is. The same goes for Baker and Hacker's suggestion (p. 268) that, to accomplish a logical construction of arithmetic, Frege needed a *logical* connection between a concept and its extension. No such connection has been forged unless what is identified with the concept is plausibly so identified: to know whether it is nor not, we must, again, know what role the notion of a concept is to play.

There is no sensible answer to the question 'What are sentences names of?', taken in isolation, unless it be 'They are not names at all'. There is, equally, no sensible answer to the question 'What do predicates stand for?', taken in isolation, unless it be 'Only names stand for anything'. If Frege had been so foolish as to give answers

to these questions, taken in isolation—and a bizarre answer to the
first question, at that—he would deserve all Baker and Hacker's
strictures. In answering them, he was *not* taking them in isolation:
he was taking them in the context of a theory according to which
both questions asked after the objective feature of any expression
going to determine any sentence of which it is part as true or false.
Only by seeing this as the point of his notion of reference can we
understand his theory: only by considering a concept as the reference
of a predicate, where 'reference' is so understood, are we in a
position to enquire whether his account of what a concept is is the
correct one. Without this principle to guide us, we can only flounder,
as Baker and Hacker do; whether or not, like them, we then blame
our floundering on Frege is a matter of temperament.

6. NATURAL LANGUAGES AND FORMAL LANGUAGES

Baker and Hacker are wrong to deny that Frege had a semantic
theory for his formal language; was his theory intended to apply to
natural language? They are certain that Frege was not concerned, in
his early period, with the analysis of sentences, but only with that of
their contents: 'what is analyzed in logic', they say, 'are judgeable-
contents, not type-sentences or their meanings. Whether function/
argument analysis can be applied to sentences . . . is irrelevant for
whether it is the proper tool for analyzing judgements' (p. 144; see
also pp. 134–5 and 156–8). Concerning his mature period, however,
they become ambivalent. They describe him as having come to hold
'that the business of logic is closely entwined with the analysis of
language' (p. 247), acknowledge that the new conception of concepts
and relations 'is intertwined with a doctrine about the logical
analysis of atomic singular statements' (p. 238), and express shock
at his saying that no one who lays down logical rules can avoid
appealing to linguistic distinctions (p. 239). They describe his
application of the principle of logical analysis to 'the grammatical
structures of declarative sentences' (p. 247): whereas, according to
his early doctrine, 'the logical category of proper names cannot in
principle be isolated by any syntactic criteria' (p. 169), in his mature
period he 'advanced certain syntactic criteria for distinguishing
"proper names" from other expressions' (p. 250). It is difficult to see
in Frege's writings the evidence for any such abrupt volte-face; in
Grundlagen, syntactic criteria for identifying proper names are

freely used (§§38 and 57 in particular). In the end, Baker and
Hacker want to play down Frege's interest in natural language even
in his mature period. They deny that 'he advanced beyond the
commonplace idea of a rough correspondence between logic and
grammar' (p. 248); their final verdict is that 'his concern with
natural language . . . is incidental and at best indirect' (p. 398).

Baker and Hacker rightly emphasize the importance of Frege's
logical symbolism to his philosophy as a whole. In their view, it did
not serve to represent the structure of sentences of natural language
(p. 72), but, rather, 'revealed the *true* structures of thought' (p. 69).
Their defence of their failure to mention Frege's formulations
concerning sense and reference in part I of *Grundgesetze* therefore
comes as a surprise to the reader. It occurs in a passage denying that
Frege proposed a truth-conditional account of sense: and the omission
requires defence, since that part of *Grundgesetze* contains Frege's
full-dress formulation of his theory of logic, a definitive statement
set out with a minimum of justification but a maximum of exactitude.
The defence is that, although this was indeed 'Frege's sole explanation
of sense in terms of "truth-conditions" ', it 'is explicitly concerned
only with well-formed formulae' of his formal system (p. 375). What
if it were? If the logical system represents the structure of thought,
we should have a truth-conditional account, if not of linguistic
meaning, then at least of thought; and this, on Baker and Hacker's
own account, would be central to Frege's interests.

The reader of *Frege: Logical Excavations* cannot take for granted
that he is in accord with its authors about the aim of a system of
formal logic, for it is very unclear what they take that aim to be. The
aim they ascribe to Frege, of representing the structure of thoughts,
is also unclear, since, although they use the phrase incessantly, they
never stop to enquire after the application of this metaphor. This
precludes them from enquiring, either, into the general relation
between the structure of a thought and that of a formula or sentence
that expresses it. Their sole observation on this point is a blatant
non sequitur. They infer that 'there is no logical necessity that the
structure of a thought be reflected in the structure of a sentence
expressing it' (p. 66) from Frege's thesis that a thought might be
grasped (though not by us) without being clothed in words or signs:
this is like arguing that, since not everyone has been photographed,
a portrait need not resemble the sitter.

Baker and Hacker are right, as I now think, not to *presume*, as I did in *Frege: Philosophy of Language*, that the analysis of language was one of Frege's prime concerns, but to go into the complex matter of his attitude to language, which they do in ch. 3 and §5 of ch. 9; but because they ask none of the fundamental questions just listed, they fall into confusion in doing so, and, as so often, attribute the confusion to Frege. It requires philosophical elucidation what it is to think *in* a language, they say (p. 66); 'Frege provided *none*.' He left it a mystery how we apprehend the structure of thoughts (p. 75); he gave no criterion for judging when the structure of a sentence is, and when it is not, a clue to this (p. 74), a quandary which rendered him 'schizophrenic' (p. 260). His later advocacy of 'the doctrine that' his symbolic 'formulae . . . mirror the grammatical structures of declarative sentences' (p. 261) they explain as required in order to show his formal theory to be a *logic*; but they comment that nothing within the theory 'hangs on the doctrine', adding that 'his demonstration of the logicist thesis' does not, 'of course, . . . in any way' depend on it. What is necessary to show the theory to which Frege claimed to have reduced arithmetic to be a logical theory is surely essential to his demonstration of logicism; nevertheless, Baker and Hacker are confident that they have provided 'insuperable obstacles' (p. 66) to regarding Frege as having contributed to the philosophy of language.

7. SENSE AND TRUTH-CONDITIONS

One of the root causes of this series of errors is Baker and Hacker's failure to grasp Frege's theory of sense. Their argument, in §§1 and 2 of the last chapter, against ascribing to him a truth-conditional theory of sense is rendered farcical by their admitted failure to understand what, in general, such a theory may be. Any general explanation of the notion of a truth-conditional theory makes it vacuous, they claim (p. 378); their remedy is to identify such a theory with the specific theory advanced by Wittgenstein in the *Tractatus*. They then have no difficulty in pointing out differences between this theory and Frege's. In a passage containing no fewer than twenty-one footnote references to me, they might have noticed that, in *Frege: Philosophy of Language*, I was at pains to point out, more than once, the differences between Frege's theory and Wittgenstein's (pp. 246–7, 323–7, 590, 633, 636, 680, 682). Had they done so, they might have been deterred from inferring that

Frege lacked 'the modern conception of a theory of meaning' based on truth-conditions (p. 377) and that 'the concept of truth-conditions is altogether alien to' him (p. 354).

The notion of a truth-conditional theory of sense is not in the least vacuous. Such a theory must have two essential features. First, the theory of sense must rest upon a theory of semantic value as a base; and, secondly, the semantic value of a sentence must be taken as consisting in its being true or being false. Many semantic theories fail this second condition, employing, for instance, truth-values relativized to possible worlds or to times; Heyting's theory for intuitionistic mathematics is an extreme example, repudiating as it does the assumption that every sentence is determinately either true or not true. In Frege's system (not, of course, in Wittgenstein's) the theory of *Bedeutung* constitutes the semantic theory, and fulfils the second condition. Since sense is explained as the way the reference is given—namely, to one who understands the expression, in virtue of his understanding—it fulfils the first condition also. Although, so far as I know, *Grundgesetze*, vol. i, §32 is the only passage in which Frege uses the word 'condition', the very same conception is expounded by him in numerous places. To grasp the thought expressed by a sentence is to have a particular way of conceiving of the references of its constituents. For those of them which are functional expressions, this will involve a grasp of how the reference of each complex within the sentence, including the sentence itself, is determined by the references of its parts; and so the grasp of the thought will consist in a particular way of conceiving that which determines it as true or as false.

This theory leaves much concerning our grasp of sense to be explained; but it is foolish to carp at this, since it gave the first plausible account in the history of philosophy of what it is to grasp a thought or to understand a sentence as expressing one. It is absurd to complain that Frege failed to elucidate the notion of thinking in a language. His account of sense does precisely this; or, at least, it does so provided that we can supplement it by an explanation of what it is to treat a sentence as being determined as true in a certain way. Here we should note a bias towards an explanation of thought by way of explaining an expression of it not acknowledged by Frege. Frege held that it is the thought that is primarily said to be true or false, the sentence being called true or false only in a derivative sense; and this means that it is the sense of the sentence that primarily has the reference, and the sentence only derivatively. Frege generalized this to all expressions: for instance, it is the sense of a proper name that primarily refers to the object.

In practice, however, he never conformed to this order of priority when expounding the sense/reference distinction. He never first introduces the notion of sense, subsequently explaining that of reference as a feature of the sense: he speaks first of the *expression* as having reference, and proceeds to argue that it also has a sense or to say in what its sense consists. This order of exposition is demanded by the conception of sense as the way the reference is given: it follows from this conception that the notion of sense cannot be explained save by appeal to that of reference, and so we must first have the latter notion. If we have the notion of reference in advance of that of sense, we cannot have it as a property of the sense, but only of the expression: the thesis that it is the sense to which reference is primarily to be ascribed is therefore incorrect. This comes out clearly in part I of *Grundgesetze*. The stipulations that determine under what condition each formula has the value *true* lay down what the *reference* of each expression is to be. Sense has yet to be mentioned: so, if we could understand what it was for an expression to have a reference only in terms of the possession by its sense of a corresponding property, those stipulations ought to be unintelligible. On the contrary, it is by invoking those stipulations that Frege explains in what the sense of each expression consists: to grasp how its reference is to be determined is to grasp its sense.

Frege believed it possible in principle to grasp a thought otherwise than as expressed linguistically; but his account of sense does not show how that is possible. It leaves it obscure how a sense can be grasped otherwise than as the sense *of* something to which reference can be ascribed; it explains nothing to say that the reference might be ascribed directly to the sense, since we must know what it is to ascribe reference before we can recognize it as a sense. This is one instance of several in which the inner dynamic of Frege's thinking drove in a linguistic direction to a greater extent than even he was aware.

8. LANGUAGE AND EXPRESSION

The metaphor used in speaking of the structure of a thought relates to what is essentially involved in grasping it. This idea has an obvious intuitive force: to grasp the thought that 239 is prime requires possession of the concept of a prime number; to grasp the thought that Phobos is a satellite of Mars requires a conception of one body's being a satellite of another. Now the complexity of a sentence obviously plays a part in our identification of the thought thereby conveyed; but this is not enough to qualify it as *expressing* the thought. If I speak of the weakest additional premiss needed to make a certain inference valid, I thereby pick out a unique thought, but I do not express it, because you can understand my words without grasping the thought. Only when understanding the form of words used requires a grasp of what belongs to the structure of the thought do those words express the thought: only so do those words do more than enable the hearer to identify the thought, namely, communicate the thought to him. It follows that the expression of a thought can only be by reflection of its structure. It is this which distinguishes a *language*, in the wider sense in which we speak of formal languages and programming languages as well as of natural languages, from a code.

Frege obviously took natural languages to be languages in this sense; that is why he held the structure of a sentence to correspond, by and large, to the structure of the thought it expresses. It is therefore quite wrong to say, with Baker and Hacker, that there is, on Frege's view, no necessity why a sentence should reflect the structure of the thought: that is essential to its being an *expression* of the thought. This follows from the fact that, in so far as we have from Frege an explanation of what it is to grasp a thought, it is the *same* explanation as that given for recognizing the thought expressed by a sentence, stripped of the reference to linguistic items: to grasp a thought is to have a particular way of conceiving what determines it as true, just as to grasp the thought expressed by a sentence is to have a particular way of conceiving what determines the sentence as true. Frege of course held that sentences of natural language serve other purposes than the expression of thoughts: certain features of their structure relate to these other purposes. It is a further mistake to suppose that Frege had no principle to guide him in distinguishing those features which reflect the structure of the thought from those that do not. Given his (truth-conditional) theory of sense, the principle is evident. We have to subject the sentence to logical analysis, that is, to arrive at a semantic account of it. A semantic account will explain the manner in which the sentence is determined as true or false in accordance with its composition, and, in doing so, will respect the roles played by its constituents in other sentences. Such an account, if successful, reveals which features of the sentence are essential to the expression of the thought, and thereby makes apparent the structure of the thought itself.

Not only are natural languages languages in the sense explained; Frege considered his formal language to be one in the same sense. That was why he claimed for it the status of a *lingua characterica*.[4] It could be used as a *calculus ratiocinator*, like Boole's, to give a partial representation of the structure of the thoughts involved in some particular inference, with a different coding for each instance: but it was intended as a language in which thoughts could be fully expressed and deductive reasoning carried on. Not only that, but it was an approximation to a logically perfect language, its formulas serving no purpose but to express thoughts and judgements, their structure perspicuously displaying the structure of the thoughts and devoid of the defects which make natural languages imperfect instruments.

The opposition which Baker and Hacker set up between representing the structure of thoughts and representing that of ordinary sentences is thus a false one. Because both sentences of natural language and the formulas of Frege's symbolism express thoughts, they reflect their structure; for this reason, a formula cannot but reflect, in a perspicuous manner, those features of the structure of the corresponding sentence essential to the expression of the thought. Frege was neither schizophrenic nor even in a quandary.

9. LOGIC

It is difficult to discover from *Frege: Logical Excavations* that Frege made any contribution to philosophy whatever. This may seem hard to maintain for the inventor of quantificational logic; but Baker and Hacker consider that 'a formal calculus is of very limited philosophical significance and has limited philosophical use' (p. 392). It is very obscure what use they think it has at all. They use the phrase 'logical analysis', but manifest no awareness of what such an analysis may

---

[4] See 'Booles rechnende Logik', in *Nachgelassene Schriften*, 9, 10, 13; *Posthumous Writings*, 9, 10, 13. On th ephrase '*lingua characterica*', see the editors' note 2 on p. 9 of *Nachgelassene Schriften*, omitted from *Posthumous Writings*.

be. This is well illustrated by their shallow criticisms of Frege's analyses. 'Would anybody infer from the fact that "All mammals are red-blooded" is synonymous with "If anything is a mammal, it is red-blooded" that "mammals" in the first sentence functions grammatically as a predicate?', they ask (p. 256). Even when 'grammatically' is replaced by 'logically', no one has made that inference from the mere synonymy of the sentences: it depends on the direction of explanation. In asking their rhetorical question, they simply ignore the difficulty of treating a plural subject as functioning analogously to a singular term, namely, as standing for a compound object or aggregate. Frege's remarks, in a number of places, concerning the notion of an aggregate provide strong grounds for believing a semantic account along such lines to be impossible. He argues that we need to substitute for the notion of an aggregate that of a concept. To make this substitution just *is* to interpret the plural subject-term as functioning as a predicate, and hence to explain the first sentence as equivalent to the second, in which it overtly so figures. Baker and Hacker are not offering an alternative semantic treatment: it seems, rather, that it is because they not only feel no need for one, but fail to grasp why anyone should feel that need, or perhaps what it is a need for, that they miss the point so completely.

Clinching evidence of their failure to understand the task undertaken by logicians, or to grasp semantic notions, is provided by their summation of their subject's achievement in this field. 'Frege's concept-script', they say, 'is simply an alternative form of representation to natural language. It allows us to present certain inferences in a manner more readily surveyable and more mechanically checkable than their normal representation in ordinary language' (p. 389). It does far more, of course: its syntax is apparent from the surface form of its formulas, and, on the basis of that syntax, we can construct a semantic theory for it in a very direct manner. Natural languages lack this merit. Having paid their subdued tribute to Frege's logical symbolism, Baker and Hacker go on to discuss its defects, and list six features of natural language which they claim to be logically significant but to be unrepresentable in quantificational logic. Since they forswear advocating the abandonment of that logic (p. 390), the exercise is pointless, since the need either to modify or to supplement a logical theory does not show its invention not to have been a great step forward. The list would have a point if they supposed that, while *some* inferences are best surveyed when expressed in logical symbolism, for others natural language is more suited. If they think this, they are mistaken, because they lack the right idea of what it is to 'survey' inferences: I greatly doubt that there are any inferences not representable in quantificational logic but of which we can give a satisfactory semantic account when they are expressed in some fragment of natural language. Baker and Hacker proclaim the need to 'clarify the structures of [our] concepts' (p. 391), but do not believe that a logician's analysis of inferences involving them will contribute to such clarification; their scepticism is surely due, once more, to their not understanding what logicians aim to do. This emerges again in their attack on Davidson's theory of action sentences as 'ludicrous'. The inferences with which he was concerned involve no unclarity, they say, but 'are transparently valid'; they therefore 'set a problem *for the predicate calculus*' (ibid.). The problem whether those inferences are representable in quantificational logic is important, and will not be solved by sneers; but Baker and Hacker's principal mistake is to think it the *only* problem. As with any inferences tackled by formal logic, we need a plausible semantic account of the sentences involved, whether by appeal to existing formalism or otherwise. From such an account, the validity of the inferences must follow. Baker and Hacker appear to have missed the point of this requirement, which, in ordinary cases, is to test the adequacy of the semantics, not to vindicate the inferences; in such cases, the logician is taking their 'transparent validity' as a *datum*. Misunderstanding the nature of formal logic has led, in *Frege: Logical Excavations*, to much misunderstanding of Frege.

10. CONTINGENCY

Most of the foregoing relates to Baker and Hacker's thesis (A), that Frege's work has no interesting connections with that of subsequent philosophers and logicians; I come now to thesis (B), that it is inconsistent and confused. It will be recalled that Baker and Hacker see as a major motivation for introducing the sense/reference distinction that Frege wanted to guarantee the logical character of class abstraction—the step from a concept to its extension. They interpret this as meaning that 'the extension of these concepts must be determined by logical considerations alone', that 'the extension of the concept . . . can be calculated *a priori* from the concept' (p. 268), and contrast this with the 'commonly held' view that 'which objects . . . fall under the concept . . . can be determined only by observation and not by close inspection of the concept' (p. 269). Hence 'the proof that arithmetic is a branch of logic requires . . . an internal, *a priori* connection between concepts and their extensions which is at odds . . . with our conception of a concept' (p. 270).

This stems, in part, from Baker and Hacker's conviction, already noted, that Frege aimed to capture, by his use of the word 'concept', our ordinary conception of a concept; but more than this has gone awry. There is indeed a sense in which it is a truism that, under Frege's mature use of 'concept', 'whether or not a given object falls under' a concept is 'built into the identity of the concept' (p. 270). In the same sense, 'it is an intrinsic feature of a function that it takes a particular value . . . for a given argument' (p. 252); and we may read the statement that 'according to his account of concepts as functions, the relation between an object and a concept under which it falls . . . is always an *internal* relation' (ibid.) in the same sense. For concepts and functions, on Frege's mature doctrine, are purely extensional, and hence are *constituted* by what objects fall under them and what value they take for each argument. But talk of an a priori connection, and opposing this to determining by observation which objects fall under a concept, are quite out of place. The means of determining whether an object falls under a concept relate to the way in which the concept, and the object, too, are *given*, and thus to the *senses* of the predicate and the proper name, not their references, namely, the concept and the object in themselves. Similarly, if we use the term 'a priori' (which Frege did not in his mature period), we must apply it to *thoughts*: there are, for Frege, no facts in the realm of reference, and the value *true*, in itself, is neither a priori nor a posteriori. It is therefore both irrelevant and gratuitous for Baker and Hacker to say that 'in his view, it is unintelligible to hold that the value of a well-defined function may depend on observation or experiment' (p. 244 n.) and that 'it is of the essence of a *function* that it be possible to *calculate* its value for any given argument' (p. 312): irrelevant, because discovering what the value is can only be relative to some way in which the function is given, i.e. to the sense of a functional expression; and gratuitous, because there is no hint of any such doctrine in Frege. (In *Grundlagen*, §47, he makes it plain that a statement about a concept can have an empirical content.) The confusion is compounded by Baker and Hacker's attributing a different doctrine to Frege in his early period, when his conception of a function demanded that 'we admit observation and experiment as legitimate procedures, in addition to calculation, for determining the values of functions' (p. 146). In that period, according to them, a concept was on Frege's view a function from objects to judgeable contents, and truth-values were extrinsic to judgeable contents. Since it can hardly be that observation or experiment is needed to discover the content of a sentence, given the object referred to, the remark must refer to functions whose values are ordinary objects. Since the content of '3' or of 'Denmark' is an object, and that of '3!' or 'the capital of Denmark' another object, on Baker and Hacker's systematization of Frege's sloppy use of 'content', there would seem to be no room for any difference between Frege's conception of such functions in the two periods; the alleged difference about observation and calculation is therefore mysterious.

These are not occasional infelicities of expression; they occur repeatedly in part 2 of *Frege: Logical Excavations* and represent Baker and Hacker's deepest objection to Frege's mature doctrine of concepts, an objection resting on a thoroughgoing confusion between sense and reference. They appear to believe that Frege abolished contingency. On p. 252 they say that Frege's 'conception of concepts conflicts with the . . . common conception [which] admits the possibility that an invariant concept might have different extensions in different possible worlds'; on p. 289 that 'there is no evidence that he thought that *a posteriori* identities were contingent'; and on p. 312 they come right out and assert that 'the route from sense to reference must be independent of matters of fact'. No contrary interpretation has any 'direct warrant in [Frege's] texts', they declare (p. 313 n.). Since 'the connection between sense and reference must be internal', and since 'the truth-value of a sentence must be determined alone by the argument and function . . . (i.e. independently of matters of fact)', 'it is futile . . . to seek to broaden his account into a viable semantic theory' (p. 338). Seldom can so spirited an attack on a great philosopher have failed so dismally through such clouded perception of his doctrines.

11. SENSES AND FUNCTIONS

Given only the value of a function for some argument, it is not possible to recover the function or the argument. For this reason, it is inappropriate to regard either the argument or the function as a *constituent* or *part* of the value, since we naturally suppose that anything is uniquely analysable into its ultimate constituents, and that the parts of a thing may be discerned by scrutiny of it. According to Frege, the term '4!', whose reference is 24, is made up out of the 'proper name' '4', whose reference is 4, and the incomplete or unsaturated functional expression 'ξ!', whose reference is the factorial function. To say that the reference of the part is part of the reference of the whole would therefore be wrong, or at best utterly misleading, in such a case. The case is, however, typical. We should, accordingly, *never* say that the reference of the part is part of the reference of the whole; and Frege, despite an initial wobble in 'Über Sinn und Bedeutung', came expressly to deny this. The model of function and value conflicts with that of part and whole.

The expression '4!' represents 24 as the value of the factorial function for the argument 4: but we cannot explain the structure of the representation itself simply by appeal to the model of function and argument. Even if we can already identify the expression '4!', we cannot explain how it is made up out of its parts by saying that it is the value of a function that maps '4' on to '4!', for there are many such functions. To talk about expressions and their structure, we need the notions of part and whole, not those of function and value. For similar reasons, the *senses* of complex expressions cannot be explained in terms of function and value, either. Given the thought expressed by the sentence 'The earth spins', we cannot explain the sense of the predicate 'ξ spins' as that function which carries the sense of the name 'the earth' into that thought, for there is no unique such function; moreover, we must already know the sense of the predicate in order to grasp the thought, whereas we must be able to identify the value of a function in advance of knowing that it is the value of that function. The relation of the senses of the constituents to the sense of the sentence must also be construed on the model of part and whole, not that of function and value. That is precisely what Frege did: he consistently held that the sense of a part is part of the sense of the whole.

I argued on these grounds in *Frege: Philosophy of Language* that the sense of an incomplete expression is not to be understood as itself being a function. Baker and Hacker are highly conscious of the point, and make it repeatedly; but they deny that Frege saw it. That is, they agree with me that Frege regarded the sense of a predicate as part of the sense of a sentence containing it; but they also agree with those I was arguing against, that the sense of the predicate is a function whose value is the sense of the sentence: what they deny that Frege saw is the incompatibility of the two models. Given their mistaken view that, in his early period, Frege regarded concepts as functions whose values are judgeable contents, they have a case in respect of the early doctrine. One would naturally think that the sense/reference distinction resolved the tension: the reference of a predicate could now be taken to be a function, and the truth-value of the sentence as its value, while its sense could be taken as a part of the thought expressed by the sentence. Baker and Hacker deny this: allowing that Frege could now independently specify the value of a concept for an object as argument, namely, as one of the two truth-values, they allege that 'curiously enough, the same muddle is immediately reintroduced at the level of *thoughts*, conceived as the values of sense-functions' (p. 281).

Those, like Geach, who have contended that the senses of predicates should be taken as functions from the senses of names to thoughts, and that Frege's talk of them as parts of thoughts 'should be charitably expounded, not imitated', have had a reason; in fact, two. The first is Frege's insistence that the senses of incomplete expressions are themselves incomplete. Baker and Hacker offer the same ground: 'to describe the sense of a . . . predicate as unsaturated is to classify this entity as a function' (p. 323). Frege is indeed at fault for never having explained the mode of incompleteness of senses, and perhaps for not having given his mind to it. Nothing inhibits us from saying, however, that the incompleteness of the sense of a functional expression consists, not in its being a function, but in its being a way of conceiving of a function, the way a function is given to us. With this, the whole of this allegedly unresolvable tension in Frege's mature doctrine is resolved; or, rather, it would be, but for the second reason for regarding incomplete senses as functions.

Baker and Hacker contend (pp. 301–7) that the only way to understand Frege's account of sense as 'mode of presentation' is in terms of the presentation of an object or a truth-value as the value of some function: 'two expressions have the same sense only if they indicate an entity as the value of the same function for the same argument' (p. 305). They charge that the impossibility of explaining the senses of 'simple expressions, whether proper names or concept-words', in this way 'is an absolute gap in Frege's discussion of sense' (p. 307). Indeed, 'there is no such thing as a mode of presentation associated with a simple name' (p. 308). This yields another ground for holding that 'a thought is literally the value of a function (one thought-constituent) for an argument (another thought-constituent)' (p. 324), i.e. that the senses of predicates and functional expressions are themselves functions. For complex expressions, the reply is as before: the sense of an incomplete expression is not a function, but a 'mode of presentation' of the function which is its reference. For *simple* predicates and functional expressions, however, Baker and Hacker could not entertain this reply, since they admit no mode of presentation embodied in a simple expression: for simple expressions, sense cannot in their view be distinguished from reference (cf. p. 319). All this provides a *reductio ad absurdum*, not of Frege's theory of sense, but of Baker and Hacker's interpretation of it: even if we were forced to conclude that no two expressions incapable of verbal explanation could have distinct senses but the same reference, it would be absurd to *identify* their senses with their references.

12. ALTERNATIVE ANALYSES

We expect an analysis of something into its ultimate constituents to be unique, and Frege's use of the part/whole metaphor indeed suggests that. The possibility of alternative ways of analysing a single thought, asserted by Frege, therefore creates a difficulty both for the part/whole metaphor and for the exegesis of Frege. Geach very aptly quoted Ramsey apropos of the first difficulty, with no reference on Ramsey's part to Frege; Geach's solution was to replace the part/whole model by that of function and argument, under which there is no problem about multiple representations of a thought as the value of various functions for various arguments. Baker and Hacker press these points repeatedly against Frege; according to them, the tension threatens the integrity of his formal symbolism, since it is supposed to represent the structure of thoughts. On the one hand, 'the possibility of essentially independent representations of a single judgeable-content is not available in concept-script' (p. 152), because the formula must display the *whole* structure of the content; on the other, it is 'in principle impossible that a sentence expressing a judgeable-content should have a unique translation into concept-script' (p. 174). The sense of a complex expression depends on how it presents its referent as the value of a function: but since we may analyse it as doing so in a variety of ways, we are forced to the 'conclusion that there is no such thing as *the* sense of any complex expression' (p. 310; cf. pp. 317–18).

The difficulty can only be resolved, I believe, by distinguishing the two processes which, in *The Interpretation of Frege's Philosophy*, I called analysis and decomposition (having referred to them in *Frege: Philosophy of Language* merely as two sorts of analysis). The distinction was not expressly drawn by Frege, but is, in my view, implicit in his writings. Baker and Hacker think it worthwhile to claim, in two separate footnotes (pp. 158 and 163) that I addressed myself to the question in response to their 'harping' on it in a seminar of theirs which I attended. This is not so. In *The Interpretation of Frege's Philosophy* I was responding principally to Geach's observations; and I was in any case only spelling out more fully a distinction already drawn in *Frege: Philosophy of Language*, as I recall Gareth Evans pointing out to Baker and Hacker in the seminar. Unfortunately, they appear not to have understood it yet: they interpret it as the distinction between a complete and an incomplete analysis, whereas, for me, analysis and decomposition are quite different processes.

The process of decomposition is that described, in rather loose language, in *Begriffsschrift* and in 'Booles rechnende Logik'. Stated as applied to sentences or formulas, it consists in regarding an expression, or each of two expressions, as replaceable in all or some of its occurrences by some other expression of the same type: the incomplete expression thought of as extracted from the sentence by this process is the part of the sentence invariant under such replacements. As Baker and Hacker correctly observe, this process was characterized by Frege as one of concept-*formation*: it is a way of arriving at a *new* concept. In order to engage in this process, we must therefore already grasp the judgeable content or thought being decomposed, or expressed by the sentence being decomposed. We must in fact do more: if, for example, the expression imagined as replaceable was a proper name, we must know how to determine, from the sense of any proper name, the thought expressed by a sentence in which that proper name is inserted into the argument-place of the newly formed predicate. Just because we must grasp the judgeable content or thought before decomposing it, the concept attained by decomposition, or the sense of the new predicate, is not to be taken as intrinsic to the content or thought: that is why Frege says in *Begriffsschrift* that it is a matter of how we choose to regard the judgeable content. Thus, in order to grasp the thought expressed by '$17 > 1$ & $\forall n \, (n | 17 \Rightarrow n = 17 \lor n = 1)$', it is as unnecessary to conceive of it as made up out of '17' and the predicate that results from removing all three occurrences of that numeral as it is to conceive of it as made up out of '1' and the predicate formed by removing both of *its* occurrences. Since the newly attained concept—here that of primality—is not a constituent of the content, the possibility of distinct decompositions of the same content poses no problem.

The main point of decomposition lies in the fact that the newly formed predicate *is* a genuine constituent of other sentences, namely, quantified ones, as Frege also points out in *Begriffsschrift*. Since it is, we must ascribe a sense to it; and there is nothing to hinder us from regarding *its* sense as a function from senses of names to thoughts, since it will never be a constituent of a thought which is one of its values; it is only the sense of a simple predicate that we cannot consistently regard as such a function. Decomposition is not a reiterable process: it can be used only to yield an incomplete expression, since complete ones—sentences and proper names—do not need to be extracted from more complex ones; and it can be applied only to a complete expression. For this reason, we never have occasion to consider expressions for functions whose values are themselves functions or concepts. A function, for Frege, must always have objects as values, a principle missed by Baker and Hacker, who twice envisage functions having functions or concepts as values (p. 237, under (ii) and p. 267, under (vii)), and even ascribe recognition of such a function to Frege.

Analysis, on the other hand, takes place in stages, because the sentence, or the judgeable content or thought, is to be viewed as having been formed by successive operations. The purpose of analysing a sentence is to display that structure essential to its expressing the thought, and thus the structure of the thought expressed. The analysis of any part of the sentence displays those of its constituents a grasp of whose sense is required for a grasp of the sense of that part. The process is trivial for a logical formula, which is designed to display its essential structure on its surface. For a sentence of natural language, on the other hand, analysis in this sense is the syntactic part of logical analysis: it consists in finding a representation of the structure of the sentence that will serve as a basis for a correct semantic account.

Complex predicates can be constituents of sentences, though not of those from which they can be extracted by decomposition, if the word 'constituent' is reserved for what is encountered in the course of analysis; but it is only the senses of simple predicates and other simple incomplete expressions which cannot be characterized as functions. The complete analysis of any sentence or thought into its ultimate constituents is indeed unique; in my terminology, there are only alternative decompositions. The distinction completely resolves the difficulties laboured by Baker and Hacker. Frege's doctrines can hardly be interpreted save in the light of it; in its light, all becomes clear. This is not to claim that Frege was always fully conscious of the distinction: if he had been, he would have stuck to his conception of *fruitful* definitions, as expounded in *Grundlagen*, §88, instead of maintaining that definitions are in principle dispensable and leave the content unchanged. The thought that 17 is a prime number has the concept of primality—the sense of 'ξ is prime'—as a constituent, whereas the thought expressed by the complex sentence which is its definitional equivalent does not, though we can attain the concept by viewing the latter sentence in a particular way, that is, by effecting an appropriate decomposition of it. Here there is genuinely a tension between what Frege says in different places; but not one capable of bringing his entire system tumbling headlong in ruins, as Baker and Hacker so desperately wish to believe it does.

13. A STRAIGHTFORWARD AND COMPELLING ARGUMENT

Baker and Hacker present a train of reasoning they call 'straightforward and compelling' (p. 174). Given 'a judgeable content expressed by the formula "$\Phi(A)$"', they argue that 'nothing could prevent our introducing a concept Φ' by the . . . stipulation' that Φ' is to agree with Φ save on a pair of objects B and Γ distinct from A, that $\Phi'(B) = \Phi(\Gamma)$ and that $\Phi'(\Gamma) = \Phi(B)$. Baker and Hacker conclude that 'the object and the judgeable content fail to determine the remaining "constituent" . . ., viz. the concept'; the ideal of a unique canonical symbolic representation of any judgeable content is thereby rendered incoherent.

The consequence, if genuine, would indeed be 'dramatic', as they claim; for it would overthrow the whole principle of concept-formation by decomposition. The fallacy in the argument is very simple to detect, however: it lies in the assumption that every function from objects to judgeable contents is a concept. Let us assume that decomposition is applied directly to judgeable contents, and consider how we arrived at the concept Φ, and so at the representation $\Phi(A)$, in the first place. Suppose we did so by decomposition of the judgeable content, which we may call 'P'. We had, then, to apprehend P, not just as a whole, but as having the object A as a part. A may in fact have been a part several times over, that is, have had several 'occurrences' within P. We selected certain of these, and then imagined A as replaceable, in each of them, by any one of a range of other objects, B, Γ, and so on; we had, for this purpose, to grasp what judgeable content would result from each of these replacements. By this means, we obtained the concept Φ as a function mapping each object on to the judgeable content resulting from the replacement of A by that object. (I am not endorsing this account, but simply applying Frege's account of decomposition to Baker and Hacker's systematization of his doctrine of content.)

Given that, for each replacement, a determinate content results, this process uniquely determines the function Φ. Different decompositions would yield different representations of P; by selecting different occurrences of A within P, we should find one of the form $\Psi(A)$. Relatively to the choice of A, and of specific occurrences of A, however, no further definition of functions can call in question the uniqueness of Φ. Φ' is indeed a well-defined function, and $\Phi'(A) = $ P; that is not enough to justify the representation of P by the formula $\Phi'(A)$, since Φ' has not been shown to be a concept extractable from P by decomposition, or, indeed, a concept at all. Φ' will be a concept if there are in P some occurrences of A such that $\Phi'(x)$ will, for each object x, be the result of replacing them by x; there is no reason to suppose there are any such occurrences, and it is easy to see that there cannot be.

The same refutation could be repeated if we took decomposition as applying to the sentences that express the judgeable contents, but that may be left as an exercise for the reader, who will then see, even more clearly than, it is hoped, he does already, that the straightforward and compelling argument has no force whatever, but is simply a piece of legerdemain. We may notice, by the way, that the talk of discerning, and replacing, parts within a judgeable content is highly metaphorical, and patently relies on assuming such contents to have a structure very similar to that of sentences. We saw earlier that Frege wrote to Russell that a decomposition of the thought parallels that of the sentence; but we may ask which is prior. Since Frege consistently believed that thoughts are accessible to us only through their linguistic expression, the impression conveyed by *Begriffsschrift*, that the process has to be understood as applied to sentences or formulas in the first place, is almost certainly correct.

14. TYPE AMBIGUITIES

In decomposing a sentence, we must of course have in mind its sense: otherwise we shall arrive at an incomplete expression to which we cannot attach a sense, and shall not be engaged in concept-formation. We have also to be aware of the logical types of expressions occurring in the sentence, so as to know what replacing one expression by another consists in. Baker and Hacker maintain that Frege cannot consistently distinguish a proper name from an expression for a concept of second-level: '"$\Phi(A)$" . . . can with equal propriety be characterized as stating that the concept Φ falls under a second-level concept . . . On this . . . interpretation, Frege apparently concluded . . . the symbol "A" must . . . be viewed as the name of a second-level concept' (p. 166). This shows that 'the differentiation of proper names from concept-words is . . . a matter of how the sentence . . . is viewed' (pp. 167–8).

This reasoning is based on a misunderstanding of the classification of expressions into types, and hence of the process of extracting expressions of higher type. An ability to discriminate 'proper names' from other expressions is the foundation of the entire process. The extraction of a predicate of second level cannot be understood until it is known what a predicate of first level is, and what it is for it to occur in a sentence and to be replaced, in a given occurrence, by another predicate of first level. All this has to be explained, since a predicate is an incomplete expression: you cannot tell whether it occurs in a sentence, or what would be the result of replacing it, just by looking to see if some string of symbols or words occurs and considering the substitution of another string for it. The only case in which this procedure is adequate is the basic one, when what is to be replaced is a proper name, since that is a complete expression and occurs in a sentence, and can be replaced within it, in a straightforward sense. Not every word or string of words may be significantly considered as replaceable, however: not, for instance, the symbol '$>$' in 'If $5 > 3$, then $5 + 2 > 3 + 2$'. That is why the whole theory rests on the presumption that we can distinguish a proper name from other words or strings of words.

A predicate of second level, being incomplete, is no more a separable bit of a sentence than one of first level: it is therefore in principle incapable of being identical with a proper name. It is, rather, what is left of a sentence when (say) one or more occurrences of a predicate of first level have been removed. Thus we might remove the predicate '$\xi > 3 + 2$' from the foregoing arithmetical statement to form the second-level predicate 'If $5 > 3$, then $\Phi(5+2)$'. As an extreme case, we may remove 'If $5 > \xi$, then $5+2 > \xi +2$' to obtain '$\Phi(3)$', which stands for that concept of second level under which fall all and only those first-level concepts under which 3 falls; but it is not '3' that stands for this second-level concept, since an expression standing for a concept or function must be unsaturated and hence have argument-places. The proper name '3' is not type-ambiguous at all.

15. CONCLUSION

No one can read very far in *Frege: Logical Excavations* without perceiving the animus against Frege; the book is relentlessly dedicated to proving that he was virtually worthless as a philosopher. It is a very bad idea to devote a book to such an aim. Virtually no one could produce a good book in this way, avoiding the merely captious and thinking through his victim's ideas sympathetically before evaluating them. Even the authors cannot suppose that there is much philosophical profit to be gained from reading it, save to be inoculated against being 'mesmerized' by Frege. It is unlikely to destroy Frege's reputation, which is evidently their aim; but it might badly retard the understanding of him, which is why I have thought it worth while to comment on it in such detail. This pair of authors might have given us an illuminating comparative study of Frege and Wittgenstein; it is regrettable that they have preferred to attempt a hatchet job on a philosopher they lack the goodwill to understand.

9

Second Thoughts

*A revised version of a 'Reply to "Dummett's Dig",
by Baker and Hacker'**

1. ARE JUDGEABLE CONTENTS OBJECTS?

Did Frege consider the judgeable contents of which he spoke in his early period (up to 1885) to be objects, or, in the terminology he used before *Die Grundlagen der Arithmetik*, individual things? The point is not of great intrinsic importance, but bears on our view of Frege's development. In *Frege: Logical Excavations*, Baker and Hacker represented Frege as having, in his early period, as fully articulated a logical doctrine as that expounded in the writings from 1891 onwards. In particular, he included judgeable contents within the category of objects (p. 148), and treated sentences as names of objects, assimilating them to proper names; on this they characteristically comment (pp. 124–5), 'Is it not incongruous to hail his logical system as a triumph when this is built on an idea commonly viewed as an unmitigated disaster?' Correlative to this first claim is a second: that he already identified (first-level) concepts with functions from objects to objects; the only difference was that he took their values to be judgeable contents rather than truth-values. Baker and Hacker attached such importance to these claims as to assert that 'any defence of [Frege's] thinking which undermined [their] literal truth . . . would be ludicrous as an interpretation of his work'.

This view is grossly unhistorical. In *Begriffsschrift*, he had not only expounded his invention of quantificational logic, but had

---

* 'Dummett's Dig: Looking-Glass Archaeology', by G. Baker and P. M. S. Hacker, itself a response to my review (reprinted as the preceding essay in this volume) of their *Frege: Logical Excavations* (Oxford and New York, 1984), appeared in *Philosophical Quarterly*, 37 (1987), 86–99. I have revised the present essay for this reprint so as to remove the more polemical passages, the justice of which could not be judged by a reader without access to the article being answered, and to concentrate attention more on Frege's views and less on those of Baker and Hacker. This essay was first published in *Philosophical Quarterly*, 38 (1988), 87–103.

developed its theory to an astonishing extent, presenting a second-order logic incorporating his method of converting inductive into explicit definitions, and containing a complete formalization of its first-order fragment. The informal explanations embody deep insights into the philosophical framework of formal logic: but it was not to be expected or demanded that these should have been fully worked out or flawlessly formulated; nor, I think, are they. Unlike Frege's mature period (1891–mid-1906), his early period was one of sustained (and extraordinarily rapid) development: neither his terminology nor his ideas were stable. Just as most of the labour that went into *Begriffsschrift* must have been devoted to the formal work, so most of that which went into *Grundlagen* must have been devoted to applying his logical theory to the logical construction of number theory; yet he had also made an immense advance in clarifying the philosophical foundations of this work. Even so, the clarification was not yet complete. Realizing this, he dedicated all the time he could spare from teaching over the next five years to attaining a comprehensive system of logical doctrines to serve as the base for the formal work of *Grundgesetze der Arithmetik*. It is therefore fundamentally misguided to attribute to him, during his early period, a comparable though different system; still more, to do so for the purpose of excoriating the doctrines so attributed, and thereby depreciating his great achievements during that period as resting on faulty foundations.

The question whether we can ascribe to Frege, in his early period, a thesis that judgeable contents are individual things is simply answered. Such a thesis can be expressed, in the formal mode, as 'Sentences are singular terms', meaning 'Sentences are of the same logical type as the expressions normally recognized as singular terms'. Now, in his early period, Frege said none of these things. The question therefore becomes whether he *treated* sentences as being of the same logical type as singular terms. According to Frege's mature doctrine, if one expression can meaningfully occur in *any* place in which another can meaningfully occur, it can meaningfully occur in *every* place in which the other can meaningfully occur: the test for being of the same logical type is then unambiguous. This is not so for the early period. The only point of any substance made on this topic in 'Dummett's Dig' is that, in the *Begriffsschrift* symbolism, sentences and singular terms can both flank the identity-sign (though not, so far as appears, in the same identity-statement). In 'An Unsuccessful Dig', on the other hand, I had pointed to the content-stroke as creating a context in which only sentences, and not terms, can occur. We may therefore say that sentences are of a *similar* logical type to singular terms; but we cannot say that they are of the *same* logical type: correlatively, that judgeable contents are something *like* individual things, but not that they *are* individual things. That, I believe, is the whole truth of the matter.

Baker and Hacker cite five pieces of 'evidence' in their favour from *Begriffsschrift* and the associated writings.

(i) 'Greek capitals have a *dual* use in concept-script. They are the arguments of first-level functions . . . And they are the sentences of the notation and argument-expressions for the truth-functions . . . In this second role, they are said to *stand for* or *mean* judgeable-contents.' This is somewhat inaccurately expressed. Baker and Hacker do not take the functions spoken of in *Begriffsschrift* to be either expressions or functions from expressions to expressions: their speaking of capital letters as the arguments of functions therefore illustrates how easy it is to slip into the carelessness about use and mention with which they reproach Frege. It is also somewhat odd to say that capital letters *are* sentences (Frege says that he uses them as abbreviations). Moreover, capital Greek letters do not actually figure in the symbolic formulas. Frege uses them as syntactic variables in informal examples and in statements of the rule of inference, and also in the specifications, given at the side of steps in the formal proofs, of the substitutions being made in previously proved formulas, in order to indicate the argument-places in a functional expression. In any case, the appeal to Frege's use of such letters is completely self-defeating; for, though he indeed uses them both as sentential and as individual variables, he also uses them as predicate-variables in the proofs of theorem 77 and of the formula intermediate between theorems 92 and 93. The argument, if valid, would therefore show that he regarded, not only judgeable contents, but 'functions' (in the sense of concepts) as objects. Frege's procedure, in these two proofs, is indeed illegitimate, in that he is citing a formula involving first-order quantification to justify a transition involving second-order quantification: for instance, he substitutes '$\Gamma(y)$' for '$f(\Gamma)$'. But this fact only makes the matter worse: the capital Greek letter represents an individual variable on one side of the substitution, and a predicate-variable on the other. It would have been better to fasten on the use of italic letters; but even this would have reduced to the argument about the identity-sign, rather than supplying an independent ground.

(ii) 'Sentences of concept-script are explicitly equated with singular referring expressions, namely, sentential nominalizations, e.g. "The violent death of Archimedes at the conquest of Syracuse". Such a *singular subject term* contains the *whole content* of a possible judgement. In this way every judgement is expressed by attaching to a name the formal predicate "is a fact" (represented in concept-script by the judgement-stroke).' This argument proves the exact opposite of the conclusion Baker and Hacker wish to draw. In *Begriffsschrift*, Frege indeed attempts to explain his distinction between a judgement and a judgeable content by describing his symbolic notation as a language in which there is only a single predicate for all judgements. In such a language, it is essential to a predicate to have assertoric force; indeed, the whole content of its sole predicate consists in having assertoric force. By contrast, the concept-expressions of the language must uniformly lack assertoric force. Frege was well aware that natural languages do not have a single predicate for all judgements, and that their predicates sometimes carry assertoric force and sometimes lack it, which is why he speaks of an *imaginary* language which would resemble his symbolic notation in this respect: the purpose of representing the expressions for judgeable content of this imaginary language by nominalizations of German sentences is just to drive home that they would be devoid of assertoric force, not at all to suggest that they have any other resemblance to proper names. The same applies to his interpretations in German of sentence-letters of his notation by phrases beginning 'the circumstance that . . .'; this, of course, cannot consistently be maintained for subsentences. The *Begriffsschrift* account of the judgement-stroke implies, not that expressions for judgeable contents are of the same kind as names of individual things, but that they are in no way comparable to them. The single predicate of the symbolic language differs wholly from the concept-expressions of that language; for the application of the judgement-stroke does not yield an expression for a judgeable content, but for a judgement, which is something quite different. The judgement-stroke neither is nor designates a function, and the expression for a judgeable content to which it is attached therefore does not designate the argument of a function. There is thus no analogy between names of individual things and expressions of judgeable contents: what Baker and Hacker cite as showing that Frege conceived both as belonging to a single category actually shows that they have utterly different roles in the language.

(iii) is the point about the identity-sign, which indeed has some substance; but its substance is not great. As Frege remarks in 'Booles rechnende Logik und die Begriffsschrift', he uses identity-statements connecting expressions of judgeable contents only for giving definitions and then using these definitions in subsequent derivations. The essential instrument for this purpose is axiom 52, saying that if $c = d$, then if $f(c)$, then $f(d)$; when expressions of judgeable contents are substituted for 'c' and 'd', f is taken as the identity function, to obtain: if $c = d$, then if c, then d. German letters, bound by the quantifier, are never required to range over judgeable contents; and even the italic letters in axiom 52 are not required to range *simultaneously*, but only *indifferently*, both over them and over individual things. What clinches the conclusion that Frege's use in *Begriffsschrift* of the identity-sign does not imply that judgeable contents and individual things are of the same logical type is a remark about axioms (31) and (41), governing double negation, at the end of the Preface:

> I noticed subsequently that formulas (31) and (41) can be combined into the single:
>
> $$\vdash\!\!\!\!\!\!-(\underline{\quad\quad}_{\tau}\underline{\quad}_{\tau}\underline{\quad}\, a = a)$$
>
> which would make some further simplifications possible.

Combined, (31) and (41) say that 'a' and 'not not a' have the same truth-value; on any account, a statement that they have the very same judgeable content ought to be much stronger. Nothing could illustrate more clearly the folly of crediting the author of *Begriffsschrift* with a fully worked-out system of philosophical logic.

(iv) Baker and Hacker's fourth piece of evidence is a retrospective remark from the very beginning of 'Über Sinn und Bedeutung': 'Is [identity] a relation? A relation between objects? Or between names or signs for objects? In my *Begriffsschrift* I assumed the latter'. Baker and Hacker say, 'Clearly "designations" of judgeable-contents . . . are treated as *names* of judgeable-contents. Did Frege none the less not conceive of judgeable-contents as *objects*? His own testimony demolishes this quibble', and go on to quote the above remark.

Neither in *Begriffsschrift* nor in 'Booles rechnende Logik', nor yet in any of the three short published articles about *Begriffsschrift*, does Frege speak of a 'designation' of a 'judgeable content'. To turn up an occurrence of the word 'designation' (*Bezeichnung*), Baker and Hacker can therefore cite only the unpublished 'Booles logische Formelsprache und meine Begriffsschrift', which tallies closely with the lecture 'Über den Zweck der Begriffsschrift', but does employ the word '*Bezeichnung*'. The article is concerned to compare Boolean symbolism with Frege's own; the word '*Bezeichnung*' can mean 'notation', is obviously so employed here, and could throughout be rendered 'symbolic expression' or the like. From this flimsy evidence, Baker and Hacker infer that Frege regarded an expression for a judgeable content as a *name* of that content, a term which he does not use once in this connection in any writing of the period, published or unpublished. Even if Frege *had* spoken of 'names of judgeable contents', it would not be a quibble to question whether he regarded judgeable contents as objects: for in *Grundgesetze* he calls functional expressions 'names' of concepts, relations, and other functions. As for the quotation from 'Über Sinn und Bedeutung', what concerns Frege in this opening passage is whether identity is a relation between expressions or between what they stand for: the remark records that, in *Begriffsschrift*, Frege had taken it as a relation between expressions. It does not testify that every expression there allowed to stand before or after the sign of identity was thought of by him as standing for an object; he speaks of a relation between objects because that is, on any view, the central case, because, by the time he was then writing, he had become clear that it is the only case, and because he did not wish, in that essay, even to discuss the use of the identity-sign between sentences.

(v) is not a citation of evidence at all, but an argument. Most of it attempts to deduce the first claim, that judgeable contents are objects in Frege's early doctrine, from the second, that concepts are functions, which has yet to be argued in 'Dummett's Dig'. Amplifying a claim made earlier that, in his early work, Frege took 'everything to be either a concept (or, more generally, a function) or an object, just as he later . . . did', Baker and Hacker assert, first, that *Begriffsschrift* 'analyzed all judgeable-contents into function and argument. Every judgement is taken to be complex; whether it be an atomic proposition, a disjunction or conjunction, or a general-ization, its representation in concept-script depicts it as the value of a function for some argument(s)'. These observations are simply false: neither the quantifier nor the sentential operators are charac-terized in *Begriffsschrift* as being or as denoting functions of any kind. In general, in his early period, Frege did not have the same interest in obtaining a comprehensive classification of everything into logical types that he later had. Lacking the distinction between sense and reference, he did not have his later conception of the realm of reference, but only of the external world—a very different domain, in which there are no concepts, no properties of concepts, no numbers. A schema of all possible logical types would therefore not yet be an ontological classification, that is to say, a classification of 'everything'—of all that there is—but, rather, of conceptual contents. Whether or not, when he wrote *Grundlagen*, he held every conceptual content to be either an object or a concept, might be disputed: but it is a gross anachronism to attribute such a view to *Begriffsschrift*.

Baker and Hacker go on, under (v), to ask, 'Can one make intelligible *Frege's* conception of a function independently of his taking the values of functions to be objects?' Their asking this question is remarkable. In *Frege: Logical Excavations*, they twice represented Frege, in his mature period, as admitting functions whose values are concepts. In 'An Unsuccessful Dig', I criticized this, saying that he recognized only functions taking objects as values; I intended this also to refer to the period after 1890. Yet in 'Dummett's Dig' they demand of me how one can interpret Frege's view of functions if one does not take their values invariably to be objects. The important question is *why* functions can only have objects as values. The reason is this. Suppose one wants to construct an expression for a function from objects to first-level concepts. One will therefore start with an expression for a first-level concept, and remove from it (one or more occurrences of) some proper name. What one will be left with, however, is simply an expression with two argument-places, which will stand for a first-level relation; there is no way to indicate that one of the two argument-places is to be filled first, and no point in doing so. It is obvious that this reasoning, of itself, tends only to show that the value of any function must be the referent of some saturated expression; to deduce that it must be an object, one must already know that every saturated expression stands for an object. When the expression is one for a judgeable content, this is precisely the point at issue; the argument therefore begs the question.

Finally, Baker and Hacker enquire, 'Could Frege have made sense of treating expressions of generality as names of second-level functions while denying that their values (judgeable-contents) are objects?' Ignoring the multiple *petitio principii* in this question, we may simply answer 'Yes'. If Frege had regarded the quantifier as standing for a function from first-level concepts to judgeable contents, but had held that judgeable contents form a category distinct from individual things, he would have been construing that function as of a distinct type from functions from first-level concepts to individual things. By taking judgeable contents as the values of a certain function, he would no more have been constrained to construe them as objects than one who speaks of truth-functions is constrained to regard truth-values as objects, or Russell, by speaking of propositional functions, to regard propositions as individuals. Admittedly, in his mature period, Frege distinguished different types of functions only by the number and types of their arguments, not by the type of their values, because he had come to believe all saturated expressions to be of the same logical type. The question at issue is whether he believed that, or had so much as asked himslf the question, during his early period; an affirmative answer cannot be defended simply by assuming it. One cannot evaluate either his functional conception of concepts or his (later) doctrine that sentences stand for objects if one fails to see that the former does not depend upon the latter.

2. CONCEPTS AS FUNCTIONS

The question whether, for Frege in his early period, concepts are functions is independent of the question whether judgeable contents are individual things; for they might be functions of a different logical type from, say, arithmetical functions. In *Begriffsschrift* Frege used the notion of a function to explain the process of decomposing a sentence or judgeable content to obtain a predicate or concept; and we may distinguish three related questions of interpretation. (1) Granted that he unquestionably attached fundamental importance to this process throughout his early period, did the notion of a function then have the same importance for him?

(2) Did he conceive of the process as applied primarily to judgeable contents or to linguistic or symbolic expressions? (3) Was the result of supplying an argument for a function of the kind spoken of in *Begriffsschrift* a judgeable content or an expression of one? *Frege: Logical Excavations* gives very definite answers. It lays the greatest emphasis on the doctrine that concepts are functions from objects to judgeable contents, as being an ingredient of the system of philosophical logic on which it represents Frege as having based all his work throughout his early period. Furthermore, Frege was exclusively concerned with judgeable contents, not with their expressions; it is to judgeable contents that the process of decomposition is applied, and it is they that are the values of the functions extracted by this process. Any appearance that he is concerned, rather, with sentences (expressions of judgeable contents) is due solely to typical mathematician's carelessness about use and mention.

In fact, *Begriffsschrift* is virtually the only one of Frege's early writings in which the notion of a function is employed. There is a mention of it in an overt reference to *Begriffsschrift* in example 19 of 'Booles rechnende Logik'. One other occurs in an example given in the lecture 'Anwendungen der Begriffsschrift', delivered in 1879. There is little to show that Frege continued to attach any importance to it after that year, until he revived it in the very different context of his mature theory. About question (2) I remarked in 'An Unsuccessful Dig' that he 'surely viewed [the process of decomposition] as applying to both' judgeable contents and sentences, observing that 'in his early writings, he expressed himself in both ways. In ['Booles rechnende Logik'], he spoke of decomposing the judgeable content, as he also did in a single sentence in [*Begriffsschrift*]'. I cited a later observation, from a letter to Russell of 1902, to explain this oscillation, namely, that 'to the decomposition of the sentence there corresponds a decomposition of the thought'.

In *Frege: Logical Excavations*, Baker and Hacker deride Geach for explaining functions, as they figure in *Begriffsschrift*, as having symbolic expressions for their arguments and values. In this, they fly in the face of the plain sense of Frege's own words. It is undoubtedly true that, throughout his early period, Frege was as careless as other writers about observing the distinction between use and mention; this holds good even in *Grundlagen*. Nevertheless, as I urged in 'An Unsuccessful Dig', Frege, when explaining his notion of a function in §§9 and 10 of *Begriffsschrift*, 'speaks so persistently in terms of *expressions*, and does so, in particular, in the four italicized formulations, that it is impossible to doubt this way of expressing himself to be deliberate'. Baker and Hacker cite in support of their interpretation Frege's remark about a quantified sentence: 'The whole splits up into function and argument according to its own content, and not just according to our way of regarding it.' They comment, 'Here [Frege] explicitly specified the *judgeable-content* as the value of a function for an argument.' If by 'the whole' Frege had meant a content, 'its own content' would have referred to a content of that content. If Frege's remark had meant that, in the case in question, the *content* split into function and argument, then it would also mean that, in the case with which it was contrasted, that of a singular sentence, our way of regarding it split into function and argument. From this it is clear that Frege's explanation, in 'Booles rechnende Logik' and *Grundlagen*, of the process, if taken as applied to judgeable contents, rather than to their expressions, would risk incoherence; for the distinction between a split that is in accordance with the content and one that depends only on our way of regarding the matter is difficult to state when it is the content itself that is being thought of as split up. Precisely what is at issue here is the distinction I have drawn between decomposition and analysis.

Baker and Hacker's explanation in *Frege: Logical Excavations* in terms of mathematicians' carelessness left no other interpretation open than that, in speaking of a symbol as replaceable by another at one or more occurrences within an expression, Frege intended us to understand the replacement of one object by another at one or more occurrences within a judgeable content. This, of course, is implausible because we have no idea what an occurrence of an object within a judgeable content would be, or how one might set about replacing it by another object; such language would be blatantly parasitic upon the application of the terminology to expressions. *Frege: Logical Excavations* had given no hint, however, that Frege's formulation in terms of expressions was deliberate, let alone correct. This makes it the more remarkable that, in 'Dummett's Dig', Baker and Hacker should have accepted my contention that Frege's formulation was deliberate, and, indeed, unavoidable.

Indeed, they have not gone all the way. What they have conceded is that the functions of which Frege spoke could be characterized only in terms of operations upon expressions: but they still maintain that such functions were intended to be ones mapping objects on to judgeable contents—Frege went astray in specifying the function to be 'the part of the expression that here appears as invariant'. Having admitted that the references throughout §§9 and 10 to expressions and operations upon them mean exactly what they say, it is pointless for Baker and Hacker to continue to insist that his characterization of the functions with which he is concerned does not mean what it says, opposing to his considered formulations three or four passing remarks in the Preface and elsewhere. He explicitly characterizes functions, in *Begriffsschrift*, as parts of expressions. It is true enough that, in that work, he frequently slides about between speaking of expressions and of their contents, without close attention to which he is doing. That cuts both ways, however; his 'mathematician's carelessness' can much more economically be invoked to explain the passing remarks as carelessly referring to contents when expressions are meant than, as Baker and Hacker do, to explain the many full-dress statements as involving the opposite mistake. It would be reasonable to suggest that Frege thought of the *contents* of the invariant parts as themselves functions; but nothing can be cited that compels us to suppose that.

The fact, however, is that, in 'Dummett's Dig', Baker and Hacker recognize that, whatever kind of function it is, the specification of it requires us to talk about expressions, whereas it was just this point the neglect of which vitiated so much of the criticism of Frege contained in *Frege: Logical Excavations*. In accordance with Frege's instructions, we consider the sentence 'Cato killed Cato', and regard the second occurrence of the name 'Cato' as replaceable by another name. By this means we arrive at a function. It does not matter here whether we are aiming at a function mapping the name 'Cato' on to the sentence 'Cato killed Cato', or one mapping the man Cato on to the judgeable content expressed by the sentence, or the sense of the name 'Cato' on to the thought expressed by the sentence, or the man Cato on to the truth-value of that thought; in no case can we specify the function we have in mind simply by mentioning the one argument and the corresponding value. In fact, we cannot specify it just by operating with the notions of function, argument, and value; we have to mention the base sentence and the range of sentences resulting from it by replacing the name 'Cato', at its second occurrence, by other names.

It was for this reason that I said, in 'An Unsuccessful Dig', that 'to talk about expressions and their structure, we need the notions of part and whole, not those of function and value', and that 'for similar reasons, the *senses* of complex expressions cannot be explained in terms of function and value, either . . . but on the model of part and whole' (section 11). With Baker and Hacker's belated recognition of this point, their 'straightforward and compelling argument' against Frege, discussed in section 13 of 'An Unsuccessful Dig', collapses. Of course, if we could directly discern occurrences of objects within judgeable contents, we should not need to attend to the occurrences of their names within expressions of those contents, and it was in these terms that I feigned to discuss the 'straightforward and compelling argument', so as not to go back over old ground; it would still remain that we should need to specify the functions in terms of the *parts* of the judgeable contents. But it is not merely the 'straightforward and compelling argument' that collapses, but the entire polemic, which occupies vast tracts of both parts of *Frege: Logical Excavations*, against the alleged tension, in Frege's early and mature theories, between the part/whole and function/value models. There would in fact be no obstacle to considering the sense of the unsaturated expression 'Cato killed . . .' as a function mapping the sense of 'Cato' on to the thought that Cato killed Cato; nor, in the terminology of the early period, to considering the concept of being killed by Cato as a function mapping Cato on to the judgeable content expressed by 'Cato killed Cato'. The reason is that the sense of 'Cato killed . . .' is not a constituent of the thought expressed by 'Cato killed Cato': as it is expressed in *Begriffsschrift*, the latter sentence splits into 'Cato killed . . .' and 'Cato' according to our way of regarding it, not according to its content. We may therefore assume a grasp of the thought, or of the judgeable content, that does not depend upon a prior grasp of the concept (of the sense of the one-place predicate). The judgeable content expressed by 'Cato killed someone' does involve that concept; in the later terminology, the sense of the predicate is a constituent of the thought expressed by that sentence. But this does no harm, since this thought or judgeable content will not be a value of the function in question. In order to see that Frege was not guilty of the confusion of which, in *Frege: Logical Excavations*, they had repeatedly and scornfully accused him, Baker and Hacker needed to do two things. They needed, first, to perceive the reason that made an approach through the linguistic expression essential. This they did in 'Dummett's Dig', without acknowledging that they had radically shifted their ground. Secondly, they needed to understand the sentence from *Begriffsschrift*, which they themselves quote, about two ways of splitting up. Even with the first alone, they have gone a considerable way towards demolishing their own book.

3. THE VALUE OF *BEGRIFFSSCHRIFT*

Baker and Hacker accuse me of limiting the achievement of *Begriffsschrift* 'to the invention of a *notation*', of condemning it because it fails to meet *my* 'standards for a proper exposition of the predicate calculus' and of failing 'to see that the key to the invention of the predicate calculus was Frege's treating expressions of generality as names of *second*-level concepts'. This is a surprising attack from those who wrote, in *Frege: Logical Excavations*, that 'Frege's concept-script is simply an alternative form of representation to natural language' (p. 389), that 'a formal calculus is of very limited philosophical significance and has limited philosophical use' (p. 392), that 'Frege did not produce anything remotely like a philosophical grammar' (p. 337), that it is 'incongruous to hail his logical system as a triumph when this is built on an idea commonly viewed as an unmitigated disaster' (p. 125), and that 'the whole framework of [*Begriffsschrift*] would collapse' if it were rightly admitted that his explanation of 'judgeable content' was incoherent and his use of the verb 'express' inconsistent (p. 103). Like the Indian ('Arabic') notation for the natural numbers, the quantifier-variable notation embodied an analysis of the structure of what is symbolized, and for that reason allowed of perspicuous and simple rules of transformation; it is therefore wrong to contrast its claim to be the key to the invention of modern ('quantificational') logic with that of the structural analysis it embodied. In *Begriffsschrift*, Frege did not yet classify the quantifier as standing for a second-level concept, not yet having that general notion; but he of course presented it as operating on expressions for what he was later to call 'first-level concepts', and could not be said to have introduced the quantifier-variable notation unless he had done so. Naturally, he did a great deal more than introduce the notation. It would be an absurd impertinence to 'condemn' *Begriffsschrift*, which was a work of genius. That its formulation of the calculus is defective at certain points—though remarkably few—would be recognized by anyone with any competence in logic; it is ludicrous to attribute this concession to any idiosyncrasies of mine.

4. SENSE AND REFERENCE

Against my observation that, in explaining his notion of reference, Frege always started with proper names, Baker and Hacker assert that in *Function und Begriff* he first explains it for equations and declarative sentences generally, 'and barely hints at extending it to proper names'. This is quite false: he introduces the notion of reference, on pp. 3–5, for complex numerical terms, and begins to speak of the references of equations and other sentences only on p. 13, arguing for his identification of them as truth-values by appeal to the references of numerical terms and of names such as 'the Morning Star' and 'the Evening Star'. The fact that he puts forward this argument, based on the principle that, if the reference of the parts remains unchanged, so must that of the whole, is of fundamental importance. If reference were first introduced as the relation of a sentence to its truth-value, no reason could be given, or would be needed, for this identification: but who could then guess how the notion of reference was to be extended to subsentential expressions, including singular terms? In 'Über Sinn und Bedeutung', 'Einleitung in die Logik', 'Logik in der Mathematik', 'Aufzeichnungen für Ludwig Darmstaedter', his letter to Russell of 1904, and his draft letter to Jourdain of 1914, Frege explains the distinction between sense and reference, in the first instance, as it applies to 'proper names': it is always their relation to their bearers that serves as the prototype. Baker and Hacker would have done better to cite *Grundgesetze* as a counter-example: but, in *Grundgesetze*, Frege was not *explaining* the distinction, but merely stating it.

'Dummett's account', Baker and Hacker say, 'makes no place for the notion of sense in the explanation of Frege's formal system of logic'; on the contrary, 'Frege implied that it is an essential feature of his concept-script that its formulae have senses as well as reference.' It is difficult to make out the substance of so vague a charge. If the accusation means that I cannot allow that Frege's symbolic formulae express thoughts, or that I must dismiss this as unimportant, it is completely false; but if it means that I think that the validity of a logical deduction depends only on the references of the parts of the sentences that figure as premises and conclusion, and that this was so for Frege, it is true. That indeed appears, from subsequent formulations, to be their meaning: 'Dummett goes astray', they say, 'in declaring that, as a logician, Frege could limit his attention to reference.' On the contrary, 'the possibility . . . that consideration of semantic values . . . may suffice to discriminate between sound and unsound reasoning' was 'not available to Frege'. I am said to have 'deluded myself' 'into thinking that Frege thought the concept of reference sufficient for a logician'.

This is completely wrong: it betrays a failure to grasp the point of Frege's notion of *Bedeutung*. It is at the outset difficult to grasp their argument. They state that Frege 'characterised logic as the study of relations between genuine thoughts, i.e. thoughts known to be true': but this rendering is excessively free. Frege never suggested that thoughts not known to be true are in any way spurious; what he actually said, in the passage of 'Logik', 1897, to which they refer, was that 'logic is the science of the most general laws of truth' (or 'of being true'). In 'Über die Grundlagen der Geometrie', he says, of the question whether a thought is independent of certain other thoughts, 'With this question, we enter a domain that is otherwise alien to mathematics. For although mathematics, like all the sciences, issues in thoughts, thoughts are not among the objects that it studies.'[1] Even more clearly, in 'Ausführungen über Sinn und Bedeutung', taking the side of extensionalist as against intensionalist logicians, he says that 'logical laws are primarily laws in the realm of references and relate only derivatively to sense'. This observation tallies with the fact that the model-theoretic criterion of validity used by logicians makes no appeal to any notion corresponding to that of sense. It would not, indeed, hold for a deductive argument whose validity turned on the sense of some non-logical expression. In a theory formalized in Frege's manner, however, the only device for appealing to that would be a definition of the expression; by this means, every deductive argument is converted into a purely logical deduction.

What, then, led Baker and Hacker to rank Frege with the intensionalists? A very trivial mistake. They argue that, if we attend only to the references of the premisses and conclusion of a valid argument, these will, in each case, be the value *true*, since the reference of a sentence is its truth-value and we can validly infer

[1] *Jahresberichte der Deutschen Mathematiker-Vereinigung*, 15 (1906), 425–6.

only from true premisses. It is not a sufficient analysis of the validity of an argument to say that it has true premisses and a true conclusion: hence validity depends upon more than reference. Now, quite obviously, in saying that logical laws hold primarily in the realm of reference, Frege is allowing that one must attend to the structure of the sentences which serve as premisses and conclusion of an argument; his point is that its validity, considered as a purely logical argument, turns only on the references of the parts of those sentences, and that one does not need to appeal to their senses. By looking at the reference of the whole, one indeed cannot discern the references of the parts; that is the point of Frege's thesis that the reference of a part is not part of the reference of the whole. Baker and Hacker think that, if reference were all that mattered for validity, one would have to be able to discern the references of the parts in that of the whole. That is why they deny that what is in fact Frege's view is 'not available to' him, and why they charge me with thinking that 'the semantic value of a formula is intrinsically complex', a thesis which I have never propounded.

Baker and Hacker ask, 'What does it mean to speak of how a concept or a function is *given*?' An example is needed to make the matter clear. The addition function may be given set-theoretically, that is, in terms of its application, or by means of the recursion equations, or, relatively to a particular notation for natural numbers, by means of a computation procedure, or by some combination of these. According to how the function is given, the sign '+' will vary in sense, while its reference remains unchanged. It will depend on how the function is taken as having been given in what manner arithmetical equations and other propositions are to be proved.

The methodology of Baker and Hacker's polemics is perplexing. They themselves may denigrate Frege and lambast him for advancing incoherent, self-contradictory, and nonsensical views; but if I suggest that a tension could be resolved by an adjustment in the doctrine, this renders me open to attack '(Dummett *corrects* Frege's conception'—Baker and Hacker's italics). If I reiterate something I have always said, and with which Baker and Hacker agree, e.g. that Frege did not formulate the semantic definition of logical consequence,[2] this is to be reported as 'Dummett now concedes that . . .'. If, on the other hand, I expressly record a change of view,

---

[2] *Frege: Philosophy of Language* (London, 1973, 1981), 81–2.

then the very page on which I do so is to be cited in support of the
unqualified attribution to me of the earlier view. Thus Baker and
Hacker write, 'he strives to explain Frege's notion of a concept
independently of the definition of a concept as a function whose
value is always the True or the False [*Frege: Philosophy of Language*],
pp. 234 f.; cf. [*The Interpretation of Frege's Philosophy*], pp. 166 ff.,
294 ff.)'. The first passage they cite from *The Interpretation of
Frege's Philosophy*[3] is a chapter actually entitled 'The Functional
Character of Concepts', in which I declared my conversion to the
view that Frege's conception of concepts as functions is both correct
and of considerable importance; the second passage, about Sluga's
conception of thoughts as initially simple, is entirely irrelevant. The
point is closely connected with the thesis (T) that truth-values are
the referents of sentences. If thesis (T) holds, but thesis (O), that
truth-values are objects, fails, then concepts are of a different
logical type from functions from objects to objects; but they still
may be functions in the generic sense in which, say, functions from
concepts to objects are. In both books, I laboured to distinguish
thesis (T) from thesis (O),[4] emphasizing that thesis (O) is objection-
able, but, in the context of a semantic theory of this general type,
thesis (T) is not. Yet Baker and Hacker appear still not to have
grasped this distinction; describing me as holding 'that one obliterates
the fundamental distinction in semantic role between sentences and
names by assimilating sentences to names in treating them as having
truth-values as referents'.

Baker and Hacker further describe me as being 'in difficulties
when he attempts, on Frege's behalf, to explain how to extend the
sense/reference distinction from proper names to other kinds of
expressions'. A reader might suppose Baker and Hacker to be in
possession of a better explanation: but, in *Frege: Logical Excavations*,
all they had to say was that Frege 'offers no argument whatever for
supposing that a . . . "predicate" stands for or designates any entity
at all' (p. 257). In 'Dummett's Dig', they go on to say that '[Dummett]
thinks it problematic whether incomplete expressions have referents
at all', but 'tries to salvage his position by reconstructing the
reference of an expression as its semantic value'.

I offered an interpretation, backed by arguments, which explains

[3] (London and Cambridge, Mass., 1981.)
[4] *Frege: Philosophy of Language*, 183; *The Interpretation of Frege's Philosophy*,
174–5.

10
Which End of the Telescope?*

It is unhistorical to read back into Frege ideas which originated only
with his successors; but equally so to project on to those successors
the discovery of ideas already present in his philosophy. Only by
avoiding both faults can we see how the various ideas are related
and what was genuinely original in Wittgenstein and other philosophers who came after Frege.

In a review[1] of the second edition of my *Frege: Philosophy of
Language* and of my *The Interpretation of Frege's Philosophy*,
Mr Stuart Shanker holds that I commit the first of these two errors;
and I am certain that he commits the second. Shanker's purpose is
to depict Frege as sharing the accepted opinions of his time, and his
work as therefore in no way a genuine source of the analytical
movement in philosophy. Rather, he sees analytical philosophy as
resulting from the partial absorption of the revolutionary ideas of
Wittgenstein, the sole originator; and he is accordingly determined
to repudiate as an anachronism any understanding of Frege's ideas
as anticipating or inspiring salient components of the thought of
twentieth-century philosophers of the analytical school. The attempt
to portray Frege as unconcerned with language and as purveying
irredeemably 'mentalistic' explanations necessarily makes incredible
the achievements whose originality no exegesis can call in question—
the invention of mathematical logic and of the very notion of a
formal system. Interpreting a philosopher is not a matter of collecting
proof-texts, but, rather, of identifying the ideas original with him
and those, whether original or not, that genuinely engaged him,
disentangling them, if necessary, from those he simply took over
from others without subjecting them to adequate scrutiny. Frege's
writings undoubtedly contain some clearly stated but unoriginal
views which he was at no pains to develop and which are in some
tension with original features of his thought: to insist on these to the
extent of denying the existence of those original features, in the face

---

* Not previously published.
[1] *Dialogue*, 21 (1982), 565–71.

of the plain sense of Frege's words, exhibits, not respect for the past, but, rather, idolatry of the present.

Shanker's objections to my interpretation of Frege can be summarized under four heads. Under each head, there are several points, which require separate discussion, but, in summarizing Shanker's views, it would be misleading to separate them, since he clearly sees them as connected. Under each of the four heads, therefore, I shall first give a summary of Shanker's views, and then set out my comments seriatim.

1. INFERENCE AND LOGICAL CONSEQUENCES

It was not Frege, Shanker claims, but Wittgenstein, who, in the *Tractatus*, introduced the semantic conception of logical validity (p. 566). It is erroneous, according to Shanker, to invoke the context principle as showing Frege to have had any particular interest in sentences rather than their contents: on the contrary, he regarded logical relations as holding, not between sentences, but between judgeable contents or thoughts (p. 568). He 'never questioned the premise that inference is a mental process' (p. 568), and thought it possible to infer anything from given premises only if they are true (p. 566). His 'conception of assertion remains irretrievably imbued with psychologism' (p. 566), in that it was for him the expression of an inner act of judgement; this landed him 'with the paradoxical consequence' that one 'cannot assert a false thought' (p. 567).

Frege and the Notion of Semantic Consequence

The modern notion of semantic consequence treats it as primarily a relation between a set S of logical formulas and a single such formula A, holding when A comes out true under every interpretation under which every formula in S comes out true. We may regard it as inducing a corresponding relation between a set S' of actual sentences and another such sentence A' when it holds between S and A, and S' and A' are obtainable from S and A by some uniform system of replacements of schematic letters by sentences, terms, functors, and predicates. Frege did not, indeed, have this notion, or even an approximation to it. This was not because he lacked the semantic notion of an interpretation of a logical formula or set of formulas, but, rather, because the idea of considering a formula under a range of such interpretations does not seem to have occurred to him. In part I of *Grundgesetze der Arithmetik*, he in fact came extremely close to our conception of a semantic interpretation, by giving a complete categorization of the logical types of expressions of his symbolic language, and laying down what sort of thing is to be the reference of an expression of any of these types: the only thing missing is the requirement of an initial specification of the domain of the individual variables. He did not, however, go on to use these formulations to define the notion of semantic consequence or of validity: rather, he treated them merely as providing a framework for any specific stipulation of the single intended interpretation of a formal language.

Wittgenstein and the Notion of Semantic Consequence

Thus Frege made a great advance towards attaining the concept of semantic consequence, but fell markedly short of doing so: there is no reason either to begrudge him recognition for the advance or to conceal his failure to reach the goal. It is, however, preposterous to credit the *Tractatus* with possession of the notion Frege failed to attain, save possibly at the level of sentential logic, since, unlike Frege, the book lacks even the conception of a semantic interpretation. Since the *Tractatus* contained the first account of truth-tables, one might accord to it an account of semantic consequence as applied to sentential formulas only, although, strictly speaking, Wittgenstein envisages initial assignments of truth-values only to elementary propositions. But the book contains nothing concerning the semantic values to be assigned to individual constants, function-symbols, or predicate-letters, let alone the specification of the domain. Wittgenstein's ideas are entirely different, and rest on the assumption that every proposition can be exhibited as a truth-functional combination of finitely or infinitely many elementary propositions: this assumption, which, when applied to propositions involving higher-order quantification, is tantamount to the axiom of reducibility, plays no role in the explanation of the now standard notion of semantic consequence, to which it is quite irrelevant whether there are any elementary propositions. It is no service to historical accuracy to credit Wittgenstein with achievements that were not his.

220   *Which End of the Telescope?*

Sentences and Thoughts

Logical relations do indeed hold primarily between thoughts, on Frege's view, just as it is thoughts that are primarily said to be true or false: but it was not this thesis, as Shanker appears to suppose, that blocked Frege from arriving at our notion of semantic consequence, any more than it blocked him from proposing an (epistemic) notion of analyticity. It is, after all, primarily a thought that is analytic or synthetic; but by including an appeal to definitions in his explanation of 'analytic', Frege showed that what he was directly concerned to characterize were those sentences that express analytic truths, rather than the thoughts that are analytically true, since definitions are of words or symbols. It is instructive to contrast Frege's definition of 'analytic' in this respect (as well as in respect of its epistemic character) with Bolzano's:[2] since for Bolzano analyticity is a property of propositions in themselves, rather than of the sentences expressing them, he does not need to make any appeal to definitions.

What Shanker has overlooked is that, even though Frege held that it is thoughts of which it is said, in the first instance, that one follows from others or is inconsistent with yet others, it was also his view that we human beings can grasp thoughts only as expressed in language or symbolism: it is as so expressed that we recognize an inferential transition as valid or invalid. That is why formalization serves to guarantee validity and to make explicit the underlying assumptions, as is argued in *Grundlagen der Arithmetik*, §§90–1. By overlooking this feature of Frege's thought, Shanker has adopted a picture of him incompatible with his having been the first mathematical logician and the first advocate and practitioner of the formalization of mathematical theories. In what terms can a logician formulate logical laws? In what terms can be propose the formalization of a theory? Obviously, only in terms of linguistic or symbolic *expressions*: there is no such thing as a logical law stated as applying solely to thoughts, independently of the forms of sentence that express them, or as a theory formalized in terms of the structure of thoughts rather than of formulas. Frege endorsed Leibniz's conception that the aim of a symbolic notation was to 'peindre non pas les

---

[2] B. Bolzano, *Wissenschaftslehre* (Sulzbach, 1837), ii, §148.

paroles, mais les pensées'.[3] But that does not imply that his symbolic notation was not itself a language: a great improvement on natural language for the purpose of displaying the structure of thoughts and hence of carrying out deductive reasoning, but still a language and not a system of diagrams. On the contrary, that was precisely what he insisted that it was, in contrast to Boole's notation: not a mere *calculus ratiocinator* but a *lingua character(ist)ica*, in which mathematical and other thoughts could be expressed, not just encoded. Although logical relations hold primarily between thoughts, they have to be stated in terms of relations between sentences, even if these are sentences of a formal rather than of a natural language.

If our only access to thoughts is through their linguistic or symbolic expression, it is obvious that our first access to them must be by means of natural language, rather than of a logical notation; and Frege, from the first, allowed that sentences of natural language reflect the structure of the thoughts they express, albeit imperfectly. It is by apprehending the relations of dependence and combination between the parts of sentences of natural language that we give sense to speaking of the structure of those thoughts. Logical relations therefore obtain between sentences of natural language, too, even if an exact statement of logical laws requires formulation in terms of a symbolic notation rather than of the forms of natural language.

We should not infer from the fact that a logical relation—entailment, for instance—is a relation between thoughts that, in reasoning, we are judging, concerning thoughts, that that relation obtains between them. It would no more be right to say this than to say that every judgement is about a thought, and is to the effect that it is true. When I judge that the cat is asleep, the subject-matter of my judgement is the cat, not the thought that the cat is asleep, which is, rather, its content. My judgement may well be based on a recognition that the evidence for the truth of the thought is decisive: but, to recognize this, and hence make the judgement, I do not have first to *judge* that the evidence is decisive, and hence do not have to have the concept of evidence, let alone possess an explicit criterion for its adequacy. Similarly, if I conclude from Euclid's proof that there is no largest prime, I do so by recognizing the cogency of the reasoning, but my judgement concerns prime numbers, not inferential relations,

---

[3] 'Booles rechnende Logik und die Begriffsschrift', in *Nachgelassene Schriften*, ed. H. Hermes, F. Kambartel, and F. Kaulbach (Hamburg, 1969), quoting from a letter of Leibniz's.

and I do not need to have a concept of deductive validity, let alone to be able to define it. That is why Frege says[4] that a proof that one *thought* is independent of certain others involves us in a realm alien to normal mathematics, which, like all sciences, issues in thoughts, but does not treat of thoughts as its subject-matter.

Since, according to Frege, we can grasp thoughts only as expressed verbally or symbolically, we are never in the position of having to recognize, of a naked thought, whether or not it follows from a set of other naked thoughts. Furthermore, even when we are explicitly *judging* whether or not the thought expressed by a sentence or formula follows from those expressed by other sentences or formulas, we have, of course, to grasp the thoughts concerned, but never need to judge concerning thoughts or their constituent senses. We need attend only to the *references* of the constituent parts of the sentences or formulas, and to how they determine the truth-values of the sentences or formulas of which they are parts: that is why Frege says, in the unpublished 'Ausführungen über Sinn und Bedeutung', that the extensional logicians 'are right . . . in showing that they regard the reference of the words, and not their sense, as the essential thing for logic', and that the intensional logicians 'fail to consider that in logic it is not a matter of how thoughts result from thoughts without regard to truth-value, that the step must be taken from the thought to the truth-value, or, more generally, from the sense to the reference; that the laws of logic are in the first instance laws in the realm of reference, and relate only derivatively to sense'.[5] Frege is, of course, here speaking of strictly *logical* deductions, not of those the recognition of whose validity turns on a knowledge of how certain terms are to be defined. We human beings cannot but start from the level of linguistic expression, because that is how thoughts are presented to us: and Frege is asserting that, even for an *analysis* of a logically valid deduction, we need to advert only to the theory of the references of the words or symbols, and not to theory of sense. An analysis in terms of the notion of semantic consequence, to which Shanker wished to compare Frege's views, to the disfavour of the latter, does just the same: but

---

[4] 'Über die Grundlagen der Geometrie', *Jahresbericht der Deutschen Mathematiker-Vereinigung*, 15 (1906), 425–6.

[5] *Nachgelassene Schriften*, ed. H. Hermes, F. Kambartel, and F. Kaulbach (Hamburg, 1969), 133; *Posthumous Writings*, trans. P. Long and R. White (Oxford, 1979), 122.

the contrast between them that Shanker believed himself to perceive does not exist.

The Context Principle

It was a perverse triumph on the part of Gregory Currie to interpret the context principle as having nothing to do either with sentences or with meaning.[6] Baker and Hacker would have liked to do the same, and announce that Frege implied 'no dependence of content-analysis on sentence-structure':[7] but in the end they find themselves forced to understand the principle as saying something about sentences and the meanings of words. Shanker never offers a reading of the context principle of his own; but his ruling that it does not reveal any particular interest on Frege's part in sentences, rather than in judgeable contents, appears quite arbitrary. It blinds him to the most remarkable fact about its use in *Grundlagen*: that it constitutes the first occurrence of the 'linguistic turn'. If Frege had formulated the context principle as one relating to judgeable contents and conceptual contents comprised in them, that would not have been a psychologistic formulation, on his conception of judgeable contents as objective: but he chose to formulate it as a principle governing sentences and words occurring in them. He puts it to work in *Grundlagen* in §62, when, having asked the Kantian question 'How are numbers given to us?', he answers it by an appeal to the context principle. This leads him into an enquiry into how it is possible to fix the sense of sentences containing numerical terms: he has thus converted an epistemological enquiry into a linguistic one. The urge to minimize Frege's originality has caused Shanker to overlook one of the important turning-points in the history of philosophy.

Assertion

Shanker reasons that, since assertion is for Frege the outer expression of the inner mental act of judgement, and since inference essentially involves judgement, his account of logical validity must itself be psychologistic. This is simply to overlook his distinction between (subjective) mental acts and their (objective) contents, which Shanker himself explains as the distinction between an act and its object. Frege indeed regarded judgement and inference as mental acts,

---

[6] See his *Frege: An Introduction to his Philosophy* (Brighton and Totowa, NJ, 1982), 156.

[7] *Frege: Logical Excavations* (Oxford and New York, 1984), 195.

since they are acts—something that we do—and are obviously not physical acts; but he insisted that the thoughts involved in them are *not* contents of the mind, but, as objective and accessible to all, are independent of our grasping them or judging them to be true. Logical relations are relations between such thoughts, and Frege concerned himself with logic and not with psychology; so no feature of his very undeveloped views concerning mental acts formed any obstacle to his giving what was to remain for a long time the clearest analysis of the relation between premisses and conclusion on which a valid inference must be based. The important feature of Frege's doctrine of assertion was his distinction between assertoric force and the content of the assertion—the thought asserted as true; whether it is possible to give a non-circular account of what assertion is is one of the large questions which he never addressed. To remark, as he did, that an assertion is the expression of a judgement, is not to commit oneself to holding that the former has to be explained in terms of the latter. Shanker is quite right to say that, for Frege, one can make an inference only from true premisses; but it is a calumny, with which I dealt in *The Interpretation of Frege's Philosophy*,[8] to represent him as denying the possibility of false assertions.

2. PSYCHOLOGISM, PLATONISM, AND LAWS OF THOUGHT

Frege's attack on psychologism was 'not the resounding success' that I claimed, Shanker declares (p. 567). He shared with his contemporaries 'the belief that logic consists in the study of the laws of thought' (p. 568), but insisted that it is a normative, not a descriptive, science (p. 567); and he treated our inability to understand those who denied fundamental laws of logic as a psychological limitation, instead of seeing, as Wittgenstein did, that the laws of logic *define* what we call 'reasoning' (p. 567). Frege criticized psychologism for confusing the act of judgement with its object, and so projecting the psychological character of the former on to the latter. His remedy was to adopt a platonist account of thoughts, as the objects of judgement (pp. 567–8); but that merely shifts the problem 'from that of explaining what it is that we think, to explaining what it is for us to think what we think', that is, what it is to grasp a thought (p. 568).

[8] (London and Cambridge, Mass., 1981), 4–5.

Laws of Thought

The attribution to Frege of the view that logic is a normative science is very frequent, but for all that no more than a half-truth. In earlier writings (for instance, in *Begriffsschrift*, §13), he used the phrase 'laws of thought' without a qualm; but his considered view is stated in the unpublished 'Logik' of 1879. He says there that *if* we call the laws of logic 'laws of thought', we must remember that they are laws which 'prescribe how we are to act', 'prescriptions for judging which must be complied with if the truth is not to be missed', rather than laws 'which, like natural laws, determine the actual course of events':[9] they are not laws laying down how we in fact think. But this is only *if* we choose to use the term 'laws of thought' of logical laws; and Frege thinks it 'better to avoid the term "laws of thought" altogether in logic'. His reason is twofold. The expression tempts us to regard logical laws as descriptive of our thinking; and, even when they are taken as prescriptive, to characterize them as laws we must obey if we are to arrive at the truth fails to distinguish them from any other laws. 'One could regard geometrical and physical laws as laws of thought . . . just as well as the logical ones, namely as prescriptions to which judging must conform . . . if it is to remain in harmony with the truth.' Rather, logical laws are to be regarded as the laws of truth: so regarded, they are no more normative than are the laws of geometry. The same point was made by Husserl when he argued that 'every normative . . . discipline presupposes one or more theoretical disciplines as its foundation':[10] for this reason, a characterization of logic as a normative science is quite superficial, for logic is best regarded as the theoretical science underlying the relevant normative principles; the important question is the proper characterization of the subject-matter of this theoretical but non-prescriptive science.

Disagreements over Fundamental Logical Laws

Frege admittedly gave no good account of the nature of the confrontation between those who differ over the fundamental laws of logic. Nor, however, did Wittgenstein. To give such an account, one must attend to disputes of this kind that genuinely arise, such as that

[9] *Nachgelassene Schriften*, 157; *Posthumous Writings*, 145.
[10] E. Husserl, *Logische Untersuchungen: Prolegomena zur reinen Logik* (Halle, 1900, 1913), §16.

between classical and intuitionistic logic in mathematics, or, perhaps, that between classical logic and quantum logic. For one disputant to say to the other that the laws he accepts define what he counts as reasoning would cut no more ice than for him to abuse the other as insane.

Platonism concerning Thoughts

Shanker's characterization of Frege as distinguishing the object (better, the content) of thinking, as being something non-mental, from the act of thinking is perfectly correct; and he is also right in saying that his platonism concerning thoughts failed to solve the problem of the objectivity of sense. As a positive solution, the myth of the 'third realm' has nothing to offer; but Shanker fails to see the importance of the negative part of the doctrine. On the one hand, it liberated Frege from seeking an account of thoughts in terms of psychological operations, and thereby enabled him to construct the first plausible theory in the history of philosophy of what constitutes the content of a thought, that is, the sense of a sentence, and the senses of subsentential expressions of different types. On the other, it opened the way to analytical philosophy. For the thesis that senses are not contents of consciousness required that they be constituted by something objective, non-mental and yet not in the ordinary sense physical, and accessible to all: once the myth of the third realm is discarded, what more natural to identify as constituting them than the social institution of a common language?

3. CONTEXTUAL DEFINITION AND THE PRIMACY OF SENTENCES

According to Shanker, Frege neither defended contextual definitions in *Grundlagen*, nor repudiated them, in that work or later: rather, since he did not admit that names and sentences belong to distinct semantic categories, even in his early period, when he took sentences to name judgeable contents, he drew no distinction between contextual and explicit definitions, and had no place for any such distinction: the need for such a distinction 'only results from the modern conception that sentences and names belong to distinct semantic categories' (p. 569). The primacy of sentences lay, for Frege, not in their being of a different logical type from proper names, but in their being vehicles of judgement, and hence playing a special role in inferences: 'for Frege, the primacy of sentences is entirely a consequence of the conception of inference which he inherited' (p. 570).

Contextual Definitions

That Frege expressly rejected contextual definition in his mature period cannot be questioned. In *Grundgesetze*, vol. i, §33, he laid down as one of seven fundamental principles of definition that:

> The name being defined must be simple; that is, it must not be composed out of already known names or names that have yet to be defined; for otherwise it would remain doubtful whether the definitions of the names were in harmony with each other.

(The word 'name' here applies to a symbol of any logical type.) In vol. ii, §66, he spells out this 'principle of the simplicity of the defined expression' thus:

> It is evident that the reference of an expression and that of one of its parts do not always determine the reference of the remaining part. One ought therefore not to define a symbol or word by defining an expression in which it occurs and in which the remaining parts are already known. For (to avail myself of a readily understandable algebraic metaphor) it would first be necessary to investigate whether it was possible to solve for the unknown, and whether the unknown was uniquely determined. But, as has already been said, it is impracticable to make the admissibility of a definition dependent upon the outcome of such an investigation, which, perhaps, we may not be able to carry out. Rather, the definition must have the character of an equation solved for the unknown, so that on the other side nothing unknown any longer occurs.

Shanker's claim that Frege does not draw a distinction between explicit and contextual definitions, and that, from his point of view, 'there is simply no need to distinguish' them is thus plainly false, if it was intended to cover the whole of Frege's career.

Shanker understands me as holding that, in *Grundlagen*, Frege first defended contextual definition and then repudiated it, whereas, in Shanker's opinion, he did neither. He certainly never repudiated contextual definition in that book, and in *Frege: Philosophy of Language*,[11] I expressly said that he did not. He devotes §§63–7 to a discussion of what he calls 'an attempted definition' (*Definitionsversuch*) of the operator 'the direction of *a*', with an eye to a similar

---

[11] (London, 1981), 496.

definition of the operator 'the number of Fs'; and Shanker is quite right to say that he eventually rejects the proposed definition, in §§66–7, not on the score of any general objection to contextual definitions, but for the specific reason, applying only to purported definitions on this model, that it leaves us with no way of determining the truth-value of a sentence like 'England is the direction of the earth's axis'. But it is indisputable that he begins by defending contextual definition. The proposed definition of the operator 'the number of Fs' is of course to be given by laying down the condition for the truth of a sentence of the form 'the number of Fs is the same as the number of Gs'; and the first objection to it considered by Frege, in §63, is that:

The relation of identity does not occur only among numbers. It appears to follow from this that it ought not to be defined especially for that case. We should expect the concept of identity to have already been established previously, and that then, from it and the concept of number, it would have to result when numbers were identical with one another, without the need for a further special definition of that.

Frege rejects this objection, however, saying:

Against this it is to be remarked that for us the concept of number has not yet been established, but is to be determined precisely by means of our definition. Our intention is to construct the content of a judgement that can be regarded as an identity in such a manner that a number stands on each side of this equation. We therefore are not wishing to define identity specially for this case, but, by means of the already known concept of identity, to arrive at that which is to be considered to be identical.

The objection was precisely to the contextual character of the definition; the reply, which is not withdrawn in any later passage in the book, is to the effect that such a contextual definition is legitimate—we may solve for the unknown.

Names and Sentences

Shanker claims that Frege was precluded from perceiving any distinction between explicit and contextual definitions, since he regarded sentences as names, that is, took them to belong to the same semantic category as singular terms. He follows Baker and Hacker in insisting that this applied as much to his early as to his mature period, the difference being only that, in the early period, sentences were for him names of judgeable contents, rather than of truth-values. Now there is a shift, from *Begriffsschrift* to *Grundgesetze*, in the formation rules of Frege's formal system: in *Begriffsschrift*, it is not true that a sentence (an expression for a judgeable content) can stand wherever a proper name can stand. Claims that Frege nevertheless regarded judgeable contents as objects that could be named cannot obliterate this distinction; in fact, it was not until *Grundlagen* that he came to use the word 'object' extensively or with any precision, and he did not then raise the question whether judgeable contents were objects, a question that seems alien to his early thought. It was not until his mature period that he unequivocally identified sentences as names of objects; and it was then that he developed objections of principle to contextual definitions. It is evident from this that Shanker's reasoning is astray. His ground for holding that Frege could not admit a distinction between contextual and explicit definitions rests on a misunderstanding of what contextual definitions are. He apparently thinks that a definition is an explicit one if a term stands on either side of the sign for definitional equivalence, and a contextual one if a sentence does; whereas the criterion is that, in an explicit definition, only the expression to be defined stands on one side, whereas, in a contextual definition, what stands there is a complex expression (whether a sentence or not) of which the definiendum is a proper part. Of course, if the definiendum is a predicate or other incomplete expression, it will have to appear in the definition with a free variable in each of its argument-places, with the same free variable occurring in the definiens: the occurrence of free variables does not impugn the explicit character of the definition.

The Context Principle Again

Shanker interprets me as construing the context principle as no more than a licence to employ contextual definitions, although in *The Interpretation of Frege's Philosophy* (pp. 363–4), I warned against such a reading; he is quite right to observe, as I had also done in the above-mentioned passage, that Frege's reiteration of the principle, in §106, in the course of his final summary of the argument of *Grundlagen* proves that that cannot possibly exhaust its significance for him, since the proposed contextual definition of the numerical operator had been abandoned long before. It is equally certain, however, that he took the principle as giving such a licence. Shanker believes that Frege's 'apparent abandonment of the principle' after *Grundlagen* is 'a major source of embarrassment' for my interpretation. Despite the confused discussion accorded to it, this question now seems to me to be capable of a very straightforward answer.

The crucial passages for an assessment of Frege's attitude after 1890 are *Grundgesetze*, vol. i, §§10, 29, and 32. The context principle, as originally stated in *Grundlagen*, admits a weak and a strong interpretation. On the weak interpretation, it says that:

The meaning of an expression consists in its contribution to the content of any sentence containing it.

On the strong interpretation, it says, rather, that:

An expression has been given a meaning once the truth-conditions of all sentences containing it are determined.

After the distinction between sense and reference had been drawn, such formulations, using a vague notion of 'meaning', would no longer represent any clear theses about which we could ask whether Frege would accept or reject them: we have to consider the twin results of replacing 'meaning' by 'sense' and by 'reference'. Now in *Grundgesetze*, vol. i, §32, Frege, explaining his notion of sense for the first time in the book, first explains what thought he takes an arbitrary sentence of his symbolic notation to express. More exactly, he speaks of a 'name of a truth-value' rather than of a 'sentence', the latter term being reserved for a formula complete with the judgement-stroke. He then treats of subsentential symbolic expressions having a logical unity (those expressions which he here calls generically 'names'), and says:

The names, whether simple or themselves complex, of which the name of a truth-value is composed, contribute to the expression of the thought, and this contribution of the individual component is its *sense*.

If, as I now think we should, we understand Frege as intending to give a general statement of what constitutes the sense of a subsentential expression, this formulation clearly represents a reiteration, for sense, of the weak interpretation of the context principle. Although, at the level of reference, Frege now recognizes no distinctions between names of truth-values and names of other objects, that is, between sentences and singular terms, he still accords sentences (considered apart from their assertoric force) a quite special role in the theory of sense. It seems reasonable to say that Frege's distinctions of logical type relate primarily to the theory of reference; if so, Shanker is right in denying that 'the primacy of sentences lay . . . in their being of a different logical type from proper names', and I, in the past, have been in error in thinking that Frege's distinctions of logical type formed an obstacle to his maintaining the principle that sentences are primary in the theory of sense. Shanker makes their primacy turn on their being 'vehicles of judgement', as witnessed by the judgement-stroke's being attachable only to a 'name of a truth-value', but this is only half the truth: they are primary in an account of sense.

This is only a weak version of the context principle for sense. It tells us that the sense of an expression consists in the contribution it makes to the thought expressed by a sentence containing it; but not that its sense may be determined by fixing the senses of such sentences. How, then, does it stand for the context principle as applied to reference?

In §10 of *Grundgesetze*, vol. i, Frege argues that the stipulation he has so far made (to be embodied subsequently in his Axiom V) does not suffice to determine the references of value-range terms uniquely, and asks, 'How is this indeterminacy to be resolved?' His answer is:

By its being determined, for every function as it is introduced, which values it shall obtain for value-ranges as arguments, just as for all other arguments.

He proceeds to discuss how to secure a determinate value for every primitive function so far introduced for the referent of every value-range term as argument, or, in the case of binary functions, as one of the two arguments. Having accomplished this to his satisfaction, he says:

We have hereby determined the *value-ranges* as far as is here possible. As soon as it again becomes a matter of introducing a function not fully reducible to already known functions, we can stipulate what values it is to have for value-ranges as arguments; and this can be regarded as being as much a determination of value-ranges as of that function.

In §29, he generalizes this principle, laying down that:

A proper name has a *reference* if a reference is possessed by every proper name that results from inserting the given proper name in the argument-place of a name of a first-level function of one argument, provided that this function-name has a reference; and if, further, a reference is possessed by every name of a first-level function with one argument that results from inserting the proper name in question in the [first] argument-place of the name of a first-level function with two arguments, and the same holds good for the [second] argument-place, provided that this function-name has a reference.

'Proper name' is, of course, Fregean for 'singular term'. In other words, a term is to be deemed to have a reference if a reference has been specified for every more complex term of which it is part, where, for Frege, 'terms' include sentences ('names of truth-values'). The proviso that the function-symbol into whose argument-place the given term has been inserted should itself have a reference gives an appearance of circularity, for the criterion for a function-symbol to have a reference is that a reference should be possessed by every term formed by inserting a term itself having a reference into the argument-place of the function-symbol. Frege's intention was, of course, that the stipulations which guaranteed a reference to each well-formed term or function-symbol of his symbolism should not be circular; the occurrence of the contradiction in his system is testimony that he failed to achieve this objective. The idea, as applied to value-ranges, for example, was that the stipulation governing the function-symbol should specify the value of the function for each object as argument independently of whether that object was a referent of a value-range term. The function-symbol could then be recognized as having a reference in advance of the stipulations laying down the reference of a term formed by inserting a value-range term in its argument-place, and circularity would be avoided.

We plainly have here a form of context principle for reference. The formulation in §29 could be understood according to the weak interpretation; but Frege's argumentation in §10 makes plain that he intends the strong one: namely, that it is by our laying down what is to be the reference of each complex term containing a given term that we determine the reference of that given term. The application of this form of the context principle has, however, been restricted to singular terms ('proper names'), instead of to arbitrary expressions ('words' in the *Grundlagen* formulation); at the same time, in accordance with the obliteration, in the theory of reference, of the distinction between sentences and terms, the context has been widened to comprise all complex singular terms.

It is clear that in *Grundlagen* the context principle is meant to be understood in its strong sense; and it is hardly surprising that, so understood, Frege should have taken it as a justification of contextual definition, the most striking instance of this occurring in the footnote to §60. It may seem more surprising, in view of the form of context principle for reference enunciated in §§10 and 29 of *Grundgesetze*, vol. i, that he should have come so vehemently to reject contextual definition. There is no inconsistency, however. In §§10 and 29 he is concerned with metalinguistic stipulations determining the reference of expressions of the formal object-language, and these do not need to satisfy the condition demanded of a definition, that it enable us to find equivalents not containing the defined expression for all formulas containing it. Conversely, a contextual definition specifies the reference of only one type of sentence or other complex term containing the definiendum, whereas stipulations of the kind required by Frege will specify the references of all such terms.

So far as I can see, this gives a complete answer to this question how Frege viewed the context principle in his mature period.

4. THE EARLY PERIOD AND THE MATURE PERIOD

In interpreting Frege, Shanker urges, we should not assume that the mature doctrine, set in the framework of the sense/reference distinction, is an essential clarification of the doctrine of the early period, in which the notion of judgeable content is central. Rather, we should start with the early doctrine, taking the notion of judgeable-content as 'the foundation on which we build our interpretation of Frege'; and we should 'see the later writings as desperate attempts to surmount . . . obstacles' to 'the progress of logicism'. 'Such a change of emphasis', Shanker adds, 'results . . . in a radically different picture of what Frege was trying to accomplish' (p. 566). The sense/reference distinction was primarily, or at least originally, intended merely to provide an improved account of identity-statements (p. 570). It is therefore just a technical modification of Frege's function-theoretic analysis of judgeable contents, added to that framework 'in order to provide a logically impeccable route from concepts to their extensions' (p. 571). By concentrating on Frege's exploitation of the contemporary development of function theory, 'we can begin to discern the outlines of an interpretation of' him different from mine, and doing more justice to history: Frege will then stand revealed as 'a late nineteenth-century philosopher of mathematics who resolutely pursues his logicist goal, tinkering with his system when he encounters obstacles' (p. 571).

Methodology

As far as we can tell from Frege's writings, published and unpublished, he saw the modifications announced in 1891 as essential improvements to his theories, which nevertheless remained substantially continuous with those he had formerly held. If this was truly his opinion, it creates a strong presumption that we should look at his work in this light. It is therefore methodologically mistaken to concentrate exclusively on the early work, extracting from it a complete doctrine covering questions that Frege never raised at that time: when he addressed himself to them, he found it necessary to modify the theories.

Sense and Reference

Sometimes a philosopher's second thoughts are less successful than his first ones; but it is a bad idea to presume that he spoiled his own work when he believed himself to be improving it, unless this can be rigorously demonstrated. Shanker offers no justification for regarding Frege's later writings as '*desperate* attempts to surmount obstacles': most people have seen them as propounding a highly plausible and coherent theory. Even Shanker acknowledges that Frege's early account of identity stood in need of improvement: if so, it would be good to know what better improvement he believes should be made than that which Frege himself proposed.

In fact, however, the sense/reference distinction did a great deal more than clean up the account of identity. It is frequently asserted, as it is by Shanker, that Frege's original motive for introducing the distinction was to obtain a better explanation of identity-statements, but there is no evidence for this: all we know is that he rightly believed that they provided an excellent first means of persuading others of the need for it. It would be more plausible to say that his original concern was to explain the general notion of the cognitive value of a statement. Obviously, identity-statements provide a motive for applying the distinction only to singular terms, and, if this were all Frege's theory amounted to, it would be far less remarkable: the important feature of it was his extension of the distinction to expressions of all logical types. It is in fact almost impossible to arrive at a coherent understanding of *Grundlagen* without invoking the sense/reference distinction that he had not yet drawn: for instance, the term 'concept', as used in that book, sometimes means the sense of a predicate or general term and sometimes its reference. We can make no sense, for example, of the thesis that the content of a statement of number consists in predicating something of a concept unless we view the concept as being the *reference* of the concept-word. Immensely powerful as Frege's first two books were, his early work does not admit of a fully coherent interpretation. To arrive at one, it requires the importation of ideas he developed later, not as a repudiation of his earlier thought, but as a development of it. To interpret all of Frege's philosophy by looking at the mature work from the standpoint of the earlier, rather than conversely, is to look through the telescope from the wrong end.

Prospects for a New Interpretation

For Shanker, arriving at such a new interpretation by thus reversing our viewpoint is merely a hope for the future. His one prescription is to concentrate on Frege's use in semantic theory of the notion of a function. This is surely a bad recipe if one wishes to place most emphasis on the early period, since, despite his employment of the word 'function' in *Begriffsschrift*, his serious use of the concept of a function only began with his mature writings. Shanker implicitly accuses me of neglecting Frege's use of this concept; I have yet to see a more effective appeal made to it in expounding Frege than I made in *The Interpretation of Frege's Philosophy* (where I confessed to having undervalued Frege's use of it in *Frege: Philosophy of Language*). Baker and Hacker aimed, in their *Frege: Logical Excavations*, to provide a new interpretation, such as Shanker desires. In accordance with this aim, they treated the early work as embodying a fully worked out doctrine rather than an unfinished first version. In doing so, they in effect reinterpreted the early work in the light of the mature doctrine; while proclaiming themselves to be the first actually to look at the texts, they in fact thereby did them more violence than anyone else has done. In particular, in interpreting his early work, they took over wholesale the use Frege made in his mature period of the concept of a function. Neither for the early nor for the mature period, however, did they arrive at any new insights concerning his use of the concept; rather, they appealed to it principally in order to accuse Frege of incoherence, on the ground that the models of part

11
Frege and Wittgenstein*

Everyone knows that Wittgenstein was soaked in Frege's writings and in Frege's thought. Doubtless many philosophers unnamed by Wittgenstein can be shown to have given him ideas. Others, to whom he does refer, provided him with material that he found interesting to reflect or comment on: but Frege is very nearly the only one whom he quotes with approval. It would be an exhausting and a thankless task to cull from Wittgenstein's writings every passage containing an overt or covert reference to Frege, or for the understanding of which it is necessary to know Frege's ideas, and I have not attempted it; I dwell on only a few points that have struck me as of especial interest.

Some of Wittgenstein's work builds on, elaborates, or complements that of Frege: and then, I think, Wittgenstein is at his happiest. One example is the famous doctrine of Frege concerning the necessity for criteria of identity (a phrase which Frege introduced into philosophy). It is stated in the *Grundlagen* thus: 'If we are to use the sign *a* to designate an object, we must have a criterion for deciding in all cases whether *b* is the same as *a*.' The principle here enunciated by Frege is perfectly general, and the idea is fundamental for the first third of the *Philosophical Investigations*, and, indeed, throughout that book. Yet Frege himself worked out its implication only to terms for abstract objects, or, to speak more precisely, to terms of such forms as 'the direction of *a*', 'the number of Fs', and so on; that is, to terms formed by means of expressions for functions of first or second level which do not, or do not obviously, carry their arguments into objects specifiable without appeal to those functions. It was left to Wittgenstein to apply the principle that the understanding of a singular term involves the apprehension of an appropriate criterion of identity to terms of other sorts, including for what would ordinarily be thought of as concrete objects.

Again, consider Frege's insistence that the sense of an expression is not connected with any psychological process, for instance the

* First published in I. Block (ed.), *Perspectives on the Philosophy of Wittgenstein* (Oxford, 1981), 31–42 (paper delivered in 1976).

evocation of mental images, a principle he expressly associated with the objectivity of sense, with the fact that a thought is communicable without residue from speaker to hearer by means of language. Frege thought it necessary to safeguard the non-psychological character of sense by holding that senses exist timelessly and in independence of whether there is available any means of expressing them. This highly unWittgensteinian thesis he supported by a number of bad arguments, such as that, even before there were men, it was already true that the earth goes round the sun, and would have been true even if there had never been any men; and surely what is true is a thought, and a thought is the sense of a sentence. But this did not save Frege from getting into difficulties over the question: Even granted that senses are not mind-dependent, still grasping a sense, or understanding a word or phrase, as expressing a sense, is surely a mental act, something that belongs within the province of psychology. Frege never found a satisfactory answer to this objection: it receives its answer from Wittgenstein's observation (*Philosophical Investigations*, §154), 'Try not to think of understanding as a "mental process" at all. . . . In the sense in which there are processes (including mental processes) which are characteristic of understanding, understanding is not a mental process.'

Or, finally, take Frege's views about the relation between sense and reference. Sense determines reference, but reference does not determine sense; nevertheless, when we lay down what the reference of some expression is to be, we thereby provide a sense for it. As I remarked in *Frege: Philosophy of Language*[1] and as, I understand, Peter Geach has worked out in much more detail, it is difficult to expound this doctrine without inconsistency save by invoking the distinction drawn in the *Tractatus* between *saying* and *showing*. In laying down what an expression is to stand for, we *say* what its reference is, not what its sense is; but, by choosing, as we must, a particular manner of doing this, we *show* what sense it is to have. The distinction between saying and showing is not only consonant with Frege's ideas, but almost required for a coherent statement of them. Indeed, had Frege had this distinction at his command, a great deal of misunderstanding of his doctrine of sense would surely have been avoided. Not only, in laying down the reference of a term, do we not *state*, but only *show*, its sense; but surely we ought

---

[1] (London, 1973), 227.

to add, we cannot state the sense of an expression, save as being the same as that of some other expression, something which, within one language, there is no reason to suppose can always be done. That does not mean, in my view, that a theory of sense is mute, that a theory of sense can only be shown, not stated, since while we cannot state the sense of an expression, we can state what it is to grasp that sense and attach it to that expression. Whether or not Frege would have agreed with this last remark, I do not know; but I do feel reasonably certain that, if he had had the distinction between saying and showing to hand, he would not have laid himself open to the charge, which I continue to believe is a misinterpretation, of having held a 'description theory' of proper names.

All these are cases in which Wittgenstein built upon doctrines of Frege to produce what is not only a legitimate, but the only true, development of them. In other cases, Wittgenstein fought against the power of Frege's thought; and in such cases, I believe, he was almost always at his worst. In most of them, in my opinion, Frege was in the right and Wittgenstein in the wrong; but, even when this is not so, Wittgenstein seldom succeeded in framing cogent arguments to show that Frege was wrong. Take, for example, his repeated attacks upon Frege's doctrine of assertion. The first hundred-odd paragraphs of the *Philosophical Investigations* almost all compel assent; although there may be large questions about how one should go on from there, it is almost impossible to read those paragraphs and maintain any reservations about this definitive treatment of the topics with which they deal. But from this classic landscape, paragraph 22—that in which he attacks Frege's doctrine of assertion—sticks out like a gasometer. To vary the metaphor abruptly, the boxer's punches suddenly become feeble, and miss their mark or are easily blocked.

Or, again, consider the celebrated passage towards the beginning of the *Blue Book*[2] in which Wittgenstein comments on Frege's criticism of the formalist philosophy of mathematics as ignoring the sense, and thus, as Wittgenstein says, the life of the mathematical formulas. He characterizes Frege's conclusion as that '. . . what must be added to the dead signs in order to make a live proposition is something immaterial, with properties different from all mere signs', and retorts, 'But if we had to name anything which is the life

² L. Wittgenstein, *The Blue and Brown Books* (Oxford, 1958), 4.

of the sign, we should have to say that it was its *use*.' If, as Waismann did, one interprets the 'use' of a mathematical statement as its extra-mathematical application, the idea is very unconvincing. What is the application of the proposition that every number is the sum of four squares? Even if one can think of one, could someone not perfectly well understand this proposition without having the least suspicion of that application? If it is the application of mathematical concepts that ultimately gives them their meaning, then, one must surely say, the injection of meaning may be very remote from the particular proposition considered. One cannot ask for the application proposition by proposition, but, at best, for the applications of the basic concepts; once these are grasped, the mathematical theory takes on a life of its own. But, in this sense, did not Frege do full justice to the relation between a basic mathematical concept and its application? Did he not write, 'It is applicability alone that raises arithmetic from the rank of a game to that of a science: applicability therefore belongs essentially to it'?[3] It was not Frege who formulated the Peano axioms or presented number theory as a self-contained axiomatic system; on the contrary, he insisted that the natural numbers could be explained only by reference to their use as cardinal numbers in empirical, and other, propositions; and he thought that the real numbers must, similarly, be explained by reference to the general conception of a measure of the magnitude of a quantity. In any case, what *is* an application of a mathematical proposition? We are all so used to the fact that there is such a thing as applied mathematics that we do not stop to notice what an odd idea it is that a theory, or a proposition, can be 'applied' to some other subject-matter. I do not mean to deny that mathematics gets applied: I am contending only that an appeal to the application of mathematics cannot help us philosophically until we can say in what such an application consists; and we cannot say this until we have a prior account of the significance of a mathematical statement.

Almost certainly, however, Wittgenstein did not intend to restrict the notion of the 'use' of a mathematical statement to its empirical applications, but had in mind, not only its application within mathematics, but, more generally, its role in the mathematical theory. But what is to show that Frege did not succeed in giving a general account of this? True, Frege took sense to be immaterial

---

[3] *Grundgesetze der Arithmetik*, ii (Jena, 1903), §91.

and to exist independently of our grasping it; but this does not exhaust his conception of the sense of a sentence: he said a great deal more about what such a sense consists in, above all, that, in grasping the sense of a sentence, including a mathematical sentence, what we grasp is the condition for that sentence to be true. Perhaps these are not, after all, the right terms in which to explain our understanding of mathematical statements; perhaps it can be shown that the use which we learn to make of such statements is incapable of being explained in this way. But, then, it has to be shown: one cannot simply oppose the notion of use to Frege's notion of sense, as if it were something Frege had obviously left out of account. I am not, of course, here criticizing Wittgenstein's famous conception of meaning as use: I am criticizing only a formulation which makes it appear that, in arriving at this conception, Wittgenstein had discovered something which immediately shows Frege to have been thinking along the wrong lines.

When Wittgenstein is moved to make direct criticisms of Frege, the criticism is usually curiously ineffective, and fails to do justice to Frege's thought. It is one thing to make this observation, however, and quite another to say that, whenever Wittgenstein diverges from Frege on any essential point, he gets on to the wrong track. That would be to make a devastating condemnation of Wittgenstein, if it could be made out; for there is no doubt that the differences between them are not just a matter of style, or of passing remarks, or of disagreements over inessentials: many of Wittgenstein's most fundamental ideas concerning meaning are irreconcilable with those of Frege.

The first attempt to make a radical modification in Frege's conception of how language functions was the picture theory, perhaps, better, the diagram theory, of the *Tractatus*. In Frege, a proper name (singular term) is complete (*selbständig*), and so is a sentence; and the things which they stand for, an object and a truth-value, are similarly complete. But a one- or two-place predicate is incomplete, and so is the concept or relation for which it stands. The incompleteness of the predicate is not a mere semantic property: it does not consist just in its having to be understood as standing for something incomplete, a mapping of objects on to truth-values. Rather, it is itself incomplete: it is not just a string of words that can be extracted from the sentence and stand on its own, not even a disconnected string; its occurrence in the sentence depends, in general, upon the occurrence in different places in the sentence of the same proper name. It is, thus, not a detachable bit of the sentence, but a feature that the sentence has in common with certain other sentences. The completeness of names and of sentences, conversely, is similarly not a mere semantic property: they are themselves complete—they are objects—in the way that predicates are not.

Now this, notoriously, leads to difficulty. If the fundamental conception of Frege's theory of meaning—that to grasp the sense of a sentence is to know the condition for its truth—is right at all, then surely the identification of the reference of a sentence with its truth-value is correct. Admittedly, this forces us to treat intensional contexts in some special way; but, then, we are already forced to do this by Frege's identification of the semantic values (references) of proper names with their bearers. If the reference of 'Napoleon' is a man, and that of 'Mont Blanc' a mountain, then we already know that names, at least, cannot have their standard reference when they appear in intensional contexts. But, if the reference of a sentence is its truth-value, we are very easily led into the disastrous step which Frege took of assimilating sentences to proper names: sentences are just complex names of a special kind of object. This step produces intolerable consequences, and so we must seek to undo it: but how? Not, surely, by denying that sentences have reference at all. The whole theory of reference is an attempt to give an account of how a sentence is determined as true or false in accordance with its composition: and, if Frege's fundamental conception of the theory of meaning is correct, such an account must be possible, and must underlie any account of sense, which is what determines reference. But sentences can occur as constituent parts of other sentences; and so they must be assigned a reference if the whole theory is to fulfil its appointed task. (If sentences could not occur as parts of other sentences, we should be in no difficulty.) Nor, while sentences are regarded as being complete in the same way that proper names are, does it seem reasonable, in the context of Frege's fundamental conception of a theory of meaning, to deny that what a sentence has as its reference is its truth-value. The only recourse, which I should myself favour, is to deny that truth-values are objects; and this seems a weak response. Of course, we have a strong intuition that sentences are not of the same syntactic or semantic category as proper names, and this implies, at least within a Fregean framework, that the things they stand for will be of different logical types too: but to say that truth-values are not objects hardly illuminates the nature of this type-difference. We can say various things in support. We can, for instance, as Peter Geach has pointed out, say that the principle of the interchangeability of any expression α with ⌜what 'α' stands for⌝ works very badly, if at all, for sentences. Or, again, we can observe that, while with names and even with predicates it seems plausible to say that the references of our words are what we talk about, we have not the least inclination to allow that we use a subsentence of a complex sentence to talk about its truth-value. Still, these incongruities seem rather witnesses to the difference between objects and truth-values than explanations of it. If we are going to get such an explanation, it will surely depend upon a much more searching enquiry into what truth-values are.

The picture or diagram theory surely appeared as a brilliant solution of this difficulty. If a predicate is a property, rather than an object, why not take it as a property, not of the sentence, but of the name or names that appear in its argument-places? The predicate will not consist in the property of the atomic sentence that the same proper name occurs in various places between certain other words: rather, (a token of) the predicate will consist in the property of the name that certain tokens of it occur in those places. If we say that, then we can replace the sentence as object—the string of words— by the sentence as fact—the fact that a certain name has a certain property, or that two names stand in a certain relation. And then, abiding by the principle, which is not in Frege, but is partially suggested by his doctrine of predicates and of concepts, that a linguistic ingredient of a given logical type will stand for an entity of the same logical type, we shall arrive at the conclusion that the sentence—considered as fact—must itself stand for or represent a fact, or, rather, since it need not be true, a state of affairs; and now the temptation to think that names and sentences stand for or represent things of the same logical type is totally dissolved.

This would have been a brilliant solution had it worked. Unfortunately, it does not work. A sentence cannot be a fact because it states just one thing; and the hearer, if he understands the language, must know just what it is that it states. A diagram is not a fact, it is an object; and there are many facts about the diagram. If we understand the method of representation, then we shall know which facts about the diagram represent, and which do not: for instance, which lines are drawn in black, and which in red, may or may not be significant; and we may well overlook some of these facts although we see the diagram and understand it. The diagram will show, for example, that the only man in the village with great-grandchildren has a wife older than himself, and also that only the three oldest men in the village have wives older than themselves, and so on; and what show these different facts are different facts about the diagram, facts not all of which we may notice, and, save with the simplest diagram, some of which we are sure *not* to notice, when we look at the diagram. But a sentence is not like this: though the sentence may imply many things, it *says* just one thing, and, if you understand it at all, you must know what it says; you cannot, just by studying the sentence more closely, elicit new things that it says that you had not noticed before. Well, it may be replied, that is because the diagram is, as you said, not itself a fact but an object: any one fact about the diagram signifies just one fact about what it represents; and the sentence is being claimed to be a fact, not a diagram or picture— hence the inappropriateness of the name 'the picture theory'. But, if a sentence is to represent in the way that a fact about the diagram does, there must be something that plays the role of the diagram, other facts about which will also represent; and what is that? If what represents some state of affairs is a fact about the properties or relations of certain objects, the names or signs, then we must start with some arrangement of these objects in virtue of which that fact obtains, and this arrangement will correspond to the diagram. What can that arrangement be but the sentence, considered, now, not as a fact but as an object with a certain complexity? Thus, if we try to take the picture or diagram theory seriously, we are, after all, forced back on to considering the sentence, once again, as an object; and, since there are not *different* facts about the sentence, as object, which represent different states of affairs, we are forced to conclude that the sentence does not represent as a diagram does, but in a different way altogether.

In his later work, the conception of meaning as use led Wittgenstein into a much more radical divergence from Frege's theory of meaning, although that conception itself owes something to Frege's ideas. For Frege, as I have remarked, it is of the essence of sense that it is communicable. It happens, indeed, that different speakers attach different senses to the same word; but the communicability of sense implies that it must always be objectively discoverable when this is so and objectively discoverable what sense each attaches. But, also, sense is not psychological; it is not because a speaker's utterance of a word occurs in response to some inner mental process, and that utterance triggers off a similar process in the mind of the hearer, and they share a common psychological make-up, that the one understands the other. Their agreement over the sense of the utterance consists in an agreement on the conditions under which it is true. Since sense is objective and communicable, it must be possible to determine from what they say, and how they react to what is said, what truth-conditions they attach to sentences. What makes this possible is that every utterance effects more than just the expression of a thought: the speaker also indicates, tacitly or explicitly, the type of linguistic act that he is performing, e.g. asserting that the thought is true, asking whether it is true, etc.; he thereby attaches one or another type of force to his utterance. Each type of force bears a uniform relation to the sense of the sentence: whether or not it is possible to give a non-circular characterization of the type of linguistic act effected by the utterance of a sentence with this or that variety of force, Frege never said. What is clear, however, is that, on this conception, everything involved in communication, both the sense expressed and the force attached to that expression, is determined by what lies open to view. Since no contact between mind and mind, save that achieved by the medium of linguistic interchange, need be assumed, and since the sense of an utterance and, presumably, the force it carries are objectively determinable, they can only be determined by the observable employment of the language. If a non-circular account of the different varieties of force is attainable, then we may describe how the speakers' use of their sentences determines what they convey by means of them. But, even if such an account is not attainable, that use, and nothing else, determines the content of their utterances: no other supposition would be compatible with the doctrines about language expressly propounded by Frege.

It is easy to see how, when these principles, learned from Frege, had been encapsulated in the slogan 'Meaning is use', Wittgenstein came, in his middle period, to give a verificationist turn to them. There is a tendency to be apologetic about this, as if verificationism were a rather discreditable complaint; but so far as I can see, no discredit attaches to this tendency at all. The cardinal error of logical positivism lay in treating all synthetic propositions as standing on the same level (unless they proved to be pseudo-propositions), that is, in ignoring the articulated structure of language. In the most characteristic forms of positivism, each sentence was treated as if it were in principle intelligible in isolation from the rest of language, being given meaning by some direct association with a set of possible sequences of sense-perceptions, each of which would constitute a verification of it. It was this unnatural picture which led to the complete sundering of analytic or would-be analytic propositions from the main body of language, since they could be established, if at all, only by linguistic operations, and hence had to be regarded as having a meaning of a completely different kind. To obtain a plausible conception of verification, it is necessary to recognize that no sentence can be understood without a mastery of some segment of the language, and that, in establishing a sentence as true, argument, including deductive argument, may always, and often must, play a part. So far as I know, there is no hint in Wittgenstein's writings of the positivists' mistake.

Verificationism naturally first appeared as a sharpening of Frege's conception of sense as given by truth-conditions: someone shows what he takes as the condition for the truth of a sentence by showing what he takes as establishing or excluding the truth. But it appears to me that Wittgenstein came to see it as a rival to Frege's conception. Frege assumed a notion of truth for which the principle of bivalence held good: save for failure of reference, every thought was determinately either true or false. But this means that, when there is no effective means, even in principle, to decide whether a thought is true or false, a knowledge of the condition for it to be true cannot be exhaustively accounted for in terms of a knowledge of those special conditions under which it may be recognized as one or the other. But, then, there seems no other way by which we may account for the supposed knowledge of the truth-condition in terms of actual use, of principles governing the actual employment of the sentence expressing the thought. Hence, if meaning is to be explained solely in terms of use, in such cases we must abandon the idea that a grasp of the sense consists in a knowledge of the condition for the sentence to be true, where the notion of truth is subject to the principle of bivalence, or even the idea that we have any such notion of truth. Rather, the understanding of the sentence consists in an ability to recognize what is taken to establish its truth, and, perhaps, what is taken as ruling it out.

But a much more radical idea superseded this. It is marked, in part, by Wittgenstein's embracing the redundancy theory of truth (of which there is an explicit expression in the *Remarks on the Foundations of Mathematics*, in the Appendix on Gödel's theorem). If an enunciation of the equivalence between a sentence A and the sentence ⌜ It is true that A ⌝ is the *whole* explanation of the meaning of the word 'true', then that word has, as it were, a home only *within* the language, and is of no use in giving an account of the language as from the outside: and this rules out, not only an account of meaning in terms of truth-conditions, but, equally, one in terms of verification. Passages like *Philosophical Investigations*, §§304 and 317, and, particularly, the middle paragraph of §363, are the expression of a total rejection of Frege's approach to language. For Frege, an utterance is an assertion, a question, a command, a request, a piece of advice, an instruction, an expression of a wish, or one of some small and determinate number of other things. What the particular content of the utterance is is a matter of its sense; what type of utterance it is, is a matter of the force attached to it. So, as I remarked, there must be a uniform explanation, or at least way of grasping, the significance of each type of utterance, the nature of each type of force, and, in particular, of assertoric force: uniform, that is, over all the possible particular contents, the senses, of utterances of that type. 'What is the language-game of telling?' *That* is the question that must have an answer if Frege's approach to language is at all correct: and here the difference between an account of sense in terms of truth-conditions and in terms of verification is quite beside the point; neither is workable unless we can distinguish sense from force. *Philosophical Investigations*, §363, is an overt repudiation of the possibility of such a distinction, or, at least, of any uniform account of what it is to make an assertion. And this, of course, explains Wittgenstein's hostility to Frege's doctrine of assertion. The confused objection of *Philosophical Investigations*, §22, is not the point. *Philosophical Investigations*, §23, is more to the point: if no definitive list of types of force can be made, then no complete account of a language can be arrived at by Frege's strategy. Even that is not the real point, however: we might be content to let some of the minor cases take care of themselves, if only we could deal with the most prominent uses of language. The real point is to deny that there is any 'language-game' of such generality as that of assertion; and, if there is not, then, it seems to me, there is no general distinction between sense and force.

What is the ground for this denial? That is something I have never been able to understand. Perhaps it is just that it seems so difficult to achieve a general account of assertoric force, of the language-game of assertion. Perhaps some watertight formulation can be arrived at along Gricean lines; but then to invoke the concept, not only of intention, but of belief, appears to be begging the question, since most of the beliefs formed on the testimony of others could not be intelligibly ascribed to anyone who had not the command of a language. If we forswear all appeal to propositional attitudes, however, we hardly know how to begin. But, now, what is supposed to be the alternative? Is it just that a systematic account of how a language functions, or of what we know when we know a language, is impossible? But, then, how can this be? It is something that we do, something that we learn to do: how can it be impossible to say what it is that we do, what it is that we learn? Of course, in one sense, we already know what we do: but we do not know how to *say* what it is we do. The simple language-games described by Wittgenstein, like the one about people going into a shop and saying things like 'Five red apples', are supposed to be some kind of model. But the practice of speaking any one of these tiny languages *can* be systematically described: so, if they are really a model, such descriptions can be given also for larger and larger fragments of language, and eventually the whole of it. Yet, as soon as one starts to think how one might set about doing this for even some quite restricted language that still permits anything resembling the discourse of everyday, rather than the employment of language as an adjunct to one specific activity, one's first thought is the necessity of some distinction between sense and force. Or, if one imagines a language with only assertions, what seems to be needed is an account of the particular content of each utterance in terms of some central notion such as truth or verification, set against the background of some uniform explanation of the significance of an utterance with some arbitrary given content, so determined. It is not that I think this would be easy to do: my difficulty, as I said, is to understand what alternative it was that Wittgenstein had in mind, something that I have never learned either from his writings or from those of philosophers who acknowledge him as their master.

12

Frege's Myth of the Third Realm*

One natural criticism of Frege's attack on psychologism is that it over-shot the target. Given his strict dichotomy between the radically subjective and the wholly objective—his rejection of any inter-mediate category of the intersubjective—it follows from the fact that the senses of words and of sentences can be grasped by different individuals that they exist eternally and immutably in complete independence of us: but is this not a textbook example of philosoph-ical mythology? Even if the conclusion is true, it cannot be proved by such means, which would equally prove that the moves of chess pieces exist eternally and independently of the games we play. There are sentences which no-one has ever framed, and such sentences have senses just as do those which are uttered; these are legitimate grounds for saying with Frege that a thought does not depend for its existence upon our grasping or expressing it. There are many different moves which pieces have had in obsolete or still-practised variations of chess, such as those of the pieces called Camel and Giraffe in Tamerlane's 'great chess'; and there must be countless other possible moves that might be assigned to pieces in versions of chess that have never been played or thought of. It is harmless to say that 'there are' such moves; but it would be insane to deny that moves are *of* (actual or possible) chess pieces. This 'of' of logical dependence is not properly expressed by saying that a certain move exists only if there is a piece that has that move, since, as just noted, we can speak of moves that have never been assigned to any piece. It means, rather, that to conceive of any move is to conceive of a piece as having that move. Chess moves are objects by Frege's criteria, for they can be named and have predicates applied to them. There is nothing wrong with Frege's criteria, nor with the principle of classifying things as objects, properties, or concepts, relations, and functions of various types. Frege's mistake is to assume that all objects are self-subsistent (*selbständig*): on the contrary, some are intrinsically 'of', or dependent on, other objects.

* First published in *Untersuchungen zur Logik und zur Methodologie*, 3 (1986), 24–38.

It would be insane to treat chess moves as not dependent in this sense on chess pieces; but it is perfectly possible to come to conceive of what Frege called 'thoughts'—what are expressed by utterances of sentences, what are judged to be true or false, what are believed, known, doubted—as independent of language and of thinking beings. This is precisely what Frege did; and it is in his doing so that he became guilty of philosophical mythologizing.

A belief in what Russell, Moore, and other British philosophers called 'propositions', conceived as non-mental entities expressed by sentences and forming the objects of propositional attitudes, was common to the whole realist school with which Frege may loosely be associated. In Bolzano they appear as '*Sätze an sich*', in Meinong as '*Objektive*'.[1] Whether Bolzano, Brentano (in his earlier phase), Husserl, or Meinong committed the error I am attributing to Frege is a matter for the exegesis of those writers. Exegesis is needed, since none of them explains logical dependence as it was explained above. One therefore cannot, for example, deduce that Husserl was mythologizing about the ideal meanings of sentences from the fact that, like Frege, he regarded them as immutable,[2] or from the fact that, like Frege, he took them to exist independently of being grasped or expressed:

What I mean by the sentence . . . or (when I hear it) grasp as its meaning, is the same thing, whether I think and exist or not, and whether or not there are *any* thinking persons or acts.[3]

---

[1]   One of the few sustained criticisms of this belief is that of Gilbert Ryle in his 'Are There Propositions?', *Proceedings of the Aristotelian Society*, 30 (1929–30), 91–126. Ryle's attack fails because it is founded on the assumption that there are facts, distinct from propositions, and that a believer in propositions must explain the truth of a proposition as its correspondence with a fact. Not only is Ryle's explanation of the ontological status of facts derisorily feeble and cursory, but the argument, to the effect that we do not need to posit propositions as well as facts, is powerless against those, such as Frege, who rejected the correspondence theory and declared facts to be nothing but true thoughts or propositions.

[2]   'The actual meanings of words fluctuate, often changing in the course of the same train of thought; and for a great part they are by their nature determined by the occasion. But, properly regarded, the fluctuation of meanings is really a *fluctuation in what is meant*. That is, what fluctuate are the subjective acts which bestow meaning on the expressions; and they change not merely individually, but, rather, according to the specific characters in which their meaning lies. But the meanings themselves do not change: such a way of speaking is indeed nonsensical, assuming that we continue . . . to understand by 'meanings' ideal unities'. *Logische Untersuchungen*, First Investigation, (Halle, 1901, 1913), vol. i, §28.

[3]   Ibid., §31.

After all, a chess move cannot change, though a piece can acquire a different move; and the move remains the same, whether or not it is assigned to any piece, and even whether or not chess was ever invented. Husserl comes very close to the mythological conception when he says that

There is as such . . . no necessary connection between the ideal unities which in practice serve as meanings and the signs to which they are attached.[4]

But even this could be defended by saying that there is no necessary connection between a move and the piece, identified by shape or initial position, to which it is assigned. To know whether they are guilty of mythology or not, one must go deep into the philosophies of these thinkers.[5]

Whatever the truth is about other philosophers, Frege's conception of thoughts and their constituent senses is mythological. These eternal, changeless entities inhabit a 'third realm', distinct from the physical universe and equally distinct from the inner world of any experiencing subject. Despite their separation from the physical world, many of these thoughts are *about* that world, and are true or false, not indeed by corresponding to anything in it or failing to do so, but, in so far as they are about the external world, in virtue of how things are in that world. Somehow we grasp these thoughts, and sometimes judge them to be true or false; indeed, it is only by grasping them that we become aware of the external world, rather than only of our own inner sensations and feelings. Somehow, too, we associate senses with words, and so communicate thoughts and judgements to one another.

As long as this perspective is dominant, all is mysterious. There is no way of explaining how thoughts relate to things in other realms of reality, that is, what makes them about anything. There is no way of

---

[4] Ibid., §35.

[5] An interesting defence of Husserl in this regard is to be found in D. Willard, 'The Paradox of Logical Psychologism: Husserl's Way Out', in J. N. Mohanty (ed.), *Readings on Edmund Husserl's 'Logical Investigations'* (The Hague, 1977), 55–66. Willard is actually maintaining that Husserl, alone of the anti-psychologistic theorists of logic, is able to explain how logic bears on actual thought and discourse. I have failed to see why he takes this to be a problem for them: certainly his remarks on Frege are vitiated by a misunderstanding of Frege's notion of an idea (*Vorstellung*). One can, however, read his essay as expounding the thesis that, of the friends of propositions, only Husserl avoided mythology by recognizing their logical dependence, in just the present sense, on specific acts of thinking.

explaining how we grasp them: no wonder Frege wrote, 'this process is perhaps the most mysterious of all'.[6] Above all, there is no way of explaining how we attach senses to words or expressions, that is, what makes them senses *of* those words and expressions. All this is obscured for us by Frege's having had very good, if not fully complete, explanations of all these things. It is just that these explanations cannot be reconciled with the mythological picture. When we have Frege's theory of meaning in view, our perspective has wholly altered: the third realm has receded to infinity.

John Searle has written:

It is at least misleading, if not simply a mistake, to say that a belief, for example, is a two-term *relation* between a believer and a proposition. An analogous mistake would be to say that a statement is a two-term relation between a speaker and a proposition. One should rather say that a proposition is not the *object* of a statement or belief but rather its *content*.[7]

The difficulty is to know whether we have a clear enough grasp of the distinction between object and content to be able to apply it so confidently. The notion of the object of a mental act or attitude seems straightforward enough in those cases in which grammar is a satisfactory guide, namely, when the object can be identified as the referent of the accusative of the verb (if we allow verb-plus-preposition as a form of transitive verb). The building is the object of my admiration because it is the building that I admire; the size of the audience is the object of my surprise because it is what I am surprised by. When we have verbs for propositional attitudes, such as 'believe' and 'hope', what they govern is a clause in indirect speech, or, in the case of 'believe', a term for a principle, hypothesis, doctrine, or the like. Searle's claim is that, in this case, grammar misleads us.

In his early period, Frege used the term 'content' for that which we judge true or false, and for its constituents; but such conceptual content was not, for him, the content of the mind or of the mental act, but of the linguistic expression. At every stage of his career, he spoke of contents of the mind or of consciousness only in contrast with thoughts and the senses which compose them. Neither mental contents nor thoughts were, for him, qualities of mental acts: the

---

[6] 'Logik', 1897, in *Nachgelassene Schriften*, ed. H. Hermes, F. Kambartel, and F. Kaulbach (Hamburg, 1969), 157.

[7] *Intentionality* (Cambridge, 1983), 18.

former he took to be inner objets of awareness, and the latter mind-independent objects of the mental acts of grasping and judging and of mental attitudes such as believing. He did not, indeed, speak of either as objects of mental acts, but this is largely because 'object of . . .' did not belong to the terminology he used. He plainly conceived of thoughts as objects of mental acts, however, as many passages show;[8] he did not operate with any distinction between the object and the content of a mental act.

Searle is nevertheless quite right. It is in taking thoughts as the objects of mental acts that Frege goes astray. The first false step is an apparently innocent one, namely, to hold that truth and falsity primarily attach to thoughts, and only derivatively to sentences.[9] Now the truth-value of a sentence stands to the thought expressed as reference (*Bedeutung*) to sense: the thesis is thus that it is the sense of the sentence to which the reference is primarily to be ascribed, and only derivatively the sentence itself. By parity, this must hold for all expressions: it is the sense, not the expression, which primarily refers. Admittedly, this consequence is seldom explicitly drawn by Frege. It is, however, expressed in the celebrated remark: 'The regular connection between the sign, its sense and its

---

[8] In the celebrated footnote to 'Die Verneinung: Eine logische Untersuchung' (in *Beiträge zur Philosophie des deutschen Idealismus*, 1 (1918), 151), he recommends using the word 'judgement' for an act of judging, 'as a leap in an act of leaping', but goes on to remark that to judge is to recognize something as true, and to identify what is recognized as true as a thought. (From what he further says, it is apparent that he wishes to take 'recognize . . . as true' to be a verb with a unitary sense, though split into three words: imitating Quine, we could say that the thought is the object of our recognizing-true.) In a footnote to 'Der Gedanke: Eine logische Untersuchung' (in *Beiträge zur Philosophie des deutschen Idealismus*, 1 (1918), 74), he says: 'The expression "to grasp" is as much a metaphor as "content of consciousness" . . . What I hold in my hand can indeed be regarded as the content of my hand, but yet it is the content of my hand in quite another, and more extraneous, way than the bones and muscles of which the hand consists or than the tensions they undergo.' The grasping of a thought is here compared to grasping a physical object—a hammer on p. 77; the thought is in the mind only in the sense in which the hammer is in the hand (but not in the body).

[9] 'It is . . . clear that it is not to the sequence of sounds which constitute the sentence but to its sense that we ascribe truth' ('Logik', 1897, *Nachgelassene Schriften*, 140). 'For the sake of brevity I have here spoken of the sentence as true or false, although more properly it is the thought expressed in the sentence that is true or false' ('Logik in der Mathematik', *Nachgelassene Schriften*, 251). 'When we call a sentence true, we really mean its sense' ('Der Gedanke, 60). An early expression of the thesis is the eighth 'Kernsatz zur Logik': 'The linguistic expression of a thought is a sentence. One also speaks of the truth of a sentence in a transferred sense' (*Nachgelassene Schriften*, 189).

reference is such that to the sign there corresponds a determinate sense and to this in turn a determinate reference' (my italics).[10] The same conception is illustrated by the diagram in Frege's letter of 1891 to Husserl.[11] And this must be so if senses are logically independent objects. If a sense is intrinsically the sense *of* an expression, then a reference may be associated with it as being the reference of any expression with that sense; and this would remain so even if it were only the sense of some expression never in fact uttered, or of an imaginary expression not actually belonging to the language, or of an expression of an imaginary language. If, on the other hand, it is possible to conceive of a sense otherwise than as the sense of some actual or possible expression, the association of a reference with it must accrue to it directly.

The conclusion may seem harmless: for, taking the state of the world as given, is it not in virtue of its sense, and of it alone, that an expression has the reference it has? It is indeed; but it no more follows that the reference is to be ascribed to the sense than it follows from the fact that it was in virtue of his speed that an athlete won a medal that it was the speed that won the medal. When Frege expounds his distinction between sense and reference, he never treats sense as prior to reference. He never *first* introduces the notion of sense, subsequently explaining that of reference as a feature of the sense: he speaks of the *expression* as having both sense and reference, arguing that it has both and explaining the relation between them. Though, in the case of sentences and in that of incomplete expressions, he occasionally feels constrained to argue that references can be ascribed to them, this is largely a matter of getting across to the reader his generalized notion of reference; once this is grasped, the propriety of ascribing references to expressions of all logical types is not open to question. In the full-dress exposition given in part I of *Grundgesetze der Arithmetik*, the notion of reference appears as prior to that of sense. The primitive symbols are explained by stipulating what their references are to be. These serve jointly to determine the conditions under which the referent of any formula of the system is the value *true*. The formula will then express the thought that these conditions are fulfilled:[12]

---

[10] 'Über Sinn und Bedeutung', *Zeitschrift für Philosophie und philosophische Kritik*, 100 (1892), 27.
[11] *Wissenschaftlicher Briefwechsel*, ed. G. Gabriel, H. Hermes, F. Kambartel, C. Thiel, and A. Veraart (Hamburg, 1976), 96.   [12] *Grundgesetze*, vol. i, §32.

and the sense of each part of the formula consists in its contribution to the thought so expressed, that is, in its role in determining the condition for the reference of the formula to be the value *true* rather than the value *false*. The original stipulations did not mention sense: they did not lay down the *senses* of the primitive symbols, but their referents. If reference—including truth-value—could be understood only via the notion of sense, namely, as either an attribute of a sense or as an attribute derivatively ascribed to an expression in virtue of its having a sense with the corresponding attribute, these stipulations would have been unintelligible: it is because we can understand what is involved in assigning a reference to an expression in advance of our having the general notion of sense that we could understand the stipulations. In understanding them, we indeed thereby came to grasp the senses of the expressions concerned: to grasp how the referent of an expression, whether simple or complex, is to be determined just *is* to grasp its sense. But, to grasp this, we must take the referent to be the referent *of the expression*: we could not take it as the referent of the *sense* in advance either of grasping that particular sense or having the general concept of sense.

This order of exposition is demanded by Frege's conception of sense as embracing everything that must be grasped concerning an expression—and only that—which, given the state of the world, determines its reference. If the sense is the route to the referent, or the way the referent is given, the general notion of sense cannot be explained except by appeal to that of reference; we must therefore have the latter notion first. If we have the notion of reference in advance of that of sense, we cannot be conceiving of the possession of a reference as a property of the sense, but only of the expression: it is to the expression that reference is therefore primarily to be ascribed, even though it has the specific reference that it has in virtue of its sense. On this conception, then, it is an expression which primarily has a reference: in particular, utterances of sentences are the primary bearers of truth and falsity. Since a sense is a way of referring to something, and it is the expression which refers, senses are intrinsically the senses *of* expressions. Frege says that he is concerned with thoughts rather than with sentences;[13] but his detailed theory of sense does not show what explanation could be given of thoughts without alluding to a means of expressing them.

[13] e.g. 'Der Gedanke', 66 n.

He says also that there is no contradiction in supposing beings who grasp thoughts without clothing them in language,[14] and he may well be right; but his theory of sense gives no indication how this can be so.

Sense, for Frege, is not a mental content. I can grasp a sense, but the sense is not *in* my mind: indeed, there is *nothing* in my mind that determines what sense it is that I am grasping, just as one cannot tell, by looking only at my hand, whether I am holding an apple or an orange. It is the conception of sense as the way the referent is given that leads to this conclusion: whatever goes to determine the referent must be part of the sense, and so we cannot speak of a route to the sense, or of the particular way in which the sense is given. The sense is not a half-way station *en route* to the referent: the sense itself is the whole route. This conception is, however, at war with that of senses as self-subsistent objects which we apprehend: a way in which something else is given cannot be a self-subsistent object in its own right. Senses, if they were self-subsistent objects, would be the only objects *not* given to us in any particular way, but whole and entire in the fullness of their being. It may be said that this is just the difference between *grasping* something and thinking *about* it: when I think or speak about a thought, referring to it as, say, 'the labour theory of value' or 'the fundamental theorem of algebra', I am picking it out from other thoughts in a particular way, just as I pick out a city from other cities by thinking of it or referring to it as the capital of Poland. The problem then becomes how it is possible to *grasp* objects: if we can grasp senses, why cannot we grasp other objects, without their being given to us in a particular way? The only explanation consistent with Frege's other views is that thoughts, and senses generally, are not self-subsistent objects at all, but ways in which other things (not only objects) are given to us; the way in which something else is given does not itself need to be given in any way. A way in which an object can be given may, indeed, itself be given in a particular way, for example as the sense of the name 'Suomi'; but, in that case, the object is not thereby given.

Frege should not have said, therefore, that senses are the objects of mental acts of grasping: he should have said that they are ways in which we refer to something (not exclusively, of course, to an object); in particular, on his account, a thought should be explained

---

[14] 'Erkenntnisquellen der Mathematik und der mathematischen Naturwissenschaften', *Nachgelassene Schriften*, 288.

as a way of referring to a truth-value. More exactly, a distinction is needed between inner reference, when someone has a thought he does not voice, and reference made when speaking to another: using 'adverting to' and 'mentioning' to distinguish these, Frege should have said that grasping a sense is having a way of adverting to something, and expressing it is a way of mentioning that thing. Here reference must be understood in Frege's highly extended sense, which goes well beyond thinking or talking *about* something, as we normally understand this notion.

This is a model only for grasping and expressing thoughts and other senses, not for judgement or belief. We may leave to other parts of philosophical psychology the explanation of belief in terms of judgement: but we cannot leave judgement unexplained without raising suspicion that it cannot be fitted in to the model. Surely judgement is an act which has a thought as its object: how could it be represented as a way of carrying out an act with some different object, as grasping a thought may be represented as having a way of adverting to a truth-value? The question forces us to look critically at Frege's semantic apparatus. A definite description, say 'the oldest city in the world', is not an expression of a thought: we may obtain one by adding an identificatory phrase such as 'is Jericho', and, by so doing, we have, in a clear sense, advanced from an object to a truth-value. We should expect, then, that a term standing for a truth-value does not yet express a thought, but that we succeed in expressing one if we add the identificatory phrase 'is (the) true'. Yet, on Frege's account, a term for a truth-value already expresses the thought, and the addition of the identificatory phrase leaves unaltered not only the truth-value referred to but even the thought expressed: we have not advanced either from a truth-value or from a thought to a truth-value, but have remained stationary. This is baffling in itself. 'The oldest city in the world' and 'Jericho' both (I believe) denote the city of Jericho, but do so in different ways: 'The oldest city in the world is Jericho' therefore expresses an identification of them, i.e. the thought that the object picked out in one way and that picked out in the other are identical. Similarly, '2 + 2 = 4' and 'the true' both denote the value *true*, but in different ways: so (inserting the conjunction 'that' to satisfy the grammatical requirement of converting the former into a substantival phrase) 'That 2 + 2 = 4 is (the) true' ought also to express an identificatory thought distinct from the sense of the first term. How does it come about that any means of referring to a truth-value just is an identification of that truth-value as the value *true*?

More baffling still is the question 'What is judgement?' Frege calls it a recognition that a thought is true. A thought cannot, of course, be the value *true*: to say that a thought is true is to say that the truth-value of that thought is the value *true*. It is natural to say that 'The oldest city in the world is Jericho' expresses a recognition of the oldest city in the world as being Jericho (more naturally yet, a recognition of Jericho as the oldest city in the world). That, however, cannot be the sense in which Frege speaks of recognizing a thought as true, for then such recognition would be expressed by 'That 2 + 2 = 4 is true', which merely expresses a thought—namely, that 2 + 2 = 4—not a judgement. No wonder, then, that Frege says that the judgement-stroke is *sui generis*:[15] like the sign that represents it, judgement is *sui generis*, too. Recognizing a thought as true is not a matter of recognizing that the truth-value of the thought is the value *true*: it is doing something to the thought of a different kind, which we may call 'acknowledging' it. 'Acknowledging' might be written 'recognizing-true'; but, apart from the violation of the language that would result from saying 'recognizing-true the thought', this is unnecessary, and even misleading, since, in judgement, we do not need expressly to advert to the notion of truth.[16]

Nevertheless, it is in making judgements that we encounter the two truth-values: 'these two objects are recognized, even if only tacitly, by everyone who makes a judgement, who holds anything to be true'.[17] It is plain that, without allusion to judgement, there is no way of distinguishing the two truth-values from each other. That is why it would be senseless to imagine a language whose speakers went in for the linguistic act of denial rather than for that of assertion: truth is given to us as that at which we aim when we say anything (in the sense of 'say' that occurs in 'I do not say that'). As Frege repeatedly insists, one can grasp a thought without judging it to be true: but one could not grasp any thought without knowing what judgement is, because then one could have no notion of truth.

[15] 'The sign belongs to a kind of its own', *Grundgesetze*, i, §26.
[16] 'Here we must recognize that the assertion does not lie in the word "true", but in the assertoric force with which the assertion is uttered', 'Meine grundlegenden logischen Einsichten', *Nachgelassene Schriften*, 271. 'It is the form of the assertoric sentence which is really that by means of which we predicate truth, and we do not need for that the word "true"', 'Logik', 1897, *Nachgelassene Schriften*, 140.
[17] 'Über Sinn und Bedeutung', 34.

Since, if we start with thoughts, considered as merely expressed, not asserted, judgement becomes, not simply inexplicable, but mysterious, it is better to start with sentences whose utterance constitutes assertion, and explain the expression of unasserted thoughts in terms of them. This fact is often misperceived by critics of Frege as implying that he was wrong to separate assertoric force from sense. On the contrary, without such a separation we cannot explain the use of sentences as constituents of more complex ones, or the community of sense between assertoric sentences and ones carrying other kinds of force (interrogative, imperative, etc.), that is to say, the obvious fact that the word 'dog', for example, has the same sense in 'Take the dog for a walk' and 'The dog is not here'.

By starting with sentences carrying assertoric force, we ensure recognition of the special place of sentences in semantic theory. The significance of a sentence is not properly explained by regarding it as referring to a truth-value in a particular way; or, better, we do not know what it is for it to refer to a truth-value unless we regard it as capable of being used to make an assertion. Frege's attribution of reference to sentences is justified by, but only by, the possibility of using them as subsentences in more complex ones, since the notion of reference is required to explain the determination of a sentence as true or false in accordance with its composition: the parts of the sentence contribute to that via their referents. The reference of a sentence bearing assertoric force is, as such, irrelevant to its sense: all that matters for that is whether the sentence is (in the context of utterance) true or false in the sense of yielding a correct or incorrect assertion. This is obscured for us by the special character of Frege's two-valued semantic theory, according to which all that matters for the (ordinary) reference of a sentence, i.e. for explaining its role as a subsentence, is its being true or not being true. That this is not essential for semantic theories in general can easily be seen by considering many-valued semantics. In such a semantic theory, the distinction between more than two truth-values is needed only for explaining sentence-composition: whether an assertion is correct or not depends only on whether the sentence asserted has a designated or an undesignated value, not on which particular value it has; and so the content of the assertion—the thought expressed by the complete sentence—depends only on the condition for the sentence to be true in the sense of having a designated value, and not on the more detailed conditions for its having each one of the many distinct 'truth-values' as its referent. When we see the sentence in this way, as of itself directed towards assertion, we no longer have the problem of explaining what assertion is when applied to a name of a truth-value.[18] A sentence has the sense it has in view of its being apt for assertion, and of its being made so apt by its composition. Having this sense, it can then also be used non-assertorically, as a part of a more complex sentence or as subject to some non-assertoric force.

Does this help us with our problem? With reference, the rationale of the distinction between object and content is apparent: we refer to something—the object of reference, which may or may not be an object in Frege's sense—and we do so in a particular way, that way constituting the content of that mode of reference. Assertion and judgement, however, do not have both object and content. If the thought asserted or acknowledged is the content, in the sense of the *way in which* we are asserting or judging, then there is nothing to serve as the *object* of the assertion or judgement; that is, there is nothing *which* we are asserting or *which* we are judging to be true. We may indeed speak of an external object in the sense of what we are talking about or thinking about; but this does not fill the required role. For one thing, to say that the tree is dead and that it is bearing fruit are not two *ways* of talking about the tree, but instances of saying different things about it; for another, we have no uniform means of picking out what is being talked about. In some cases, this notion has an obvious application; in others, it does not, and there is no natural principle for extending it to these other cases.

The solution lies in attending to the logical priority of expressions over their senses—the fact that senses are *of* expressions. When someone hums a tune, the tune is the object of his humming only in a grammatical sense: the tune, being a type as opposed to a token, is a *species* of musical performance to which the humming belongs. Similarly, a sentence is a species of utterance. The thought expressed by the utterance of a sentence on an occasion is the significance of that utterance, given the language and the occasion; more exactly,

---

[18] In *Grundgesetze*, Frege actually reserves the word 'sentence' for a formula to which the judgement-stroke is attached, a formula without it being called a 'name of a truth-value'. This terminology is in the right spirit; but it does not of itself resolve the difficulties that arise from the fact that Frege starts from an account of the references of formulas and of their constituents, and considers the judgement-stroke as something added.

an important ingredient in its significance. The significance of an utterance is the difference that is made to the situation by the fact of the utterance's having occurred. An event makes a difference to a situation by its potential for making a difference to what subsequently happens; the utterance of a sentence has such a potential in virtue of the existence of the social practice of speaking the language to which it belongs. The thought expressed is thus a *feature* of the utterance, accruing to it in consequence of a variety of facts: the sentence of which the utterance is a token; the context of the utterance; and the language considered as a conventional practice. There is nothing wrong with regarding the thought as an object to which we can refer and of which various things can be predicated, and it is overwhelmingly convenient so to regard it. If we regard the thought in this way, we cannot but treat it as an object in a grammatical sense, i.e. as the referent of grammatical accusatives. But it is very far from being a self-subsistent object. A complete description of what has happened when someone expresses a thought would involve stating the relevant part of a theory of meaning for the language. Even if we do not know precisely how to frame such a theory, we know that it need not mention thoughts or senses. It must describe the practice of using the language, which, on Frege's model, involves explaining what determines the reference of each expression and the truth-value of each assertoric utterance. It may also need to provide an account of a speaker's understanding of words and sentences, that is, his grasp of how their references and their truth-values are determined, the mode of his grasp of this, and the manner in which it is manifested. It will thereby state everything that determines the sense of any possible utterance in the language: it therefore need make no reference to such objects as thoughts or the senses that compose them. In the same way, Frege himself mentions senses in part I of *Grundgesetze* only in order to explain what, in general, he takes the sense of an expression to be: but his explanation entails that the stipulations he has already made concerning the mechanism of reference for expressions of his formal language display the senses that those expressions have, without having themselves employed the notion of sense. I am not here advocating a reductionist notion of self-subsistent objects, according to which a self-subsistent object is one to which any complete description of reality must refer. A self-subsistent, or logically independent, object is, rather, one of such a kind that it would be in principle possible to make reference

13

Thought and Perception: The Views of Two Philosophical Innovators*

Brentano recognized, but notoriously did not so much as attempt to solve, a problem that was therefore left to his followers to resolve. It is unclear how far he really recognized it as a problem, since, in his writing, what promise to be discussions of it always slide off into some other topic, leaving the original problem unresolved. His most famous doctrine was that what distinguishes mental from physical phenomena is their intentionality, although Brentano himself never used precisely that term. This means that they have the characteristic of being directed towards external objects: no one can be simply contemptuous or simply irritated, but only contemptuous *of* something or irritated *by* something.

Mental phenomena are thus, for Brentano, all of them mental *acts* or attitudes of differing kinds; and this characteristic of being directed towards something was propounded by him as the defining feature of such mental phenomena. The contrast expressly drawn by Brentano is between mental and physical *phenomena*, rather than between mental and physical *acts*. What he understands as 'physical phenomena' appear to be phenomenal qualities, such as colours and auditory tones, and complexes of them; he says:

> Examples of physical phenomena . . . are: a colour; a shape; a panorama which I view; a chord which I hear; warmth; cold; an odour which I smell; and also similar images which appear in the imagination.[1]

Brentano's distinction between physical and mental phenomena thus differentiates things of a sort that many philosophers have regarded as being among the contents of the mind from those of another sort—mental acts—that are more uncontroversially mental.

---

* Forthcoming in D. Bell and N. Cooper (eds.), *The Analytic Tradition: Meaning, Thought, and Knowledge* (Oxford, 1990).
[1] Franz Brentano, *Psychologie vom empirischen Standpunkt* (Leipzig, 1874), bk. 2, ch. 1, §2; quoted from the English translation *Psychology from an Empirical Standpoint*, ed. Linda L. McAlister (London, 1973), 79–80.

Brentano explains what he wishes to include among such mental phenomena as follows:

> Hearing a sound, seeing a coloured object, feeling warmth or cold, as well as similar states of imagination are examples of what I mean by this term ['presentation' (*Vorstellung*), identified as a species of mental phenomenon]. I also mean by it the thinking of a general concept, provided such a thing actually does occur. Furthermore, every judgement, every recollection, every expectation, every inference, every conviction or opinion, every doubt, is a mental phenomenon. Also to be included under this term is every emotion: joy, sorrow, fear, hope, courage, despair, anger, love, hate, desire, act of will, intention, astonishment, admiration, contempt, etc.[2]

Brentano's celebrated original statement of the thesis of intentionality was as follows:

> Every mental phenomenon is characterized by what the Scholastics called the intentional (or mental) inexistence of an object, and what we might call, though not quite unambiguously, reference to a content, direction towards an object (which is not to be understood here as meaning a thing), or immanent objectivity. Every mental phenomenon includes something as object within itself, although they do not all do so in the same way. In a presentation (*Vorstellung*) something is presented, in a judgement something is affirmed or denied, in love something is loved in hate something is hated, in desire something is desired, and so forth.[3]

The doctrine here propounded makes the object intrinsic to the mental act. Brentano insists that what he calls 'physical phenomena' never exhibit anything like the characteristic of 'intentional inexistence', and concludes that we may 'define mental phenomena by saying that they are those phenomena which contain an object intentionally within themselves'. Since his 'physical phenomena' are not acts in even the most general sense, and cannot be referred to by transitive verbs, it would be literally ungrammatical to speak of them as having, and therefore, equally, as lacking, objects. What Brentano means is best seen by contrast with what we should ordinarily call a physical act, for instance that of kicking a football. The object of such a physical act is extrinsic to it *qua* physical act. Up to the point of contact, the act of kicking the football would have been exactly the same if the ball had not been there: it is only to the

---

[2] *Psychologie vom empirischen Standpunkt*, 79 in English trans.
[3] Ibid., §5; 88 in English trans. (here slightly altered).

intention underlying the act that the object is intrinsic, in that I should not have had precisely the same intention if I had meant just to make a kicking motion without impact. In a different terminology, the relation of a physical act to its object is external, that of a mental act to its object internal.

Not only does Brentano's characterization of a mental phenomenon make the object intrinsic to it: it also appears to attribute to the object a special kind of existence, namely, intentional inexistence or mental inexistence, as embodied in that act. On such an interpretation, an object may have either or both of two modes of existence: it may exist in the actual world, external to the mind; and it may also exist in the mind, as incorporated in a mental act directed towards it. There would then be no more difficulty in explaining how there could be a mental act directed towards something that had no actual existence than in admitting the actual existence of objects to which no mental act is directed: in the former case, the object would have intentional inexistence but no existence in actuality, while in the latter case it would exist in actuality while lacking any intentional inexistence. To admit the possibility of the latter case is necessary if we are to be realists about the external world; to admit the possibility of the former is necessary if we are to recognize that the mind is not constrained by external reality. It is but a short step from such a position to the thesis that the object of any mental act is always to be considered as enjoying only mental inexistence, but *represents* the external object, if there is one. On this development of Brentano's view, a mental act is always directed towards something that, as an ingredient of the act, is essentially a content of the mind; and, at this stage, we should be fully entrapped in the bog of empiricism.

But that was not the road down which Brentano travelled. It seems probable that when, in the original edition of *Psychology from an Empirical Standpoint*, published in 1874, he originally introduced, or reintroduced, the term 'intentional inexistence', he did mean to ascribe to the objects of mental acts a special kind of existence in the mind, distinguishable from actual existence. But he withdrew from the edge of the bog. He not only declined to take the next step into full-blooded representationalism: he came to repudiate the conception of a shadowy mental existence altogether. He continued to maintain that the object of a mental act is intrinsic to the act, but nevertheless now insisted that it is external to the mind: not merely external in the sense in which one may contrast an external object with the correlate of a cognate accusative, as one might say that the internal object of thinking is a thought, the external object that which is thought about, but external in the full sense of not being a constituent of the subject's consciousness, but a part of the objective world independent of him and of the mental act which he directs towards it. If, for instance, I intend to marry a woman, or promise to marry her, it is *that woman* whom I intend or promise to marry, and who is therefore the object of my mental act, expressed or unexpressed; the object of that act is not my mental representation of the woman, but the woman herself. Thus in 1909 Brentano wrote, 'It is paradoxical in the extreme to say that a man promises to marry an *ens rationis* and fulfils his promise by marrying a real person.'[4]

Thus when the object of a mental act exists in actuality, it is that very object, considered as actually existing, that is the object of the mental act. But does this not leave it open that the object also has a different type of existence, as an ingredient of the mental act, and that, when the object of a mental act lacks actual existence, it has only this mental kind of existence? No! Not according to the later Brentano: for, on his later view, there are not, properly speaking, any kinds of existence at all: there is only actual existence, and all other ways of speaking, though frequently convenient, are strictly speaking improper:

> All mental references refer to things. In many cases, the things to which we refer do not exist. We are, however, accustomed to say that they then have being as objects [of the mental acts]. This is an improper use of the verb 'to be', which we permit ourselves for the sake of convenience, just as we speak of the sun's 'rising' or 'setting'. All that it means is that a mentally active subject is referring to those things.[5]

This passage contains another retraction. In the last passage quoted earlier from *Psychology from an Empirical Standpoint* (§5, p. 88), he went out of his way to assert that the object of a mental act need not be a thing. Brentano used the word 'thing' after the mode

---

[4] Letter to Oskar Kraus dated 1909 and quoted by Kraus in his Introduction to *Psychologie vom empirischen Standpunkt*, 2nd edn. (Leipzig, 1924); English trans., p. 385.
[5] Supplementary Remark 9, added to F. Brentano, *Von der Klassifikation der psychischen Phänomena* (Leipzig, 1911), which was a reissue of bk. 2 of *Psychologie vom empirischen Standpunkt* with eleven Supplementary Remarks; English trans., p. 291 (here slightly altered).

generally then current in German philosophical writing, namely, to mean a concrete particular, which, for him, might be either material or spiritual: in effect, a substance in the sense of Descartes. He had originally held that the object of a mental act need not be a thing in this sense; in particular, he had allowed that it might be what he referred to as a 'content', that is, the content of a proposition. His later view was that the object of a mental act could only be something '*real*', that is, not necessarily real in the sense of actually existing, but thing-like: all mental acts must have concrete particulars as their objects. This naturally led him into very involved explanations of the host of apparent counter-examples. His general strategy for such explanations was to admit a large range of different 'modes of presentation'—types of mental act involving different relations to their objects. He thus repudiated the entire range of ideal objects admitted by Husserl and Meinong—those objects characterized by Frege as objective but not actual, and whose existence he insisted that we must acknowledge if we are to avoid the twin errors of physicalism and psychologism. Brentano was, in particular, especially scathing about Meinong's 'objectives'—the equivalents of Frege's thoughts.

More germane to the present purpose is the fact, blandly stated by Brentano in the last passage quoted, that 'in many cases the things to which we refer'—the objects of our mental acts—'do not exist'. As Dagfinn Føllesdal quite rightly observes, in his essay 'Brentano and Husserl on Intentional Objects and Perception',[6] Brentano's insistence that, when the object actually exists, it is that very object, and not any mental representation of it, which is the object of the mental act tallies exactly with Frege's insistence that, when I speak of the moon, it is the heavenly body itself, and not my idea of the moon, that is the reference of the phrase I use, and hence is that *about* which I am talking.

But all this only provokes the obvious objection that it fails to explain how there can be a genuine mental act, even though there is no object in actuality. There plainly can: someone may be contemptuous of or irritated by something illusory; or, again, he may suffer a hallucination or other sensory delusion. A visual or auditory illusion does not consist in simply seeing or hearing without seeing or hearing anything: the character of intentionality still attaches to

---

[6] In H. L. Dreyfus (ed.), *Husserl: Intentionality and Cognitive Science* (Cambridge, Mass., 1982), 32.

mental acts of this kind. To have that character is to be directed towards an object; but, in such a case, there *is* no object.

Brentano seems to have thought it sufficient to observe that, 'If someone thinks of something, the one who is thinking must certainly exist, but the object of his thinking need not exist at all.'[7] But this is obviously quite inadequate: for what does the phrase 'the object of his thinking' stand for here? Meinong's answer, 'An object that does not happen to exist', was not available to Brentano, who vehemently denied the admissibility of any notion of being distinct from existence. If, on the other hand, it were answered that the phrase does not stand for anything at all, that would be to equate the statement 'The object of his thinking does not exist' with the statement 'His thinking does not have an object': and that would flatly contradict Brentano's salient principle that one who is thinking must be thinking of something, which is difficult to construe otherwise than as meaning that there is something of which he is thinking. Nor was it open to Brentano to say that, in *such* a case, the object of the mental act is, after all, a constituent of the subject's mind; for it would then have been impossible to resist saying the same in a case in which the subject is thinking of an actual object or is having a veridical perception.

This, then, was the problem which Brentano bequeathed to his successors. Husserl's solution was to generalize the distinction between meaning and object (i.e. between sense and reference) from 'expressive' acts (that is, linguistic acts) to mental acts of all kinds. For singular terms, the linguistic distinction lies to hand. The notion of using a singular term to talk about a particular object, or of referring to something by means of such a term, is not a philosopher's invention: it is part of the equipment we already have when we come to the philosophical analysis of language. It has never been necessary to argue that singular terms, in general, have reference: it is a starting-point. The further distinction drawn by Husserl from the time of his *Logische Untersuchungen*[8] onwards, between objective meanings and subjective ideas, parallel to the similar distinction drawn by Frege and, before him, by Bolzano, is not part of everyday modes of thought, however; the distinction was intrinsic to his recoil from the psychologism of which he had

---

[7] *Von der Klassifikation der psychischen Phänomena*, Supplementary Remark 1; *Psychology from an Empirical Standpoint*, 272.

[8] (Halle, 1900–1).

originally been an exponent, but whose implacable enemy he now became.

To complete sentences, and to subsentential expressions other than singular terms, intuition of course demands that we ascribe meanings; but assigning to them anything analogous to reference goes against the grain of common sense: everyone's reaction, on reading Frege for the first time, is therefore to think his extension of *Bedeutung* from singular terms to all significant expressions unwarranted. The problem is thus the opposite to that which arises for singular terms. For them, what requires justification is the ascription to them of a sense distinct from their possessing a particular reference: for expressions of other categories, it is the ascription to them of a reference as well as a sense.

This problem did not trouble Husserl, however. He was at one with Frege in regarding all meaningful expressions as having, or purporting to have, objective correlates, taking this for granted because of his inheritance from Brentano. For a follower of Brentano, all mental acts are characterized by intentionality, and therefore have objects, or at least purport to have them. In itself, of course, an utterance is not a mental act: but its significance is due to its being accompanied by a mental act, called by Husserl the meaning-conferring act, which, as being a mental act, must have, or purport to have, an object.

Husserl was not concerned to convince anybody that expressions of categories other than singular terms also had objective correlates: the intentionality of mental acts was so axiomatic for him that he saw no need to demonstrate it in particular cases. He therefore paid little attention to the question what the objective correlates of such expressions should be taken to be, the correct answer to which so exercised Frege. Even if he had attended to it more closely, he would have been perplexed to answer it: for he lacked any general principle for extending the notion of objective reference from singular terms to other categories. Frege had such a principle: namely, that the reference of an expression is what is common to every expression which could be substituted for it in any sentence without affecting the truth-value of that sentence. Moreover, on Frege's theory, the reference of an expression constituted its contribution to determining the truth-value of any sentence containing it: the references of the parts jointly formed the mechanism by which the truth-value of the whole was determined. For each logical type that he recognized, Frege appealed to these principles in order to determine what sort of thing we should take the reference of an expression of that type to be. Husserl, by contrast, did not care very much what the objective correlate of an expression is taken to be, as long as it is recognized as having one. He did not identify the reference of a predicate with a concept in Frege's sense; rather, he tended to think of it as the object to which the predicate applies. The most salient instance of his indifference to how we identify the objective correlates of expressions concerns whole sentences, of which he wrote:

> If we consider assertoric sentences of the form *S is P*, for example, the object of the statement is normally regarded as being that which constitutes the subject, and thus that *of* which something is asserted. A different conception is, however, also possible, which takes the *whole* state of affairs corresponding to the statement as the analogue of the object denoted by a name and distinguishes it from the meaning of the statement.[9]

He states no preference for either option: he merely records that there are these two ways of ascribing an objective reference to the sentence, and appears indifferent to the choice between them.

Husserl, like Frege, regarded the sense of an expression as being that in virtue of which it has the particular objective reference that it has.

> An expression attains an objective reference only through its meaning what it does, and . . . it can therefore be rightly said that the expression designates (names) the object *in virtue of* its meaning, and that the act of meaning is the particular way in which we refer to the object at a given time.[10]

But since, unlike Frege, he had no systematic theory of the kind of objective reference possessed by expressions of different types, he lacked the basis for any systematic account of how meaning determines reference. This makes a fundamental difference between him and Frege, since Frege's theory of reference is the foundation of his theory of sense. For Frege, the crucial first step towards characterizing the sense of any expression is to decide what kind of thing, and what in particular, constitutes its reference. Its sense is required to take the form of a means by which that reference may be given to one who knows the language, in virtue of his knowing it: hence, while a

[9] *Logische Untersuchungen*, First Investigation, §12.   [10] Ibid., §13.

theory of reference does not yet amount to a theory of sense, it constitutes its indispensable foundation.

For Husserl, as for Frege, the existence of meaningful expressions which miss their mark by lacking any objective correlate is unproblematic in the light of the distinction of meaning from objective reference. We must not confuse lack of reference with meaninglessness, or even logical inconsistency with meaninglessness, for, if we do, we shall be unable to explain how a true denial of existence succeeds in being meaningful. In the period following his *Logische Untersuchungen*, Husserl's fundamental thought was that the notion of sense could be generalized from expressive (linguistic) acts to all mental acts: the notion thus generalized he termed 'noema'. The object of any mental act is given through its noema: since it is intrinsic to the noema to be directed towards an object, it is the noema that imparts intentionality to mental acts, and it is in virtue of it that an act has whatever object it has. It was by introducing this distinction between the object of a mental act and its noema that Husserl believed that Brentano's problem could be resolved. A noema must inform every mental act, giving it the quality of being directed towards an object; but it is no more perplexing that a noema should miss its mark, so that no external object corresponds to it, than that an expression should have a sense that fails to determine any actual objective reference for it. Delusive perceptions are accordingly no longer problematic: they possess the feature of intentionality as well as do veridical ones, but simply happen to lack any actual object.

Husserl insisted that, in the standard case, the meaning of the words employed in a linguistic act is not an object of our thought: 'in the act of meaning, the meaning is not present to consciousness as an object', he said: 'if we perform the act, and live in it, as it were, we naturally refer to its object and not to its meaning'.[11] Frege hardly ever discussed what we are conscious of when we are speaking, regarding this as irrelevant to the objective properties of our words, namely, their references and their senses; but he distinguished sharply between speaking of the ordinary referent of an expression, which is the normal case, and the special case in which we are using it to speak of its (ordinary) sense. Husserl similarly maintained that it is the (external) object of any of our acts of

---

[11] Ibid., §34.

perception of which we are aware. Far from its being the noema that we directly apprehend, it does not normally serve as an object of the observer's awareness at all, still less of his perceptions. Just as, in the normal case, a speaker is talking and thinking about the objective referent of his utterance, not about the meaning in virtue of which his words have that reference, so a subject perceives an object in virtue of the noema of the perceptual act, and does not perceive or otherwise apprehend that noema.

Husserl's theory is thus to be distinguished from a sense-datum theory, according to which sense-data are the primary objects of awareness. In the case of perception, Husserl thought that we can, by an act of reflection, make the noema the object of our attention: but he held that this is an extraordinarily difficult thing to do, which only the philosopher can achieve, and that it is the fundamental task of philosophy to fasten attention on noemata and attain a characterization of them.

The only one of Frege's writings to contain any substantial remarks about sense-perception is 'Der Gedanke'. There, using the term 'thing' to mean a material object, he wrote as follows:

Sense-impressions . . . on their own do not disclose the external world to us. There are, perhaps, beings who only have sense-impressions, without seeing or feeling things. To have visual impressions is not yet to see things. How does it come about that I see the tree in just that place where I see it? It obviously depends on the visual impressions that I have, and on the particular kind of visual impressions that arise because I see with two eyes. On each of my two retinas there is formed a particular image, in the physical sense. Someone else sees the tree in the same place. He, too, has two retinal images, which, however, differ from mine. We must assume that these retinal images determine our impressions. We thus have visual impressions that are not only not identical, but markedly divergent from one another. And yet we move about in the same external world. Having visual impressions is, indeed, necessary for seeing things, but it is not sufficient. What has still to be added is not anything sensible. And yet it is precisely this which opens up the external world for us; for without this non-sensible component each person would remain shut up within his own inner world . . . . Besides one's inner world, one must distinguish the external world proper of sensible, perceptible things and also the realm of that which is not sensorily perceptible. To recognize either of these two realms we stand in need of something non-sensible; but in the sensory perception of things we have need, in addition, of sense-impressions, and these belong wholly to the inner world. Thus that on which there primarily rests the distinction between the different manners in which a thing and a thought are given is something assignable, not to either of the two realms, but to the inner world (p. 75)

Frege is here distiguishing between three realms of existence of which we are each conscious: the inner world, private to each individual and comprising the contents of his consciousness; the external world of material objects, which we all inhabit together; and the 'third realm' of thoughts and their constituent senses, which, like the external world, is accessible to all in common, but whose contents, though they can be grasped by human minds, are immaterial and immutable, and do not act on the senses or on each other. At an earlier phase, Frege had recognized objects of many kinds as being objective, unlike the contents of consciousness, but causally inert, unlike material objects, and hence not what he called 'actual': among these were logical objects such as numbers. But at the time of writing 'Der Gedanke', he had probably ceased to believe in logical objects: he could therefore take thoughts and their constituent senses to exhaust the population of the third realm. The non-sensible component of perception, converting it from a sense-impression wholly part of the inner world into the perception of a material object, thus opening up the external world to us, clearly belongs to the third realm. Frege does not tell us whether it must be a complete thought, say to the effect that there is a tree in a certain place, or whether it may be a mere thought-constituent, such as the sense of the concept-word 'tree', involving our seeing the object *as* a tree, nor whether, if it is a whole thought, the act of perception involves judging that the thought is true, or whether it is sufficient merely to grasp the thought without advancing from it to the truth-value. Most likely, he meant that perception involves a judgement to the truth of a complete thought: for he accepted sense-perception as a source of knowledge, and knowledge issues in judgements; so, at least in the normal case, perception must involve judging some state of affairs to obtain, rather than merely entertaining the thought that it does.

Frege's notion of grasping a sense or a thought requires examination. There is, first, the distinction between grasping a thought as being the sense of a particular sentence, and grasping the thought that happens to be expressed by that sentence, without necessarily recognizing the sentence as having that sense. A second distinction, never drawn by Frege himself, is that between a dispositional and an occurrent grasp of a sense or thought. Consider the opening passage of 'Gedankengefüge':

It is astonishing what language can do, in that, with a few syllables, it can express unsurveyably many thoughts, so that it can find a clothing even for a thought that has been grasped by an inhabitant of the earth for the very first time in which it will be understood by someone else to whom it is entirely new. This would not be possible, if we could not distinguish parts in the thought corresponding to the parts of a sentence, so that the structure of the sentence can serve as a picture of the structure of the thought.

Our ability to understand a sentence expressing a thought that is entirely new to us is here explained in terms of our existing grasp of the senses of the constituent parts of that sentence; our grasp of them is surely dispositional. But when Frege speaks of the very first time that an inhabitant of the earth grasps a given thought, he is, presumably, speaking of grasping a thought in an occurrent sense. The earth-dweller has long had the *capacity* to frame or understand the thought, as has the one to whom he communicates it: but this is the first time that he, or any other human being, has expressly entertained that thought.

It is the dispositional notion of grasping the sense of an individual word that is primary: what interests us is whether someone will understand the word when he hears it, and whether it will be available to him when he has occasion to use it, rather than whether he has its sense in mind at a particular moment, save when he hears or uses a sentence containing it. Similarly, we are more interested in whether someone does or does not possess a given concept than in whether he is currently exercising his grasp of it. By contrast, what is important about a sentence is not whether someone is capable of understanding it, but whether he understands it on a particular occasion on which he hears it; and what is important about a thought is not whether someone is capable of grasping it, but whether he is currently considering whether it is true or understanding someone else to have asserted it: so it is the occurrent notion of grasping a complete thought that is primary.

Grasping a sense, understood dispositionally, is evidently not a mental act, but a kind of ability: and this tallies with Wittgenstein's dictum that understanding, which he expressly compares to an ability, is not a mental process. But Frege allowed that, while thoughts are not mental contents, grasping a thought is a mental act, although one directed towards something external to the mind; and he must here be construing the notion of grasping a thought in its occurrent sense. Wittgenstein strove to dispel the idea that there is an occurrent sense of 'understand': but it is difficult to see how this can be successfully maintained. We cannot, for instance, simply reduce the conception of understanding an utterance to that of hearing it while possessing a dispositional understanding of the relevant words and constructions: for it is possible to be perplexed by a sentence on first hearing, through a failure to take in its structure, and to achieve an understanding of it on reflection.

Nevertheless, these considerations prompt us to ask exactly what it is to grasp a sense or a thought, according to Frege's conception. For him, it is the sense that is the logical notion: grasping the sense of an expression or of a sentence is a psychological process, irrelevant when our concern is to characterize the sense itself; in consequence, he seldom devotes any attention to the process. One of the few exceptions occurs in his lectures of 1914 on 'Logic in Mathematics'. In *Grundlagen der Arithmetik*, Frege had insisted that definitions are scientifically fruitful; it would be inconsistent both with his earlier views on content and his later views on sense to dismiss this fruitfulness as a purely psychological matter. In the lectures, he has changed his view in favour of the Russellian one that definitions are no more than abbreviations, and hence logically unimportant. He then comments.

A thought is by no means always present to our consciousness clearly in all its parts. When we use the word 'integral', for example, are we always conscious of everything that belongs to the sense of this word? Only in very rare cases, I think. Usually just the word is present to our consciousness, though associated with a more or less dim knowledge that this word is a sign that has a sense, and that, when we wish, we can recall this sense. . . . We often have need of a sign with which we associate a very complex sense. This sign serves us as a receptacle in which we can, as it were, carry the sense about, in the consciousness that we can always open this receptacle should we have need of what it contains.[12]

Frege even attempts to use these reflections in order to reinforce his distinction between the logical and the psychological, arguing that 'from this consideration it is apparent that the thought, as I

---

[12] *Nachgelassene Schriften*, ed. H. Hermes, F. Kambartel, and F. Kaulbach (Hamburg, 1969), 225–6; *Posthumous Writings*, trans. P. Long and R. White (Oxford, 1979), 209.

understand the word, in no way coincides with a content of my consciousness'. This only proves, however, that my taking a word to have a certain sense does not depend on my bearing that sense continuously in mind: the passage speaks of the sense as sometimes being 'present to the consciousness', and hence supplies no reason for its not being a *content* of my consciousness.

The conception here sketched by Frege differs strongly from Husserl's view that an utterance assumes a meaning by an interior act investing it with that meaning. For Frege a word simply *has* a sense: he does not discuss, here or elsewhere, what confers that sense upon it, but it is clear that he does not think that its bearing that sense in the mouth of a speaker depends upon his performing any mental act of endowing it with that sense. Quite the contrary: even in thinking to himself, he may use the word without adverting to its sense, confident only that he can call the sense to mind when he needs to. When will he need to? When doing so is necessary in order to judge whether a sentence containing it is true, or to decide what follows deductively from that sentence or whether it follows from certain others. This suggests, therefore, that we should interpret his grasp of the sense as an ability which is called into play in determining the truth-value of the sentence, or in attending to particular features of the manner in which its truth-value is determined: the subject employs the word in the confidence that he has this ability, and can recall the contribution the word makes to the truth-conditions of the sentence when it becomes necessary to attend to it.

This interpretation appears in general accord with Frege's explanation of that in which the sense of a word consists. It is nevertheless far from certain that he would have accepted it. He had two modes of writing about sense: the first when he was concerned with the relation between sense and reference, and the second when he was invoking the mythology of the third realm in order to elaborate the ontological status of senses. The interpretation of a grasp of sense as an ability fits very well all that he wrote in the former mode, but not the conception of senses as non-actual but objective and immutable objects. In the latter mode, he thought of the sense of a word or of a sentence as something that we apprehend by an exercise of an intellectual faculty somewhat analogous to sense-perception: so, although it is not a content of consciousness, a sense or thought may be an object of conscious attention. This conception makes awareness of a sense highly disanalogous with awareness of a material object. For, first, there is nothing corresponding to the sense-impression which forms an integral part of the perception of a physical object: my awareness of the thought, which is *not* a content of my consciousness, is not mediated by something which *is* a content of my consciousness, namely, an impression of that thought. And, secondly, no *further* sense or thought plays the role which, in sense-perception, Frege believed was played by some constituent of the third realm. In perception, the sense-impression must be accompanied or informed by the sense of some means of referring to or picking out the object, or, more likely, by the thought that such an object is present. When we *refer* to a thought or sense, we do so by means of a further sense, for instance that of the term 'the principle of double effect', whose referent is the first thought or sense: but grasping a sense is something quite different from referring to it or thinking of it. Grasping a sense is immediate. Frege held, with Kant, that an object cannot be given to us save in a particular way; for him, the particular way in which it is given constitutes a sense to which that object corresponds as referent. But there cannot be different ways in which one and the same sense can be given, since everything that goes to determine the referent is part of the sense: more exactly, we ought to say that grasping a sense is not an instance of being *given* an object. The third realm is thus far more directly accessible to us than the external world of physical objects. For all that, the human mind is not capacious enough to be able to attend simultaneously to many senses, or to all the details of a very complex one: but language enables it to handle complicated thoughts, since we can attend to the *words* without, at each moment, attending to all their senses.

This conception is plainly unsatisfactory, precisely because, although it denies that senses are contents of consciousness, it makes adverting to a sense an act of consciousness. Frege's account indeed reflects an experience familiar to anyone who has devised or followed a mathematical proof: a recently defined term may be used for several steps without appeal to its definition; at a crucial point the definition is invoked, but requires a certain effort to recall. The mythology of the third realm gets in the way of a clear account, however. Frege's positive theory, that the sense of an expression consists in the manner in which its referent is determined, as a step in the determination of the truth-value of any sentence containing that expression, is independent of the mythology. The mental processes accompanying the use of the expression on the part of someone who grasps its sense are irrelevant to that sense, according to Frege: they do not enter into the explanation of what it is for it to have that sense. This shows that the psychological has to be distinguished from the logical. What Frege set aside as psychological cannot so easily be dismissed from consideration, however. Sense is distinguished from reference precisely by the fact that it can be grasped—can be apprehended directly, rather than in one or another particular way: were it not so, there would be no place for a notion of sense, as distinct from reference, at all. If, then, we are to have a firm grip on the concept of sense, or to give a clear explanation of it, we need to know exactly what it is to grasp a sense.

Frege was not disposed to explain a grasp of sense as an ability; and this is probably why he paid no attention to the distinction between a dispositional and an occurrent grasp. It was his realism that blocked him from construing a grasp of sense as an ability. A realist interpretation of sense has to link it, not with *our* procedures for deciding the truth-values of sentences, but with their determination as true or as false by the way things objectively are, independently of our knowledge. On such a view, therefore, a grasp of sense must consist, not in the ability to determine the truth-values of sentences, or to recognize them as having one or other truth-value, but in the *knowledge* of what renders them true or false. The notion of sense thus becomes an ineradicably cognitive one: grasping a sense is not a practical skill, but a piece of knowledge. What the mode of that knowledge may be is then a perplexing problem. Thus, in the end, Frege does not supply us with a clear account of what it is to grasp a sense; and, among other reasons, we need to know this in order to assess the thesis that sense-perception involves the grasp of a thought or sense.

The interpretation of a grasp of sense as an ability makes the grasp of sense the primary concept: any account of what sense is must be embedded in the account of a grasp of sense. On such a theory, sense is merely the cognate accusative of the verb 'to understand'; but this does not accord with Frege's mythology, which takes a sense to be an independently existing object with which the mind somehow makes contact. A further obstacle to Frege's interpreting a grasp of sense as an ability, had he considered doing so, was that this would have conflicted with his conception of the relative priority of thought and language, which viewed senses as intrinsically capable of being, but not intrinsically being, the senses *of* linguistic expressions. He held, namely, that it is not intrinsic to thoughts to be expressed in language, and that there is no contradiction in supposing beings who can grasp them in their nakedness, divested of linguistic clothing; but he added that 'it is necessary for us men that a thought of which we are conscious is connected in our consciousness with one or another sentence'.[13]

This latter difficulty not only relates to the notion of grasping a sense, but is intrinsic to Frege's various doctrines concerning sense itself: on it turns the question whether his two modes of discussing sense can be reconciled. On the interpretation of a grasp of sense as an ability, to grasp that a word has a certain sense is to apprehend how its presence contributes to determining the sentence in which it occurs as true or as false. If another word, in the same or another language, makes the same contribution, it has the same sense, and anyone who understands it may be allowed to have grasped the sense of the original word, considered independently of its being the sense of any particular word: but that leaves it unexplained what it would be to grasp that sense, but not *as* the sense of any actual or even hypothetical word. *We* cannot do that, according to Frege: but we ought to be able to explain what it would be to do it.

It might be suspected that the context principle was generated by overlooking the occurrent/dispositional distinction. Dispositionally construed, grasping the sense of a word does not have a context. The sense of the word may provide for its occurrence in certain contexts and not in others: but the word itself is understood in isolation, in that, if someone understands it at all, he thereby grasps its contribution to the sense of any larger context in which it can intelligibly occur. Nevertheless, we cannot quite dispense with an occurrent conception of the grasp of the sense of a word: for one may be quite familiar with the fact that a particular word has two distinct senses, and yet, when someone utters a sentence containing it, take it (perhaps wrongly) in just one of those senses. A disposition must be capable of being actuated or realized; the context principle may thus be understood as saying that the dispositional grasp of a sense can be activated only in the occurrent grasp of a thought of which that sense is a constituent. That is why the appeal to sense

---

[13] 'Erkenntnisquellen' (1924), *Nachgelassene Schriften*, 288; *Posthumous Writings*, 269.

which is involved in sense-perception must consist in the grasp of a complete thought.

Frege's ground for holding that sense-perception involves the grasp of a sense is, presumably, that sense-perception normally requires the awareness of one or more objects, whereas an object can only be given to us in one or another particular way. This thesis means that we cannot ever simply be aware of an object, in the sense that our state of awareness can be completely described by indicating the object of which we are aware: the way in which the object is given is always a sense which can be a thought-constituent. A sense-impression may be an impression of some particular object, but, being a mere content of consciousness, does not point beyond itself to that object: only a sense—a thought-constituent—has that capacity to point to something as its referent.

Despite its considerable plausibility, the theory fits rather badly with Frege's view of the relation between thought and language. We saw that to conceive of a grasp of sense as an ability conflicts with his thesis that there is no intrinsic impossibility in grasping a thought in its nakedness, without a verbal clothing: but his account of perception jars, conversely, with his further thesis that human beings can grasp only those thoughts which they attach to sentences as their senses. This thesis cannot be reduced to the contention that none of us can have a thought which he is incapable of expressing; rather, he says, in effect, that we can think only in words or symbols. Plainly, the notion that sense-perception involves the grasping of a thought or the making of a judgement wars powerfully with this view, for it is far from plausible that sensory perception always involves, or is even often accompanied by, any conscious linguistic operation.

In the First Logical Investigation, Husserl came close to Frege's view of perception, saying that 'if we imagine a consciousness prior to all experiences, it is a possibility that it has the same *sensations* as we do. But it will see no things and no events involving things, it will perceive no trees or houses, no flight of birds or barking of dogs.' But in the Sixth Investigation he expressed a wholly contrary view, construing our recognizing what we see as, say, a dog as an *accompaniment* rather than an ingredient of the act of perception, a judgement *prompted* by, but not inseparable from, it. It was in *Ideen* that he introduced his notion of noema, and developed a new account of sense-perception as informed by a noema. This new account is not to be equated with that given by Frege in 'Der

Gedanke', since Husserl explicitly characterizes his notion of noema as a *generalization* of that of sense: thus in the posthumous third volume of *Ideen* he says, 'The noema is nothing but a generalization of the idea of sense to the field of all acts.'[14] The remark rules out the possibility of Husserl's consistently explaining sense in the same way as Frege: for Frege's explanation does not allow for any generalization. For him, a sense is conceivable only as a constituent of thoughts, and, as he remarks in 'Der Gedanke', 'thoughts stand in the closest connection with truth'. On Frege's view, a sense is, as it were, an instruction for taking a step towards determining a thought as true or as false; such a step can be represented as the determination of a referent of the appropriate logical type, and the instruction as a particular means of determining it. Thoughts are *sui generis*: every thought may intelligibly be characterized as true or as false, and whatever can intelligibly be so characterized is a thought. The constituents of a thought are therefore similarly *sui generis*. Whatever serves the purpose of a sense—whatever constitutes a particular means of determining an object or a function—*is* a sense, forming a part of various thoughts; whatever does not serve that purpose cannot in any respect resemble a sense. Sense must be conceived quite differently if it is to be a notion capable of generalization, as Husserl wished to generalize it to the wider notion of noema.

It might be thought that Husserl's generalization consists solely in stripping the sense from its connection with any linguistic expression, and that it therefore does not follow that his conception of sense must have differed radically from Frege's. This interpretation appears to accord with some of Husserl's explanations, as when he says in *Ideen*:

> The words 'mean' and 'meaning' relate in the first instance only to the linguistic sphere, of 'expressing'. It is, however, almost inevitable, and, at the same time, an important advance, to extend the meanings of these words, and to modify them appropriately, so that they become applicable in a certain manner . . . to all acts, whether they are connected with expressive acts or not.[15]

The interpretation cannot be sustained, however. Husserl distinguishes between two ingredients of the noema of a mental act: that

---

[14] E. Husserl, *Ideen*, iii (The Hague, 1952), 89.
[15] *Ideen zu einer reinen Phänomenologie* (Halle, 1913); English trans. by W. R. Boyce Gibson, *Ideas* (London, 1931).

which is capable of being expressed in words, which he sometimes calls 'the noematic sense', and which forms what he terms the 'central nucleus' of the noema; and that which is not so expressible, and forms the outer layer of the full noema. Thus he says:

'Within' each of these experiences there 'dwells' a noematic meaning; and, however closely related, and, indeed, as regards a central nucleus, in essence identical, this remains in different experiences, it nevertheless differs in kind when the experiences differ in kind. . . . Thus within the *complete* noema . . . we must separate out *as essentially different* certain *strata* which group themselves around a *central 'nucleus'*, the sheer '*objective meaning*' which . . . can be described in purely identical objective terms.[16]

He further specifies that:

Every intention in the noematic sense, as the noematic nucleus, of any act whatever can be expressed by meanings. . . . 'Expression' is a remarkable form, which allows itself to be adapted to every sense (to the noematic nucleus), raising it to the realm of Logos.[17]

It is plain that by 'meanings' Husserl intends 'linguistic meanings'. A noema thus consists, in its central part, of a sense that can be attached to a linguistic expression, but may inform a mental act without being so attached, and, in addition, of further layers not linguistically expressible. The noematic sense represents a generalization of linguistic meaning only in that it is detached from language; but the other layers constitute a more radical generalization.

What, then, is the noema of an act of sense-perception? It would be a complete mistake to equate it with the sense-impressions incorporated in the perceptual act, collectively called 'hyle' by Husserl. His view of them is the same as Frege's: having sensations does not in itself amount to seeing things or events involving things. The noema is what endows the perceptual act with an object; like a sense, therefore, it points beyond itself to an object in the external world. Sense-impressions, on the other hand, do not, in themselves, point to anything beyond—we simply *have* them; and here 'in themselves' does not mean 'when they occur in isolation', but merely 'considered as such'.

The noema must, then, have the following properties:

1. it is that which renders the perception the perception *of* an object;

---

[16] *Ideas*, §91.
[17] Ibid., §124.

2. it may be a common ingredient of different acts of perception, just as a sense may be the sense of different utterances;
3. and it may vary while the object remains the same, just as there may be different senses with the same reference.

It therefore consists, in the first instance, in our interpreting our sense-impressions as representations of external objects.

Surprisingly, Husserl makes little effort to use the notion of noema in order to explain what makes a particular object that towards which a given act of perception is directed. His concern, when discussing the noema of such an act, is wholly concentrated upon the perceiver's apprehension of the object, not merely as an external object, but as having certain general characteristics. The principal consequence, for him, of the fact that every act of perception is informed by a noema was that we always perceive an object as having such characteristics: as being of a certain kind, say, or as having a certain three-dimensional shape, or again as disposed to behave in certain ways.

For all that, if the notion of noema is truly a generalization of that of sense, it must also explain what makes one object, rather than another similar to it, the one which is, at a given time, perceived by a particular subject. Nowadays we are inclined to explain it in causal terms: the object perceived is that which gives rise to our sense-impressions. The theory of noema must deny this, holding that what determines the object of perception, or of any other mental act, is internal to the act, because intrinsic to the noema which informs it, just as what determines the object that is being spoken of or thought about is, on Frege's account, internal to the thought expressed or entertained. The object of discussion is the referent of the sense associated with the singular term used; the object under consideration is the referent of the sense constitutive of the thought; and the object of perception must similarly be the objective correlate of the noema.

It would be possible to reconcile the causal theory with that of noema, by holding that the noema informing any act of perception always involves reference to a particular object via the notion of causality, namely, as being the cause of the subject's sense-impressions, as when I think of someone as the person my noticing whom initiated my present train of thought. Since Husserl leaves the question unexplored, there is no way of saying whether or not he would favour such a solution. As remarked, he discusses the noema of a perceptual act largely in terms of the general characteristics of the perceived object; and, in some passages, he carries this very far:

> The factual world of experience is experienced as a *typified world*. Things are experienced as trees, bushes, animals, snakes, birds; specifically, as pine, lime-tree, lilac, dog, viper, swallow, sparrow and so on. The table is characterised as being familiar and yet new.[18]

Husserl presumably here means that the table is new, inasmuch as that particular table has not been seen before, but familiar in being a *table*. He continues:

> What is given in experience as a new individual is first known in terms of what has been genuinely perceived; it calls to mind the like (the similar). But what is apprehended *according to type* also has a horizon of possible experience with corresponding prescriptions of familiarity and has, there- fore, *types* of attributes not yet experienced but expected. When we see a dog, we immediately anticipate its additional modes of behaviour: its typical ways of eating, playing, running, jumping and so on. We do not actually see its teeth: but we know in advance how its teeth will look—not in their individual determination but *according to type*, inasmuch as we have already had previous and frequent experience with similar animals, with dogs, that they have such things as teeth and of this typical kind.[19]

According to Husserl, then, the noema of a visual perception of a dog renders the perception intrinsically that *of a dog*, in that, even if it were illusory, a characterization of the perceptual experience would have to include its being of a dog. In such a case, it is therefore embodied in the noema that informs the perceptual act that what I am seeing is a dog. A possible first reaction to this passage is that Husserl's earlier account of perception is truer to the facts of such a case. However much of a unity may be formed, in experience, by our recognition of the animal as a dog, or of the object as an animal, and our perception of it, the two are, on this view, distinguishable acts: registering what is seen as a dog accom- panies the act of perception, and is not a component of it.

I believe this reaction to be mistaken, but shall not here pursue the point. What plainly cannot be detached, even conceptually, from the perception is the percipient's apprehension, relative to

---

[18] From the posthumously published *Erfahrung und Urteil*, trans. J. Churchill and K. Ameriks (Evanston, 1973), 331; cited in Dreyfus (ed.), *Husserl*, 18–19.
[19] Ibid., 19.

himself, of the region of three-dimensional space occupied by the object: its rough distance from him, its orientation, and its shape, including, of course, that part of it not actually presently accessible to the senses. Equally integral to the perception is his impression of the rigidity and cohesion of the object seen: whether he takes it to be something that will disperse, like a puff of smoke, flow, like water or treacle, droop, like a piece of string, move of itself, like an animal or a functioning machine, or retain its present shape and position. Such characters as these all have to do, as Husserl says, with the expectations generated by our perception of the object. In particular, the shape the object is seen as having governs not only our expectations of its appearance from other viewpoints, but also of its behaviour, such as whether (if it is solid) it will rest, topple, roll, or slide. Our apprehension of the world as revealed to us in sense-perception is guided, from a very early stage of our lives, by a rudimentary terrestrial physics and geometry, backed by a basic classification of types of substance according to their behaviour. At least this much may be reckoned as belonging to the noema.

Frege and Husserl's accounts of perception both approach what must be the truth of the matter, but neither is acceptable as it stands. What shows this more sharply than their internal weaknesses is the impossibility of adapting them to explain the perceptual processes of animals or of infants not yet in possession of language. We cannot say that animals are locked into their inner worlds of sensation and are unable to attain an awareness of physical reality: yet there are strong objections to ascribing to them thoughts of the kind that are expressible in language. Frege himself voiced such an objection when he pointed out that we cannot attribute to a dog such a thought as 'There is only one dog barring my way', since he does not have the concept 'one'. He nevertheless admits that the dog may well be able to distinguish between being attacked by one hostile dog and by several. The dog's awareness cannot accurately be expressed in language, because any sentence that suggests itself is conceptually too rich for the purpose. Human thought-processes differ radically from the analogous processes in animals, and, in particular, by their capacity to be detached from present activity and circumstances. Our thoughts may float free of the environment: we may follow a train of thought quite irrelevant to our surroundings or what we are engaged in doing. An adult human being may be suddenly struck by a thought as he is walking along. He may have hit on the key to solving a mathematical problem, or he may suddenly have remembered that he has left his spectacles at home; in the latter case, he may turn round and go back for them. An animal, or, equally, an infant, cannot act in such a way. An animal may solve quite complex problems, by a process that may reasonably be called thinking, as was illustrated by Köhler's chimpanzees: but its thought-processes cannot float free, but can occur only as integrated with current activity.

The proper characterization of the mental processes of animals is thus an exceedingly delicate task; but, without accomplishing it, we can hardly attain an adequate account of our own. It is surely a mistake to suppose that, because, by means of language, we can engage in thought-processes both far richer and more precise than those of which animals are capable, we do not also engage in ones very similar to theirs. A cat can perceive a dog just as a human being can: there is no good reason to suppose that utterly different accounts should be given of feline and of human perceptions of such an object. Frege and Husserl were obviously right to hold that perception is not simply a matter of sensation, but that it has a further component at least analogous to thought. Frege simply identified it with thought, whereas Husserl wanted it to be a generalization of thought; but the one failed to show how thought could be fused with sensation, while the other failed to explain how the notion of thought was capable of generalization.

Husserl was the founder of phenomenology, Frege the grand-father of analytical philosophy, two schools which today are generally regarded as utterly diverse and barely capable of communicating with one another. Yet the analogy between the ideas of Frege and those of Bolzano has frequently been remarked on, and Bolzano was the salient influence on Husserl's *Logische Untersuchungen*. Just after the publication of that book, Frege and Husserl would have appeared, to anyone who knew the work of both, remarkably close in their philosophical views: what was it in the thought of each that set their followers on such divergent paths? Frege was the first philosopher in history to achieve anything resembling a plausible account of the nature of thoughts and of their inner structure. His account depended upon his conviction of the parallelism between thought and language. His interest was in thought, not in language for its own sake: he was concerned with those features of language irrelevant to the expression of thought only in order to set them aside. Nevertheless, his strategy for analysing thought was to analyse the forms of its linguistic or symbolic expression; and this strategy became the characteristic mark of the analytical school. Although he continued to reiterate that it is inessential to thoughts and thought-constituents that we grasp them as the senses of sentences and their parts, it is quite unclear that his account of the senses of linguistic expressions is capable of being transposed into an account of thoughts considered independently of their verbal expression.

For this reason, Frege's theories are of little assistance towards an explanation of unverbalized thought. Unverbalized thought is of importance to an account of human psychology because it is involved in perception and in our manipulation of objects, for example in driving a car, when it can be a highly active process. It also bears upon the philosophical analysis of language itself, since the problem of correctly characterizing a speaker's knowledge of his mother tongue, unsolved by Frege, remains unsolved. Even if we reject realism, it cannot be classified as a practical skill like the ability to swim, since it is not a technique for doing something of which we know in advance what it is to do it; and yet it plainly cannot wholly consist of verbalized knowledge. Husserl's ideas, however, do not supply the guidance in this matter that we fail to derive from those of Frege. It is of little use to propose a generalization of the notion of meaning unless we first have a clear conception of what meaning is and can then see in which direction it is possible to generalize it. Frege's notion of sense seems incapable of generalization, and Husserl provided no clear alternative notion: his proposal was therefore purely programmatic. It was just as this point that the philosophical heritage of each diverged. That of Frege prompted an exclusive concentration on language, yielding rich dividends but rendering adequate accounts of various important concepts impossible; that of Husserl turned philosophical attention away from language, but left an essential vagueness at its centre.

Where both failed was in demarcating logical notions too strictly from psychological ones. Together, they quite rightly attacked the psychologism of their day, from which no genuine progress could be expected; but, by setting up too rigid a barrier between the logical and the psychological, they deprived themselves of the means to explain what it is to grasp a thought. That is a notion that cannot be relegated to psychology, but is one of which any adequate philosophical account of thought owes an explanation. These failings

14
More about Thoughts*

1. TWO FUNDAMENTAL THESES

In his exceedingly illuminating article 'Thoughts',[1] Dr David Bell
sets out a number of requirements that he believes that any successful philosophical theory of thoughts must meet. He believes that
Frege's theory of thoughts comes closest, of any yet propounded, to
meeting them; and he argues that, among the theses essential to that
theory, are those he labels 'Thesis 1' and 'Thesis 3':

THESIS 1. A thought is isomorphic with the sentence whose sense it
is.

THESIS 3. Every unambiguous sentence has a unique function-
argument analysis.

These theses, he contends, are indispensable for the ability of
Frege's theory to handle those of the requirements on an acceptable
theory of thoughts which he lists under the head of 'rationality', in
particular that it yield an account of the logical relations between
thoughts.
   Despite his admiration for Frege's theory, Dr Bell claims to
detect within it two distinct incoherences. These, he thinks, are
difficulties not peculiar to the theory maintained by Frege, which
contains certain features that might call for modification on other
grounds: rather, they affect any theory of thoughts, and no resolution
of them is generally available, or, at any rate, generally accepted.
We have, then, first to decide whether the incoherences Bell
perceives are genuine; if they are, we have to see what modifications
in the theory would be needed to correct them. The first alleged
incoherence bears on Theses 1 and 3; so we may start by considering
whether Bell is right in maintaining that these two theses are
essential to Frege's theory, or whether one or other could be
jettisoned without fatal damage to it.

* First published in *Notre Dame Journal of Formal Logic*, 30 (1) (1989), 1–19.
[1] *Notre Dame Journal of Formal Logic*, 28 (1987), 36–50.

Not only was Thesis 1 held by Frege: he regarded it as a key component of his theory. It is implicit in his doctrine that the sense of part of a sentence is part of the sense of the whole, and explicit in remarks like 'This would not be possible if we could not distinguish in the thought parts to which the parts of the sentence correspond, so that the construction of the sentence could serve as a picture of the construction of the thought'.[2] Now structure can be ascribed to thoughts only metaphorically, as Frege acknowledged; so the tenability of the thesis depends upon the defensibility of the metaphor. A natural response—virtually a conditioned reflex for professional philosophers—is that Thesis 1 is meaningless in the absence of independent notions of structure for thoughts and sentences. That is a misunderstanding: the two notions are interdependent, and must be explained together. For different purposes, structure may be ascribed to sentences according to different schemes of analysis: the type of structure with which Thesis 1 is concerned is that revealed by what, in his formulation of Thesis 3, Bell calls 'function-argument analysis'. Since functions, for Frege, belong to the realm of reference, Bell clearly means to speak of the semantic theory that constitutes Frege's theory of reference: the structure of a sentence is that which underlies Frege's account of the determination of its truth-value in accordance with its composition. Our understanding of the sentence depends upon our grasp of what determines it as true or as false: so the structure in question is that relevant to our grasp of the thought it expresses. But, conversely, our access to the thought is through that, or some other, sentence expressing it: we arrive at a notion of the structure of the thought via that of the semantic structure of the sentence.

It may appear that, if our conception of the structure of the thought is correlative to that of the (semantic) structure of the sentence, Thesis 1 is vacuous. It is not vacuous, however: rather, it vindicates the attribution of structure to thoughts. Sentences do not encode thoughts, but *express* them: it is only because we can conceive of the thought as having parts corresponding to the parts of the sentence that we can distinguish expressing the thought from a systematic means of identifying it. A thought may be identified, for instance as the weakest additional premiss that would make Smith's argument valid, otherwise than by expressing it: you can understand

---

[2] 'Gedankengefüge', 36.

the means of identifying it without yet knowing what thought it is. But your grasp of the thought depends upon your grasp of the senses of constituent expressions within a sentence expressing it: that is why Frege was entitled to speak of the sense of such a constituent as consisting in its contribution to the sense of the whole, and as a part of that sense (that thought). You cannot have the thought that planets travel in elliptical orbits, for example, without having the concept of an ellipse: and you cannot have the concept of an ellipse unless you are able to think, of some other closed curve, that it is an ellipse.

It might at first sight be doubted whether Frege would have endorsed Thesis 3: but, on reflection, we can recognize that it is integral to the very idea of a semantic theory, such as he advanced, that the construction of each unambiguous sentence be unique. Different sentences of natural language can of course express the same thought: a sentence may be transformed, without altering the thought expressed, so that its verb is changed from active to passive and its object becomes the new subject. Such distinctions are irrelevant to logic, and hence the two sentences may be represented by the same symbolic formula. It is to this formula that Frege's theory of reference directly applies; and the theory treats each such formula as constructed in a unique way from atomic sentences by logical operations. One might therefore regard a Fregean analysis of a sentence of natural language as taking place in two stages: its representation by a formula of his logical notation, and the syntactic analysis of the formula into parts to which references may significantly be ascribed. Frege no doubt believed that his theory of reference constituted the unique correct semantic theory, but I do not think that Bell needed or meant to endorse such a claim. The uniqueness of the analysis of the sentence is relative to the semantic theory adopted; within that theory, the construction of each sentence must be unique, on pain of ambiguity. For example, a salient feature of Frege's theory is that, although a sentential connective like 'if . . . then . . .' does not always stand between complete sentences, the manner in which complex sentences are constructed from atomic ones makes a truth-functional explanation of the connective (as standing between complete sentences) adequate for all occurrences. It follows that, given a sentence representable by a formula of the form 'If A then B', where 'A' and 'B' *are* complete sentences, the first step in analysing the formula must necessarily be to break it up into the connective and those two subsentences; any other strategy of analysis will destroy the adequacy of the truth-functional explanation.

Bell observes that Theses 1 and 3 together imply the corollary that every thought has a determinate structure, corresponding to that of a sentence expressing it. This corollary is then threatened by any example either of a single unambiguous sentence whose structure is not unique, or of two sentences with different structures that express the same thought; and Bell contends that it is from this that the first of the two incoherences he perceives in Frege's theory arises. For he maintains, on pp. 45–6, that Frege was compelled to admit that certain pairs of sentences with 'radically different function-argument structures' can express the same thought, and, further, that there are general grounds for this admission. The Fregean examples he offers are the pairs A, B, and D:

SENTENCE A1. *a* is parallel to *b*.
SENTENCE A2. The direction of $a =$ the direction of *b*.

SENTENCE B1. For every *a* $f(a) = g(a)$.
SENTENCE B2. The value-range of $f =$ the value-range of *g*.

SENTENCE D1. There exist unicorns.
SENTENCE D2. The number of unicorns is not nought.

To these we can add pair C,

SENTENCE C1. There are just as many Fs as Gs.
SENTENCE C2. The number of Fs is the same as the number of Gs,

which is of course that pair with which Frege is really concerned in §§63–9 of *Grundlagen der Arithmetik*,[3] expressed without his technical jargon; he uses pair A merely as a convenient analogy. About pair A, he indeed said in §64 that we obtain A2 from A1 by 'carving up the content in a way different from the original way', adding that 'this yields us a new concept', a passage that Bell quotes. About pair B, he said on p. 11 of *Function und Begriff*[4] that B1 'expresses the same sense' as B2, 'but in a different way'. As for pair D, Bell is relying on the remark in §53 of *Grundlagen* that 'affirmation of

---

[3] (Breslau, 1884.)   [4] (Jena, 1891.)

existence is nothing but denial of the number nought'; but we can avoid irrelevant side-issues by fastening instead of pair E,

SENTENCE E1. Jupiter has four moons.
SENTENCE E2. The number of Jupiter's moons is four.

of which Frege says in §57 that E1 'can be converted into' E2. It is thus Thesis T which Bell regards as intrinsically difficult to reject, as having been held by Frege, but yet as incompatible with the fundamental Theses 1 and 3 also held by him.

THESIS T. The two sentences in each of the pairs A to E express the same sense or have the same content.

Concerning Thesis T Frege had, I believe, one of his tacit changes of mind; for it is noteworthy that in *Grundgesetze der Arithmetik*[5] he did *not* anywhere claim that the two sides of Axiom V (the two members of pair B) express the same sense. This was questioned by Hans Sluga in 'Semantic Content and Cognitive Sense'[6] on the ground that Frege says that he uses B2 as '*gleichbedeutend*' with B1,[7] and that according to Sluga, this word signified for him 'having the same sense', and not just 'having the same *Bedeutung*'. In view, not merely of Frege's scrupulous terminological precision in *Grundgesetze*, but of the fact that the observation follows immediately upon his preliminary explanation in §2 of the distinction between sense and *Bedeutung* (reference), this seems somewhat unlikely. If he had still believed the senses to coincide, he could have entertained no doubts about the Axiom, for he held that, if two sentences express the same thought, this will be immediately apparent to anyone who grasps the thought each expresses; yet he said on p. vii of *Grundgesetze*, vol. i, that a dispute might break out over Axiom V, and, in his Appendix to vol. ii, that he had never concealed the fact that it was less evident than the other axioms, and than a logical law ought to be. More likely, by the time he wrote vol. i of *Grundgesetze*, he had come to hold that the claims made in this regard, in *Grundlagen* and in *Function und Begriff*, were too strong. Even so, two questions remain, of which the first is:

[5] Vol. i (Jena, 1893); vol. ii (Jena, 1903).
[6] In L. Haaparanta and J. Hintikka (eds.), *Frege Synthesized: Essays on the Philosophical and Foundational Work of Gottlob Frege* (Dordrecht, 1986).
[7] *Grundgesetze*, vol. i, §3.

Why did Frege ever Assert Thesis T?

The answer is not far to seek. Let us concentrate on pairs A, B, and C, which exhibit a common pattern, strongly emphasized by Frege in *Grundlagen*. In each case, the first member states that a certain equivalence relation holds: between certain objects, in pair A; between functions, in pair B; and between concepts, in pair C. The second member states an identity between objects characterized by reference to the two terms of the equivalence relation. The relation between the first and second members of each of these three pairs is that between 'This stick and that stick are equally long' and 'The length of this stick is the same as the length of that stick'. Now Frege insists that in each case we can arrive at an understanding of the second member only if we already have an understanding of the first; our understanding of the second member essentially involves our recognition that it is logically equivalent to the first. How do we make this transition? Individually, almost certainly by being taught to make it: but how could it be made in the first place? Only by reflection: we come to see that we can express that the equivalence relation holds by stating the identity of certain (abstract) objects. Our understanding of the new form of sentence is mediated by our recognition of its logical equivalence with the old: the meaning of A2, as we ordinarily understand it, is *given* to us by the requirement that it have the same truth value as A1. Since this is so, what more natural than to say that the new sentence has the same content, or expresses the same thought, as the old one? Pairs D and E exhibit a somewhat different pattern; but a similar line of thought seems equally compelling in their case.

Criterion R, was that usually, though not unwaveringly, employed by Frege from 1891 onwards for two sentences' expressing the same thought.

CRITERION R. Anyone who grasps the thought expressed by each of a given pair of sentences must immediately recognize one as true if he recognizes the other as true.

The conclusion that the members of pairs A to E have a common content or sense is reinforced by the fact that they all satisfy Criterion R. No one can be said to grasp the content of A2, for example, unless he is aware that it is true or false according as A1 is true or false; so, by Criterion R, the content of each must be the same.

Attaining New Concepts

Now the natural objection to Thesis T is that the second member of each pair involves a concept—that of a direction, a value-range, or a number—that the first does not, and hence, by Principle K, cannot express the same thought.

PRINCIPLE K. If one sentence involves a concept that another sentence does not involve, the two sentences cannot express the same thought or have the same content.

We shall see that the objection is in fact decisive; but our present concern is still with Frege's motivation. He was not in a position to repudiate Principle K, for it is implicit in his frequently repeated thesis that the sense of a part of a sentence is a part of the thought expressed by the sentence as a whole: if that does not mean that a grasp of the sense expressed by the constituent part is a necessary condition for grasping the thought, it means nothing at all. Nor could he deny that Principle K applies to pairs like A and C: for he expressly contends in §64 of *Grundlagen* that by means of the transition from the first member of the pair to the second 'we attain a new concept'—that of a direction or of a number. Why, then, did he still think that the content of A2 could be arrived at by analysing that of A1?

This, too, is readily explained: he adopted Thesis T by false analogy with the type of sentence concerning which he repeatedly insisted that distinct analyses can be given of one and the same sentence, and that it is essential to logic that they can. The process of analysis is described both in *Begriffsschrift*[8] and in 'Booles rechnende Logik und die Begriffsschrift', the latter paper being one submitted for publication but rejected. In the simplest case, we pick out one or more occurrences of one singular term within the sentence, and conceive of it as replaceable, in all the occurrences we have picked out, by any other singular term; we may then view the sentence as composed out of that singular term and the remaining (constant) part (called in *Begriffsschrift* the 'function'), which expresses a concept. In the light of this analysis, the content of the

---

[8] (Halle, 1879.)

sentence may be viewed as saying of the thing denoted by the singular term that it falls under the concept. Since the sentence may contain more than one singular term, and each of them may have more than one occurrence, this operation can be executed in a number of different ways. We may also pick out each of two singular terms, in one or more occurrences, conceiving of each as replaceable, in those occurrences, by another singular term; we are then viewing the content as being to the effect that a relation, expressed by the constant part, obtains between the things denoted by the two terms. Yet more sophisticated forms of analysis allow us to pick out expressions for concepts or relations, again to be regarded as replaceable by other expressions of the same type. The choice of an analysis for any one given sentence is thus very wide.

Frege regarded this conception of analysis as one of his great discoveries, and characterized it by saying that 'instead of putting together the judgement from an individual thing as subject and an already formed concept as predicate, we conversely analyse the judgeable content and so attain the concept'.[9] By thus representing a complex predicate, to which a quantifier can be attached to form a sentence, as not being formed out of its parts, but as arrived at by omitting its argument from a complete sentence, he was able to treat all complex sentences as built up, ultimately, from closed atomic sentences. He did not need, like Tarski, to resort to so semantically problematic, if syntactically simple, a device as taking *open* atomic sentences as the basis; and this lends an especial purity to his semantics.

More importantly, Frege characterized the process of analysis as a means of concept-formation, more powerful than the Boolean operations and the process of abstraction generally admitted; his favourite example was our forming the concept of the continuity of a function. The analysis of a sentence enables us to discern a pattern in the sentence, a pattern it shares with every other sentence resulting from inserting an argument into the argument-place of the 'function'. We may equally well say that we discern a pattern within the content; but the recognition of this pattern was not needed for a grasp of the content, but occurs when that content has already been grasped. It is for this reason that Frege says in *Begriffsschrift*, §9,

---

[9] 'Booles rechnende Logik', in *Nachgelassene Schriften*, ed. H. Hermes, F. Kambartel, and F. Kaulbach (Hamburg, 1969), 18; *Posthumous Writings*, trans. P. Long and R. White (Oxford, 1979), 17.

that 'it has nothing to do with the conceptual content, but is solely a matter of the way we view it'. The pattern is not imposed, since it was there to be discerned; but it is selected from among many different equally discernible patterns, which is why each sentence or thought is capable of being analysed in different ways. Thus it would in principle be possible to grasp the thought expressed by 'Brutus killed Brutus' without noticing that it exhibited a pattern shared by 'Cato killed Cato', but not by 'Brutus killed Caesar': it is by noticing that common pattern that we attain the concept of suicide.

For Frege, deductive reasoning was not a mechanical process of eliciting new ways of stating what was already known: rather, analytic judgements could extend our knowledge. What explained how this could be was precisely the fact that analysis, and with it the formation of concepts, was an essential constituent of logical inference; a step indispensable to constructing a quantified sentence, and equally to recognizing the validity of an argument in which it figured. Since the form of the analysis was not uniquely determined by the content of the sentence analysed, deductive reasoning must therefore be, in some part, a creative intellectual operation. All this put Frege, almost alone amongst philosophical logicians, in possession of an account of how deductive reasoning could be simultaneously certain and fruitful.

Two of Frege's central doctrines were that one and the same content was capable of distinct analyses, and that different sentences of natural language could have the same content. Often the difference reflected a variation in the focus of attention; and hence one sentence might better accord with one analysis of the content, another with another. What made analysis a process of concept-*formation* was the fact that a grasp of the concept revealed by the analysis was not integral to an apprehension of the content being analysed. These views together render it entirely comprehensible how Frege came to claim that, by analysing the content of the first member of any of our pairs, one could extract a concept which obtained explicit expression in the second member, but that the content itself remained unaltered.

The relation thus claimed to obtain between the first and second member of a pair is in fact precisely that between a sentence and its definitional abbreviation or replacement. We may analyse the sentence '13 is greater than 1 and, for all n, if n divides 13, $n = 13$ or $n = 1$' into '13' and the concept-expression obtained by omitting all three occurrences of '13' from the sentence. By this means, we attain the concept of primality, which that concept-expression expresses. We may therefore use that concept-expression to define the predicate '. . . is prime', and then replace the original complex sentence by '13 is prime'. This last sentence obviously involves the concept of primality, whereas the whole point of regarding the analysis of the original sentence as a means of attaining that concept was that a grasp of the content of that sentence did not require us to see it as splitting up in that way, nor, therefore, to have the concept of a prime number. But, since the latter sentence has been introduced by stipulating that it have the same truth-value as the former, it seems that they must have the same content.

The Untenability of Thesis T

For all that, Thesis T must be pronounced indefensible. It cannot be justified by Criterion R, which Frege indeed often used to good effect in order to show that two sentences did *not* have the same sense, in other words as a necessary condition for expressing the same thought. But, although he never acknowledged the fact, it is far less plausible as a sufficient condition. Its inadequacy when so used is shown when it conflicts with Principle K. The principle is compelling: no one can be said to grasp the thought that a certain politician is dishonest, for example, if he lacks the concept of dishonesty. Since possession of the concept is essential to a grasp of the thought, the thought cannot be identified with one that can be grasped by someone who does not possess the concept. It follows that Principle K rules out an identity of sense between the members of each of the pairs A to E. In doing so, it contradicts Criterion R for identity of sense. Possibly Frege never noticed that Principle K conflicts with Criterion R, to both of which he was committed; but it is plain that, when they conflict, it is Principle K to which we should hold fast.

Since Frege was himself comitted to Principle K, he ought never to have asserted Thesis T; and his other doctrines in no way compelled him to do so. In *Grundlagen*, having first argued that it would be improper to define A1 as equivalent to A2, Frege eventually decided that it was not possible directly to stipulate A2 to be by definition equivalent to A1, nor C2 to C1. This by itself should have warned him that there was something amiss in holding them to have the same content. In fact, Principle K disallows identity of content even for definitionally equivalent predicates, and sentences containing them, at least given Frege's doctrine of analysis. The sentence '13 is prime' and its definitional expansion are, of course, intimately connected: the sole difference betwen them is what, in the terminology of *Begriffsschrift*, was not integral to the content of the expanded sentence, but was merely one out of different possible ways of regarding it, has become integral to the content of its definitional abbreviation '13 is prime'. The predicate '. . . is prime' has indeed the same sense as the complex predicate serving as its definiens; but this sense is not a constituent of the thought expressed by the expanded sentence.

Gregory Currie in 'Frege, Sense, and Mathematical Knowledge'[10] tries to vindicate Frege by attributing to him two distinct theories (or concepts) of sense, a weak and a strong one: the weak one is that concerned with the information conveyed by a sentence; the strong one allows Frege to justify the analytic definitions of arithmetical notions that he offers in *Grundlagen*, involving the replacement of an intuitive notion by a precise one. This is not very plausible. It is hard to see how there could be any acceptable concept of sense according to which an imprecise expression could bear the very same sense as a precise one: precision and imprecision are features of the *sense* itself, not of the manner of expressing it. Currie does not attempt to delineate the alleged strong concept of sense; he merely asserts that Frege had such a concept, which of course explains nothing. But, in any case, the replacement of an intuitive notion by a precise one, though exemplified by Frege's explicit definition of 'the number of *F*s', is irrelevant to the logical equivalence of C1 and C2. It *does* indeed bear on the definition of 'There are just as many *F*s as *G*s' (C1) to mean 'There is a one–one map of the *F*s on to the *G*s'; but this definition should be kept separate from the requirement that C1 and C2 have the same truth-value, since it would be quite possible to accept the definition of cardinal equivalence in terms of one–one mapping while refusing to take numerical terms at face value as genuine singular terms denoting objects, or, indeed, to do the converse. Frege runs the two together in §63 of *Grundlagen* because his contention that C2 is to be explained in terms of C1 would be idle unless C1 were independently definable; but, when he discusses the analogous pair A, he does not enquire

how A1 (the concept of parallelism) is to be defined, and considers
the logical equivalence of A2, not with some definiens of A1, but
with A1 itself. Once the distinction is clearly made between (1) the
definition of cardinal equivalence (equinumerosity) by means of
one–one mapping, and (2) the equation of cardinal equivalence
with numerical identity (pair C), the temptation to think that Thesis
T has anything to do with replacing vague everyday notions with
mathematically precise ones is dispelled, and, with it, Currie's
account of Frege's alleged strong concept of sense.

Frege's idea that we attain a concept by analysing a content
already given is, on his own principles, wrongly applied to the pairs
A to E. Since, by means of analysis, we discern a pattern that was
there to be discerned, the possibility of discerning it must be
apparent from a complete representation of the structure of the
sentence; but A1 cannot be displayed as dissectable into two terms
for directions and the sign of identity. It would be perfectly in order
to observe that A2 could be analysed, not only as saying of the
direction of a and the direction of b that they are identical, but also
as saying of the lines a and b that they stand in the relation that the
direction of one is the same as that of the other: in this way, given
the content of A2, we could arrive at the concept of being parallel. It
would therefore be possible to maintain that A1 is a disguised form
of A2, and can be understood only by recognizing it as conventional
shorthand for A2; its apparent form would not then be its true form,
but would conceal a tacit reference to directions. But this is precisely
the view Frege is opposing: he argues that 'this is to stand the true
state of affairs on its head', since the concept of parallelism is prior
to that of a direction. We may express this by saying that the
direction of explanation runs from A1 to A2: A1 is explained
independently of A2, but must be invoked in any explanation of A2.
It is true that Frege appears to be proposing to analyse E1 as
shorthand for E2, for E2 is interpretable by means of his definitions,
whereas he gives no independent explanation of E1, but merely
remarks that 'it can be transformed into' E2. Against this, however,
the same objection might be brought, namely, that the adjectival
use of number-words is prior to their substantival use and to the
concept of a number; and so his procedure at this point requires a
justification he does not offer. Certainly, it would be contrary to all
Frege's beliefs to propose that to say that F and G have the same
value for every argument is shorthand for saying that their value-

ranges coincide: the former statement involves only identity and universal quantification, in explaining neither of which is any allusion made, however tacit, to value-ranges.

My own view is that Frege is right about the direction of explanation as between the members of pairs A and C, and that it is a minor flaw in his presentation in *Grundlagen* that he represents statements of number like E1 as explicable in terms of statements of identity between numbers like E2. This, however, is irrelevant to the present issue. If the direction of explanation runs from the second member of any of these pairs to the first—if, for example, in the pair A, 'is parallel to' is definable by 'has the same direction as'—there is no problem: the first member can then be arrived at by analysis of the second, and is a definitional replacement of it. By what was said earlier about definition, the two sentences would still not have precisely the same content; but their contents would be bound in that intimate connection that results from definition. If, conversely, the direction of explanation runs from the first member of a pair to the second, the second cannot be obtained by analysis from the first. Frege was simply mistaken in thinking that it could; in my opinion, he came to realize his mistake, although without ever clearly perceiving that his criterion for expressing the same thought did not constitute a sufficient condition for doing so. We indeed have, in the transition from the first member of such a pair to the second, a mode of concept-formation, and one that follows a pattern common to many distinct instances; but it is a different mode from that which Frege expounded in *Begriffsschrift* and so strongly emphasized in 'Booles rechnende Logik' and in *Grundlagen*. The first of Bell's two crises for Frege's theory of thoughts, and for theories of thoughts in general, is thus resolved.

Two Kinds of Analysis

The doctrine of alternative possible analyses appears to contradict Bell's Thesis 3, with which we started. Bell resolves the matter by holding that all but one of the alternative analyses recognized by Frege are always *partial* analyses, whereas it is only a complete analysis that should be unique. The example he uses is the sentence 'Brutus killed Caesar', which can be correctly analysed into the proper name 'Brutus' and the concept-expression '. . . killed Caesar', and equally correctly into the proper name 'Caesar' and the concept-expression 'Brutus killed . . .'. This enables him to dismiss as spurious certain apparent counter-examples to unique analysability. But even if the contrast between partial and complete analyses suffices to explain the 'Brutus killed Caesar' case, it does not serve for all. The fact is, rather, that we have to do with two quite different senses of 'analysis'. The analysis spoken of in Thesis 3 uncovers what Frege refers to as the structure of the thought, as a whole composed of parts: it shows how the thought is to be represented as constructed in stages from thoughts expressible by atomic sentences, and how those thoughts in turn have as constituents the senses of simple names, predicates, and functional expressions. This conception is indeed fundamental to Frege's semantics; but it is not what he is referring to when he uses words translatable as 'analysis'. If we use the term 'analysis' for the former process, we should use some other for what Frege means when he says that one sentence or thought admits of different analyses: I have suggested 'decomposition'. The latter process does *not* purport to display the structure of the thought, in that sense of 'structure' in which a grasp of the thought depends upon an apprehension of its structure. Rather, it picks out a pattern common to that thought and a range of others, a perception of which is *not* required in order to grasp the thought. A recognition of this pattern yields a new concept which is not, in general, a constituent of the thought, though it is attained by regarding the thought as exemplifying that pattern; but, as Frege makes clear in *Begriffsschrift*, it will be a constituent of other thoughts, in particular one attributing a property to that concept (a thought expressed by a quantified sentence).

When, by omitting all three occurrences of the numeral '13', we subject to the process Frege referred to as 'analysis' the arithmetical sentence cited earlier, '13 is greater than 1 and, for all n, if n divides 13, $n = 13$ or $n = 1$', we have not taken a first step towards an analysis in Bell's sense: on the contrary, the concept-expression so obtained nowhere appears in the process of displaying the structure of the sentence as built up from atomic sentences, for this must begin by breaking it up into two subsentences conjoined by 'and'. The reconciliation between Thesis 3 and the doctrine of alternative analyses is, therefore, to be effected, not merely by demanding uniqueness only for complete analyses rather than partial ones, but by distinguishing two quite different notions of analysis.

Do Contents Have Structure?

An interpretation of Frege due originally to Hans Sluga has found a few adherents, among them Steven Wagner. The interpretation rests on construing quite literally Frege's apparently comprehensive claim quoted above, that 'instead of putting together the judgement from an individual thing as subject and an already formed concept as predicate, we conversely analyse the judgeable content and so attain the concept'. If we make no distinction between the two senses of 'analysis', this appears to imply that we initially grasp the content as unstructured. That conclusion is presented by Wagner in 'Frege's Definition of Number'[11] as Frege's doctrine, understood, as Wagner emphasizes, by analogy with Kant's epistemology of space and time. 'Contents', he tells us (p. 8), 'are *unstructured* bearers of truth-values, and propositions (as I am now using the word) are structures which the mind formulates by way of representing content to itself'; hence 'the content . . . is itself an entity prior to these propositions and more objective'. Contents exist independently of us, but we can grasp them only by imposing a propositional structure on them; grasping a content is thus itself 'a process of analysis'. The propositional structure is 'the mind's contribution'; but 'a single content may admit radically different analyses', and hence be 'represented by us to ourselves by distinct propositions'. It therefore makes no sense to ask 'whether a particular concept or term appears' in a given content, 'although this question makes sense for any of the propositions that express' it.

A little reflection should show that it is unnecessary to attribute to Frege so radically Kantian a view of judgeable contents in order to guarantee that concepts are never among their building blocks, but are always extracted from them. It could still be allowed that the contents of complex sentences have a structure depending on how they are built up from the contents of atomic sentences by operations corresponding to negation, application of the sentential connectives, and quantification; all that is needed is that the contents of the atomic sentences be initially apprehended as devoid of structure. But Frege does not appear at any stage to have believed even this. Thus he says, in 'Booles rechnende Logik', that 'in order to be capable of being so analysed, the expression of the judgeable

---

[11] *Notre Dame Journal of Formal Logic*, 24 (1983), 1–21.

content must already be articulated. From this one may conclude that at least the properties and relations that are not further analysable must have their own simple designations':[12] in other words, even atomic sentences are complex and contain simple expressions for the primitive properties and relations. He goes on to touch upon a difficulty not peculiar to his theory, saying, 'It does not follow from this that the ideas of these properties and relations can be formed unconnected with things' (that is, with objects); 'rather, they arise simultaneously with the first judgements in which they are ascribed to things.' The thought 'That leaf is green' cannot be unstructured, since, for anyone to have it, he must be capable (as Evans's 'generality constraint' requires) of thinking of other objects that they are green, and of thinking other things concerning the leaf; moreover, he must be aware that he is capable of this. The same holds good at the linguistic level: the sentence 'That leaf is green' might be new to him, but he can understand and use it because he knows what 'that leaf' means and what 'is green' means. On the other hand, to know what 'is green' means consists in knowing what is meant by saying of any one thing that it is green; one can understand the phrase only as a component of sentences. Correspondingly, one can grasp the property of being green only by knowing what it is to think, of something, that it is green. Frege offers no deep account of the matter; but, by speaking of the primitive properties and relations as 'arising simultaneously' with the judgements involving them, he rules out the idea that we *first* grasp the judgeable contents and only subsequently discern the properties and relations within them.

Wagner will reply that this is not the view he takes Frege to hold: the properties and relations arise simultaneously because *we* cannot grasp the unstructured contents without imposing a structure on them. Such a reply, however, reveals how gratuitous his contrast between judgeable contents and 'propositions' is; for, in that case, it can only be from the *propositions* that we can extract concepts, and Frege's dictum about attaining the concept by analysis cannot after all be used to support the thesis that *contents* are unstructured. There can be, for Frege, no more and less objective: there are only the wholly objective and the wholly subjective. Moreover, there is no true analogy between Wagner's doctrine of propositions and

---

[12] *Nachgelassene Schriften*, 18–19; *Posthumous Writings*, 17.

Kant's doctrine of space. Different individuals may have qualitatively very different intuitions of space; but Wagner requires that there may be two distinct propositions which we all grasp and which impose different structures on the same content-in-itself, and there is no analogue of this in Kant's account of our apprehension of objects as in space. Wagner speaks of the way *he* uses the word 'proposition'; but we need to know to which Fregean term or concept that use corresponds. Wagner ascribes his quasi-Kantian theory simply to Frege, without differentiation of period, citing both *Grundlagen* and *Grundgesetze*. In Frege's post-1890 doctrine, contents were split into thoughts and truth values. Thoughts—even those expressed by atomic sentences like 'Etna is higher than Vesuvius'—have parts, including the sense of the name 'Etna', and hence also the sense of 'is higher than'; truth-values have no structure, and there are only two of them. Thoughts presumably correspond to Wagner's propositions; but there is no place in which to locate his unstructured contents. For the early period, conversely, it is impossible to say which term corresponds to Wagner's 'proposition'.

Wagner's interpretation enables him to ascribe to the Frege of *Grundgesetze* as well as of *Grundlagen* the view expressed in 'Booles rechnende Logik'[13] that numbers 'are first created by thinking', or, at least, that this is true of the extensions of concepts with which he identifies them. But, quite rightly faithful to Frege's conclusion that we cannot introduce numerical terms by simply stipulating that C2 is to be equivalent to C1, Wagner finds himself forced to concede that, if such a stipulation were made, C2 would merely express an unstructured relation between the concepts *F* and *G*, not a genuine identity between objects (p. 9): it thus only shows how numerical terms, if we had them, could be used to restructure the content of C1. It is plain to Wagner that Frege thought it essential to be able to treat the numerical terms in C2 as genuine terms standing for objects in the domain of the individual variables. We obtain such terms by the explicit definition Frege gives of the numerical operator: but, since many alternative definitions of it would yield the logical equivalence of C2 and C1, the understanding of C2 as containing genuine terms for numbers involves more than is given by that equivalence, and it follows (p. 10) that we cannot obtain a concept of number by analysing C1. Hence, in the end,

---

[13] *Nachgelassene Schriften*, 38; *Posthumous Writings*, 34 ('yielded' should be 'created').

Wagner's interpretation proves impotent to justify assigning the same content to C1 and C2 (or, presumably, any of the other pairs).

3. BELL'S SECOND ACCUSATION

The second incoherence Bell claims to detect in Frege's theory concerns the status of thoughts (and senses generally) as objects; we may say, although Bell does not express it in this way, that it has to do with Frege's mythology of the third realm. For Frege, thoughts are objects existing independently of our grasping them. Bell claims, however, that 'it is impossible for an object to fulfil the role of a sense',[14] and quotes Frege's possibly unguarded remark that 'a truth-value cannot be part of a thought, . . . because it is not a sense but an object'[15] in support. He justifies his claim by arguing that, for Frege, 'to have an object in mind is to have grasped the sense of some expression which has that object as its reference', but that, when applied to the case in which the object is itself a sense, this leads to a vicious infinite regress.

For all objects other than senses, Frege adhered faithfully to Kant's dictum that every object must be given to us in a particular way; the sense of a singular term consists in a way in which its referent is given to us, and we can think about or be aware of an object only by grasping such a sense. When we grasp a sense, however, *it* cannot be given to us in any one way rather than another; our mode of awareness of it is not constituted by our grasp of any *other* sense. That is because everything that contributes to determining the reference of an expression is part of its sense: we do not go to the reference via the sense, as one goes from Oxford to Leeds via Birmingham; the sense is the route, and not an intermediate station. It thus appears that, if senses are objects, they are the only objects which we can apprehend immediately, without conceiving of them in any particular way. We might say that, in grasping a thought or a constituent sense, we apprehend it *as it is*, or in its entirety: not, of course, that we know everything there is to know about it, but that we identify it by its constitutive properties, that is, by what makes it the thought or thought-constituent that it is.

It might be objected that Bell's phrase 'to have an object in mind' properly applies to thinking *about* an object, or possibly also to

[14] 'Thoughts', 46.
[15] 'Über Sinn und Bedeutung', 35.

apprehending it in perception or to comparable modes of awareness of it, whereas grasping a thought is not thinking *about* it, but thinking it: in grasping the thought, we are thinking about whatever the thought is about. But the objection, as it stands, merely serves to underline, not invalidate, the contrast between grasping a thought and apprehending other objects. For if, as Frege supposed, thoughts are independently existing objects, grasping a thought can only be a mode of awareness of an object, however unlike our awareness of an object of any other kind it may be. If thoughts are objects, they are objects standing to us in an epistemic relation utterly different from all others; and this suggests that Frege's theory should be amended by denying that thoughts are objects at all.

Bell's response to the difficulty concerns thoughts as contents of the activity of thinking rather than as the senses of sentences. His solution is to hold that thinking and judging should be construed as intransitive rather than transitive verbs: not on the model of agent-act-object, but on that of agent-act; thoughts, in other words, are the referents of mere cognate accusatives. And there his essay abruptly ends. It is true that he has published a sequel, 'The Art of Judgement',[16] in which, taking off from a remarkable anticipation of Wittgenstein's observations about rules that he discovered in the *Kritik der reinen Vernunft*, he seeks help from Kant's *Kritik der Urtheilskraft*: but I shall not discuss this. Instead, I want to consider where Bell leaves us at the end of 'Thoughts'.

We have to ask whether the crisis is as grave as Bell believes it to be; and then to ask what will happen to the Fregean theory if Bell's resolution of the crisis is adopted. The end of 'Thoughts' is abrupt, because, as with Frege's attempted solution of Russell's paradox, Bell has proposed an emendation of Frege's theory without reviewing the effect this would have on the merits of the theory already canvassed. As he remarks, Frege advanced the thesis that thoughts are not merely objects, but objects that exist timelessly and independently of us, because he thought it necessary in order to safeguard their objectivity. That is, since he allowed no intermediate status between the radically subjective and the wholly objective, he thought it followed from the fact that thoughts are accessible to all that they are independent of any. The objectivity of thoughts forms for Bell another class of requirements upon an adequate theory of

[16] *Mind*, 96 (1987), 221–44.

thoughts, requirements that he recognizes Frege's theory as meeting; above all, the requirement that different individuals can grasp the same thought, and that one individual can communicate a thought without residue to another. What Bell believes himself to have discovered is that Frege's theory contrives to satisfy the requirements of objectivity only at the price of violating other requirements that come under the head of interiority, namely, that thoughts can be grasped and judged to be true by individual subjects.

We may well doubt that Frege needed to interpret the objectivity of thoughts so strongly as he did in order to meet the requirements that fall under that head, and yet feel uncertain whether the theory will continue to meet them if it is amended as Bell proposes: especially so since the emendation jettisons the Fregean principle, anticipated by Bolzano, that thoughts are not contents of the mind. Acts of thinking may be differentiated in many ways: the same thought may be grasped as the senses of different sentences, in one or more languages. But we have seen that there cannot be distinct ways of grasping it. Now when thinking and judging are construed as mental acts directed towards extramental objects which form the contents of the thoughts or judgements, there is no difficulty in seeing how thoughts and judgements made by others at other times *can* have the same contents, though it is not ruled out that some thoughts of mine may be such that nobody else's could have their content. But to say that 'think' and 'judge' should be construed as intransitive verbs is to say that which thought is grasped or judged to be true is a matter of the way in which one thinks or judges; and then it is much more doubtful whether an adequate sense can be given to saying that two people think or judge in the same way, and so may be said to have the same thought or make the same judgement. Such a sense depends upon conceptually separating the content from the act of thinking and providing it with a criterion of identity distinguishable from anything binding it to an event in the subject's mental life. Now is not that to say that we must construe that event on the model of agent–act–object? And does that not make Frege right, after all?

Reflexivity

Others of Bell's requirements on a successful theory of thoughts stand in danger from his emendation. Among these are those coming under the head of 'reflexivity'. As Bell puts it,[17] we can think and judge about thoughts and judgements; hence thoughts and judgements can figure as the objects of other thoughts and judgements as well as the contents of acts of thinking and judging. Bell rightly contends that Frege's own principles demand that the reference of such a phrase as 'the sense of the expression "*A*"'—let alone, we may add, of one like 'Boyle's law'—cannot but be an object. In thinking about thoughts, we may refer to them without expressing them, for instance by a name like 'the fundamental theorem of algebra' or a description like 'the weakest additional premiss that would make the argument valid'; and the thought is then given to us in a particular way, as other objects are. Frege's theory indeed meets the requirements of reflexivity admirably: it will surely no longer be able to meet them if thoughts and judgements are not recognized as objects at all.

Reflexivity requires, then, that thoughts and their constituent senses must be objects of some kind, which, like other objects, can be given to us in one way or another. That, Bell might reply, holds good when we are referring to them or thinking *about* them; but we have another way of apprehending them, namely, grasping them, to which other objects furnish no analogy. It is, he might say, when we grasp them that we know them directly, rather than in some particular way. This might be objected to as a confusion. To think about something is to have it as an object of reference. The way we think about it is the sense: but, for that very reason, the sense is not a second object of our thinking, but simply the way in which we are thinking about the referent; it would therefore be better not to call grasping a thought a means of apprehending it, if by this is meant being aware of it as we are aware of what we perceive and what we think about. But Bell might retort that it is this very confusion which he is aiming to expose, since it is engendered precisely by Frege's mythology of the third realm, by his treating senses as objects. More exactly, senses are objects inasmuch as they are possible objects of reference and possible subjects of thought: but Frege's mythology makes them objects of the mental act of grasping; and the error lies in conceiving that act as having an object at all.

This solution cannot be adequate. It is not merely that senses *can*

---

[17] 'Thoughts', 38.

be objects of reference, things we think about as well as contents of our thinking, but that one of several ways of referring to a sense goes via our grasp of it: Frege is therefore justified in speaking of 'oblique' reference. It does not matter here whether he is right to invoke this notion in respect of the *oratio obliqua* clause that follows a verb like 'believe': we are concerned, rather, with phrases of the form 'the thought that . . .' and 'the sense of ". . ."'. As Bell correctly observes, it is because we grasp the direct sense of the sentences in the 'that'-clause or of the expression in quotation marks that the phrase identifies a thought or a sense for us, namely, the sense of that very sentence or expression: the prefix 'the thought that' or 'the sense of' requires us to turn from the referent to the way it is referred to. Grasping a sense, although primarily a way of directing our attention upon the referent, must also involve awareness of that sense itself: otherwise we could not exploit a grasp of the sense as one way of directing attention upon it, when it is the sense that we are thinking about. It thus seems, after all, that grasping a sense must be classed as a mode of apprehending it; if so, it constitutes a direct apprehension of it.

But what is it to apprehend something directly? The difference is that between referring to a thought and expressing it. We can, in general, understand a phrase that refers to a thought without knowing which thought it is that is referred to; but we cannot understand one that expresses a thought without thereby knowing which thought that is—that is what it is to *express* a thought. However, in view of the obscurity of the notion of knowing which object satisfies a given condition—of knowing who committed the murder, for example—this intuitively natural reply does not furnish a sufficient explanation. It will not do, either, merely to say that to apprehend an object directly is to know its essential or constitutive properties. A game, for example, is constituted by its rules; so if a game is specified to me by a statement of its rules, I can identify it by its constitutive properties, even though I may not know anything else about it, such as whether it is enjoyable, when it was invented, or where it is played. But the analogy breaks down. We can distinguish, with other objects, between their constitutive properties and the way in which those properties are expressed, for instance between the rules of the game and the manner in which the rules are stated: by contrast, when a thought is identified as that expressed by a sentence, any variation in the way the sentence determines the thought, that is, in the sense of the sentence, will induce a variation in the thought.

The point is general, since any means of identifying an object is taken by Frege to be a sense: if not one expressible in the language as we have it, then at least one capable of expression in language. A means of identifying a thought may vary while the thought remains the same, but not if it is identified by being grasped. For grasping a thought is to other means of identifying it as expressing it is to other means of referring to it: any variation in the manner in which the thought is grasped will induce a variation in the thought itself. To grasp it *is* to have hold of a means of expressing it, or, if not that exactly, then of the principle whereby some possible (complex) sign would express it: it is, as it were, what is left of understanding when we take away the expression understood, comparable to the knowledge of the meaning of a word possessed by someone who has temporarily forgotten that word and is searching for it. In all other cases, a distinction obtains between what is identified and the means of identification; but, when a sense is grasped, the means of identification and the thing identified coincide. Although it can also be identified in other ways, a thought, or a sense generally, is something that can be used to identify itself, precisely because it can be expressed; and it can be expressed because it is already a means of identification, although, in the first instance, a means of identifying, not itself, but its referent. It is the use of an expression of the thought or sense to refer to that very thought or sense that prompts us to say that in grasping it, that is, in understanding the expression (actually or potentially), we apprehend it directly. This terminology is harmless provided that we explain the phenomenon in this way, and not as exemplifying a mysterious cognitive faculty for mental contact with objects of one particular kind, objects that mediate our awareness of objects of all other kinds. It would make no sense to speak of grasping other objects, or of apprehending them directly; there is therefore no substance to saying that we apprehend them only indirectly.

Now does this provoke the crisis that Bell discerns? That is far from evident. The theory requires that, when we refer to or think about anything, we refer to or think about it in a particular way, but that, in doing so, we are conscious of the way in which we are referring to or thinking about it: all that is actually essential is that we should be capable of becoming conscious of that. The theory further requires that such modes of identification should have sufficient structure for there to be a clear way of identifying *them*—a criterion of identity for the way in which a referent is given—so that it makes sense to speak of fastening upon any one such mode as an object of our thought. Finally, the theory requires that these modes of identification be capable of embodiment in linguistic expressions, by means of which they can be conveyed by one person to another. The embodiment consists, as Bell states, in an isomorphism: the contribution of features of the mode of identification or sense to the whole should be mirrored by the contribution of the parts of an expression to the manner in which the reference of the whole is determined. Given all this, it remains no mystery how a sense can become itself an object of thought, and how, among other ways, it can be reflexively identified—that is, identified *by means of itself*. When so reflexively identified, there is then naturally the impression that we are apprehending it directly, in a manner in which no other type of object can be directly apprehended. The theory thus appears to account, without any incoherence, for the facts that prompt Bell to deny that senses are objects.

The Third Realm

But is this a sufficient solution? Is not Bell still right to deny that grasping a sense is to be understood on the act–object model? Was not Frege wrong to conceive of thoughts as eternal, immutable objects, and does not his notion of the third realm remain a piece of misleading philosophical mythology? One way of rejecting it as mythology is to maintain that senses are intrinsically *of* expressions. Frege, again like Bolzano, argues that the existence of a sense does not depend upon its being expressed or even grasped; and this must be allowed, inasmuch as there are surely thoughts that have never been and never will be expressed or grasped. But this does not show that senses are not, metaphysically, *of* expressions, as the powers of a chess piece are *of* the piece. Although there are powers which no piece, in any past or future version of chess, has ever had or will ever have, to conceive of such a power is to conceive of a piece as having that power; and similarly, on the proposed view, to conceive of a sense is to conceive of an expression as having that sense, whether or not there ever has been or will be such an expression. This of course conflicts with Frege's view that there could be beings who grasped the thoughts we grasp, but not as expressed in language or symbolism. It is temerarious to deny this possibility: what we may reasonably deny is that Frege's theory of thoughts gives any explanation of how it may be so.

We need a distinction, among objects, that Frege did not draw, namely, between transcendent objects and immanent objects. A dance step, for example, is an immanent object. There appears to be no clear answer to the question whether or not we should construe the statement that a dancer danced a certain step on the model of agent–act–object. It would be unreasonable to deny that the dance step is an object: two dancers can execute the same step, and the step may have been danced many times, and hence have existed a long time, before a particular dancer danced it; a dance step has objective properties, and can be spoken of and thought about. On the other hand, the step did not exist, and could not have existed, antecedently to or independently of anyone's dancing it: it is this which distinguishes it as an immanent object from a transcendent one like a shoe. Thoughts and other senses should not be banished, as Bell wishes to banish them, from the category of objects; but they are immanent, not transcendent, objects, and hence not inhabitants of a realm altogether independent of us and our activities. Since we *can* conceptually separate the thought from the particular act of thinking, it does not harm to construe that act as having an object. To characterize the act as objectless would suggest that we *cannot* conceptually distil its content; the opposite mistake, which was Frege's, is to regard the object as transcendent.

Spontaneity

Appealing both to Kant and to Wittgenstein, Bell proposes as a requirement for a successful theory of thoughts what he calls the 'Principle of Spontaneity', which lays down that the performance of a learned or rule-governed act should not be so explained as to presuppose the prior performance of an act of the same type. He maintains that the second incoherence he claims to detect in Frege's theory entails the violation of this principle. The theory does violate the principle, in my opinion; not, however, for this reason, but because of Frege's realism. That realism requires that we are able to recognize the sense as determining the reference, even when we ourselves have no capacity to identify the referent. On this view, the sense of a proper name constitutes a condition that an object must satisfy to be its referent, and that of a predicate a condition for it to apply to any object: the sense will be definite if it is determinate, for any object, whether or not it is the bearer of the name and whether or not the predicate applies to it. But this determination is impersonal: it is effected, not by us, but by the way things are. Hence, when Frege makes his demand that it be determined, for every object, whether or not it falls under a given concept, he frequently feels constrained to add that *we* may be unable to decide this. He therefore cannot explain a grasp of the sense of a name or predicate as consisting in an ability to recognize, in favourable circumstances, that the name does or does not refer to a given object, or that the predicate does or does not apply to it. Rather, a grasp of the sense must consist simply in knowing what condition an object must satisfy to be the referent of the name or for the predicate to apply. But such knowledge can amount only to a *judgement* that the name denotes, or the predicate applies to, any given object just in case that object satisfies such-and-such a condition; and thus the grasp of a sense is explained in terms of a judgement as to the truth of a certain thought, and Bell's principle of spontaneity is flouted.

15

The Relative Priority of Thought and Language*

Historically, the common principle uniting all the very diverse versions of analytical philosophy has been the priority of language over thought in the order of explanation. The fundamental ground of this priority thesis lies in Frege's doctrine (already to be found in Bolzano) that a thought, expressible by a sentence, and the senses of the component words, which are the constituents of that thought, are not contents of consciousness; which is to say that, unlike, say, a sensation, their presence is not independent of surrounding circumstances. For this reason, even given that we know what it is to have a concept, we cannot explain a word's expressing that concept in terms of a mental association between the two. Hence, even if we were in possession of a philosophical theory of thought, we could not exploit it in framing a philosophical account of language. Rather, in explaining what it is for words to have the meanings that they do, we are forced to describe their use *ab initio*, without presupposing it as already known what it is to grasp the concepts they express: by stating what constitutes knowing those meanings, the description will therefore itself show what possession of the concepts involves.

Recently, this priority thesis has been challenged from within the analytical tradition. I shall try to understand and evaluate this challenge by examining the thought of one of the challengers, the late Gareth Evans, whose premature death was so great a loss to philosophy; his challenge is the more interesting because I do not think that the reversal of priority was an original objective for him, and was never quite explicit in his writings.

Anyone who wishes to approach the philosophy of thought via a theory of linguistic meaning must employ some concept, of sense or of meaning, finer-grained than that of reference. Evans operated with a notion of sense, akin to that of Frege, in addition to the

* Paper delivered at the World Congress of Philosophy, Aug. 1988, not previously published.

notion of reference; and he rightly insisted that a Fregean distinction between sense and reference does not depend upon the admission of terms with sense but not reference. He was much taken with an adaptation which I made of the distinction drawn by Wittgenstein in the *Tractatus* between what can be said and what can only be shown. I proposed that Frege should be understood as holding that the reference of an expression can be stated, but its sense not; rather, we *show* what its sense is or is to be by the particular way (out of a number of possible non-equivalent ways) in which we say what its reference is or is to be. Evans quotes this explanation several times, and adopts it as his own.[1] This principle, that sense can only be shown, not stated, is of crucial importance. It in effect underlies Davidson's claim that a theory of truth just *is* a theory of meaning. A theory of truth, in Davidson's sense, corresponds to a Fregean theory of reference. Davidson does not operate with the notion of sense, but he is concerned with more than that the clauses of his truth-theory should assign the correct references to the words of the language, namely, that they should do so in the right way: this concern is equivalent to the requirement that they should display the senses of the words. But, despite Evans's enthusiastic endorsement of the principle that sense can only be shown, I do not believe that it is consistent with his other views.

The principle certainly agrees with Frege's practice in his *Grundgesetze der Arithmetik*, and indeed with his explanations there. In his exposition of the intended interpretation of his formal system, he lays down what the *reference* of each primitive symbol is to be, and how the reference of a complex symbolic expression depends on the references of its constituent symbols, without saying anything about what the senses of these expressions are to be. It is only when he has completed these stipulations that he speaks of sense: and then what he says is that those stipulations together determine, for each sentence, the condition for it to have the value *true*, that the thought expressed by the sentence is the thought that that condition is fulfilled, and that the sense of each constituent expression is its contribution to the thought expressed by the whole.

This account of Frege's not merely treats language as prior to

---

[1] 'Understanding Demonstratives', in Gareth Evans, *Collected Papers* (Oxford, 1985), 295 (repr. from H. Parret and Jacques Bouveresse (eds.), *Meaning and Understanding* (Berlin, 1981); 'Does Tense Logic Rest on a Mistake?', in *Collected Papers*, p. 345; *The Varieties of Reference* (Oxford, 1982), 26 and 35.

thought in the order of explanation: it makes it hard to see how it could be extended to an explanation of what it is to grasp a thought otherwise than as expressed by a sentence of some language. One grasps the thought expressed by a sentence of the symbolism if one knows what would determine it as true; and this knowledge is derived from knowing what determines the references of its constituent expressions. Granted, what is important is the reference, and not the words or symbols, which are arbitrary; one can therefore easily envisage the possibility of an isomorphic language, with different words and symbols, put together in different ways, but governed by parallel stipulations. But, for there to be a reference, there must be *something* that refers, something of which it is the reference: one cannot stipulate what the reference is to be, if it is not the reference *of* anything, or grasp the condition for something simply to be the reference, rather than the reference of something. And, as Frege here explains the notion of sense in terms of the notion of reference, taken as antecedently understood, he leaves it equally mysterious how one could grasp a sense, and in particular a thought, otherwise than as the sense of some expression, the thought expressed by some sentence.

Frege always introduces sense as attaching to a word or expression, or, more accurately, to a particular utterance of one, and as something communicated by that utterance. It is also a constituent of the thought expressed by the sentence of which the word or expression forms part; but it appears in the first instance as a property of the linguistic item, and hence as a feature of the language spoken by many. Evans respects this; he nevertheless explains the notion of sense in such a way as to make it dependent upon a prior conception of thought. For him, the sense of a singular term is the 'particular way in which its referent must be thought of (as the referent) if the term is to be understood'.[2] He glosses this by saying that ways of thinking about any particular object are to be distinguished by the accounts that are to be given of what makes one or another thought a thought about that object. This appeal to the possibility of an *account* seems quite inconsistent with the principle that sense can only be shown, not stated. The conception of language yielded by Evans's interpretation of the notion of sense is that the utterance of a sentence constitutes a signal to the hearer to

---

[2] 'Understanding Demonstratives', in *Collected Papers*, 301.

think a thought of a certain kind. Of course, he is not required, in order to understand the utterance, to judge that thought to be true; on the other hand, it is not enough that the utterance should prompt him to have that thought—he must take the thought as being that which the speaker's words expressed. But the explanation will go from the thought to the sentence: we have first to explain what it is to have such a thought, and then we can characterize the sense of the sentence as signalling that thought.

One, at least, of Evans's reasons for adopting an interpretation of this kind is best seen in the light of his quarrel with Perry and Kaplan about the first-person singular pronoun.[3] A Fregean sense has two important properties: it is capable of being grasped; and, together with the way the world is, it determines reference. Frege's notion of the sense of an expression comes apart from that of its meaning in the language in two kinds of case: expressions in intensional contexts; and demonstrative and indexical expressions. In a case of the latter kind, the two must come apart, because sense determines reference, whereas the meaning of the expression requires it to have a different reference on different occasions of utterance. Now one can question, and Perry does question, whether a Fregean sense is required at all for indexicals. If you are exploring an underground cave and you hear a distant voice shouting, 'Help! I am trapped', you surely understand the cry, or, in Frege's terminology, grasp the thought expressed, even if you can identify the speaker only as the person who just shouted for help. There seems no need to ascribe to the pronoun 'I' a sense that you can grasp and that determines its reference on that occasion of its use: it is enough that you know the meaning of the pronoun in the language and that you heard the particular utterance. This might even be held to apply when you yourself are the speaker. Novelists sometimes describe a state in which, recovering from a bad injury, someone hears a voice speaking and only subsequently realizes that it is his own; but it is arguable that he understands what the voice says, even if it uses the first-person pronoun.

This supplies a prima-facie ground for agreeing with Perry, at least when the subject-term is an indexical or demonstrative phrase, to replace the thought as Frege conceived it by one in which the component corresponding to that term is its referent: something

---

[3] See John Perry, 'Frege on Demonstratives', *Philosophical Review*, 86 (1977), 474–97; and David Kaplan, 'Demonstratives', mimeo, Los Angeles, 1977.

like a proposition as Russell thought of it. Evans does not agree with this at all: he thinks that, to understand an utterance of a sentence with 'I' as subject, one must be able to identify the speaker more substantially than as the person, whoever he was, who said that; and this is a point of strong divergence between the two. It is not, however, the important point of divergence; for Perry acknowledges that, when a speaker A uses the first-person pronoun to express a certain proposition, some differentiation is required between his epistemic state and that of another person B who has the same proposition in mind. To allow for this difference, Perry admits a notion of a 'way of thinking' a proposition; it is this way of thinking that corresponds most closely with what Frege called the 'thought'. What distinguishes A's way of thinking the proposition from B's, Perry holds, is just that he thinks it by entertaining the meaning in the language of the pronoun 'I'. Evans's comment on this proposal is brief: he declares that it 'evades' him.

The meaning in the language of the word 'I' is given by the semantic rule that the referent of an utterance of it is the author of that utterance; here the term 'semantic' means 'belonging to the theory of reference'. Obviously, a grasp of this rule does not supply one with a Fregean sense for a particular utterance of the pronoun, but only with a means of determining the referent from the context; but Perry is keeping as close as he can to the principle that the sense of a word is shown by the canonical way of stating what its reference is. To grasp what an utterance of 'I' refers to, one has to know the general semantic rule, together with the relevant features of the context; these two items therefore characterize one's way of thinking the proposition expressed. The minor disagreement between Perry and Evans concerns what one has to know of the context, Perry thinking it enough to be able to identify the utterance and Evans thinking that one has to know more than this. The major disagreement lies in Evans's rejection of Perry's entire approach; and this means, in this instance, his rejection in practice of the principle that sense can only be shown.

Evans rejects Perry's account in favour of one that accords better with what Frege said on the subject in his late essay 'Der Gedanke' (pp. 65–6). Notoriously, Frege did not there follow the principle that the sense is shown by the statement of the rule determining its reference. Instead, he explained the use of 'I' in terms of 'a special, primitive way' in which 'everyone is given to himself' and in which he is given to no one else. He did this because he viewed the sense that a speaker attaches to a singular term as constituting the manner in which its reference is given to *him*, that is, *his* means of identifying it or picking it out. In accordance with this, Evans wishes to include in an account of the sense of the first-person pronoun a description of how a subject thinks of himself. That is why he says that Perry's proposal 'evades' him: it makes no acknowledgement of the need to explain what it is to think of a person as *oneself*. This has little, if anything, to do with knowing the semantic rule governing the pronoun 'I': Evans rejects, as 'neither necessary nor sufficient' the suggestion that 'self-conscious thought depends upon the interior exploitation of certain public linguistic devices'.

It is not, indeed, that Perry purged this feature from his explanation of our understanding of 'I': he merely concealed it. The minor point of disagreement between him and Evans is irrelevant here: for it has no substance to think of someone as the person, whoever he may be, who just uttered a certain sentence unless one is in principle capable of subsequently identifying someone as that person. Hence, even if I do not know that it was I who just said, 'I have been wounded', I must at the very least be capable of coming to realize that it was I who did so if I am to be said to have understood that utterance. For someone to know who it was who just said, 'I have been wounded', he must pick out the speaker in some particular way; and when it was myself who said it, I shall express my realization of the fact by saying, for instance to an enquirer, 'It was I who said that'. From Evans's standpoint, therefore, Perry's proposal begs the question: for it presupposes that I can identify myself as the referent of the pronoun 'I', as used by me, but leaves us as far away as ever from an account of what it is for me to do so.

There is certainly something wrong with Frege's account, which Evans does not acknowledge. Frege argues that only the individual in question can grasp the thought he expresses by saying to himself, 'I have been wounded', and concludes that, when he communicates with someone else, he must use the word 'I' in a different sense, since he cannot communicate a thought that only he can grasp. Now it is quite implausible that I am using the word 'I' in a different sense when I say to myself, 'I have been wounded', and when I say the same words to you. This can be clearly seen if we consider someone telling a story about events in which he was involved. In the course of it he says, 'At that moment I suddenly said to myself, "I have been wounded" '. If there are two senses of 'I', a sense in soliloquy, and a sense in communication, the reported utterance must have employed the 'I' of soliloquy; yet those who hear the story have no difficulty in knowing what thought the narrator had.

How can they know this? They know it because each of them is familiar with the special, primitive way in which each of us is given to himself: each, that is, in the *same* way. This way in which each of us is given to himself is not a Fregean sense, since all can grasp it and yet it does not determine a unique referent. Now, given that someone, say Dr Lauben, is thinking of himself in the special way in which each of us is given to himself, what makes it the case that he is in fact thinking of Dr Lauben? Obviously the fact that that someone *is* Dr Lauben. It is therefore far from evident that there need be any Fregean sense that he grasps and that determines him as the referent: what he *grasps* is the special way in which each of us is given to himself, and what, in addition, renders his thought one that is about *him* is the fact that it is he who is thinking it.

This is not a vindication of Perry, however; for Frege and Evans are right that the special way in which each of us is able to think about himself plays an essential role in our understanding of the utterances of sentences, whether by ourselves or by others, involving the first-person pronoun; and this is not to be equated with a mastery of the semantic rule governing the first-person pronoun. The semantic rule that an utterance of 'I' refers to the speaker applies as much to a machine that says, 'I speak your weight', as to a human speaker: it has nothing to do with self-consciousness.

The notion of sense has to do with the speakers' *understanding* of their language, that is, with their grasp of meaning. Since Frege wrote, we have become highly conscious of a distinction he barely recognized, that between the meaning of an expression in the common language and an individual speaker's grasp of its meaning. This distinction is not forced on us merely by speakers' invariably imperfect knowledge of their language—their partial understanding of some words and misunderstanding of others: we need also to attend to the connections which a speaker makes between a name and its bearer which he does not suppose to underlie its use in the language and which are not of a kind to do so. The precise content of a belief that someone expresses by means of a certain sentence depends, not on the meaning of that sentence in the common language, but on that individual's grasp of its meaning: a thought, considered as the content of a belief, cannot therefore be identified with the sense of a sentence of the common language, but, rather, with the subject's personal understanding of it. Now the claim that the philosophy of language underlies the philosophy of thought must be baseless unless the philosophy of language incorporates an account of understanding, that is, of an individual speaker's grasp of meaning. Indeed, it must do so independently of that claim: for it is evident that an adequate account of how language functions cannot ignore the fact that speech is an activity of rational agents, whose reasons for saying what they do rest upon their admittedly limited awareness of the meanings of the words they use.

Any explanation of the understanding, by speaker or hearer, of a particular utterance of an indexical must thus recognize two components: the semantic rule determining its referent; and the speaker's or hearer's means of identifying the referent so determined (the two need not coincide). The second of these components is *not* displayed by the statement of the semantic rule. Frege's celebrated character-ization of sense as 'the way in which the referent is given' is ambiguous. If, for immediate purposes, we take the 'meaning' of an expression in the language to be given by the canonical statement of what its reference is, the ambiguity is between 'the way in which the speaker knows the referent to be determined in virtue of the meaning of the expression' and 'the way in which the speaker identifies the referent in accordance with that meaning'. Evans is in the right as against Perry in that the second interpretation must supplement the first in any adequate philosophical theory of language.

If Evans is in the right, the theory of meaning is more closely bound to epistemology than is usually supposed; and he must certainly be conceded to be in the right by those who maintain that thought is to be explained in terms of language. The question before us is whether his being in the right compels us to abandon such an order of explanation: whether, in giving an account involving the second component, we are forced to explain language in terms of thought.

The answer, I believe, is that we are not: for the considerations that originally underlay the thesis that language is prior to thought in the order of explanation remain intact. Since thoughts are not, in the sense explained, contents of consciousness, a thought requires a vehicle: it is not possible for someone to have a thought at a particular time without there being some event, overt in his actions or interior to his mental life, that embodies it. But whatever actions, mental images, or the like constitute the vehicle of the thought, they cannot be identified with it, in the strong sense that to do or have them is, in itself, to have that thought: it is only when they occur against a complicated background that they warrant our ascribing the thought to the subject. We might call the ascription of the thought to him an *interpretation*, which is not to say that it is doubtful, but only that it could not, as it were, be read off from an inspection of his consciousness. A theory of thought must therefore explain the grounds of any such interpretation in terms of the background justifying it. Without restricting our attention to thoughts carried by a linguistic vehicle, we should be faced with an unmanageable heterogeneity. The background of a fully verbalized thought is, however, a uniform one: the same background, consisting of the subject's knowledge of the language, for all thoughts verbalized in a given language. This background is complex enough; but it is one of which philosophy needs in any case to give an account, and, though complex, it is necessarily systematic. It therefore offers the only hope we have of explaining the surroundings needed for someone to have such a thing as a *thought*. The necessity so clearly exposed by Evans for supplementing a semantic theory, in the narrow sense, with an account of all that is involved in an individual's personal understanding establishes that it is impossible to explain language wholly from the outside, as it were: but it gives no promise of a description of thought independent of language.

In language, thoughts are fully articulated, whereas the ascription to someone of an unverbalized, or only partly verbalized, thought can seldom be precise; that is to say, there will usually be non-equivalent verbal formulations of its content that fit the circumstances equally well, and will be equally readily accepted by the subject as stating what he thought. The priority thesis concerned priority in the order of explanation: it contained no assumption that there is no such thing as languageless thought, or even as thought by subjects—infants or animals, in particular—who do not possess language. No verbal formulation can literally represent the content of the mental processes of a creature without language, because any such formulation will involve concepts that such a creature does not command. At present we do not know what to put in the place of verbal formulations—in what other terms to characterize the content of the thought of creatures devoid of language. Most unverbalized

Appendix: Writings on Frege by Michael Dummett

Review of P. Geach and M. Black, *Translations from the Philosophical Writings of Gottlob Frege*, Oxford (1952), in *Mind*, 63 (1954), 102–5.

'Frege on Functions: A Reply', *Philosophical Review*, 64 (1955), 96–107; repr. in E. D. Klemke (ed.), *Essays on Frege*, Urbana, Chicago, and London (1968), 268–83, and as 'Frege on Functions' in M. Dummett, *Truth and Other Enigmas* (henceforth *TE*), London and Cambridge, Mass. (1978), 74–84.

'Note: Frege on Functions', *Philosophical Review*, 65 (1956), 229–30; repr. in E. D. Klemke (ed.), *Essays on Frege*, 295–7, and in *TE* as Postscript to 'Frege on Functions', 85–6.

'Nominalism', *Philosophical Review*, 65 (1956), 491–505; repr. in E. D. Klemke (ed.), *Essays on Frege*, 321–36, and in *TE*, 38–49.

Article on: 'Frege, Gottlob', in Paul Edwards (ed.), *The Encyclopedia of Philosophy*, iii, New York (1962), 225–37; repr. in full as 'Frege's Philosophy' in *TE*, 87–115, and in abbreviated form in J. O. Urmson and Jonathan Ree (eds.), *The Concise Encyclopedia of Western Philosophy and Philosophers*, London, Boston, Sydney, and Wellington (1989), 113–17.

'Platonism', address to the Third International Congress on Logic, Methodology and Philosophy of Science, 1967; first published in *TE*, 202–14.

Frege: Philosophy of Language, London (1973; second edn., 1981).

'Frege's Way Out', *Analysis*, 33 (1972–3), 139–40.

Article on: 'Frege, (Friedrich Ludwig) Gottlob', in *The New Encyclopaedia Britannica*, iv, Chicago (1974), 968–9.

'Frege', *Teorema*, 5 (1975), 149–88; English version as 'Frege's Distinction between Sense and Reference' in *TE*, 116–44.

Review of H. Sluga, *Gottlob Frege*, London (1980); David Bell, *Frege's Theory of Judgement*, London (1980); G. Frege, *Philosophical and Mathematical Correspondence*, ed. B. F. McGuinness, Oxford (1980); and P. Geach and M. Black, *Translations from the Philosophical Writings of Gottlob Frege*, third edn., Oxford (1980), in *London Review of Books*, 2/18 (1980), 13–15.

The Interpretation of Frege's Philosophy, London (1981).

'Corrections to Hacking on Frege', *Philosophical Quarterly*, 35 (1985), p. 310.

'The Origins of Analytical Philosophy', *Lingua e Stile*, 23 (1988), 3–49, 171–210; German version, trans. J. Schulte, *Ursprünge der analytischen*

Philosophie, Frankfurt am Main (1988); trans. E. Picardi, Italian version, *Alle Origini della filosofia analitica*, Bologna (1990).
Frege: Philosophy of Mathematics, forthcoming.

Index

abstraction 49–50
Ackermann, W. 3 n.
Adeleke, S. A. xi, 53, 54
analytical philosophy ix, 217, 286–7, 315
analyticity 19–20, 22, 126, 131–4, 138 n., 139–41, 146, 160, 220
application of mathematics, 56, 64, 239–40
assertoric force, 175, 202, 223–4, 239, 245, 247–8, 259
Austin, J. L. viii, 81, 132 n.

Baker, G. 158–98, 199–216, 223, 228, 235
Behrend, F. S. 53 n.
Bell, D. xii, 289–314
Berkeley, G. 136
Black, M. viii
Bolzano, B. vii, 220, 250, 268, 286, 308, 312, 315
Boole, G. 185, 221
Bosanquet, B. 72, 98, 112 n.
Brentano, F. viii, ix, x, 250, 263–9, 271
Broackes, J. 77
Brotman, H. 151 n.

Cantor. G. 41, 49, 119
Carnap, R. 33, 34
Cohn, P. M. 53 n.
completeness (of logic) 1
completeness (of ordering) 57–8, 61–3
concept-formation 193–4, 296–7
concepts 6–7, 88, 100, 142–3, 163, 165, 173–9, 188, 206–8, 235
consistency 1–16, 147–8
context principle 39–40, 81–3, 85, 89, 90, 92–3, 94, 95, 111, 124, 159–61, 218, 223, 229–33, 279
contextual definition 226–9
correspondence theory 67
criteria of identity 89–90, 159–60, 237
Currie, G. 98–9, 119, 133, 223, 299–300

Davidson, D. 187, 316
decomposition 25–6, 93, 163–5, 192–5, 207–11, 295–8, 301–2
Dedekind, R. 49

definition 5, 18–36, 38–44, 47, 195, 220, 297–8, 299, 301
see also contextual definition
Droste, M. 54 n.

epistemological atomism 89–90
Erdmann, B. 80
Evans, G. xii, 167–8, 193, 304, 315–24

Fitch, F. B. 1
Føllesdal, D. 267
Frege's writings
  published
    'Anwendungen der Begriffsschrift' (1879), 164 n., 207
    Begriffsschrift (1879) 25–7, 76, 77, 93, 126 n., 141, 161, 162, 163–5, 174, 193–4, 197, 199–200, 201–5, 206–11, 225, 229, 295, 296–7, 299, 301, 302
    Funktion und Begriff (1891) 162, 212, 292, 293
    'Der Gedanke' (1918) 98, 116–17, 119, 123–4 n., 151 n., 168, 253 n., 255, 272–3, 280–1, 319–21
    'Gedankengefüge' (1923) 94, 274, 290
    Grundgesetze der Arithmetik (1893, 1903) 83, 163, 200, 229, 293, 305, 316
      Part I 169–70, 180, 183, 219
      Part III 53 n., 54–8, 60–1, 64, 145
      i, Preface 76–7, 80, 81, 100, 116, 119, 122–3, 130 n., 134–5, 150, 151 n., 293
      i, Introduction 28, 127, 128
      i, §2, 212, 293
      i, §10, 38, 82, 230–3
      i, §26, 258
      i, §29, 230–3
      i, §30, 39
      i, §32, 182, 230, 254–5, 261
      i, §33, 227
      ii, §66, 227
      ii, §74, 98, 124, 136
      ii, §91, 240

Frege's writings
  Grundgesetze der Arithmetik (*cont.*):
    ii, §147, 136
    ii, §175 (incl. n., p. 243), 54, 56
    ii, §197, 60–1
    ii, §214, 58
    ii, §216, 58
    ii, §217, 56
    ii, §218, 58
    ii, §244, 58
    ii, Appendix, 293
  Die Grundlagen der Arithmetik
    (1884) 76, 81, 82, 83, 126–7,
    138–9, 142, 155, 160–1, 162, 165,
    176, 200, 205, 207, 229, 234–5,
    275, 294, 298, 299, 301, 305
    §3, 97 n., 130–3, 146
    §4, 19
    §5, 144, 148 n.
    §12, 141–2, 143–4, 148
    §13, 148
    §14, 124
    §24, 121
    §26, 98, 106–7, 123, 130 n., 136,
    152–5
    §27, 105, 117, 142, 174
    §§29–44, 49
    §38, 179–80
    §47, 122, 177, 188–9
    §53, 292–3
    §55, 48
    §§55–61, 32
    §§55–83, 20–1
    §57, 179–80, 293
    §60, 233
    §61, 130 n.
    §62, 90, 223, 237
    §§62–9, 32
    §63, 228, 299
    §§63–7, 227–8
    §§63–9, 292
    §64, 42, 144, 292, 295
    §§66–7, 228
    §69, 33–4
    §70, 23, 163
    §85, 98, 119, 130 n., 151 n.
    §87, 121–2, 127, 151
    §88, 23, 131, 141, 195, 208
    §89, 127, 162 n.
    §90, 140–1, 220
    §91, 141, 220
    §§94–5, 7–8
    §96, 130
    §100, 34–5
    §101, 36–7
    §104, 143
    §105, 124
  Logische Untersuchungen (1918–23)
    96
    see also 'Der Gedanke', 'Die
    Verneinung', 'Gedankengefüge'
  'Le nombre entier' (1895) 98, 119
  Rechnungsmethoden, die sich auf
    eine Erweiterung des
    Grössenbegriffes gründen
    (1874) 139, 145
  Review of Husserl (1894) 24–5
  'Über Begriff und Gegenstand'
    (1892) 23
  'Über formale Theorien der
    Arithmetik' (1886) 7–8, 124, 139
  Über eine geometrische Darstellung
    der imaginären Gebilde in der
    Ebene (1873) 139
  'Über die Grundlagen der
    Geometrie' (1903, 1906) 8–13,
    127, 213, 222
  'Über Sinn und Bedeutung' (1892)
    87, 117, 168, 190, 203–4, 212,
    253–4, 258, 306
  'Über das Trägheitsgesetz, (1891)
    149 n.
  'Über den Zweck der
    Begriffsschrift' (1883) 204
  'Die Verneinung' (1918) 253 n.
  unpublished
    Aufzeichnungen für
      L. Darmstaedter (1919) 94, 212
    'Ausführungen über Sinn und
      Bedeutung' (c. 1892) 213, 222
    'Booles logische Formelsprache
      und meine Begriffsschrift' (1882)
      204
    'Booles rechnende Logik und die
      Begriffsschrift' (1880–1) 93, 95,
      163, 164, 165, 193, 203, 204, 207,
      208, 220–1, 295, 296, 301, 303–4,
      305
    Dialogue with Pünjer (1880–3) 65
    'Einleitung in die Logik' (1906)
      65–6, 96, 212
    'Erkenntnisquellen der
      Mathematik und der
      mathematischen
      Naturwissenschaften' (1924–5)
      127 n., 137, 151, 256, 279

'17 Kernsätze zur Logik' (1876–7)
65–78, 253 n.
'Kurze Übersicht meiner logischen
Lehren' (1906) 118
'Logik' (1880–2) 75, 76, 77, 96,
103 n., 107, 124, 130, 133–4, 136,
150, 155, 156–7
'Logik' (1897) 75, 94, 96, 98, 107,
110, 116, 118, 128, 129, 130, 141,
151, 156, 166, 213, 225, 252,
253 n., 258 n.
'Logik in der Mathematik' (1914)
17–19, 23, 102 n., 131–2 n., 212,
253 n., 275–6
'Meine grundlegenden logischen
Einsichten' (1915) 258 n.
'Neuer Versuch der Grundlegung
der Arithmetik' (1924–5) 129,
137
'Über Euklidische Geometrie'
(1899–1903) 140 n.
'Zahl' (1924) 129, 145
'Zahlen und Arithmetik' (1924–5)
126 n., 137

Fuchs, L. 58 n., 59
functions 80, 100, 163–5, 176–7, 188–9,
206–11, 235
have objects as values 194, 205–6
Furth, M. 81, 134 n.

Gabriel, G. ix–x, 66, 76
Geach, P. viii, 86, 94, 164, 191, 192,
193, 207, 238, 243
Gentzen, G. 131
geometry x, 126–57, 160
grasping a sense 51–2, 165–9, 182,
183–4, 238, 256–7, 273–5, 277–80,
306–7, 310–11, 314, 321–2
Grice, P. 248
Grossmann, R. 85

Hacker, P. M. 158–98, 199–216, 223,
228, 235
Hankel, H. 7, 141–2, 144, 145
Hegelianism viii, 79–80
Heidegger, M. viii
Higman, G. 53 n.
Hilbert, D. vii, x, 3 n., 8–16, 128–9
Hölder, O. x, xi, 53 n., 56, 57, 58, 64
Huntington, E. V. 58 n.
Husserl, E. viii, ix, x, 24–5, 27–9, 33,

41–50, 174, 225, 250–1, 254,
267–72, 276, 280–8

idealism 80, 115, 124–5, 126, 136, 142,
149–57, 152, 155–7
ideas 66–73, 102–6, 110, 112, 115–16,
117, 120–1, 142–3, 148, 155, 174
intensional contexts 86, 242
intentionality viii, 263–9
intuition 126, 128–30, 148–9, 153–6,
160

Jourdain, P. E. B. 12, 127, 147 n., 212
judgement 257–9

Kant, I. x, 19, 68–9, 126–8, 130–1, 133,
135, 137–9, 141–4, 148–50, 153,
155, 157, 162, 176, 223, 277, 303,
305, 306, 307, 313
Kaplan, D. 318
Kaulbach, F. 137–8
Kleemeier, U. 121, 122
Köhler, W. 286
Korselt, A. R. 8
Kossak, E. 41
Kronecker, L. 119

language and expression 184–5, 221,
311
language and thought 91–2, 95–6,
182–3, 217, 280, 315–24
languageless thought 183, 255–6, 262,
279, 285–8, 323–4
Leibniz, G. W. 220–1
Liebmann, O. 11, 147 n.
limpness 57–8, 60–4
linear ordering 55–64
logic 75–6, 96, 134–6, 146–7, 151,
180–1, 185–7, 211–12, 225–6
intensional and extensional 212–14,
222
logical objects 80–1, 100, 273
Lotze H. vii, ix, x, 66–78, 81, 97–125,
144–5

Marty, A. 126 n., 138
meaning as use 245–6
Meinong, A. viii, ix, 250, 267–8
Moore, G. E. xii, 17, 25, 167–8, 250

natural language 179–81, 184–5,
186–7, 217
Neumann, P. M. xi, 53, 54
noema 271–2, 280–5

object and content 252–4, 260, 307, 309–10
objectivity 80–1, 97–108, 113–19, 123–5, 142, 153–4, 174, 238, 244–5, 249, 307–8
Occam's razor 38

Paul, St 131
Perry, J. xii, 318–20, 322
phenomenology ix, 286–7
Picardi, E. 20, 23, 28
picture theory 241–4
platonism 4, 112–13
psychologism 79–80, 224, 249, 287–8
Pünjer, B. 65

Quine, W. V. O. 111, 253 n.

Ramsey, F. 192
real numbers 56, 64
realism, viii 79–96, 97–9, 113, 126, 136, 151–2, 278, 313–14
redundancy theory of truth 247
reference
    of incomplete expressions 171–2, 174–5, 215–16, 241–2
    of proper names 84, 85–6, 171, 173, 174, 212, 241
    of sentences 84, 171, 172, 174–5, 177–8, 215, 228, 241, 242, 243–4, 259–60
relation between Frege's early and middle periods 160–5, 199–206, 233–6
Resnik, M. 113, 118 n., 124
Russell, B. xii, 3, 18, 96, 105, 109, 110 n., 163, 197, 206, 207, 212, 250, 275, 319
    contradiction 15, 19, 64, 83, 137, 307
Ryle, G. viii, ix, x, xii, 250 n.

Sachse, L. 65, 77
Sayce, A. H. 93
Schirn, M. vii
Scholz, H. 65
Schröder, E. 41
Searle, J. xii, 252–3

self-subsistence 249–50, 254, 255–6, 260–2, 312–13
semantic consequence 170, 214, 218–29, 220
semantic value 84–6, 170–3, 175, 215
semilinear ordering 54–5, 57–61, 63
sense determines reference 87, 175, 182, 238, 253–5, 270–1, 316, 322
senses
    as thought-constituents 26, 190–1, 280, 295, 298
    of incomplete expressions 87–8, 191, 214
    of names 88–9, 174
Shanker, S. 217–36
Sluga, H. vii, viii, ix, xii, 77, 79–96, 97–101, 103, 106–8, 111–15, 118, 123–4, 126–7, 130, 135, 146, 150, 215, 293, 303
Stolz, O. 41
structure of thought and sentence 183–5, 289–91, 303–6
synonymy 19, 29, 51, 294–5, 297–9
synthetic a priori 127–8, 130–3, 135, 137–41, 147–8, 150, 152

Tarski, A. 296
third realm 249–62, 272–3, 276–8, 306, 312–13
thoughts 72–4, 76–7, 91–2, 100, 161–2, 250–3, 255, 257–8, 261, 289–314
truth indefinable 66, 73
truth-conditions 180, 181–2, 241, 246
truth-values as objects 82, 175, 178, 215, 228, 242–3
Tugendhat, E. 85, 170–1

verificationism 245–6

Wagner, S. xii, 303–6
Waismann, F. 240
Willard, D. 251 n.
Wirklichkeit 81, 97–101, 103–6, 108–11, 114–23
Wittgenstein, L. viii, x, 96, 158, 181–2, 198, 217, 218, 219, 224, 225, 237–48, 274–5, 307, 313, 316
Wright, C. 35–6